Understanding Global Poverty

Understanding Global Poverty introduces students to the study and analysis of poverty, helping them to understand why it is pervasive across human societies, and how it can be reduced through proven policy solutions. Using the capabilities and human development approach, the book foregrounds the human aspects of poverty, keeping the voices, experiences and needs of the world's poor in the centre of the analysis.

Drawing on decades of teaching, research and fieldwork, this interdisciplinary volume is unique in its rigorous application of the multiple disciplines of anthropology, sociology, political science, public health and economics to the phenomenon of global poverty. Starting with definitions and measurement, the book goes on to explore causes of poverty and policy responses, aiming to give a realistic account of what poverty reduction programmes actually look like. Finally, the book draws together the ethics of why we should work to reduce poverty and what actions readers themselves can take to reduce poverty.

This book is an accessible and engaging introduction to the key issues surrounding poverty, with key questions, case studies, discussion questions and further reading suggestions to support learning. Perfect as an introductory textbook for postgraduates and upper-level undergraduates, *Understanding Global Poverty* will also be a valuable resource to policy makers and development practitioners looking for a comprehensive guide to the theoretical frameworks of poverty through the lens of human development.

Serena Cosgrove is an Assistant Professor of International Studies at Seattle University, USA.

Benjamin Curtis is a Senior Advisor at The Behavioural Insights Team, UK.

'Serena Cosgrove and Benjamin Curtis have produced a compelling and, at times, moving guide that comprehensively rehearses the major challenges of poverty facing our unequal world, addressing these both conceptually and with empirical evidence and examples. Their book requires that we all pay careful attention to lives lacking human dignity and access to a threshold of basic human capabilities for well-being and agency, and to who is responsible for the current deplorable state of affairs globally in which too many people – men, women and children – are deprived unnecessarily and avoidably of human freedoms. The book should be required reading for practitioners and policy makers involved in development, as well as scholars working in the field of development, all grappling with the formidable – and yet feasible – challenge of multi-dimensional poverty and its significant reduction. As the authors make clear, this is a matter of ethics and global justice – a moral imperative towards which each of us should strive individually and in solidarity with others across levels of communities and governance structures. As the authors explain, people reading this book should aspire to think more deeply about both their obligations to reduce poverty and the actions they can take to that end.'

– Melanie Walker, National Research Foundation Chair and Director of the Centre for Research on Higher Education and Development at University of the Free State, South Africa

Understanding Global Poverty

Causes, Capabilities and Human Development

Serena Cosgrove and Benjamin Curtis

Routledge
Taylor & Francis Group

LONDON AND NEW YORK

First published 2018
by Routledge
2 Park Square, Milton Park, Abingdon, Oxon OX14 4RN

and by Routledge
711 Third Avenue, New York, NY 10017

Routledge is an imprint of the Taylor & Francis Group, an informa business

British Library Cataloguing-in-Publication Data
A catalogue record for this book is available from the British Library

Library of Congress Cataloging-in-Publication Data
A catalog record for this book has been requested

ISBN: 978-1-138-23076-7 (hbk)
ISBN: 978-1-138-23077-4 (pbk)
ISBN: 978-1-315-31684-0 (ebk)

Typeset in Bembo
by Florence Production Ltd, Stoodleigh, Devon, UK

Contents

Figures

Tables

Preface

This book has three main objectives. First, it presents an interdisciplinary perspective on the problem of global poverty. Despite common rhetoric about the benefits of interdisciplinary approaches, research and teaching often remain firmly siloed within individual disciplines. The authors of this book are an anthropologist/sociologist and a political scientist, with one chapter written by a medical doctor who is a public health specialist. Some vignettes or text boxes were prepared by former students of ours whose majors were interdisciplinary as well: Humanities and International Studies. The primary authors have decades of experience in global health, international humanitarian assistance, sustainable development and working with governments. The endeavour to harmonize disciplinary perspectives within this book has not been .easy, but we believe it was both necessary and rewarding. It was necessary because poverty's multidimensional nature requires an interdisciplinary approach; no single academic discipline can provide an adequate understanding of such a complex phenomenon. It was rewarding because it forced us to think outside our own narrow academic specializations, which should help readers think outside narrow bounds too. The book thereby presents a more holistic and insightful understanding of poverty than if it were written from the perspective of a single academic discipline.

The chapters that follow draw on academic literature from philosophy, economics, anthropology, sociology, women's studies, political science and public health. We also draw on research written by international and national practitioners about what does and doesn't work on the ground for poverty reduction policies. And we draw on our own fieldwork. For this book, we have carried out research in Latin America (Chile, Argentina, Guatemala, El Salvador, Panama, Nicaragua, Costa Rica and Brazil), Asia (Indonesia, India and Kyrgyzstan), Africa (Zambia, Ghana, Rwanda and the Democratic Republic of the Congo) and several former communist countries in Europe (Bosnia-Herzegovina, Croatia, Hungary and Slovakia).

The second main objective of the book is to introduce undergraduate and graduate students to the capabilities approach: what capabilities or opportunities do people need to lead a life that they value? Though there is a considerable literature on this approach to poverty and development, there are few introductory survey texts. Those that do exist we have found too specialized, or more philosophical than empirical, or otherwise not written in an accessible way to students new to the topic. We aimed to write a book that would present readers with some of the key concepts of the capabilities approach, then apply those concepts to a number of causes of and solutions to poverty. Because this book is a survey, we emphasize breadth rather than depth in our coverage of capabilities; there are certainly subtleties and specificities that we neglect. We do not pretend to be exhaustive, but do suggest additional readings at the end of each chapter for those who want to deepen their knowledge about a particular theme or topic. That same caveat applies to our coverage of the causes and solutions. We do not pretend to be comprehensive. We chose to cover causes and solutions where we had expertise, and which we thought would be interesting to analyse through the lens of capabilities.

The third main objective is pedagogical in nature. We wanted the book to be *teachable*, much more so than most of what academics write, including other textbooks. This book emerged from a course on global poverty that we developed to complement an existing course at our academic institution called Poverty in America. Given all the research and teaching that had been synthesized for the Poverty in America course, we decided it was important to examine many of the same questions from a global perspective, preferencing voices from the global south but also recognizing that some of the same causes contribute to poverty in the global north. We believe – given that we live in an interconnected, globalized world where economic, political, cultural and environmental issues affect us all – it is just as important to understand poverty and inequality at home as well as abroad. And though the primary focus of this book is poverty in the global south from the examples we use to illustrate our points, the reader should understand that poverty and inequality permeate many of the world's countries. Inequality in high-income countries can mean that certain groups have the same levels of deprivation such as low life expectancy, hunger or illiteracy as people in low-income countries.

Thus in contrast to many textbooks, this one has (unapologetically) an ethical perspective. In Chapter 1 we state our fundamental ethical assumptions for studying poverty, which depend above all on conceiving poverty as a human problem. This means that for all the diverse definitions and methods we utilize, the focus must always be on how poverty affects human beings as individuals and not just on abstract, aggregate statistics. For this reason the book includes vignettes about real individuals affected by the topics we're discussing; ethnographic description helps us visualize and understand how it might feel to be that particular person. Compassion is an essential quality when considering the causes of and solutions to poverty because it helps us appreciate the urgency of the topic. Focusing on poverty as a human problem, too, connects to our collective responsibility to achieve the book's goals of understanding what causes poverty and how poverty can be alleviated.

Just as the book does not aim to be exhaustive and comprehensive, nor does it aim to be definitive. We try to avoid authoritatively pronouncing on what students and readers should conclude. Instead, we encourage debate and discussion. On one issue we do presume a bedrock definitiveness, namely on the need to correct the injustice of poverty. Besides our own ethics and beliefs on what constitutes good pedagogy, in this aspect of the book's approach we rely on some influential inspiration. This inspiration comes from Amartya Sen – the founder of the capabilities approach – who wrote that 'the greatest relevance of ideas of justice lies in the identification of patent injustice, on which reasoned agreement is possible.'[1] We hope this book promotes both reasoning and agreement on at least this bedrock issue. Beyond that, the book is very much aligned with Paulo Freire's pedagogy that those who have been invisibilized and marginalized by poverty and exclusion can be the authors of the solutions to the challenges they confront. In this, our book's objectives, approach and inspiration are wonderfully summed up by Melanie Walker: 'The key question is: what do I as a human being become as a consequence of what I experience in learning about human development?' For us as teachers of human development, 'the essential question is therefore: what kinds of human beings do I hope my students might one day become?'[2]

We hope that this book provides some useful answers to both of these questions.

Notes

1 Sen, Amartya. 1999. *Development as Freedom*. New York, NY: Knopf: 287.
2 Walker, Melanie. 'Teaching the human development and capability approach: Some pedagogical implications', in Séverine Deneulin and Lila Shahani, eds. 2009. *An Introduction to the Human Development and Capability Approach*. London: Earthscan: 335.

Acknowledgements

Over the nearly 7 years of researching and writing this book, we have been fortunate to work with, learn from and be assisted by many inspirational people on five continents. Our list of gratitude is long and deep, and an acknowledgement here is a frustratingly incomplete attempt to repay our debts, not least because the list is actually so much longer than what we can mention below. Thank you to all who helped us along the way, and if we haven't mentioned you by name, accept our apologies for the oversight. And of course the standard disclaimer applies: any errors in this text are our own.

Thanks to the staff at Seattle University's Lemieux Library who fetched research materials from far and wide. Thanks to all our current and former colleagues at Seattle University, particularly in Matteo Ricci College, and the International Studies Department in the College of Arts and Sciences, for providing a worthy intellectual home. A debt of gratitude to Stephen Sundborg, SJ, the president of Seattle University, whose commitment to global engagement means that research projects like this one receive university-wide support. This book would not have been possible without support from the Seattle University Endowed Mission Fund and SU's Global Engagement Grants programme. Ben thanks all his colleagues at The Behavioural Insights Team – especially Kizzy Gandy, Chloe Bustin, Stewart Kettle, Luke Ravenscroft and Simon Ruda – for both their acumen and the opportunity to work on impactful development projects.

Thanks to all the many people at development organizations we have met over the course of our fieldwork. Particular thanks to: Thomas Awiapo and CRS staff, and Cole Hoover and Lumana staff in Ghana; Sabina Čehajić-Clancy, Amir Telibečirović, Sanel Marić and Kurt Bassuener in Bosnia; Rafael and Shirley Luna and Moisés Leon in Costa Rica; Peter Henriot, SJ, Leonard Chiti, SJ and the staff of the Jesuit Centre for Theological Reflection in Zambia; Modestine Etoy and the amazing young women she works with in Goma, Democratic Republic of the Congo; the faculty, staff and students at the Gashora Girls Academy in Gashora, Rwanda; the faculty and students at Universitas Sanata Dharma in Indonesia; in India, staff from the Ernakulam, Trivandrum and Kochi Social Service Societies, from Caritas and the Karunya Trust, and from Pratham Mumbai; Danessa Luna and her staff at the Guatemalan women's organization, Asociación Generando, in Chimaltenango, Guatemala as well as their friends and contacts around the country; and last but not least, José (Chepe) Idiáquez, SJ, the rector of the Universidad Centroamericana (UCA) in Managua, Nicaragua, and students and colleagues at the UCA.

Thanks to Helena Hurd and Kelly Watkins at Routledge for shepherding this project to publication. Helena saw the relevance of an interdisciplinary textbook from her first read of the manuscript, and we are very grateful for her keen eye and support. An enormous debt of gratitude to Audrey Hudgins for many reasons, one in particular that she will understand. A huge thanks to Paula Brentlinger, not only for contributing an excellent chapter on health and poverty, but also for being a brilliant mind and dear friend over many years. Emily Lieb, a colleague at Seattle University and US historian, made valuable suggestions for including historical perspective when applicable.

Finally, and perhaps most importantly, thanks to our students. It has been a great joy to teach many remarkable young people over the years. They helped us create a wonderful learning community, both in the classroom in Seattle and in the field in a number of countries. We cannot mention all their names, but several shouldered extra duty. Janie Bube, Morgan Marler, Feeza Mohammad, Mark Olmstead, Helen Packer, Kelsea Shannon, Mara Silvers and Callie Woody accompanied us on a research trip to Bosnia in 2014. Kelly Armijo, Amelia García-Cosgrove, Andrew Gorvetzian, Lauren Kastanas, Michael Keenen, Lindsay Mannion, Jacqueline Shrader and Caitlin Terashima accompanied a research trip to Guatemala in 2013. Melissa Howlett, Kimberly Whalen, Raine Donohue, Erika Bailey, Phillip Bruan, Caitlin Terashima, Emily Chambers, Laura Gomez and Sophia Sanders assisted us on a trip to Ghana in 2012. A special thanks to students who worked as our research assistants: Sophia Sanders, KJ Zunigha, Jill Douglas, Julian Fellerman, Andrew Gorvetzian, Alex Ozkan, Michael Kaemingk, Amelia García-Cosgrove and Sy Bean.

In gratitude,
Serena Cosgrove and Benjamin Curtis

1 Building a framework for understanding poverty

Benjamin Curtis and Serena Cosgrove

Key questions

- How can poverty be defined?
- What are income and monetary definitions of poverty? What are their strengths and weaknesses?
- What is the capabilities definition of poverty? What are its strengths and weaknesses?
- Why study poverty from a multidimensional, multidisciplinary perspective?
- What does it mean to conceive of poverty as a human problem?

Introduction

It may have been the most troubling place we have ever visited. It was a slum in a major city in the developing world; for the moment, it doesn't matter exactly where. An estimated one million people live in an area of about 500 acres, significantly less space than Central Park in New York City. The population was incredibly dense, with sometimes families of eight people living in houses of maybe 100 square feet, roughly the same size as a bedroom in an average American home. If they were fortunate, people would have running water in their house for about three hours a day. Otherwise, they had to get water from a communal spigot. In either case, the water was not safe to drink. Very few people in this slum had bathrooms in their homes. Instead, they had to use the public toilets. Because of the scarcity of services and the very high population density, one public toilet would serve around 1500 people. The stench was horrifying. There were few proper streets in this settlement. Rather, it was mostly pathways through dilapidated structures, and many of those pathways had open sewage in them. There was garbage everywhere. One children's playground was on top of a giant mound of trash.

Though people might own the ramshackle structure where they lived, very few people owned the land beneath it, which means that their lives were precarious in many ways. If people did earn an income, they might be lucky to make the equivalent of USD 2 a day. Oftentimes, the working conditions were deplorable. Some people worked in a small plastics recycling industry. All day long they would sort by hand through giant piles of plastic – including things like discarded syringes – then melt the plastic down into other things. They had little to no protection from the melting plastic's hazardous fumes, and yet this is what they did every day just to earn two dollars. There was actually a whole range of jobs in this community. Some people made pottery, some made food, some made clothing. As hard as life in this slum may sound, many people came there because they could make more money than trying to farm land in the rural areas. Why, then, was this place so troubling? It was not just the sewage, the cramped living conditions, the fumes or the paltry wages. It was that no human beings should have to live like this. And yet for most of the people in this slum, they had no better option. They were poor. Their choices were drastically restricted.

Poverty can be found virtually everywhere. It is a universal human problem. However, poverty may not be the same everywhere. The very definition of 'poor' can change from place to place – and yet it can also remain the same. There are some traps that will make you poor no matter where you are. This chapter is concerned with definitions because a study of global poverty must start with trying to understand what 'poverty' means. We consider several different ways of defining poverty, though we will ultimately suggest that a lack of opportunities is a basic, underlying definition. We will consider first monetary/income understandings of poverty, then define poverty through the idea of capabilities and functionings. We will also discuss different methodological approaches to studying poverty, stressing the need to consider insights from a variety of academic disciplines. This is a necessary foundation for understanding what poverty is, what causes it, how it affects people and how it can be remedied. Subsequent chapters will build upon this foundation to expand upon the chapter's themes. One idea will remain consistent, however: poverty is a human problem, so just as with the example of the slum, we must never lose sight of the experiences, hopes, aspirations, tribulations and lives of human beings in poverty.

What is poverty?

How can we define poverty? This is one of those words that people use conversationally, with a meaning they think they understand, but often without thinking deeply about possible definitions. Stop right now and take a minute to think about how you would define poverty. What does it mean to be poor?

On the one hand, the definition could seem simple – but it is not nearly as simple as it initially seems. The simplest, most common way of defining poverty is 'not having enough money'. Why use money (or the lack thereof) to define poverty? What is money good for? The idea is that money (or income more broadly) is really a proxy to indicate a person's or family's ability to acquire goods necessary to survive. Money can be used to buy food, for example. Therefore, another potential definition of poverty is 'not having enough food'. If a person is starving not by his own choice, then he is almost certainly poor; he is lacking the means necessary to survive. This food definition of poverty is most applicable in developing countries, since in high-income countries it is very rare that people do not get enough calories (though the calories they get may not be optimally nutritious). When we add the idea of food poverty to monetary poverty, the definition of poverty becomes more complex, since we recognize that poverty is a *multidimensional* phenomenon. There is more than one way that a person can be poor, and therefore there is more than one way of defining poverty.

As this chapter progresses, we will be exploring how poverty is multidimensional. There is nonetheless a core idea to all definitions of poverty, namely a shortfall or deprivation of something, whether something tangible such as money or food, or intangible such as rights or respect. The specific meaning of *deprivation* is key here: it assumes that a person is deprived of something to which he or she is entitled. Does this presume that every person is somehow entitled to a certain amount of money? Not necessarily. What it does presume is that every person is entitled to a basic material standard of living (such as having enough food) that a certain amount of money can buy. Therefore, a shortfall of money below the threshold necessary to acquire the basic necessities (such as food) deprives a person of a minimally adequate standard of living. In addition to deprivation, then, also essential to the idea of poverty is some conception of a *threshold*: above this threshold, whether it relates to money, food, rights, respect, etc., a person is not poor, but below it, he or she is. The question of what constitutes the threshold for an adequate minimum in the areas of income, food, rights and respect is a debatable one that we will return to repeatedly.

Income definitions of poverty

Incorporating the ideas of deprivation and a threshold, we need to examine the definition of income poverty in greater detail. Income – the money a person has – is certainly a vital component of meeting one's needs. At the individual level, one's income is the sum of all income-generating activities. Those activities can be in formal sector jobs, i.e. those jobs that are regulated and taxed by the government, and/or in the informal sector, which is commonly thought of as 'under the table' work that is not reported to the government. Informal sector jobs can include domestic service work, construction, farm work, food preparation, sales in the marketplace etc., and they are very common in the developing world. At the national level, the gross domestic product – or the total market value of all goods and services produced in the country – is a way of measuring a country's economic prosperity. When this figure is divided by the number of people in a country, you have the GDP per capita, often used as an indicator of individuals' standard of living. Using data from 2016, GDP per capita in the United States was USD 57,220, and USD 499 in the Democratic Republic of the Congo (DRC). While much more will be said in Chapter 3 about such measurements, a quick glance at these figures suggests that there is much more poverty in the DRC than in the USA.

Since the end of the Second World War, lack of income has been the principal definition economists have used to describe poverty. However, given what we have already said about multidimensionality, do income/monetary definitions of poverty tell the whole story? In this book, we argue that monetary or income definitions of poverty are useful, but do not include many critical dimensions of what it means to be poor. Income has an instrumental value, which means it can be used for certain other ends, including possibly acquiring things that enable a person to live a life that she values. The instrumental value of income is a prime reason why economists use it as a proxy for wellbeing or poverty. Having enough money alone, however, does not guarantee that a person will be able to live a life that she values. For example, those who are rich but sick will probably not rate themselves high on wellbeing, even if money may help them get treatment. Similarly, it is conceivable that someone who is rich but still subject to legal or cultural discrimination of various kinds, or denied basic civil rights, cannot be said to have escaped forms of poverty.

Part of the problem is that income (or other resources, including money) are not always easily converted into things a person values. Personal, environmental and institutional factors can all limit the instrumental or proxy value of income. This is an example of how institutional factors can complicate using income as a proxy: imagine two sets of parents, each with the same income, but they live in two different countries. In country A, there is a good public education system, but in country B the public system is shoddy, so parents who want a good education for their children will pay for private schools (Sen 1999: 70). Who is better off, the parents in country A or country B? They have the same level of income, but in this example, the parents in country A are better off because they are not spending additional money to send their children to school. The point of this example is that income cannot fully capture wellbeing. As another example, imagine a family whose income is somewhat above the poverty line, but where the parents squander the money on alcohol, presents for themselves or unwise investments rather than spending the money to ensure that their children are adequately fed, educated and otherwise cared for. In this example, because the family's income is above the poverty line, it may seem that they have a basically adequate standard of living. However, the way that income is actually distributed within the family disadvantages the children. Such unequal distribution of income is all too common in many societies, with women and children most often getting less than a fair share.

It is also important to remember that income is not the same as employment. In the case of someone who has lost their job, income may be state welfare disbursements, but their self-esteem may be affected by not generating their own income. In this case again, income cannot equate to wellbeing. The problems with using income as the sole indicator of poverty magnify at the aggregate level. Imagine a country, such as the United States, with a high GDP per capita but also high levels of income inequality. In such a case where income is very unevenly distributed, there will be a small group of people with high incomes while the majority of the people have lower incomes. However, because of the way the numbers have been averaged, it appears that people are richer than they actually are: the few rich people have skewed the average. Poverty may actually be much more widespread, and much more severe, than the numbers indicate. Furthermore, economic growth – particularly in countries with high income inequality – is not the same as increased income for everyone. Because of income inequality and other structures of discrimination and marginalization, the theory that economic growth automatically benefits the poor – i.e. that 'a rising tide lifts all boats' – is not necessarily correct. When a country's economy is growing, many people might not get to share in the wealth.

Few theorists argue against the utility of income at the individual or aggregate level as one potential indicator of poverty, but it is important to recognize that income as an indicator has its limitations. The simplest definition of poverty as 'not having enough money' is therefore inadequate. While a lack of money can lead to poverty, this lack does not in itself summarize what it means to be poor. To reiterate, poverty is multidimensional: it cannot be truly understood via a single perspective, whether money, food or some other dimension. While each dimension is worth examining in some detail to understand its relationship to poverty, a more holistic, multifaceted examination will lead to a better understanding of this phenomenon. We should also return to the idea of deprivation. What does it really mean? Deprivation of what? Deprivation can take many forms, not just of the income needed to sustain oneself. In fact, a lack of money does not serve as an adequate proxy for lack of political rights, lack of safety or control over one's body, or a lack of adequate health and education. If deprivations of income and economic growth are insufficient for understanding poverty, then what other deprivations should we consider?

The capabilities approach

The capabilities approach calls attention to deprivation of opportunities, choices and freedoms. This is a powerful, provocative and multidimensional way of understanding what constitutes a good human life. It is most associated with the Nobel Prize-winning economist and philosopher Amartya Sen, but its ideas have been elaborated by a number of others as well, including the philosopher Martha Nussbaum and development ethicist David Crocker, to mention but a few. Sen developed this approach in part from a series of lectures at the World Bank in which he encouraged the Bank to expand its thinking about what poverty is. He agreed that income is an important asset in helping people get out of poverty, but he argued for a more comprehensive approach in which the basic abilities necessary for a human to lead a fulfilled life should be the goal of public policy. The capabilities approach thus provides a means of evaluating minimum requirements for quality of life, which then constitute demands of social justice and government policy to guarantee those minimum requirements.

Rather than focusing on a country's economy, the capabilities approach focuses on individual humans. It prioritizes 'the actual freedom of choice a person has over alternative lives that he or she can live' (Sen 1990: 114). The words 'freedom' and 'choice' are key: this approach emphasizes that every human being must have the opportunity to choose aspects of a life that he or she will value. As Nussbaum has written, the capabilities approach holds 'that the crucial good societies should be promoting for their people is a set of opportunities, or substantial freedoms, which people then may or may not exercise in action: the choice is theirs' (Nussbaum 2011: 18). People may value different things, both because of their individual desires and how those desires are (at least partially) socially constructed. What matters is that people have the freedom to choose what they want their lives to be.

What are capabilities? Capabilities are the processes that allow freedom of action and decisions. They are best thought of as opportunities for life choices. Can you choose your profession? Can you participate in your society? Can you choose where to live? Can you live to a ripe old age? Essentially capabilities are the freedom to do things that are important to you. A capability is not the choice or the opportunity itself; rather, it is the *potential* to choose, the freedom to choose. Writers in this tradition describe capabilities as the answer to the question, 'What is this person able to do and to be?' (Nussbaum 2011: 20), and as the freedom to enjoy functionings (Comim 2008: 4). The term 'functionings' is another fundamental concept in this approach. Think of it as the other side of the coin to 'capabilities'. It is not enough to be able to do something, to have the capability. Do you actually do it? If capabilities are what you can possibly do, then functionings are what you *actually* do, the outcomes or realizations of your choices. Functionings are people putting their capabilities into action (Sen 1999: 17). A functioning, Sen explains, 'is an achievement of a person, what she or he manages to do or be' (Sen 1985: 10).

The distinction between capabilities and functionings is not merely philosophical quibbling – it is a very important consideration in evaluating wellbeing. For example, a woman may very well have the education and vocational skill to carry out a particular job, but she is unable to use those skills in the marketplace because women are not allowed to work outside the home in her society. In this case, she is denied the capability to hold a job: she does not have the freedom to choose to work outside the home. Nussbaum gives an example of how an important capability is often not actualized as a functioning: 'Many societies educate people so that they are capable of free speech on political matters – internally – but then deny them free expression in practice through repression of speech' (2011: 21). You could have the capability to engage in political participation, but you might not choose to do so. In such a case, you have chosen not to actualize your capability as a functioning, which is justifiable because it is your own personal choice. But it is also possible that the actualization of your capability is thwarted not through your own volition, as for example if a government prevents your political participation, or you are unable to achieve the functioning of reading because you have been denied an adequate education.

A common example that may help clarify these concepts is the bicycle. The bicycle is a resource that allows its rider to convert a capability into a functioning. The capability is the opportunity to move around faster than walking, something a person might choose because she values it. A person could have this capability – e.g. if she knows how to ride, owns a bike, and social norms permit women to ride – but she may not choose to convert it to a functioning for whatever reason. The functioning itself is mobility: it is the realization of the capability to move around faster than walking. When a person is able to convert her capability to a functioning – actualizing her opportunity to move around by becoming mobile on the bike – then she derives (hopefully) some utility, some satisfaction, from doing so (Alkire and Deneulin 2009b: 42). This example helps demonstrate why the twinned concepts of capabilities and functionings are important. A person could have many capabilities but might not realize any of them. This means that a person could have a great deal of freedom in theory – she could have the freedom to choose a variety things that she could value – but that freedom may be insufficient if her choices cannot be converted to actions. Both capabilities (freedoms, opportunities) and functionings (actualizations, realizations) matter for a person's life.

Defining the central capabilities

We have already given some examples of capabilities, such as political participation or mobility. An important (but contentious) topic within the capabilities approach concerns the central capabilities, that is, the basic capabilities to which every human being is entitled. There is considerable room for disagreement in identifying the basic capabilities, in that the capabilities approach recognizes that different societies will value different things, and hence there will be some acceptable difference among cultures and individuals as to what constitutes a valuable human life. The imperative nonetheless is that communities decide democratically upon what the central capabilities are for their society. The hope is that through a participatory, deliberative process, a society can arrive at some prioritization of what every person should be free to be and to do. However, such a process must be truly democratic, inclusive of all voices in a society, so that people or groups in power are not able to dominate and impose their values.

Where the discussion truly gets contentious, however, is with identifying what the basic, *universal* capabilities should be, those that have a value regardless of cultural or societal specificities. Interestingly, Sen, the father of the capabilities approach, has refused to specify a list of basic, central capabilities, insisting on the need for the democratic process mentioned above to determine them in culturally specific contexts. Other writers, though, have proposed such a list, chief among them Nussbaum. (See also Qizilbash 2002, Gough 2003) Nussbaum claims that it is in fact possible to identify a consensus about what constitutes a valuable human life – what basic capabilities every human is entitled to – that transcends cultures. Part of her rationale is to establish a kind of moral authority with such a list, so that students, researchers, policy makers and indeed anyone can identify when a person falls below the minimum thresholds of capabilities and is thereby deprived of some basic rights. The list of all potential human capabilities could be very long indeed, but the objective of a list of 'basic' capabilities is to set out the aspects of a life essential to wellbeing.

What are the basic capabilities? Despite the disputes, there actually is some consensus, in that most writers on the subject do find areas of common ground. Many writers mention having adequate health, enough food and nutrition, and at least enough education to ensure basic knowledge and the capability of independent thought and expression (see Desai 1995 and Saith 2001). Sen himself, despite his avoidance of an explicit list, tends to mention these same features, and adds the ideas of political participation and freedom from discrimination on the basis of race, religion and gender. These common areas have not been arrived at purely theoretically; empirical research has made some similar findings as to what people consistently value. From their massive ethnographic research project called *Voices of the Poor*, Narayan and Petesch point to these as basic capabilities that people value: bodily health; bodily integrity; respect and dignity; social belonging; cultural identity; imagination, information and education; organizational capacity; and political representation (Narayan and Petesch 2002). In David Clark's research in South Africa, people mentioned jobs, housing, education, income, family and friends, religion, health, food, good clothes, recreation and relaxation, and safety and economic security as the major aspects of a valuable life (Clark 2005). While the specific meanings people may assign to each of those (admittedly somewhat vague) headings may vary, it is nonetheless apparent that there is some consonance in the fundamental *categories*, such as with health, education/information, sociability and safety.

Nussbaum's own list embraces many of these same categories, and adds a few idiosyncratic particulars. Box 1.1 enumerates and briefly explains Nussbaum's list. Her list is by no means canonical or exhaustive; it has definitely sparked dissent, and we include it here not as a complete endorsement on her view of the central capabilities but rather because it is one of the most fully developed and influential lists, and as such a useful springboard for discussions of what the central human capabilities are or should be. Note how the list is phrased: 'being able' expresses the idea that these are capabilities that people must be free to choose to realize if they want to, but they do not absolutely have to choose to realize them. That is why this is a list of basic capabilities and not basic functionings.

There is a degree of overlap or repetition in Nussbaum's list, such as with the multiple mentions of freedom of association and expression. Part of the reason for the overlap is Nussbaum's insistence that affiliation and practical reason play an 'architectonic role' for the other capabilities (Nussbaum 2011: 39). This means that affiliation and reason are essential to a person's deciding what sort of life she values. They are also essential, in Nussbaum's view, to human dignity. She envisions a situation whereby someone might be well nourished and well educated, enjoying many of the basic capabilities, and yet without the freedom to express himself politically because of government restrictions. In such a case, that person is denied his dignity, since he is being treated like an infant. He is not truly free to make choices for himself, nor is he free to participate adequately in the life of his community, which must necessarily include helping make decisions about how his community is governed.

Box 1.1 Martha Nussbaum's list of the central capabilities

1. **Life.** 'Being able to live to the end of a human life of normal length, not dying prematurely, or before one's life is so reduced as to be not worth living.' The principle here relates to life expectancy, asserting that no one should have to accept a life of seriously foreshortened mortality.
2. **Bodily health.** 'Being able to have good health, including reproductive health; to be adequately nourished; to have adequate shelter.' These capabilities relate to food security and shelter security, but also to the fact that no one should have to accept a life with especially high morbidity (i.e. susceptibility to disease).
3. **Bodily integrity.** This capability is about an individual's right to have control over and security for his or her own body. It includes freedom from violence of all kinds, including sexual assault, as well as mobility, and choice over one's sex life and reproduction.
4. **Senses, imagination and thought.** This range of capabilities upholds the principles of freedom of expression, freedom of conscience, and the right to education; it is about being able to use one's mind freely and imaginatively. The idea is that everyone should be able to think creatively and individually. Education up to minimum standards of literacy, mathematics and science is necessary to support that ability, but also to support the capability for practical reason, listed below.
5. **Emotions.** 'Being able to have attachments to things and people outside ourselves', to those who love us, to feel longing, gratitude, anger and the full complement of emotions. This item connects to the freedom that everyone must have to form intimate relationships, but it is also part of freedom of association.
6. **Practical reason.** This is intellectual freedom broadly construed, including freedom of religion. It stipulates that every human should be able to think for him or herself, and to make reasoned choices about the life one leads.
7. **Affiliation.** This refers to a bundle of ideas on being able to live beneficially in society. It again relates to freedom of association, but it is conceived not just in political terms as the freedom to form or join political parties or other societal organizations. It is also about sociability, the capability to have a variety of social relations, and to do so without being discriminated against because of one's race, gender, sexual orientation, ethnicity, caste, religion or any other ascriptive category.
8. **Other species.** 'Being able to live with concern for and in relation to animals, plants, and the world of nature.'
9. **Play.** 'Being able to laugh, to play, to enjoy recreational activities.'
10. **Control over one's environment.** This is another bundle of political and civil rights that relate to being able to manage and shape the conditions in which a person lives. This includes political participation and freedom of speech, freedom from unreasonable search and seizure, and the equal right to hold property. It also relates to work, including freedom from employment discrimination and other unfair working conditions.

Source: adapted from Nussbaum (2011)

Because these are basic capabilities, considerations of equality are important. While everyone is equally entitled to these capabilities, sometimes equality is not a sufficient standard. Nussbaum alludes to the possibility that women could have an 'equal' right to vote as men, but that their votes would only be counted as one-quarter of a man's. Similarly, everyone might have an equal right to the minimum threshold of a primary education, but that threshold is almost meaningless unless one also considers the *quality* of the primary education. Some schools may be well equipped and provide an excellent education, while others may lack resources and teach children relatively little (Nussbaum 2011: 41). Thus, though Nussbaum regards these capabilities as the 'bare minimum' that any government must secure for its people at a minimum threshold level, sometimes getting everyone to that threshold is not enough to satisfy justice concerns. The reason is that the threshold level may still disproportionately disadvantage some people.

Imagine for instance that everyone gets one malaria pill. For people who live in high or dry areas, where malaria is not endemic, one pill may be adequate. But for people who live in malaria endemic areas, the equal standard of one pill will not do enough to help them. They may need more than one pill – an unequal distribution since the people in the high, dry areas get less – in order to enjoy the same health as the people who do not live in malaria endemic areas. Finally, in Nussbaum's list there is still room for societally contextualized variation. This means that while the list attempts to establish levels below which no one should fall, different societies may establish minimum thresholds above the levels that Nussbaum suggests. In other words, there is the potential that different societies could adapt Nussbaum's central capabilities to their own cultural context, as long as they do not violate the minimum guarantees.

The idea of basic entitlements that all people must be guaranteed should bring to mind the Universal Declaration of Human Rights (see Box 1.2), and indeed there are many affinities between human rights and the capabilities approach (See i.a. Sen 2005 and 2004, Nussbaum 1997, Vizard *et al.* 2011). Both paradigms insist that human beings be treated as ends and not as means, which implies protections for certain fundamental things such as freedom of conscience, political participation and personal security. Both depend upon principles of universality, equality and interdependence necessary to safeguard our own specific rights plus each other's rights (Deneulin 2009: 60). There are, however, meaningful differences between human rights and capabilities, such that these two approaches are not identical. For instance, human rights primarily depend upon state and legal institutions, while the fulfilment of capabilities depends upon a more diverse network of formal and informal institutions, including government, cultural norms, civil society organizations, and businesses. The capabilities approach also adds the idea of functionings, paying more attention to the dynamics of the actual *realization* of fundamental guarantees than does the human rights approach.

Ultimately, though, these two approaches complement each other. The capabilities approach benefits from the moral legitimacy that human rights grant to the fundamental guarantees, and the accountability of institutions for respecting them. As the 2000 United Nations Human Development Report declared,

> Human rights express the bold idea that all people have claims to social arrangements that protect them from the worst abuses and deprivations – and that secure the freedom for a life of dignity. Human development, in turn, is a process of enhancing human capabilities – to expand choices and opportunities so that each person can lead a life of respect and value. When human development and human rights

advance together, they reinforce one another – expanding people's capabilities and protecting their rights and fundamental freedoms.

(UNDP 2000: 2)

Much more could be said about the relationship between rights and capabilities, and in subsequent chapters this theme will return. Throughout the book we will sometimes speak of 'rights to capabilities', since that is an area where these two approaches intersect: as human beings, we all have inalienable rights to certain opportunities that are encapsulated by the notion of capabilities. For example, we all have the right to realize our capability of political participation. Thus legal rights can be a way of guaranteeing capabilities. Following is a list of some rights from the Universal Declaration of Human Rights that could be considered congruent with basic capabilities.

Other important concepts in the capabilities approach

The capabilities approach moves quickly from asking whether or not someone can do something (has the capability) to whether or not they are actually doing it (realizing the capability, i.e. the functioning). The reason is that there is so much variability and heterogeneity of people's choices and differences of distribution of opportunities, not to mention the unreliability of preferences (Nussbaum 2011: 59). For this reason, in using the capabilities approach to understand poverty, we have to be careful with what 'choice' really means. Take for example the problem of 'adaptive preference', which means that our preferences (and hence our choices) adapt to our circumstances. 'When society has put some things out of reach for some people', Nussbaum writes, 'they typically learn not to want those things' (2011: 54). If a person has no conception that she could potentially choose *not* to get married at age 14 and become a mother by 15, then she has no knowledge of how her choices are unfairly limited. If all you expect is to become a child bride and spend your life having babies and caring for them, then your preferences have adapted to your circumstances. One of the normative assumptions of the capabilities approach, though, is that people deserve to be aware of a full range of life choices – they must have the freedom to choose from that range.

The freedom-limiting dynamic of adaptive preference may be especially severe for oppressed groups, in which members adjust their expectations to the restrictions (social, cultural, political, economic) in which they are embedded. Often people with few rights will not think of their situation as extreme because this is the only life that they know (Alkire and Deneulin 2009a). This is why the capabilities approach also stresses the idea of agency; it is defined as 'one's freedom to bring about achievements one values and which one attempts to produce' (Sen 1992: 57). In other words, it is the ability to actualize functionings, but most generally to pursue one's own goals. A person's agency is important to consider because it is a way of thinking about the control that person exerts over his or her own life, the choices he or she makes. We have to keep our attention on what people actually do because capabilities are only half of the story. As an example, a woman raised in a society that says she shouldn't work outside of the home may, because of adaptive preference, never seek a profession. Or she might have the capability of getting a job, but if her functioning is limited by discrimination, she is not free to choose. In this latter case, her agency is constricted.

Freedom to choose which capabilities to actualize into functionings is also a fundamental normative assumption for the capabilities approach. The choices a person makes here

Box 1.2 Selected rights from the Universal Declaration of Human Rights

Article 1:

All human beings are born free and equal in dignity and rights. They are endowed with reason and conscience and should act towards one another in a spirit of brotherhood.

Article 3:

Everyone has the right to life, liberty and security of person.

Article 5:

No one shall be subjected to torture or to cruel, inhuman or degrading treatment or punishment.

Article 7:

All are equal before the law and are entitled without any discrimination to equal protection of the law. All are entitled to equal protection against any discrimination in violation of this Declaration and against any incitement to such discrimination.

Article 8:

Everyone has the right to an effective remedy by the competent national tribunals for acts violating the fundamental rights granted him by the constitution or by law.

Article 9:

No one shall be subjected to arbitrary arrest, detention or exile.

Article 13:

(1) Everyone has the right to freedom of movement and residence within the borders of each state.
(2) Everyone has the right to leave any country, including his own, and to return to his country.

Article 18:

Everyone has the right to freedom of thought, conscience and religion; this right includes freedom to change his religion or belief, and freedom, either alone or in community with others and in public or private, to manifest his religion or belief in teaching, practice, worship and observance.

Article 19:

Everyone has the right to freedom of opinion and expression; this right includes freedom to hold opinions without interference and to seek, receive and impart information and ideas through any media and regardless of frontiers.

Article 20:

(1) Everyone has the right to freedom of peaceful assembly and association.
(2) No one may be compelled to belong to an association.

Article 21:

(1) Everyone has the right to take part in the government of his country, directly or through freely chosen representatives.
(2) Everyone has the right of equal access to public service in his country.
(3) The will of the people shall be the basis of the authority of government; this will shall be expressed in periodic and genuine elections which shall be by universal and equal suffrage and shall be held by secret vote or by equivalent free voting procedures.

Article 23:

(1) Everyone has the right to work, to free choice of employment, to just and favourable conditions of work and to protection against unemployment.
(2) Everyone, without any discrimination, has the right to equal pay for equal work.
(3) Everyone who works has the right to just and favourable remuneration ensuring for himself and his family an existence worthy of human dignity, and supplemented, if necessary, by other means of social protection.
(4) Everyone has the right to form and to join trade unions for the protection of his interests.

Article 24:

Everyone has the right to rest and leisure, including reasonable limitation of working hours and periodic holidays with pay.

Article 25:

(1) Everyone has the right to a standard of living adequate for the health and well-being of himself and of his family, including food, clothing, housing and medical care and necessary social services, and the right to security in the event of unemployment, sickness, disability, widowhood, old age or other lack of livelihood in circumstances beyond his control.
(2) Motherhood and childhood are entitled to special care and assistance. All children, whether born in or out of wedlock, shall enjoy the same social protection.

Article 26:

(1) Everyone has the right to education. Education shall be free, at least in the elementary and fundamental stages. Elementary education shall be compulsory. Technical and professional education shall be made generally available and higher education shall be equally accessible to all on the basis of merit.
(2) Education shall be directed to the full development of the human personality and to the strengthening of respect for human rights and fundamental freedoms. It shall promote understanding, tolerance and friendship among all nations, racial

or religious groups, and shall further the activities of the United Nations for the maintenance of peace.

(3) Parents have a prior right to choose the kind of education that shall be given to their children.

Source: www.un.org/en/universal-declaration-human-rights/

are rarely simple, however, nor is the principle of freedom of choice. Sen insists that evaluating a person's freedom to choose must incorporate some perspective on the quality, quantity and diversity of available opportunities (Sen 1985, 1983). If a person is forced to choose between two evils – such as whether to stay in the village that the government has burned down, or flee into a refugee camp – then is it really accurate to say that he has adequate freedom of choice? Moreover, sometimes capabilities do not really involve a meaningful choice. Does a person choose to live long, or choose whether or not to have good health? People typically have no choice about contracting such things as malaria and cholera, for example (Clark 2005). The point of these questions about choice is this: while freedom to choose is a principle worth adhering to, in practice it is often easier to evaluate achieved functionings rather than possible choices when trying to determine such things as a person's quality of life or poverty status. How to evaluate achieved functionings – in other words, to use the capabilities approach to measure human wellbeing and poverty – is a topic we will turn to in Chapter 3.

Choice and agency can work differently for different people when it comes to achieving a life that one values. For example, as Sen has acknowledged, many factors will impact the choices a person makes, including her evaluation of the possibility of attaining the functioning she desires. He cites several factors that can influence an individual's ability to convert a capability into a functioning (Sen 2005: 153; see also Robeyns 2005):

1   Physical or mental heterogeneities among persons (including such things as disability, metabolism, sex, intelligence and being prone to illness)
2   Variations in non-personal resources (including such social factors as norms, gender roles, societal hierarchies, societal cohesion or policies on public health care or anti-discrimination laws and their enforcement)
3   Environmental diversities (such as climatic conditions, geographical factors such as isolation, or varying threats from diseases or from local crime).

Going back to the bicycle example, Robeyns explains that 'if there are no paved roads or if a government or the dominant societal culture imposes a social or legal norm that women are not allowed to cycle without being accompanied by a male family member, then it becomes much more difficult or even impossible to use the good [i.e. the bicycle] to enable the functioning' (Robeyns 2005: 99). This example reminds us of two important things. First, that it is not just the goods, services and resources a person has access to that will influence how she is able to convert capabilities to functionings. Various social institutions such as cultural norms are also influential, and for this reason it is necessary to study the situation and circumstances of people's actual lives in order to evaluate what they can choose and achieve.

Second, some people may actually require more resources to convert the same capabilities to functionings (Walker 2004, 2003). This alludes again to how one conceives equality in relation to capabilities. Someone who is blind may have the capability for mobility, but will need different resources compared to the sighted person. In Walker's example, girls in South African schools may have difficulty converting the same capabilities as boys (they are equally able to read, do maths etc.) to the same functionings because of certain factors such as cultural devaluing of girls' education or threats of sexual harassment or violence. Thus one must be very careful in assumptions about equality of opportunity, since even if such initial equality truly exists, it still does not mean that there is an equal chance to achieve the life choices that a person values. Initial opportunities are at best half of the story; achieved functionings are again essential for evaluating wellbeing. And in order to assist deprived or disadvantaged people to achieve those functionings, they may need disproportionate attention or resources compared to those who are not deprived or disadvantaged.

It should be clear by now that an idea of freedom is absolutely central to the capabilities approach. However, this is not the shallow understanding of freedom that one might assume. Freedom is not only what are known as positive liberties, i.e. the freedom to do certain things, such as criticize the government, practise your own religion, live where you want, drive whatever car you want or own as many guns as you want. The idea of freedom does include positive liberties, but it also includes negative liberties, i.e. freedom *from* hunger, fear and shame. The capabilities approach embraces both notions of freedom. It does so by emphasizing the imperative of a person's freedom to choose to live a life that he values. That is a positive liberty, but it can include the freedom to avoid other things, i.e. the negative liberty to be free from things the person does not value, such as hunger or discrimination or ignorance. Why freedom is so central to the capabilities approach is because often people who are poor simply are not free to escape their destitution. They lack alternatives; they lack agency and choice. Hence they are condemned to the unfreedom of poverty, where they do not have adequate power to change their lives. Think again of that slum described at the beginning of this chapter. How much agency and choice do people who have to live in those conditions really enjoy? Are they truly free to live the life they want, and to escape the conditions of poverty? Would anyone choose to live in those slum conditions if they could choose something better?

Another way that the capability approach's emphasis on freedom avoids simplistic, jejune understandings is by recognizing that freedom is not purely individualistic. Someone who crassly insists that freedom amounts to his positive liberty to do whatever he wants fails to realize how any individual's freedom depends upon the broader society. As noted above, many social factors can impinge upon the choices we make, whether norms about gender behaviour, public policies connected to education or health care, or economic arrangements, including the distribution of wealth and power. How other people exercise their freedoms impacts how you or I exercise our freedoms. The choices we can make depend upon broader social circumstances, and we must be attentive to those circumstances when making our choices. Sometimes certain people (because of their relative status in society) will have more choices – and hence more freedoms – than other people. Sometimes, too, the actual attainment of a person's choice is not so important. Imagine a girl in the global south who decides to pursue a PhD: what matters is that she has the reasonable freedom to make that choice, and is not unfairly constrained in the actual achievement of the goal. For the purposes of the capabilities theory, though, not everyone who wants to do a PhD must complete it in order for that person to be 'free'. As Sen explains, 'the freedom to have any particular thing can be substantially distinguished from actually having that thing' (Sen 2005: 155).

Poverty and capabilities

This book, in accordance with the capabilities approach, defines poverty as unfreedom, the deprivation of freedoms necessary to lead a fulfilled life. A person is poor when she lacks the capabilities to live the life she chooses. Sen describes a number of unfreedoms that a person would surely not choose if she were free to choose something else: famine, malnutrition, excessive morbidity, lack of access to adequate health care and clean water, violations of political and civil rights. (Sen 1999) These deprivations of inherent dignity, of basic capabilities – these unfreedoms to choose something better for oneself – qualify a person as poor. In this book we do presume that there are basic or central capabilities to which every person is entitled. In examining what poverty is, what causes it and what reduces it, our bedrock definition of poverty is being deprived of the basic capabilities to which every human is entitled. Such deprivation places a person below the minimum threshold necessary for an adequate, dignified human life. Everyone by virtue of being human has dignity, but sometimes some people live in situations where their dignity is compromised or unrealized. When such situations – whether social, political, familial or economic – deny a person her dignity, then that person is deprived (Nussbaum 2011: 30). Such deprivation denies a person the freedom to choose a life that she values.

Does this seem like an adequate definition of poverty? One of the objectives of the book is to apply this definition in multiple different spheres (education, health, gender, governance) to evaluate its adequacy. Our hope is thereby to explore ways of thinking about poverty, what it means for humans who are poor, and what it means to remedy poverty. While the definition of poverty as deprivations of basic capabilities will guide our inquiry, a few other initial observations will help make this definition more nuanced. Recognize that defining poverty almost always encounters some vagueness. Qizilbash (2003) has written about both 'horizontal' and 'vertical' vagueness. Horizontal vagueness refers to which rights or capabilities qualify as 'basic'. While this book takes Nussbaum's list as a useful sketch of basic capabilities, this is an open discussion, and the chapters should promote thinking of what capabilities deserve to count as the basic ones. Vertical vagueness refers to the minimum threshold: what is the minimum threshold for the various basic capabilities below which someone can justifiably be called poor? This is also a question that should be asked of the subsequent chapters, although certain chapters will propose specific answers relevant to their topics.

Also, one has to consider the extent of deprivation. A person might be denied a number of capabilities, but is it conceivable that he still might not be poor? Imagine, for example, that someone is denied (for whatever reason) the capability of enjoying nature, such as by taking a walk in the mountains. Number 8 on Nussbaum's list involves being able to live in relation to nature. Is that person who is denied his hike 'poor'? Probably not, though the reasons for the deprivation may help determine the answer. More powerfully, though, most people would presumably not regard taking a hike in the mountains as a basic capability to which everyone is inherently entitled, the deprivation of which would fundamentally harm his dignity or the life that he values. Again, there is a permissible vagueness or uncertainty here; the individual himself has to determine what sort of life he values. Nonetheless, a principle that Clark and

Qizilbash (2005) have proposed is that poverty is best defined as a shortfall in any core or basic dimension. So even if a person experienced deprivation of one single core capability – such as being able to get an education – he would be considered poor, even if he had ample freedom in non-core capabilities such as taking a hike. From Clark and Qizilbash's research, the people who were 'core poor' because of deprivations in the basic capabilities were the homeless, those with no access to water at all, those with no education, and the unemployed (2005: 21).

Finally, be attentive to the difference between absolute and relative poverty. The idea of absolute poverty holds that there are some standards by which anyone is poor. Someone who is starving not by his own volition, someone who cannot read, someone who is so sick that he cannot work or lead the life that he wants – all of these people are poor by an absolute standard. The list of basic capabilities sets out such an absolute standard for determining poverty. Again, the claim is that in no matter what society, if someone falls below the minimum threshold of these basic capabilities, then by definition he is poor. There is a binary aspect to absolute definitions of poverty, i.e. you either are or are not poor. This matters in relation to an example that Sen often cites, which actually derives from Adam Smith, namely the ability to appear in public without shame (See Sen 1983). If a person cannot appear in public without shame then that is a kind of poverty. In Smith's famous example, a person who could not afford the minimum standard of leather shoes expected in eighteenth-century Britain would feel shame in public. No one should be forced to feel shame for a lack of some basic material good. But this shame standard can go far beyond material goods: if a person is made to feel shame because of a disability, because he is a member of a minority ethnic group or because he has made a choice for his life that contravenes an oppressive social norm, then he is experiencing a form of deprivation. Shame relates back to dignity, something to which we are all entitled.

This is not to say that simply because you do not possess the latest, neatest cell phone, and you are ashamed of that fact, you are thereby poor. There is also room for relative standards. With the shame example, then, the basic standard for whichever material good or capability can vary somewhat depending on the society. Not having completed high school might cause one to feel shame in the United States or Canada, but it probably would not in Mauritania or Afghanistan. The important thing is that the standard is relative to a *particular* society. Why this matters is that occasionally some uninformed people will claim something to the effect of 'poor people in the United States don't know how good they have it – they have cars, public schools, health care at the emergency room, plenty to eat, not like *real* poor people' in some developing country. The misguided assumption is that poor people in rich societies such as the United States are not really poor in comparison to poor people in developing societies such as Haiti or Malawi. While there is a grain of truth in this thinking, it fails to recognize that poverty in the United States must be evaluated according to standards of living in the United States and not Malawi. Hence some definitions of poverty will be relative and context dependent, while others corresponding to the basic capabilities will be absolute and apply in every country.

Critiques of the capabilities approach

Inevitably, the capabilities approach has attracted criticism from some scholars of development and poverty, who raise several objections. One objection sometimes made is that the capabilities approach is too individualistic, since its emphasis is on the freedoms enjoyed by individuals and not groups. However, the approach's proponents such as Sen have always emphasized that an analysis of capabilities is not incompatible with application to groups or social structures. In fact, the approach explicitly acknowledges that social and group factors can impinge upon the conversion of capabilities to functionings, for instance through norms or formal state institutions. It is certainly possible to consider the freedoms and rights of groups, or the possibilities of collective action, via the capabilities approach; Chapter 5 on geography and spatial poverty does so. Moreover, Sen has given powerful reasons for why individuals need to be the primary focus for capabilities. The individual, in his account, is the main unit of moral concern. What we have to care about with social justice is individuals, because individuals are what constitute groups, whether the family, the ethnicity or whatever other collectivity. Also, prioritizing an analysis of the group or its rights can actually overlook deprivations or inequalities within the group. The classic example is with women or children, who may be disadvantaged with resource allocation within the family (Alkire and Deneulin 2009).

Two other objections are worth mentioning for their relevance to this book's application of the capabilities approach. The difficulty of agreeing upon a set of basic capabilities has attracted much attention because, critics allege, it makes the approach very difficult to operationalize, i.e. to use, to apply, to measure in the real world. We will turn to some of the issues with measuring capabilities in Chapter 3. But one of the alleged problems with operationalizing the approach is that consensus on what basic capabilities should be is unattainable, certainly at the global level, and perhaps even within countries. Even if Sen's ideal of a democratic, deliberative approach to arrive at societally contextualized basic capabilities were tried, so the complaint goes, it will be distorted by power imbalances within the society. Critics claim that disputes about what counts as 'basic' will be politically impossible to overcome. For the time being, we will leave the validity of this objection open for debate, and return to the question in the book's conclusion.

Lastly, it has also been alleged that the capabilities approach (particularly Nussbaum's list of the central capabilities) is a product of imperialistic, Western thinking. The claim is that Nussbaum's philosophy, heavily inspired by Aristotle, ignores or excludes potential non-Western views of 'the good life' and valuable freedoms. In its extreme form, this argument accuses the capabilities approach of justifying further imposition of Western values on non-Western societies. Nussbaum not surprisingly rejects such accusations, pointing out that many of the capabilities approach's main theorists are from non-Western societies (Nussbaum 2011: 104). She also says that the only imposition the approach justifies is to protect the weak from the strong. While Nussbaum mounts a cogent defence of the approach from this accusation, we will again leave this debate open for discussion as the book proceeds.

Principles for studying poverty

From these definitions of poverty and broad methods (whether emphasizing income or capabilities), this book builds on three main principles: 1) using multiple disciplines to study poverty, 2) a consistent emphasis on poverty as a *human* problem, and 3) the importance of debate and deliberation. These principles are intertwined. First, our multidisciplinary approach to studying poverty grows out of the multidimensional nature of poverty. Poverty, as we have argued earlier, cannot be understood merely as not having enough money. Therefore, poverty should not be studied just as a topic for economics and economists. Poverty relates to health, education, civil rights, international politics, gender, cultural norms and environmental concerns, among other things. Many academic disciplines, whether in the humanities, the social sciences or the natural sciences, can provide valuable insights about poverty and its related issues. Anthropology, psychology, political science, law, philosophy, history, cultural studies, biology, chemistry and theology can add a great deal to the study of poverty.

When studying poverty, it is vital to approach the subject not just abstractly or with a rigid scholarly distance. Different disciplines have different strengths. Some, such as political science or economics, tend to take what might be called a more abstract approach. Think of it this way: often, though not always, economists and political scientists examine poverty while flying at 30,000 feet. From such an altitude, you can see patterns that may not emerge from a ground-level view. You can generalize far more. Most visible tend to be big institutions (governments, for instance, or major international organizations such as the World Bank). While the view at altitude tends to provide insights on larger causal forces, structural factors, and how big systems and actors work, it can lack finer-grained detail. Generalizations are helpful and necessary, but they can lose sight of individual human beings. Anthropology and sociology are often better operating at ground level, providing the thick descriptions of actual human lives, exploring the details of individuals' experiences, plumbing the intricacies of culture and institutions and how they relate to poverty. From the ground level, it is easier to see what might be called the 'micro-politics' of poverty, the quotidian interactions of individuals and groups who experience or cause deprivation.

This brief comparison of a few disciplines is inevitably simplified. But it should demonstrate why one can gain a simultaneously broader and deeper understanding of poverty from a multidisciplinary approach rather than from a single discipline. The necessity of studying poverty from multiple disciplines has a deep connection to studying poverty as a human problem. The disciplines that work 'closer to the ground' have an advantage in showing the human face of poverty, even if they may be less amenable to generalization. Faces and voices give an immediacy that may provide a more compelling entry point into studying poverty than the more distant, high-altitude analysis of political science or economics. Moreover, seeing individual humans' stories as they relate to poverty should help stimulate empathy by appealing to our common humanity. When hearing the experience of a poor person, how can you listen and not imagine yourself in his or her place? Indeed, there is a strong argument that we have an ethical obligation to do so. Therefore, always emphasizing the human aspects of poverty should help make a direct connection to the ethical demands of poverty, namely what we (whether professors, students, rich people or poor people) owe those who are suffering.

The ultimate object of studying poverty is not states, economies, businesses or cultures but actual human beings. Though obviously the dimensions of poverty extend widely, and a sophisticated body of theory and analysis from a variety of disciplines must be brought to the study of this topic, what is the point of all the theory and analysis if it loses sight of the human beings involved? Even for the most eminent economists at the World Bank, or the most highly placed leaders at the United Nations, if they treat their work as more a problem of equations or policy implementation rather than actual human suffering, are they not losing sight of the real point of studying poverty? That is why this book continually emphasizes the faces and voices of people in poverty: because they are a constant reminder of why, as fellow human beings, we should care about this problem, and why we should work to remedy it.

The method we use in this book is well attuned to the overall ethos of the capabilities approach. A critical reason why we foreground this approach in the book is because it lends itself to multidisciplinary study. For example, arriving at a list of basic capabilities can depend upon theory from both philosophy and theology, then incorporate empirical research from sociology and anthropology to evaluate the theoretical work, and finally lead to generalization and causal analysis from economics or political science. Additionally, the capabilities approach avowedly puts human beings at the heart of its concerns. Remember that its fundamental question is: what are people able to be and to do? As Drèze and Sen have written, this 'is essentially a "people-centered" approach, which puts human agency (rather than organizations such as markets or governments) at the centre of the stage. The crucial role of social opportunities is to expand the realm of

---

Box 1.3 Freedom and human wellbeing

On the roads around Lusaka, the capital city of Zambia, you will see men and women sitting by piles of stones. They sit right next to the asphalt, cars and trucks whizzing past them. They sit there all day long, in the intense heat or in the torrential downpours. All day long, day in and day out, they sit there with a hammer, breaking large stones into smaller stones. They breathe in the pollution from the vehicles and the dust from smashing rocks. They endure injuries to their hands and muscles from the gruelling work. Every so often they will sell a pile of stones to someone who needs it for a construction project. They will earn the equivalent of a few dollars for a week's worth of work. Who would choose this work, if they had a choice? The stone breakers are often the poorest of the poor, lacking education, skills or assets such as tools beyond a hammer that might help them earn a less brutal living. What freedom do people in this situation have to choose a different life for themselves?

On an island in the southern Indian state of Kerala there is a village of Dalit people. The Dalit are the lowest in India's caste system, formerly known as 'untouchables', victims of systemic cultural discrimination. The island where they live often floods during the monsoon season, which means their dwellings are insecure. Most of the men from the village work as day labourers, which is also insecure: some days you get work and money, and others you don't. The women make money by harvesting coconuts. They earn three cents for every coconut they sell. When a girl gets married, according to custom her family has to pay a dowry. Dowries can cost up to USD 1600, plus gold. How can you amass that kind of money if you earn three cents for every coconut? Families often have to take on massive debt to be able to afford a dowry. Fortunately, Kerala has a decent system of public education, so many of the villagers go to school up to the tenth grade. Beyond that, however, tuition is no longer free, so they cannot continue. Why not leave the island and go live somewhere less flood-prone? Why not find some other means of generating an income besides harvesting coconuts? Why not refuse to pay the dowry if it is such a financial burden? These choices are actually not open to the villagers – they are not free to choose. In many ways, they live in unfreedom, and that is what it means to be poor.

human agency and freedom, both as an end in itself and as a means of further expansion of freedom' (Drèze and Sen 2002: 6). The idea is again that the individual human is the fundamental unit of analysis, and the point of the analysis is to determine the opportunities (and the constraints on those opportunities) that a person has to live a life that she values. Nussbaum's emphasis on dignity also connects here. When people are unjustly denied the development of their capabilities, the inherent dignity to which they are entitled is violated.

As its third guiding principle, this book consistently incorporates debates and encourages deliberation. The reasons are several. In the development field, there often isn't a scholarly consensus about some contentious issues. Bitter debates rage around certain topics, and many of the book's chapters consider these debates in some detail. Though sometimes we do offer what we judge to be the best or most justifiable answers to a given question, we generally avoid definitive pronouncements. Definitiveness is hard to attain in development, and there is almost never a single right answer. Do not expect ideal, master lists for how to 'solve' poverty. Rather, in our view the best approach is more provisional, and embraces competing perspectives. This approach is partly motivated by capabilities theory. Sen says in *The Idea of Justice*, 'When we try to determine how justice can be advanced, there is a basic need for public reasoning, involving arguments coming from different quarters and divergent perspectives' (2009: 92). This book therefore aims to inculcate and support the general belief (espoused by other writers in the capabilities tradition such as Crocker 2008) in deliberation. By presuming debate and competing viewpoints on many topics, rather than a single definitive answer, we want to encourage reasoning, debate, and close analysis of the viewpoints. Our hope is that the chapters engage readers in such reasoning, to show the analysis from different quarters and divergent perspectives, to urge readers to debate the issues themselves. In not pretending always to offer comprehensive answers, we recognize the importance of context and interpretation, and the need continually to reconsider one's ideas about a topic as difficult as poverty.

The multidimensional perspective, the human focus and the emphasis on debate and deliberation are all essential for answering questions of what poverty is, what causes it and how it can be reduced. They all aid in understanding the possibilities for human wellbeing. They are pedagogical strategies to shed some light on this book's ultimate question: what does it mean to be a human living in poverty? This is an enormous question, with many different potential answers, and we do not intend to answer it at the outset. Instead, we hope that readers return to the question again and again, seeking new answers after every chapter. Only in the conclusion will we pull some of these threads together. For now, and to launch this book into its subsequent chapters, we will simply pose an array of questions that all stem from the objective of treating poverty as a human problem.

What does it mean to be a human living in absolute poverty versus relative poverty? What are the basic entitlements, the central capabilities to which we all have a right? How does lacking those basic entitlements affect the human being? How does being poor affect one's psychological health? Relatedly, how does living in poverty affect one's sense of self-worth? How does living in poverty affect one's physical health and one's learning? How does living in poverty affect one's ability to get what one wants, whether materially, emotionally, politically or spiritually? How, in sum, does living in poverty affect one's humanity? Answering this last question naturally requires us to try to define 'humanity', and even if such a definition may be debatable, multifarious and frustratingly incomplete, asking the question, and trying to answer it, is one of the most valuable things we can do to lead an informed and ethical life.

Make no mistake: though this book is not an ethics manual, ethical concerns pervade its inquiry. Focusing on poverty as a human problem connects to our collective responsibility as human beings to achieve this book's goals of understanding what causes poverty and how it can be alleviated. These are goals that humans, working together, can and should attain. Moral considerations are also interlaced with the capabilities approach. The idea of basic capabilities, and the need for development to promote human freedom, both presume certain moral standards of what is acceptable for human life, society, and public policy. The validity and practicality of these standards should also be interrogated as the book proceeds. A final moral concern is that studying poverty is fundamentally about our own humanity. This is because we humanize ourselves by considering the basic rights and capabilities to which we are all entitled (Walker 2009). We humanize ourselves, and hopefully our societies and the world, when we take on the challenges of understanding the minimum requirements of human dignity, how people are unjustly deprived of their dignity, and how we can justly help them to recover it. In the final chapter of the book, we examine ethical questions in more detail, but throughout all the chapters that follow, we urge readers to think consistently and profoundly about their own ethical engagement with the study of poverty.

Conclusion

The essential ideas in defining poverty are deprivation and multidimensionality. Deprivation assumes that an individual is denied something to which she is entitled. Multidimensionality stresses the need to look at many different indicators of poverty and its diverse impacts on the human experience. The income/monetary definition and the capabilities approach both have utility for defining poverty. This book will rely most consistently on the capabilities approach because it is synthetically able to incorporate aspects of other definitions, and always puts human beings at the centre of its analysis. It is inherently multidimensional in that it considers a variety of potential areas, from health to cultural expression to rights, that relate to poverty. And by establishing an idea of basic capabilities, it puts forward a definition of poverty based on the deprivation of certain opportunities to which every human being is entitled. The capabilities approach stresses inherent freedoms, and holds this as the key question to evaluate wellbeing and poverty: 'What is each person able to do and to be?'

Poverty is unfortunately a universal human phenomenon. It exists in one form or another in every society, and nearly everywhere individual humans are suffering from this problem. Around the world, the majority of poor people are women who are in turn responsible for caring for dependents (children, the elderly and the disabled). Though the capabilities approach focuses on individual freedom, this book will also pay particular attention to how disadvantaged groups (women, minorities, marginalized communities) often suffer more from poverty, and frequently have the least opportunity to develop their capabilities and functionings. Understanding how different groups experience poverty – i.e. rural versus urban, men versus women, adults versus children and youth, or people without disabilities versus people with disabilities – can help identify opportunities for intervention as well. Studying poverty is not merely an intellectual exercise; the goal of learning is action, in this case action to reduce poverty so that every person can live a life that he or she values.

Discussion questions

1   What does freedom have to do with poverty?
2   What are the problems with examining global poverty only in terms of the global south and not the global north?
3   What do you see as the relative advantages and disadvantages of the income and capabilities approaches? Is the capabilities approach relevant only for developing countries, or could it work for any country around the world?
4   What does it mean to treat human beings as ends and not as means?
5   What capabilities do you think are essential for a dignified life? Do you think the list should be left open like Sen advocates or do you think the global community needs to agree on a list like Nussbaum's? What would you add to or subtract from Nussbaum's list?
6   What would the deliberative process look like for a society to decide on its list of central capabilities?

- Attempt to construct such a process in your class, and conduct a debate to identify agreed-upon central capabilities.
- Do you think that it is possible to come to a truly democratic agreement on basic capabilities, whether globally, within countries or even within your classroom?

7   What do you think of the critiques that the capabilities approach is guilty of imposing Western values on the rest of the world?

Further reading

Brighouse, Harry and Ingrid Robeyns, eds. 2010. *Measuring Justice: Primary goods and capabilities*. Cambridge, UK: Cambridge University Press.
Clark, David A. 'The Capability Approach', in David A. Clark, ed. 2006. *The Elgar Companion to Development Studies*. Cheltenham, UK: Edward Elgar.
Comim, Flavio, Mozaffar Qizilbash and Sabina Alkire, eds. 2008. *The Capability Approach: Concepts, measures and applications*. Cambridge, UK: Cambridge University Press.
Deneulin, Séverine and Lila Shahani, eds. 2009. *An Introduction to the Human Development and Capability Approach*. London: Earthscan.
Nussbaum, Martha. 'Poverty and Human Functioning: Capabilities as Fundamental Entitlements', in David B. Grusky and Ravi Kanbur, eds. 2006. *Poverty and Inequality*. Stanford, CA: Stanford University Press.
Pogge, Thomas, ed. 2007. *Freedom from Poverty as a Human Right*. Oxford: Oxford University Press.
Sen, Amartya. 1999. *Development as Freedom*. New York, NY: Anchor Press.
Sen, Amartya. 'Capability and Well-Being', in Martha Nussbaum and Amartya Sen, eds. 2003. *The Quality of Life*. Oxford: Oxford University Press.
The Universal Declaration of Human Rights: www.un.org/en/documents/udhr/

Works cited

Alkire, Sabina and Séverine Deneulin. 'A Normative Framework for Development', in Séverine Deneulin and Lila Shahani, eds. 2009a. *An Introduction to the Human Development and Capability Approach*. London: Earthscan.
Alkire, Sabina and Séverine Deneulin. 'The Human Development and Capability Approach', in Séverine Deneulin and Lila Shahani, eds. 2009b. *An Introduction to the Human Development and Capability Approach*. London: Earthscan.

Clark, David A. 'The Capability Approach: Its Development, Critiques and Recent Advances', Global Poverty Research Group paper, GPRG-WPS-032, 2005.

Clark, David A. and Mozaffar Qizilbash. 'Core Poverty, Basic Capabilities and Vagueness: An Application to the South African Context', Global Poverty Research Group paper GRPG-WPS-026, July 2005.

Comim, Flavio. 'Measuring capabilities', in Flavio Comim, Mozaffar Qizilbash and Sabina Alkire, eds. 2008. *The Capability Approach: Concepts, measures and applications*. Cambridge, UK: Cambridge University Press.

Crocker, David A. 2008. *Ethics of Global Development: Agency, capability, and deliberative democracy*. Cambridge, UK: Cambridge University Press.

Deneulin, Séverine. 'Ideas Related to Human Development', in Séverine Deneulin and Lila Shahani, eds. 2009. *An Introduction to the Human Development and Capability Approach*. London: Earthscan.

Desai, Meghnad. 'Poverty and Capability: Towards an Empirically Implementable Measure', in *Poverty, Famine and Economic Development: The selected essays of Meghnad Desai*, Volume II. 1995. Aldershot, UK: Edward Elgar.

Drèze, Jean and Amartya Sen. 2002. *India: Development and participation*. Oxford: Oxford University Press.

Gough, Ian. 2003. 'Lists and Thresholds: Comparing Our Theory of Human Need with Nussbaum's Capabilities Approach', WeD Working Paper 01, The Wellbeing in Developing Countries Research Group, University of Bath.

Narayan, Deepa and Patti Petesch. 2002. *Voices of the Poor from Many Lands*. Washington, DC: The World Bank.

Nussbaum, Martha. 2011. *Creating Capabilities: The human development approach*. Boston, MA: Harvard University Press.

Nussbaum, Martha. 'Capabilities and human rights', *Fordham Law Review*, 66 (1997): 273–300.

Qizilbash, Mozaffar. 'Vague language and precise measurement: the case of poverty', *Journal of Economic Methodology*, 10.1 (2003): 41–58.

Qizilbash, Mozaffar. 'Development, common foes and shared values', *Review of Political Economy*, 14.4 (2002): 463–480.

Robeyns, Ingrid. 'The capability approach: a theoretical survey', *Journal of Human Development*, 6.1 (2005): 93–114.

Saith, Ruhi. 'Capabilities: The Concept and its Operationalisation', Queen Elizabeth House Working Paper 66, February 2001.

Sen, Amartya. 2009. *The Idea of Justice*. London: Allen Lane.

Sen, Amartya. 'Human rights and capabilities', *Journal of Human Development*, 6.2 (2005): 151–166.

Sen, Amartya. 'Elements of a theory of human rights', *Philosophy & Public Affairs*, 32.4 (2004): 315–356.

Sen, Amartya. 1999. *Development as Freedom*. New York, NY: Knopf.

Sen, Amartya. 1992. *Inequality Re-examined*. Oxford: Oxford University Press.

Sen, Amartya. 'Justice: means versus freedoms', *Philosophy and Public Affairs*, 19 (1990): 111–121.

Sen, Amartya. 'A sociological approach to the measurement of poverty: a reply to Professor Peter Townsend', *Oxford Economic Papers*, New Series, 37.4 (1985): 669–676.

Sen, Amartya. 'Poor, relatively speaking', *Oxford Economic Papers*, New Series, 35.2 (1983): 153–169.

United Nations Development Programme. 2000. *Human Development Report: Human rights and human development*. Oxford: Oxford University Press.

Vizard, Polly, Sakiko Fukuda-Parr and Diane Elson. 'Introduction: the capability approach and human rights', *Journal of Human Development and Capabilities*, 12.1 (2011): 1–22.

Walker, Melanie. 'Teaching the Human Development and Capability Approach: Some Pedagogical Implications', in Séverine Deneulin and Lila Shahani, eds. 2009. *An Introduction to the Human Development and Capability Approach*. London: Earthscan.

Walker, Melanie. 'Human Capabilities, Education and 'Doing the Public Good': Towards a Capability-Based Theory of Social Justice in Education', paper presented at the Australian Association for Research in Education, November–December 2004.

Walker, Melanie. 'Framing social justice in education: what does the 'capabilities' approach offer?' *British Journal of Educational Studies*, 51.2 (2003): 168–187.

2 Development and its debates

Benjamin Curtis and Serena Cosgrove

Key questions

- What is 'development'? What is the history of this term, concept, and field?
- How are human development and capabilities relevant to poverty reduction?
- Who does development? Who are the major actors at the national and international levels?
- How are the meaning and practice of development contested? What are some of the major controversies in this field?

Introduction

What does it mean to help people escape poverty? When you think of anti-poverty programmes, what do you think of? Some people might think of handouts, whether of money or food or clothing, to people who lack those things. Some might think of providing health care, for example setting up a clinic in a remote area that has little access to medicines or trained health workers. Bringing roads, electricity and clean water to that remote area might be another answer. Though it may seem more distant from the lives of people suffering from poverty, buying agricultural or manufactured products from their country could be a further way of increasing their incomes and expanding their life choices. Less obvious measures for combating poverty could include signing worldwide compacts to mitigate the damage of climate change, or providing troops for international peacekeeping missions, or opening a country's borders to eager immigrants seeking to better their lot. Some of these measures may seem surprising, and nearly all of the above can be controversial, but without exception they are actual examples of programmes to reduce poverty and promote 'development'.

This chapter studies the idea of development, and in particular what is controversial about it. In studying global poverty, naturally one should also explore how poverty can be reduced, perhaps with the goal of eliminating poverty altogether. Most chapters in this book provide an analysis of programmes for fighting poverty, including in health, education and financial services. But before diving into the details, it is necessary to think in broader terms about how the global community works today to promote prosperity and wellbeing. There are in fact a range of philosophies, practices, and actors working to accomplish those goals. Some of them are even opposed to each other, or mutually contradictory. This chapter will lay out the major competing philosophies, explain the major actors who work in the development sector and discuss some of the most salient critiques and debates in this field. In some cases, there is no 'right answer' to these debates – but the chapter will show that there are nonetheless some principles for doing development that are most strongly justified, and most recommendable for reducing poverty and improving people's lives.

What is development?

Most scholars agree that the idea of 'international development' begins shortly after the Second World War. In its broadest form, this idea holds that via the application of certain policies, the parts of the world that are 'underdeveloped' can be brought up to the levels of prosperity and wellbeing of the rich Western countries. Since the 1940s, the theory and practice of development have transitioned through multiple paradigms, some of which actively disagree with each other. The importance of these development paradigms is that they all, in one way or another, espouse a particular vision of what poverty is and how it can be reduced. There are many different periodizations of these paradigms, but a few of the major categories include:

1   **Modernization theory** predominated in the 1950s and the 1960s as the wave of decolonization created many new, 'developing' countries. According to modern-ization theory, a society's path to prosperity involves overcoming backward traditions to acquire the social and economic characteristics of the high-income Western countries. Scholars such as Walt Rostow (1960) argued that societies progress along a series of stages from an agricultural economy with more rigid social structures towards a 'modern', industrialized, consumer society. The focus of much develop-ment policy in these decades was to identify the strategies that would help countries transition to an industrial economy.

2   **Dependency theory** inverts the modernization perspective to examine economic development from the perspective of the 'periphery', i.e. the non-industrialized countries. Influential in the 1960s and 1970s, dependency theory argued that the economic development of the West retarded the development of the rest by exploiting the latter's resources, making them dependent on the high-income, industrialized countries. Moreover, according to this perspective, globally unequal development actually serves the interests of elites in Western countries, who benefit by keeping the periphery poor. Representative writers include Raúl Prebitsch, Paul Baran, André Gunder Frank and Immanuel Wallerstein.

3   **Neo-liberalism** was dominant in the 1980s and 1990s, though its ideas remain influential today. This approach generally stresses free market economics as the optimal route to development, including liberalizing trade policies and privatizing state-run enterprises so as to spur more rapid economic growth. It is famously associated with the so-called 'Washington consensus', a prescriptive set of policies promoted by Washington, DC-based institutions including the World Bank and the International Monetary Fund. As conditions for loans to developing countries, these institutions often insisted on 'structural adjustment', which required developing countries to adopt measures including tax reform, deregulation, strict budget discipline and policies to encourage foreign direct investment. Writers commonly associated with neo-liberalism are Friedrich Hayek and Milton Friedman.

4   **Human development** is in some ways a reaction against the economic focus of modernization theory and particularly neo-liberalism. It emerged in the later 1970s,

and gained momentum in the 1990s. Because it is this book's guiding approach to poverty, human development is discussed in more detail below.

5   **Sustainable development** is a broad collection of ideas questioning the costs to the environment of existing models of economic growth. Attention to these issues has grown since 1987 when the Brundtland Commission called for 'development that meets the needs of the present without compromising the ability of future generations to meet their own needs' (Brundtland 1987). The sustainable development ethos focuses on how to encourage conservation and more sustainable management of natural resources. Though sustainability is usually conceived in environmental terms, it can have additional dimensions such as social sustainability, which emphasizes that economic growth must be more equitably shared at national and global levels. The sustainability ethos can be compatible with other paradigms including human development. (See i.a. Redclift 2005, Elliott 2012, and this book's Chapter 10 on the environment and poverty reduction.)

This is by no means a complete listing of development theories, and even when theories (such as modernization) become passé or discredited, some of their ideas often form part of the intellectual heritage of subsequent paradigms, so there isn't a strict sequence in development theories either. Similarly, none of these paradigms is without its critics, and most of the theories do offer some insights. Depending on one's viewpoint, the entire idea of development itself is riddled with flaws and problems, as we discuss in a subsequent section. In fact, there is now a field of 'post-development' studies (see e.g. Rahnema and Bawtree 1997, Rapley 2004, Sidaway 2007). While we will use the language of development, our strong preference is to emphasize human development, and in particular poverty reduction.

Human development

Human development is often identified with the capabilities approach, though they are not completely synonymous (see e.g. Nussbaum 2011, Deneulin and Shahani 2009). Human development intentionally expands the notion of wellbeing beyond an economic one. In so doing, it makes its own normative claims about what development *should* be, and what policies should be pursued to achieve it. These normative claims inform the basic definitions of human development, whose purpose is 'to enlarge people's choices' (Alkire and Deneulin 2009: 26), to expand 'the opportunities open to each person' (Nussbaum 2011: 14), in short to promote freedom in all sorts of areas, whether politics, economics, social opportunities or basic security. Mahbub ul Haq, one of the principal theorists of human development, enunciated an expansive purview for this approach, saying that it 'covers all aspects of development – whether economic growth or international trade; budget deficits or fiscal policy; savings, investment or technology, basic social services or safety nets for the poor' (ul Haq 2004: 17). How can human development encompass such diverse areas? The answer is the guiding goal of 'creating an enabling environment for people to enjoy long, healthy, creative lives', in short to widen people's choices and enrich the lives they lead (ul Haq 2004: 17).

Ul Haq points to these five key principles of human development:

1   Development must put people at the centre of its concerns.
2   The purpose of development is to enlarge all human choices and not just income.

3   The human development paradigm is concerned both with building human capabilities (through investment in people) and with using those human capabilities more fully (through an enabling framework for growth and employment).

4   Human development has four essential pillars: equality, sustainability, productivity and empowerment. It regards economic growth as essential, but emphasizes the need to pay attention to its quality and distribution, analyses at length its link with human lives, and questions its long-term sustainability.

5   The human development paradigm defines the ends of development and analyses sensible options for achieving them (ul Haq 2004: 19).

These principles need to be examined in some detail. The first principle means that the fundamental locus of concern is human beings and human lives – not economic systems, governments or industrial policies. This principle accords with one of the guiding ideas of this book, which is that poverty is a human problem, and problems of poverty and development must never lose sight of the individuals who are both suffering and potentially benefiting. The second principle connects directly to the perspective of capabilities. People must be free to make choices – they must have the capability to choose, and to actualize their capabilities as functionings. The third principle states that development must secure people's basic capabilities, and that doing so requires society-wide policies to create the 'enabling framework' to support capabilities and functionings.

The fourth principle is a bundle of concepts which Sabina Alkire and Séverine Deneulin (2009) have elucidated. The pillar of equality (more appropriately stated in this case as 'equity') recognizes that some people, such as those who are poor, women or from minority groups, may be chronically and systematically disadvantaged in terms of their opportunities in life. They therefore may need additional resources to guarantee their basic capabilities. Sustainability, they explain, refers to achieving positive results that will endure over time. Besides the need to protect environmental resources for future generations, there are also financial and social dimensions of sustainability. The former refers to the need to finance development so that future generations are not harmed through countries falling into debt traps. The latter refers to involving communities in development projects to ensure that those projects have lasting positive effects. The pillar of productivity relates to the idea that everyone is entitled to an economic livelihood and that economic growth can enlarge people's choices. The final pillar, empowerment, relates again to community involvement. It stresses the need for people to have agency in political processes that affect them, so that they can ensure that development projects do truly benefit them, and so they can hold politicians and development professionals accountable.

As the fifth principle indicates, the conception of development's purpose is different between the economic and human development paradigms. Classically, in the economic development paradigm the purpose of development is to increase people's incomes. The rationale again is that higher incomes will translate to higher wellbeing. Sen reminds us, however, that the objective of building a manufacturing economy is ultimately not to expand a country's exports and raise the value of the goods it produces. Economic growth and higher incomes should be conceived above all as means of expanding human freedoms, not as ends in themselves. One reason why is that economic development does not always lead to poverty reduction. If only a small slice of the population accrues the benefits of economic growth while vast numbers remain hungry, sick, illiterate or disempowered, then clearly economic growth is not a sufficient solution. Furthermore, some scholars have claimed that economic growth is unsustainable without a focus on the key aspects of human development such as education and health (Ranis, Stewart and Ramirez 2000).

The human development perspective holds that people must be free to decide what sort of life they want to live. Yet like the other development paradigms, it is still prescriptive, since it emphasizes human freedom as the central moral good. Remember that poverty (as explained in the previous chapter) can be defined as unfreedom. 'Development', Sen has written, 'requires the removal of major sources of unfreedom: poverty as well as tyranny, poor economic opportunities as well as systematic social deprivation, neglect of public facilities as well as intolerance or overactivity of repressive states' (Sen 1999: 3). Thus Sen defines things such as education and health not as 'outcomes' of development, but as 'constituent components' of development. They can contribute to economic growth, but that is not the only rationale to pursue improvements in education and health. The additional and more powerful rationale is that improving individuals' education and health should strengthen their freedoms and rights, and doing so is the definition of development. The idea of 'development as freedom' directs attention to the ends of development, its ultimate goals, rather than stopping at its means, namely increasing incomes. Again, this is not to deny the utility of studying economic development – it is just to emphasize that though economic development has dominated research and policy, it is a decidedly incomplete way of understanding poverty.

Development policy and capabilities

Development policy should best be conceived as promoting human development, which means that development must concern itself with capabilities. Multiple different actors have responsibility for development, but governments have a particular duty. Nussbaum insists that 'the job of government is understood to be that of raising all citizens above the threshold on all ten [central] capabilities' (2011: 109). A national government's work in helping citizens reach minimum capability thresholds can take several forms. It can entail a consistent commitment to and enactment of pro-poor policies. It can also mean a legal framework in the country's constitution that includes direct mention of all the capabilities that people will enjoy. These legal guarantees can help create the institutions to assure everyone's capabilities reach minimum justice levels. Not only national governments have a duty here, since other actors including the United Nations agencies, the World Bank and the International Monetary Fund also have a role to play. They must support the institutionalization of capabilities in countries around the world, even as national governments assure basic capabilities for their citizens.

There are several justifications for government's role in ensuring basic capabilities.[1] Poor people often lack security, whether of food, income or bodily integrity. Concerted public action in the form of government policies is one of the most effective ways of mobilizing resources to make people's capabilities more secure. So for example, a policy to guarantee women access to reproductive control or other services for bodily health would be a way of securing their capabilities to make choices about their sexual and reproductive lives. Women would not have to choose to avail themselves of these services. What matters is that they have opportunity freedom (so that the services exist, they are available to be chosen) as well as process freedom (so that women could make the choice for themselves, they are not constrained or prevented from choosing what they want). The reason basic capabilities are so important as objects of policy is, first, because they are the fundamental rights to which all human beings are entitled. Second, these capabilities are foundational to many others. Without bodily health, for example, one will simply not have the opportunity to choose many other aspects of a life that one might value. Therefore, basic capabilities are a sensible focus for development policy. Programmes to guarantee people access to these opportunities – such as reproductive health, or schooling – are a way of ensuring that people have the freedom they should have.

Government has a vital role in development because it is unreasonable and illogical to assume that poor people can simply 'lift themselves up by their own bootstraps' to get out of poverty (as one can sometimes hear in American attitudes). If an adolescent child must work as a trash picker on an urban dump site so that his family has enough to eat, and he is therefore suffering from poverty by having his health harmed by terrible working conditions and being denied an opportunity to get an education, it is senseless to urge that child to 'pull himself up by his own bootstraps'. Escaping poverty does not depend solely on individual effort; it requires concerted, societal effort. People who are highly vulnerable and discriminated against need government so that their rights are protected. Government, in contrast to much discourse in the United States, is not merely a 'threat' to liberties (such as by taxation, regulation, or by taking away a person's guns). Government can also, vitally, protect liberties, such as by instituting and enforcing laws to protect people from discrimination and exploitation, and to guarantee them public goods such as basic health care and education.

Thus we see that the capabilities approach is not only a way of defining poverty and wellbeing, but also of defining what development should be. 'The purpose of global development', according to Nussbaum, 'is to enable people to live full and creative lives, developing their potential and fashioning a meaningful existence commensurate with their equal dignity' (2011: 185). The perspective of the capabilities approach on development policy is convincingly summarized by Ingrid Robeyns:

> [The capabilities approach] asks whether people are being healthy, and whether the means or resources necessary for this capability are present, such as clean water, access to doctors, protection from infections and diseases, and basic knowledge on health issues. It asks whether people are well-nourished, and whether the conditions for this capability, such as having sufficient food supplies and food entitlements, are being met. It asks whether people have access to a high-quality educational system, to real political participation, to community activities that support them to cope with struggles in daily life and that foster real friendships. For some of these capabilities, the main input will be financial resources and economic production, but for others it can also be political practices and institutions, such as the effective guaranteeing and protection of freedom of thought, political participation, social or cultural practices, social structures, social institutions, public goods, social norms, traditions and habits.
>
> (Robeyns 2005: 95)

In other words, the public policies, institutions, and structures must be in place to guarantee people their basic capabilities. Designing development policy with the objective of guaranteeing those capabilities should be the overarching goal of development. In the chapters that follow, we will be examining a number of prominent causes of poverty, and studying in particular how these causes deprive people of basic capabilities. Our study of policies to reduce poverty will focus on how basic capabilities can be supported along the lines Robeyns sketches above.

Development or poverty reduction or poverty eradication?

Is there a difference between development and 'poverty reduction'? What should the global community be aiming for – poverty eradication? Though there is some overlap between these terms, they are not synonymous, and their differences in meaning are not surprisingly contentious. In fact, just as there are different paradigms of development, there are different definitions of poverty reduction. According to the United Nations Development Programme, reducing poverty means 'public policy interventions that help to modify the social, cultural, and economic conditions that created poverty in the first place' (UNDP 2013). Those interventions can target a number of areas, such as gender equality and women's empowerment, democratic governance, adaptation to climate change and the elimination of stigma with HIV/AIDS. The Asian Development Bank characterizes poverty reduction as depending upon pro-poor, sustainable economic growth and sound macroeconomic management with good governance. It also requires strengthening human capital, social capital, the status of women and social safety net protections for people who suffer from disabilities, natural disasters or conflict. Lastly, poverty reduction necessitates attention to environmental issues including air and water pollution and degradation of natural resources such as deforestation which dispropor-tionately affect the poor (Deolalikar *et al.* 2002).

The 2000 World Development Report stressed that poverty reduction must involve empowerment, security and opportunity for poor people. Empowerment is defined as making state institutions more responsive and accountable to poor people. It can be achieved by strengthening poor people's participation in political processes and local decision making, and removing discriminatory barriers to participation whether because of gender, ethnicity, race, religion etc. Security refers to protecting the poor from adverse shocks such as ill health, crop failure, natural disasters and violence. It can be achieved by better management of the economy and through a more robust social safety net. Opportunity means increasing poor people's access to assets such as land and education, and increasing the rates of return to these assets (World Bank 2000). Clearly, poverty reduction can mean many different things. But note some consistencies here. First, the idea of poverty reduction depends upon a multidimensional understanding of poverty: poverty is more than one thing, and people can suffer from it in a variety of ways. Second, most definitions of poverty reduction do tend to emphasize economic growth with equity, good governance, certain aspects of human development such as health and education, and social protection policies specifically designed to benefit the poor.

However, the broad scope of poverty reduction also raises some difficult questions. Owen Barder, for example, points to a number of problematic trade-offs with both the idea and practice of poverty reduction. One is the 'broad versus deep' trade-off: should poverty reduction aim to help as many people as possible, or focus on a smaller number of people in more severe, chronic poverty? The 'today versus tomorrow' trade-off asks whether poverty reduction should focus resources on helping people in poverty today, or on reducing the conditions that may make people poor in the future? Similarly, there is a trade-off between poverty reduction programmes with a more temporary focus – to help people in the short term – versus programmes that aim for a long-term, sustainable impact (Barder 2009). Further complicating the picture is that many of the criticisms of development (see the next section) can also be levelled at poverty reduction. It is accused of still following a neo-liberal model of development, letting large donors set priorities and thereby preserving the clout of the big international development agencies. In practice, too, many poverty reduction strategies take the same basic form as development strategies through transfers of funds from a rich country government to a developing country government. This means that state institutions in the developing country still retain primarily responsibility for poverty reduction (Hydén n.d.).

Given these difficulties, should one focus on 'poverty alleviation' or 'poverty relief' or 'poverty eradication'? These terms appear in the study and practice of international development (and occasionally in this book), though they, too, are not without their complications. Poverty alleviation is akin to the idea of poverty reduction, in that it presumes an amelioration of the suffering and/or deprivation associated with poverty. However, some critics claim that the 'alleviation' term connotes not a real elimination of the factors causing poverty, but just their temporary lessening – a Band-Aid, perhaps, but not a cure. Poverty relief, likewise, can connote a short-term focus, merely relieving the suffering of poverty at the immediate time. Certainly such a focus is necessary sometimes, as in situations of famine, natural disaster, or insecurity provoked by armed conflict. But 'relief' as a term does not embrace the idea of systemic change to prevent poverty in the future. So why not use the term 'poverty eradication', then? Ultimately, of course, the goal should be that no human suffers from poverty. But is that a realistic goal? On the one hand, the push to eliminate extreme poverty – the deprivations of fundamental, basic entitlements of food, health, rights or central capabilities – is a moral imperative to which the global community should strive. On the other hand, poverty may never be fully eradicated because even if absolute poverty came to an end, there would still be relative poverty. Definitions of poverty will vary from society to society, even if the fundamental, universal entitlements were met for all human beings, so some people in some societies may still be poor because they could have so much less than others in the same society (see Feres and Villatoro 2012).

Keeping all these contentious definitional complications in mind, this book favours the terminology of poverty reduction. One reason is that this is a book about *poverty* and not about development per se. This book studies how poverty can be defined and measured, what causes it, and how the deprivations associated with it can be reduced. Additionally, the idea of poverty reduction is more closely attuned to the multidimensional and multidisciplinary approach to poverty the book espouses, in a way that economic development is not. Remember that the ultimate end of poverty reduction and development broadly conceived is improvements in human wellbeing, not just increases in income. Poverty reduction through a focus on development of basic human capabilities can thus avoid some of the problematic assumptions inherent in prioritizing economic growth. In their most simplistic form, those assumptions can treat capitalism as an unquestioned good. The perspective of poverty reduction can help to avoid the strain of neo-liberal ideology that holds a doctrinaire view of US-style capitalism as the highest, or only valid, model of economic organization.

Additionally, by emphasizing poverty reduction and human development, we hope to avoid the sometimes implicit, sometimes explicit attitude in development discourse and practice that the rich world can 'save' the poor. Such paternalistic attitudes fail to respect people's own agency, and can fall prey to even more offensive stereotypes about people in the developing world. It is not the job of rich countries to 'save' the poor. Rather, what this book will explore is what people in rich countries do owe people in developing countries. While we will offer several answers that we think are well reasoned, this should be a debate, albeit one conducted without unexamined paternalistic attitudes. Subsuming these previous principles is the admonition to be very cautious about Western impositions on the global south. Never should we presume that because, say, the United States and the United Kingdom are rich, they have figured out the formula for granting every person the freedom to live valued lives. Instead, we should very carefully consider when and how models from rich Western countries may be instructive for poor Southern countries, and also be very cautious about even using such broad categories as 'West' and 'South'. This book's perspective on poverty reduction is by no means free of the problems of the development paradigm(s) – but it does at least foreground the imperative of reducing 'unfreedoms', and putting the quality of individual human lives at the centre of concern.

Critiquing development

Both the concepts of development and poverty reduction are based on an idea of improving peoples' lives. But even that idea can and should be questioned (see i.a. Rist 2002, Sachs 2009, Escobar 2011). In particular, it is worth asking whether development (and hence improvement) depends on a problematic Western idea of 'progress'. Underlying the postwar conception of development is a binary: countries are either 'developed' or 'developing'. According to this conception, if countries are in the latter category, then they must attempt to move into the former category.[2] The content of what 'development' entails has changed over the decades, and will doubtless continue to change in the future. Modernization theory holds out one vision of development, neo-liberalism another, and human development another. But in every case, it might be alleged that the end goal – becoming 'developed' – involves adopting Western models. After all, industrialization, international trade, impersonal bureaucratic management and more or less free markets have brought enormous wealth to Western societies, have they not? And later, non-Western industrializers such as Japan, South Korea or Singapore have all become rich following this basic model, haven't they? Therefore, it can be claimed that achieving progress – whether defined as income growth or improvement in human development terms – depends upon accepting the Western conception of what 'progress' looks like. Often that Western conception has envisioned progress as a linear, deterministic, one-size-fits-all path from 'undeveloped' to 'developed'.

In order for countries to develop, then, their governments must enact policies derived from the successful Western experience. But can such policies actually transform, say, a traditional tribal pastoralist society into a high-wage, export-oriented, industrial democracy such as Germany? The assumption behind many development efforts is that they can. Indeed, the assumption is that the right policies can help less-developed countries speed up their development, achieving in a matter of decades what many Western countries took centuries to accomplish. Hence the conception and practice of development has been extremely policy prescriptive. It has assumed that the key to success in the development endeavour is to get policies right. In other words, if Peru would only adopt the same policies as Canada, then Peru could attain Canadian-style levels of prosperity. Following the blueprint of successfully developed countries should help any country attain that vaunted Western model.

Implicit in this assumption is the idea that planning works. Plans, devised by technical experts, should lead to success if correctly implemented. Who are the experts, though, and what do they know about local conditions? How responsive are those plans to the needs and desires of the individuals and communities who are their objects or beneficiaries? Development has often been guided by a belief in the power of technocratic management – that smart people, accurately identifying the key problems and solutions, can prescribe the steps necessary for progress. Critics of these ideas are not alleging that all planning is futile, or that the Western policy blueprint is inevitably faulty. Some planning is necessary to make almost any endeavour more efficient and hopefully successful. The criticism is rather that too strong a faith in planning can lead to inflexibility and a one-size-fits-all mindset that insufficiently respects diverse contexts. It is crucial to ask at what point planning becomes excessively top-down and unaccountable, failing to incorporate the voices of the people being affected by the planning.

Combining all the preceding caveats about development leads to another, and very important question: Is development just a new form of paternalistic Western politics, colonialism in another guise? In previous centuries, Western imperialism was motivated by ideas of the 'civilizing mission' and the 'white man's burden'. This ideology asserted that Western countries had the power and the duty to lift up benighted peoples in other parts of the world, to make them more modern for their own good. Did the belief in the civilizing mission not die with colonialism? Does it still inform many Western attitudes about non-Western countries? Part of this ideology held that non-Western peoples needed tutelage, that they were 'half-devil and half-child', in the words of Rudyard Kipling's poem *The White Man's Burden* (1899). While few would use that exact language today, critics allege that Western approaches to development are still domineering and disrespectful of other countries' autonomy.

The most concrete form of this critique targets the major institutions of global development such as the International Monetary Fund and the World Bank. It is alleged that many of these institutions are products of Western dominance. It is difficult to deny that the IMF and the World Bank in particular have been 'heavily influenced by the material and intellectual power of the United States, OECD countries, corporate capitalism and neo-classical economics in US universities' (Hulme 2010: 51). Historically, the head of the IMF has always been from Europe, and the head of the World Bank from the United States. These two institutions in particular are often attacked for being excessively top-down and technocratic, lacking in accountability to those whom their policies affect. Critics have claimed that the IMF and the World Bank, as major promoters of neo-liberalism, have often harmed developing countries with their policies (see i.a. Gore 2000, Wade 2002, Babb 2005, Sheppard and Leitner 2010). The structural adjustment programme in particular is criticized for actually increasing poverty by forcing countries that receive loans to slash spending on social services.

Has then this Western model of development essentially tried to remake the world along the lines of the consumer societies of Europe and North America? At worst, development could be an imposition of a model unsustainable on a planetary scale: if a billion Chinese want to consume like Americans, then the Earth will be despoiled in no time at all. But how can people in the Western countries tell people in China *not* to aspire to Western levels of comfort and consumption? At best, even if not an imposition, development might just be empty posturing on the part of Western countries. Attaining North American or European levels was never realistic for the vast proportion of the world's population, and so development was a false promise that the West never intended to keep. Indeed, by holding out a development model based on Western ideas and experience, countries across the globe were being asked to buy into a system that was not only unsustainable, but predicated on inequalities (Sachs 2000). According to this line of critique, capitalism and global governance as they have been instituted since the 1940s so consistently benefit Western countries that 'development' never really envisioned an equal share of prosperity and resources for all the 'developing' countries.

Finally, who ever asked people from those non-Western, or traditional, or rural cultures if development was what they aspired to? In encouraging societies around the world to follow the development model, what has been lost in traditional cultures? Unquestionably those cultures have been disrupted by urbanization, industrialization and globalization. Ancient ways of life practised by peoples in Africa, Asia, Latin America and elsewhere have been irrevocably altered by economic and social changes. Did those peoples have any choice in the matter? Are they really any better off if they become 'developed'? These are only a few of the relevant questions to be asked of the idea of both development and poverty reduction. Here we will present no conclusive answers. Instead, it is important consistently to interrogate the understandings of poverty and development presented throughout this book – and to ask whether policies for reducing poverty really do represent any kind of 'progress'. These are debates that will continue to jolt this field for the foreseeable future, as they should. They are debates worth having, since they force anyone who cares about poverty to ponder very carefully what it means to do something about it.

Who does development?

The discussion to this point should make clear that there are many difficulties in promoting poverty reduction and development. The challenge for both practitioners and students in this field is to do development better, at all levels from the national to the local to the regional. As a set of guiding principles, doing 'better' involves asking questions such as these: Does the development project respond to local needs? In other words, does the project include an assessment of on-the-ground conditions rather than having been devised in far-away Geneva, London or Washington, DC? Are local and national actors and institutions involved? Most of the time, the closer development is planned to where it will be carried out the better. The more that people affected by development are consulted the better. The more they get to participate, the more they will learn to demand accountability and responsiveness from their institutions. This is important for project sustainability but also for the capacity building of local people so that they learn how to conceive, implement and carry projects forward. Does the project empower local groups, especially civil society, to feel that they can play a role in their countries? Does the project promote the inclusion of all people? As mentioned previously, sometimes local elites and wider populations perpetuate discriminatory practices that have led to the exclusion of communities from certain rights, opportunities and capabilities. This is why projects need to incorporate provisions for the inclusion of women and marginalized groups.

Poverty reduction programmes can take many forms, including multi-year programmes targeting multiple countries supported by international agencies; local government projects; projects implemented by international non-governmental organizations (INGOs) or local non-governmental organizations (NGOs); and other types of projects besides. In general, though, poverty reduction programmes usually fall under three broad categories:

1   Official development assistance (ODA), which typically involves financial transfers (grants or low-interest loans) from a donor government. When the donor government gives to another government, it is bilateral aid. Multilateral aid is given by a government to an international organization such as the United Nations. By total global dollar amounts, most aid is ODA. Because these investments can be quite large, they have the potential to be big projects tackling big problems. However, this kind of aid is also the most criticized, as we discuss in the next section.

2   Humanitarian aid provided in cases of natural disasters, widespread famine or drought, and human disasters such as armed conflict. Whereas ODA is generally intended for long-term ends, humanitarian aid aims to reduce suffering in the short term. Examples of this kind of aid can be supplying food or water, providing medical care or shelter, or protecting civilians in conflict situations. Even fierce critics of ODA often agree that humanitarian assistance is necessary for helping local populations cope with unexpected disasters. However, there is an emerging body of research and journalism that points to how this type of aid, too, can get misused if it falls into the greedy hands of rebel groups or corrupt officials. This debate will be examined in Chapter 8 on conflict and poverty.

3   Development assistance provided by INGOs to national and local NGOs. Many international development researchers and practitioners agree that strengthening civil society organizations – including NGOs – is beneficial on two levels. First, it can channel aid dollars to a local organization capable of implementing the project, and second, it can strengthen civil society, which helps people hold local governments accountable. Nonetheless, in many different countries, ranging from Mali to Bosnia-Herzegovina, it has been alleged that INGOs sometimes play such an important role in a country's development that the government becomes less accountable, leading local citizens to look primarily to organizations such as Oxfam and World Vision to help them meet their needs (see Moratti and Sabric-El-Rayess 2009, Esquith 2013).

The different actors involved in international development can be broken down into the following categories:

1   **Multilateral and supranational institutions**. This category refers to when countries work together (multilateralism) to create governance that operates above national governments. Examples of institutions in this category include the International Monetary Fund, the World Bank, the World Trade Organization, and the United Nations and its many agencies (such as the United Nations Children's Fund, UNICEF; the United Nations High Commissioner for Refugees, UNHCR; the United Nations Development Programme, UNDP; and United Nations Entity for Gender Equality and the Empowerment of Women, UN Women). The Organization for Economic Cooperation and Development (a club of high- and middle-income democracies), the African Union and the Asian Development Bank also fit in here.

2 **Development agencies associated with national governments**. The agencies of high-income countries are major players around the world, such as the United States Agency for International Development (USAID), the German Agency for Technical Cooperation (GTZ), the British Department for International Development (DFID), or the Canadian International Development Agency (CIDA), to name but a few. These donor agencies sometimes work with the development agency, or ministries of agriculture, economics or health of the recipient government to implement projects. Development agencies from countries in the global south have recently become more active as worldwide donors; the Brazilian Cooperation Agency (ABC) is involved in multiple projects in the Portuguese-speaking parts of Africa, for example.

3 **Non-governmental organizations**. As mentioned above, there is an extensive network of NGOs and INGOs working to address poverty, and they operate both in individual and multiple countries. Some of the best-known NGOs include BRAC (Building Resources Across Communities, which started in Bangladesh but now works in a number of countries), CARE, Save the Children, Médecins Sans Frontières, the International Red Cross and Mercy Corps. Sometimes these organizations, such as World Vision, have a religious affiliation; other development NGOs with a faith connection include Caritas and Catholic Relief Services, Muslim Aid, and World Jewish Relief.

4 **Public and private foundations**. Often supporting INGOs, these foundations also work with local NGOs in the global south. The most famous example is the Gates Foundation, but there are many others, such as the Ford Foundation and the Open Society Foundations. Besides funding NGOs, such foundations can work together with multilateral institutions and governments. These collaborations have formed prominent development partnerships such as the Global Alliance for Vaccination and Immunization (GAVI) and the Global Agriculture and Food Security Program (GAFSP).

5 **Universities and think tanks**. In both the global north and the global south, universities play an important role in development through research and sometimes project implementation. Examples include major public health research centres at the University of Washington or Johns Hopkins University, the Abdul Latif Jameel Poverty Action Lab (J-PAL, affiliated with the Massachusetts Institute of Technology) which has specialized in impact evaluations, and the London International Development Research Centre, founded by a consortium of higher education institutions in the UK. Prominent development think tanks include the Center for Global Development headquartered in Washington, DC, the International Development Research Centre in Ottawa, the Indira Gandhi Institute of Development Research in Mumbai, and the African Population and Health Research Center in Nairobi. Universities and think tanks partner with governments, multilateral institutions or civil society organizations to improve development policy or focus on a particular problem such as malaria, HIV/AIDS, tuberculosis or gender inequality.

When the types of aid and these different actors are taken into consideration, a complex network of programming, service provision, advocacy, organizing, and possibilities for empowerment comes into focus. It is our hope that the chapters that follow will help clarify the interconnections and potential for addressing global poverty that this web of agencies and organizations can achieve.

With the question of who does development, it is also important to ask who works for these agencies and organizations: who implements the projects, and who benefits from them? Scholars in development ethics such as David Crocker (1991) call for a critical reflection on these issues, and particularly how to strike a balance between 'insiders' and 'outsiders' in planning, carrying out and evaluating development efforts. Insiders in this case are the local people who have an intimate understanding of their situation and its cultural contexts; outsiders are the foreigners who may have a thematic or issue-specific knowledge necessary to implement a project. In Crocker's view, the ideal is for insiders and outsiders to reach a shared vision and plan for what is to be achieved. Crocker aligns more with a 'universalist' camp, who argue that the most effective development will be a result of finding common ground and getting locals and foreigners to work together. A more 'particularist' perspective is that only members of a group should assess a group's needs and propose action or projects. The divide here is not merely philosophical. It applies on a daily basis in development work, since outsiders seeking to make change routinely come into communities about which they may know little.

The most sensible perspective is to recognize that there are liabilities and merits to being either an insider or an outsider. We are all cultural insiders and outsiders in different contexts, places and times. Sometimes insiders need to carry out development, and sometimes an outsider view is useful to see something taken for granted. The key challenge for insiders is not to overlook contributing factors to poverty or suffering because they see it as 'natural or acceptable'. The challenge for outsiders is to avoid ethnocentric responses to local situations and acknowledge the limits of their contextual knowledge. Ultimately, a crucial principle we emphasize throughout this book is local buy-in and participation: without it, there is little chance that projects will be sustainable. If local populations, including project beneficiaries, are not included in the design, implementation or evaluation of development initiatives, those initiatives may well fail. They may not be financially sustainable, since without the participation of local populations the project's benefits might end when funding ends. They may also not be socially sustainable, since without the participation of local populations the project might not even benefit those populations. Thus an answer for who does development, and how to make development sustainable, requires the inclusion of local people and institutions in planning and implementation.

The aid debate

One of the perennial debates about development is whether 'foreign aid' is beneficial or harmful. Periodically producing a flurry of books and articles, the fundamental dispute is whether ODA is effective – and some critics doubt that ODA should be given at all (see Engel 2014 for a survey). Because this debate about aid continually percolates in the development industry, and connects to many of the critical questions about development raised above, it is worth rehearsing in some detail. First we will survey the usual arguments against development assistance, then the arguments for, and finally suggest a synthesis between the opposing sides. The goal is to explore this debate but simultaneously to transcend it. By examining the opposing arguments, ultimately we will suggest not only which of them are more convincing, but more importantly, what the future of development assistance could be to promote poverty reduction.

The argument against aid incorporates many of the previous critiques of development as a whole. The most prominent critics include William Easterly (2006, 2014) and Dambisa Moyo (2009). Among the many varying critiques, it is commonly claimed that since the development age began in the late 1940s, aid has generally failed for four interlocking reasons. First, the foundational premise for aid to developing countries is based on a false analogy. The Marshall Plan, implemented between 1948 and 1952 to rebuild the economy in several western European countries, was largely successful. But it is not a reasonable point of comparison for development assistance to countries in the global south. The Marshall Plan was aid for reconstruction: there was a foundation upon which to rebuild much of war-ravaged Europe, since the countries that received Marshall Plan aid had been industrialized before the war. This is different from development's typical task of bringing industrialization and democratic political systems to countries with limited or no experience of such things. Moreover, the Marshall Plan worked because the aid flows never represented significant portions of national income. As Dambisa Moyo claims, 'At their peak, aid flows were only 2.5 per cent of GDP of the larger recipients like France and Germany, while never amounting to more than 3 per cent of GDP for any country for the five-year life of the programme' (Moyo 2009: 36). In contrast, ODA to developing countries often amounts to a much larger percentage of the country's GDP, so it is very different in kind and amount from the assistance given to Europe after the Second World War.

This leads to the second reason that aid fails: aid dollars can actually harm economic development. When aid flows compose over 60 per cent of a government's budget, the influx of dollars creates an effect eerily similar to diamonds, gold or oil. Aid dollars begin to resemble the rents received from natural resources under a phenomenon called 'Dutch disease'. These dollar flows raise prices and choke off economic growth in areas such as manufacturing or agriculture (Rajan and Subramanian 2011). Thus aid can hurt a country's economy. Aid can also promote corruption. Like the rents from commodities such as diamonds and oil, aid comes in to a government's coffers – whether as a loan or a grant – and officials are tempted to misuse the money, even putting it into their own pockets. The extent to which this routinely happens is disputed, but there is some empirical support. According to Collier's research, in Chad only 1 per cent of the money intended for rural health clinics actually reached them (Collier 2007). Increased levels of corruption harm economic development partly because companies are less likely to invest in an environment where bribes and under-the-table negotiations drive up the cost of doing business.

Third, aid harms political development. Corruption in the political system is only one aspect. There is also empirical support for the idea that aid promotes autocracy. Rents from commodities such as oil and diamonds often result in authoritarian political systems – and aid can act in a similar way to these rents (see i.a. Bueno de Mesquita and Smith 2009, Collier 2007). One way that aid can foment an autocratic, repressive government is through the need to protect the corruption cycle. In corrupt systems, government officials want to keep their bribes coming. They therefore have an incentive to undermine or suppress the non-governmental organizations acting as watchdogs. Autocrats and corrupt officials do not want citizens requesting budget transparency. (Kono and Montinola 2009) In short, aid dollars can act in a way similar to the 'resource curse', in which too great a reliance on inflows of aid or an export such as oil can harm development and poverty reduction. (For more on corruption and the resource curse, see Chapter 7 on state institutions and governance.)

Fourth and finally, despite these well-known problems, aid keeps flowing. According to this argument, there is a lot of rhetoric about the importance of meeting anti-corruption milestones, but too seldom is anyone held accountable. Organizations such as the IMF and the World Bank are sufficiently satisfied with the status quo that they do not radically re-evaluate the impact of their development assistance. Project evaluation is often so short term that there is no long-term evidence to sustain the policies in place, and hence no incentive to examine the contradictions caused by aid. It is not in the interests of the stakeholders (whether international institutions or national governments) to change the rules of the game. At the bottom of it all, critics allege, aid is not about helping countries emerge from aid. Aid is about furthering a neo-colonial model of resource extraction and profit, as well as assuring a world view that represents the political commitments and economic interests of the North. Aid flows to Iraq, the Congo, Sierra Leone, El Salvador, Colombia and Mexico are not about supporting locally led development and increased self-determination. The United States and other countries from the global north are not interested in facilitating deep democracy and local economic development. Rather, they are interested in preserving the currently unequal distribution of global power and wealth.

From the opposite camp, arguments *for* development assistance are led by people such as Jeffrey Sachs (2005) and Peter Singer (2009). Singer in particular emphasizes the essential facts on the distribution of world wealth. Roughly a billion people live on less than USD 1.25 a day. There is no denying the extent of poverty on the planet – there are many, many people who need help. On the flip side, countries just in North America and Europe, whose population accounts for about 15 per cent of the world total, control some 50 per cent of the world's net worth. Thus there is also no denying that some countries have vastly more resources than others. By any reasonable calculation, these rich countries (and people in those countries) can afford to devote more of their budgets to aiding poorer countries – the most common target is 0.7 per cent of GDP. Aid proponents say that this is not too much to ask.

The case for foreign aid rests on the powerful claim that because the rich world *can* help, it *should* help. The vastly greater resources that rich countries possess can alleviate suffering and catalyse improvement in economies and lives throughout the world. Development aid, in its various forms, has the power to combat diseases like malaria, HIV/AIDS, and even less headline-grabbing afflictions such as river blindness or schistosomiasis. It also has the power to build roads, ports, electricity grids, dams, sewage systems and communications networks. Aid can help transfer technologies such as medicines or pest-resistant crops, it can provide on-the-ground technical assistance, and of course it can build schools and hospitals. In the direst circumstances, aid can supply food, shelter and medicine for victims of disasters, whether natural or caused by humans.

It is indisputable not only that aid can work – it does work. There is a tremendous amount of evidence to support the benefits of development assistance. For instance, the World Health Organization helped push for the distribution of around 300 million bed nets between 2008 and 2010, and malaria deaths for children in sub-Saharan Africa have dropped by 51 per cent in roughly a decade. Thanks in part to support from the US President's Emergency Plan for AIDS Relief (PEPFAR), some ten million people infected with HIV received anti-retroviral medications. Money from the Global Fund to Fight AIDS, Tuberculosis and Malaria has led to the global mortality rate from tuberculosis dropping by 45 per cent since 1990. The GAVI Alliance (founded and funded in part by the World Bank) has helped immunize more than 500 million children.

Aid helped spread the Green Revolution, bringing vastly increased agricultural productivity – and with it, food security – to communities around the globe. In education, aid has massively expanded children's access to schools; as but one example, the German government spent millions of euros to help Ghana eliminate school fees. Subsequent chapters in this book will contain many more stories of development programmes that work to reduce poverty. Many of these programmes have received money from governments in the rich world. These are aid dollars that have obvious, demonstrable benefits.

According to this argument, because aid can and does work, any statement that 'all aid is bad' paints with far too broad a brush. It is true that aid has sometimes imposed a neo-colonial model on southern countries. It is also true that some aid has been wasted by corrupt regimes. And historically aid has sometimes been hamstrung by narrow political and economic interests in the donor country. Likewise, more aid dollars do not necessarily mean more improvement, and aid can contribute to Dutch disease. Too often there has indeed been a lack of accountability for donor organizations and too little consultation with the people who are supposed to benefit from poverty reduction programmes. However, it is deeply problematic to assert that aid *causes* corruption, repression and civil society breakdown. That assertion can be difficult to support empirically, since often aid has gone to states that already had problems with corruption, repression and weak civil society. In fact, for every case of Iraq, Sierra Leone and El Salvador, there is also Botswana, Namibia, South Korea or Malaysia, all places where aid has undeniably had beneficial outcomes.

A number of studies suggest that overall aid does have a positive economic effect, even if it is modest. As Paul Collier concluded from his survey of the literature, over the last 30 years aid has added probably 1 per cent to the economic growth of the poorest countries, which though not huge is important because otherwise they might not have grown at all (Collier 2007). Similarly, a review of influential studies concluded that on the whole, increases in aid are associated with increases in economic growth and investment (Clemens *et al.* 2012). As Collier states, even a modest contribution to growth means that aid 'has made the difference between stagnation and severe cumulative decline. Without aid, cumulatively the countries of the bottom billion would have become much poorer than they are today' (Collier 2007: 100). Even if some scholars will contest that particular finding, aid's positive effects beyond economic growth are easy to see. Aid has made great contributions to human development, for example by nearly wiping out polio, and helping over two billion people gain access to safe drinking water in the past 20 years. Thus even if aid were somehow conclusively shown not to foster positive economic growth, it is very easy to show how aid has improved the quality of life for poor people throughout the world. Empirically, aid's beneficial effects are consistent, generalizable, and readily apparent.

In the end, the debate between 'good aid' and 'dead aid' runs aground because the two camps often take extreme, unrealistic positions. The most useful question to ask in this debate is not 'does aid work?' but rather 'how can it work *better*?' (see i.a. Birdsall *et al.* 2005, Riddell 2007, Cohen and Easterly 2009, Ramalingam 2013). The perhaps most justified critiques of aid centre on official development assistance – systemic aid, the bilateral flows from government to government, or the large projects and loans financed through the IMF and the World Bank. Some of these critiques are legitimate, and projects do not always work optimally. But even when ODA projects do go well, remember that there are other kinds of aid, such as humanitarian assistance.

The importance of humanitarian aid is difficult to argue with, since no one deserves to be left alone when they are desperate after a natural or human-caused disaster. Nonetheless, one must still interrogate the motivations and management of the organizations that deliver such aid.

There is also much good work being carried out by private foundations and INGOs. This aid flow has traditionally been small compared to the large sums moving through bilateral channels. Many of these programmes may be pilot projects, relatively small models with a limited impact. But there are consistent efforts to take such projects to scale. The Gates Foundation has partnered with the INGO PATH to scale up their research and programmes for getting vaccines to everyone. The International Fund for Agricultural Development has for a number of years pushed to scale up its rural development programmes in countries including Albania, Ethiopia and Peru, in areas such as market access, village-level investment planning and small-scale irrigation. There are many other small, similar, innovative projects that have not cost tens of millions of dollars to be successful, things such as training for small entrepreneurs, education to improve health and hygiene practices, programmes to empower women and girls, inexpensive, low-technology water delivery systems, or community forest management programmes. These projects have often relied on a more bottom-up approach in which local communities determine their needs, or national governments consult their citizens to set up transparency and accountability strategies from the start. Such approaches do not rely on large influxes of money but instead leverage local economies, ownership and knowledge.

Of course, a pure bottom-up approach relying on entrepreneurship or individuals' economic incentives is not going to counter the big, structural causes of poverty such as disadvantageous geography, armed conflict, the disease burden or bad institutions. Microfinance alone is just not going to solve Somalia's problems. Moreover, individuals working individually are rarely going to provide public goods. As noted previously, there is a reason government exists: neither individuals, entrepreneurs in poor countries or foreign direct investment is reliably going to build roads, hospitals, water treatment plants or ports. Whatever the problems with ODA – and they definitely exist – there is simply no immediate replacement for support for things such as infrastructure, education and health interventions, which typically rely on governments in order to make a wider impact.

In order to make development assistance work more effectively, then, it should follow some general principles. More aid dollars should be given to poor people, not to poor governments. In giving aid to poor people, aid projects should be designed primarily based on what the people want, not what donors think they need or want to give them. Thus aid projects *must* include participation and buy-in from recipients. Effective aid projects should also involve coordination between donor agencies to avoid needless and wasteful replication. Independent evaluation of project outcomes also must increase. Because some aid is always going to involve governments in the recipient country, and because bad governance is consistently associated with poverty, bilateral, official aid should be given preferably only when the recipient country has already demonstrated commitment to improving its institutions such as its civil service and legal system. When possible, aid should also be targeted at the level of local rather than national governments. Procuring supplies and labour at a local level helps the local community and can build capacity by involving local partners, rather than relying consistently on international experts.

Further, the deadlock in the aid debate may be resolvable by focusing on areas where aid has most often had positive effects and should therefore receive the preponderance of resources in the future. Health programmes are critical here, and continued support for reducing the disease burden in poor countries is a tangible area where rich countries can help ameliorate the conditions that lead to poverty. A chief strategy, and one of the most recommendable strategies based on its past success, is technology transfer. For instance, transferring technologies in the health field, such as licences for pharmaceuticals, or technical materials and equipment, has had many benefits. Creating partnerships to transfer technologies for renewable energy is a promising and necessary field as both developed and developing countries confront the challenges of climate change.

Likewise, technical assistance – partnering with people in poor countries for capacity building in various fields – can be beneficial when done right. Examples of technical assistance include expert advising on climate adaptation strategies, programmes for urban water supplies, reform of the judicial system or efforts to improve agricultural productivity. Doing it right means responding to developing countries' expressed needs, ensuring complete transparency and accountability for donors and recipients, and encouraging south–south technical assistance when appropriate. Finally, there remains an important role for bilateral and multilateral aid to fund infrastructure projects. Roads, rail lines, water and sanitation, electricity and communication networks can demonstrably improve not only poor people's lives, but also poor countries' economies. A critical role for development assistance will continue to be supporting these public goods when no one else will. What one always has to remember in the debate about aid is that people's lives are at stake. The question is not really whether aid is good or bad, but rather how aid can prevent human beings from dying prematurely, how it can help people live lives that they value. Though the debates about how to achieve those goals will continue, the guiding objective should be to make ODA consistently effective so that it reaches the people who deserve it, so that it emboldens citizens to know where aid dollars are going and where they should be invested.

Conclusion

The recommendations we have just given are in some ways facile. Broad principles such as technical assistance, capacity building and local buy-in are useful as guidelines, but they admittedly fall short in their detailed, practical application. For instance, in a new maternal health programme in a remote village in South Asia, how *specifically* can one build capacity and generate local buy-in? A major difficulty is that once beyond broad principles, the specific answers on how best to carry out anti-poverty programmes can vary considerably based on the local context. The good news is that today in the development field there is more awareness of the need to pursue policies based on a society's historical, social and political context. Moreover, there is acknowledgement from development professionals that the entire idea of 'development' needs to be reconsidered to some extent. A country's level of development, for example, should be evaluated based not on how well it approximates to, say, Canada, but rather in relation to the progress it has made compared to where it started.

One of the key things to remember is that doing development is *hard*. Creating effective poverty reduction programmes is not at all easy. Indeed, development has many different, sometimes possibly contradictory components. As one illustration, consider the Center for Global Development's Commitment to Development Index.

This measure ranks a number of high-income countries on how much they do to help the poor around the world. The analysis relies on seven different dimensions of development: aid, trade, finance, migration, environment, security and technology. Some countries, such as Sweden, top the chart for aid, but score much less well on their contributions to security in developing countries. Overall, the Scandinavian countries are ranked highest for their overall commitment to development, and the United States in 2015 ranked 21st out of 27 countries – ahead of those at the bottom (Japan and South Korea), but well behind countries with much smaller economies than the United States such as Portugal or New Zealand. According to this measure, the United States could be doing much more to promote development around the world. But what should it be doing? That question immediately returns to the dilemmas and controversies of this field. Ultimately, in a book analysing causes of and solutions to poverty, it is nearly impossible to avoid some of the problematic assumptions of development and poverty reduction. The important thing is to acknowledge those problems, and throughout the rest of the book as well as in one's individual engagement with the world, continue to interrogate the flaws in our knowledge of how to promote human flourishing.

Discussion questions

1   Why is it so hard to do development well?
2   What do you see as the distinctions between the terms 'development', 'poverty reduction', 'poverty alleviation' and 'poverty eradication'? Which terms or goals are preferable, and why?
3   Does one side of the aid debate seem more convincing? Why? What key conclusions should we take from this debate?
4   Examine the Commitment to Development Index at www.cgdev.org/initiative/commit ment-development-index/index. What do you see as the benefits and flaws of this index?

- What do the seven different dimensions of development consist of? In your view, which seem the most important for poverty reduction?
- Explore how the different countries rate on this index. Compare several different countries in their respective strengths and weaknesses.

Notes

1   The basic capabilities do not necessarily need to be those from Nussbaum's list. Though we agree with her general perspective that there are some fundamental, universal entitlements, what counts as 'basic' in any given society could be partially context specific.
2   Note, too, that the usual assumption is about countries rather than societies or peoples. The Western model of the nation-state dominates the international order, and so also structures thinking and practice about how development must take place.

Further reading

Deaton, Angus. 2013. *The Great Escape: Health, wealth, and the origins of inequality*. Princeton, NJ: Princeton University Press.
Escobar, Arturo. 'Beyond the search for a paradigm? Post-development and beyond', *Development*, 43.4 (2000): 11–14.

Gates Foundation. 2014. Annual Letter, 'Three Myths that Block Progress for the Poor', available at http://annualletter.gatesfoundation.org/

Payne, Anthony and Nicola Phillips. 2010. *Development*. Cambridge: Polity Press.

Radelet, Steven. 'A Primer on Foreign Aid', Center for Global Development, Working Paper 62, July 2006.

Sachs, Wolfgang. 'Development: The Rise and Decline of an Ideal', Wuppertal Institut für Klima, Umwelt, und Energie, Paper no. 108, August 2000.

Works cited

Alkire, Sabina, and Séverine Deneulin. 'The Human Development and Capability Approach', in Séverine Deneulin and Lila Shahani, eds. 2009. *An Introduction to the Human Development and Capability Approach*. London: Earthscan.

Babb, Sarah. 'The social consequences of structural adjustment: recent evidence and current debates', *Annual Review of Sociology*, 31.1 (2005): 199–222.

Barder, Owen. 'What is Poverty Reduction?' Center for Global Development, Working Paper 170, April 2009.

Birdsall, Nancy, Dani Rodrik and Arvind Subramanian. 'How to help poor countries', *Foreign Affairs*, 84.4 (2005): 136–152.

Brundtland Commission on Environment and Development. 1987. *Our Common Future*. Vol. 383. Oxford: Oxford University Press.

Bueno de Mesquita, Bruce, and Alastair Smith. 'Political survival and endogenous institutional change', *Comparative Political Studies*, 42.2 (2009): 167–197.

Clemens, Michael A., Steven Radelet, Rikhil R. Bhavnani and Samuel Bazzi. 'Counting chickens when they hatch: timing and the effects of aid on growth', *The Economic Journal*, 122 (2012): 590–617.

Cohen, Jessica, and William Easterly, eds. 2009. *What Works in Development? Thinking Big and Thinking Small*. Washington, DC: Brookings Institution Press.

Collier, Paul. 2007. *The Bottom Billion: Why the poorest countries are failing and what can be done about it*. New York, NY: Oxford University Press.

Crocker, David A. 'Insiders and outsiders in international development', *Ethics & International Affairs*, 5.2 (1991): 149–173.

Deneulin, Séverine, and Lila Shahani, eds. 2009. *An Introduction to the Human Development and Capability Approach*. London: Earthscan.

Deolalikar, Anil B., Alex B. Brillantes Jr., Raghav Gaiha, Ernesto M. Pernia and Mary Racelis. 'Poverty Reduction and the Role of Institutions in Developing Asia', ERD Working Paper No. 10, Asian Development Bank, May 2002.

Easterly, William. 2014. *The Tyranny of Experts: Economists, dictators, and the forgotten rights of the poor*. New York, NY: Basic Books.

Easterly, William. 2006. *The White Man's Burden: Why the West's efforts to aid the rest have done so much ill and so little good*. New York, NY: Penguin.

Elliott, Jennifer. 2012. *An Introduction to Sustainable Development*. New York, NY: Routledge.

Engel, Susan. 'The not-so-great aid debate', *Third World Quarterly*, 35.8 (2014): 1374–1389.

Escobar, Arturo. 2011. *Encountering Development: The making and unmaking of the Third World*. Princeton, NJ: Princeton University Press.

Esquith, Stephen L. 'The political responsibility of bystanders: the case of Mali', *Journal of Global Ethics*, 9.3 (2013): 377–387.

Feres, Juan Carlos, and Pablo Villatoro. 'La viabilidad de erradicar la pobreza: un examen conceptual y metodológico.' United Nations, Comisión Económica para América Latina y el Caribe, March 2012.

Gore, Charles. 'The rise and fall of the Washington Consensus as a paradigm for developing countries', *World Development*, 28.5 (2000): 789–804.

Hulme, David. 2010. *Global Poverty: How global governance is failing the poor.* London: Routledge.

Hydén, Göran. 'Governance, Development and Poverty Eradication', mimeo, no date.

Kono, Daniel Yuichi and Gabriella R. Montinola. 'Does foreign aid support autocrats, democrats, or both?' *The Journal of Politics,* 71 (2009): 704–718.

Moratti, Massimo and Amra Sabic-El-Rayess. 'Transitional Justice and DDR: The Case of Bosnia and Herzegovina', International Center for Transitional Justice Research Unit, June 2009.

Moyo, Dambisa. 2009. *Dead Aid: Why aid is not working and how there is a better way for Africa.* New York, NY: Farrar, Straus and Giroux.

Nussbaum, Martha. 2011. *Creating Capabilities: The human development approach.* Boston, MA: Harvard University Press.

Rahnema, Majid, and Victoria Bawtree, eds. 1997. *The Post-Development Reader.* London: Zed Books.

Rajan, Raghuram G. and Arvind Subramanian, 'Aid, Dutch disease, and manufacturing growth', *Journal of Development Economics,* 94.1 (2011): 106–118.

Ramalingam, Ben. 2013. *Aid on the Edge of Chaos: Rethinking international cooperation in a complex world.* Oxford: Oxford University Press.

Ranis, Gustav, Frances Stewart and Alejandro Ramirez. 'Economic growth and human development', *World Development,* 28.2 (2000): 197–219.

Rapley, John. 'Development studies and the post-development critique', *Progress in Development Studies,* 4.4 (2004): 350–354.

Redclift, Michael. 'Sustainable development (1987–2005): an oxymoron comes of age', *Sustainable Development,* 13.4 (2005): 212–227.

Riddell, Roger. 2007. *Does Foreign Aid Really Work?* Oxford: Oxford University Press.

Rist, Gilbert. 2002. *The History of development: From Western origins to global faith.* London: Zed Books.

Robeyns, Ingrid. 'The capability approach: a theoretical survey', *Journal of Human Development,* 6.1 (2005): 93–114.

Rostow, Walt. 1960. *The Stages of Economic Growth: A non-communist manifesto.* Cambridge, UK: Cambridge University Press.

Sachs, Jeffrey. 2005. *The End of Poverty.* New York, NY: Penguin.

Sachs, Wolfgang. 'Development: The Rise and Decline of an Ideal', Wuppertal Institut für Klima, Umwelt, und Energie, Paper no. 108, August 2000.

Sachs, Wolfgang, ed. 2009. *The Development Dictionary.* London: Zed Books.

Sen, Amartya. 1999. *Development as Freedom.* New York, NY: Knopf.

Sheppard, Eric, and Helga Leitner. 'Quo vadis neoliberalism? The remaking of global capitalist governance after the Washington Consensus', *Geoforum,* 41.2 (2010): 185–194.

Sidaway, James D. 'Spaces of postdevelopment', *Progress in Human Geography,* 31.3 (2007): 345–361.

Singer, Peter. 2009. *The Life You Can Save.* New York, NY: Random House.

ul Haq, Mahbub. 'The Human Development Paradigm', in Sakiko Fukuda-Parr and AK Shiva Kumar, eds. 2004. *Readings in Human Development: Concepts, measures and policies for a development paradigm.* New York, NY: Oxford University Press.

United Nations Development Programme. *Fast Facts: Poverty reduction and UNDP.* January 2013. New York, NY: UNDP.

Wade, Robert Hunter. 'US hegemony and the World Bank: the fight over people and ideas', *Review of International Political Economy,* 9.2 (2002): 215–243.

World Bank. 2000. *World Development Report 2000: Attacking poverty.* New York, NY: Oxford University Press.

3 Multidimensional poverty measurements

Benjamin Curtis

Key questions

- What are the objectives of measuring poverty?
- What are the key issues in measuring deprivation and constructing poverty lines?
- Where do poverty statistics come from, and what are the difficulties with national accounts methods, household surveys, and income versus consumption measures?
- What are the major monetary measures of poverty, and what are their strengths and weaknesses?
- What are the major measures of poverty relevant to capabilities, and what are their strengths and weaknesses?
- What are qualitative measures of poverty such as participatory poverty assessments, and what are their strengths and weaknesses?

Vignette 3.1

Aneni is a 28-year-old woman who lives in a little town outside of Masvingo, Zimbabwe. She works as a small trader in the market, selling fruit, vegetables, and some basic products such as soap and soft drinks. Aneni is smart and hard working, and she has successfully built her business up from scratch. In a good month, she may earn the equivalent of as much as USD 300, which is impressive since the average income in Zimbabwe is closer to USD 100 a month. Aneni even earns enough to be able to afford to send her two older children to school, which is important to her since she herself completed only the first grade. On the other hand, though Aneni is the main breadwinner for her family, partly because of cultural norms she has to give much of what she earns to her husband, Chindori. He has had very little paid work in months, and too often spends some of the family's money on alcohol. Sometimes there is not enough money for when a family member falls sick, as happened to Aneni last year when she was incapacitated for a week with a bout of malaria. The line between good and ill health can be precarious for Aneni and her family. One of her children died when he was only 3 months old, and Aneni worries about having to endure another childbirth as complicated as her last one. Fortunately, she has been able to convince her husband to use a condom.

Introduction

Given Aneni's situation – by no means an unusual one for a woman in the developing world – should she be considered poor? In terms of her income, she is fairly well off when compared to many Zimbabweans. But does a lack of control over one's own earnings constitute a kind of poverty? And what about the fact that Aneni has had so little formal education? Likewise, do her health problems allow us to classify her as poor in some ways? The often complex task of identifying and measuring poverty is the focus of this chapter. This task – and the question of whether Aneni is poor – is obviously important, since identifying who is poor can determine who exactly needs help, and what kind of help they need. Moreover, good measures of the breadth and depth of poverty are necessary to know whether policies to reduce that poverty are working. Without good measures, how can we know if we are making progress in the fight against the various dimensions and causes of poverty?

Deriving accurate measures to understand 'who is poor' is not simple, however. It is complicated by a variety of statistical problems, conceptual challenges, and even philosophical disagreements. As an initial example of these complications, estimations for the percentage of people who were poor in 17 Latin American countries ranged from 13 to 66 per cent, depending on which definition and measurements for poverty were used (Szekely *et al.* 2000). This chapter will survey the theoretical and empirical problems, challenges and disagreements in global poverty measurement. We will also examine the most commonly used measures of poverty to answer questions of where in the world poverty is concentrated, and among which populations. The chapter begins with some of the fundamental conceptual issues in measuring poverty before examining specific monetary and capability measures, as well as a third measure called participatory poverty assessments.

How to measure deprivation?

Poverty lines

As we discussed in Chapter 1, poverty is often conceived of as deprivation. Measuring deprivation in areas such as monetary income, food, health, education and/or rights presumes first establishing a threshold above which a person is not deprived, and below which she is. This threshold is typically referred to as a *poverty line*. Constructing a poverty line involves identifying elementary, minimum requirements for the different potential dimensions of poverty such as income or nutrition. Different dimensions of course can have different poverty lines, and poverty lines can apply differently for different groups of people. For instance, a food poverty line that is often used is 2100 calories a day: a person whose consumption of food falls below that limit is considered to be deprived, or food poor. But the 2100 number is for an 'average person' – a small child will need less, or someone doing hard physical labour in extreme conditions could well need more. Constructing a poverty line is essential as part of the process to establish a target of basic requirements to which every human is entitled. Poverty lines are also useful because they establish a measure – whether of income, caloric intake, minimum years of schooling, etc. – that enables comparisons between different years, locations, and people.

However, as alluded to with the issue of the 'average person's' basic human requirements, there are a number of theoretical and practical difficulties with poverty lines. First of all, remember that poverty can be both absolute and relative. Poverty lines can be absolute (i.e. a common threshold across all humanity) or relative (a threshold contextualized to certain societies or groups of people). The measures of USD 1.90

and 3.10 a day are absolute poverty lines, established to provide an equal benchmark across the globe. Such absolute poverty lines are useful for cross-country comparison. But poverty lines are more often constructed to be relative; a minimum of monetary income or years of schooling will be different in Denmark than in Sudan. The comparison between Denmark and Sudan illustrates a common principle: in poor countries, deprivation in 'absolute consumption' tends to define poverty. This means the absolute minimum that people need to live. In richer countries, the minimum is drawn not according to what is needed merely to survive, but rather according to what is needed to live a life which is considered acceptable in that country.

A second question with poverty lines is whether a 'bright line' of deprivation is truly meaningful in terms of either human experience or human behaviour. Take for example an income poverty line of USD 1000 a year. How much difference is there, really, between a person who makes USD 1050 a year (and is therefore above the poverty line, and not considered poor) and a person who makes USD 950 a year (and is therefore considered poor)? The simplest calculation of poor people using a poverty line – what is known as the 'headcount method' – only tallies the number of people below the line. It does not take into account *how far* people fall below the poverty line.

There is an alternative calculation called the 'poverty gap method' that can compute the depth of poverty. The formal definition of the poverty gap is the mean shortfall of the total population from the poverty line, expressed as a percentage of the poverty line. As its name implies, this measure attempts to capture the 'gap' between individuals and the poverty line, providing an answer as to just how far people fall below that line. A poverty gap index is typically calculated for regions of a country to show where people are poorest, and not just where the largest numbers of poor people are located, as per the headcount method. The poverty gap calculation's focus on the depth of poverty draws attention to those people who are suffering the most extreme deprivation. As Angus Deaton comments, though, this method is relatively seldom used in part because it can seem too complex to both governments and publics (Deaton 2004).

Deaton points here to a third issue that sometimes arises with poverty lines: they can be fudged in a variety of ways to achieve political ends. For instance, if a government wants to claim its policies have significantly reduced poverty, it can target those policies at people who are just below the poverty line, helping them move above the threshold. In so doing, the government has 'reduced poverty' according to the headcount numbers, but it has done little for the very poor. In extreme cases, a poverty line can even be completely recalculated to redraw it downwards, which results in a reduction of the numbers of poor people purely through maths and not through improving their lives. None of this is to say that poverty lines are useless. Rather, the lesson from the theoretical and practical difficulties with poverty lines is always to keep in mind that the number of people who are considered deprived is the result of a complex, sometimes politicized, and potentially error-prone process. The precise statistics that national governments and international organizations provide about poverty are often not nearly as clear-cut as you might assume.

Issues of units and levels

Even if poverty lines might seem fuzzier rather than 'bright', it should still be a relatively straightforward procedure to identify particular individuals who are poor, right?

Unfortunately here, too, the endeavour is not so simple. Though care for individual suffering is usually at the heart of research in poverty, attaining reliable data on individual experience is problematic because most of the data collected apply to households, not individuals. For example, information on income and access to sanitation/clean water in many developing countries is often measured for households, but not for individuals. In some households, individuals' access to resources may be restricted, thereby limiting an individual's capabilities. Women, for instance, may completely lack any legal ownership of the household's assets, such as seeds, tools or furniture. Even if household assets are equitably distributed within the family, there are other complicating issues. Large families might have relatively high total incomes or consumption, but that translates to low incomes per person when divided on an individual basis (Streeten 1998).

Besides the unit problem of whether data refer to individuals or households, there is also the problem of data collection at the local, national or global levels. Measuring poverty at the local level is comparatively easy, relying on actual surveys of households. Accurate data at the national level can be more difficult, since it involves aggregating all the local data, inevitably obscuring certain variations or specificities to produce a picture of poverty for the country as a whole. Finally, deriving data about the total numbers of poor people at the global level is actually deeply controversial, fraught with methodological problems. Those problems are examined in a subsequent section. The key point is again that identifying who is poor and how their situation can be ameliorated is more difficult than it might at first seem.

Measuring consumption versus income

The next important question is how to determine precisely which households or individuals fall below the poverty line. The primary way to answer this question in developing countries has been through household surveys that gauge consumption rather than income. Consumption refers to the usage of a variety of goods and services, everything from food to transportation. Measuring consumption rather than income is more likely to produce an accurate picture of deprivation for several reasons. To begin with, households' consumption of such goods and services is a better indication of their standard of living than their incomes, which really serve to enable that consumption. Also, income can be difficult to calculate, especially in the poorest countries. Time can be a critical consideration in identifying poverty: a person's income can fluctuate radically according to the season (for example, if it is harvest season) or across years (years of drought will harm harvests and hence depress incomes). Similarly, valuing the income from agriculture, particularly subsistence agriculture (when the family's production does not enter the market) can be difficult. Finally, households may be more reluctant to report accurately on income rather than consumption because they are seeking to avoid taxation on that income (Sahn and Younger 2010). For all these reasons, most governments throughout the developing world conduct household surveys of consumption, sending workers around cities, towns and villages to interview families on their consumption levels. Those reported levels then help the government establish a poverty line and who falls below it.

Predictably, these household surveys end up as approximations due to a variety of complications with families' reported consumption. For instance, one category of consumption that the surveys have trouble accounting for relates to public goods such as health care or schools. Such goods can boost a family's standard of living, but they are not always factored into consumption per se. Likewise, since data are gathered in surveys that ask respondents to report their own consumption over a period of time, the respondents may not accurately recall their actual consumption. There is another significant problem related to under- and over-counts of certain groups of people. Evidence suggests that richer people are less likely to respond to such surveys and/or they will under-report their consumption or incomes. It can also be hard to reach the poorest of the poor, since they may not have fixed addresses or may avoid contact with government workers for their own reasons (Deaton 2010). The outcome of these under- or over-counts is that researchers arrive at an inaccurate picture of income or consumption levels in a country or region, which can then lead to incorrect conclusions about the extent and depth of poverty there. As a concrete example, it has been estimated that such surveys reached only 71 per cent of the population for sub-Saharan Africa in the years around 2005; if almost 30 per cent of the population remained uncounted, then income and consumption data may very well be unrepresentative (Anand, Segal and Stiglitz 2010).

A few other concerns bedevil the effort to gather accurate data about the numbers of poor people. With household surveys, different countries can use different methods, and sometimes even within countries the survey methods may change from year to year. Additionally, in many cases the surveys themselves are not conducted every year, or at least they do not survey the same people year to year. The result is that the survey data are not always comparable, either across countries or across years. The picture of poverty in Uganda may not be easily comparable to the picture from Papua New Guinea purely because of different methods used to identify the poor. Another objection is that household surveys, whether they measure consumption or income, can neglect other important aspects of poverty such as individuals' feelings of relative deprivation, health status, or inequities within the household (Ravallion 2010). Still, household surveys are widely used, their methodology continues to be improved, and they are often more suitable for getting a picture of poverty than is the other principle method of deriving poverty counts, the national accounts method.

The national accounts method measures broad macroeconomic data for an entire country, including production outputs of goods and services, wages and salaries, redistribution of income through government taxes, and how income is spent or saved. National accounts statistics thus purport to measure consumption, but they have been found often to understate consumption in very poor countries and to overstate rates of growth of average consumption (Deaton 2010). Moreover, economists have observed a growing disparity between poverty counts arrived at via the household survey and national accounts methods. In India, for example, these two measures in 1950 produced poverty count estimates that were roughly 'at parity', but more recently the survey data produced poverty counts half those produced by the national accounts data (Deaton 2001). This suggests that the two methods are actually counting different things, and thereby providing highly divergent answers as to who is poor. What lesson should you take from these complications with both household surveys and national accounts? The answer is that it is essential to understand where poverty-related data are coming from, how those data were derived, and what the relative strengths (and weaknesses) are of competing methods. And finally, you must consult multiple sources to compile the most accurate statistical picture of poverty.

Monetary measures of poverty

Whatever the source of data, the actual measures used to describe poverty depend in part on one's definition of poverty. As we discussed in the Introduction, there are two main definitions of poverty that together can capture a wide range of what it means to be poor: the monetary or income approach and the capabilities approach. Both of these approaches have a different assortment of statistics to gauge poverty. The monetary measures are the most widely used, in part because data for these measures are relatively available – which is not to say, however, that there are no problems with the data behind the monetary measurements, as we will see. Measuring capability poverty is more complicated, but efforts have been made in recent decades to devise better ways of calculating capability deprivation. We will consider in turn the philosophy behind both approaches' measurements, as well as the measurements themselves.

Monetary poverty measures involve calculating a person's income, consumption and production at market prices, and a calculation of whether these three things add up to meet the minimum needs set by the poverty line. There are several key assumptions behind the monetary approach to measuring poverty. First is the claim that measurements such as a person's annual income are the best, easiest proxy for measuring all sorts of other deprivations that are often more difficult to measure. For example, if a person's income is below 50 per cent of the society's poverty line, then he seriously lacks what has been established as the minimum income necessary for basic wellbeing, and he must be deeply deprived in a variety of ways. Therefore, though other measures such as health and education are also appropriate, a lack of income is held to represent fundamental deficiencies. Two other assumptions of monetary measures are objectivity and externality. These assume that poverty can be objectively measured by an external observer such as a researcher or government worker. There is nothing inherently wrong with these assumptions, but they contrast with ideas holding that poverty is best measured subjectively by those who experience it. Finally, monetary measures also depend upon an individualistic approach which presumes that poverty should be defined with reference to individuals rather than to groups (Stewart *et al.* 2007).

Monetary income is still the most widely used indicator of poverty. Income levels as measured by gross domestic product (GDP) per capita present a picture of overall monetary assets for a country's population. Using these numbers, countries are often classified into low-income, low-middle, high-middle and high income categories. (See Table 3.1's list of highest and lowest income countries.) Comparisons of income across countries have to be converted using a standard metric so that income in India is measured with the same yardstick as income in Paraguay. The most common metric is purchasing power parity (PPP), which is a way of comparing prices and incomes across countries with different currencies; a PPP dollar is a standardized, universally comparable unit of currency to allow for monetary comparisons. While GDP per capita provides a broad overview of a country's economic development and average individual income, a different measure zeroes in on poverty. This is the statistic on the percentage of population living on USD 1.90 or less a day, and USD 3.10 or less a day. (See Figure 3.1.) The precise numbers have changed over the years (the low end has risen from 1.08 to 1.25 to 1.90 USD), but these measures are important because they enable a cross-country comparison on numbers of people in extreme poverty. They provide a global picture of where the poorest people are. They thereby are also designed to help focus policymakers' attentions on the neediest. Likewise, the simplicity of the 1.90 a day and 3.10 a day poverty lines

---

Box 3.1 Measuring poverty through food

How well does hunger work as a measure of poverty? Several facts are undeniable: people need money to get food, and the poorest people in the poorest countries tend to spend most of their money on food. Food, since it is indispensable for life, is also a basic human right. Access to food is often operationalized through a person's ability to acquire approximately 2100 calories a day. The connection to income happens via a calculation of what it costs in any particular society to acquire a basket of 2100 calories. This is the cost of subsistence, the smallest amount of money people need to afford the basic 2100 calories. One definition of extreme poverty is a household that spends 80 per cent of its income on food, but whose members still receive only 80 per cent of their calorie requirements.

   Though food or caloric intake is used as a basic poverty measure, it has certain weaknesses so that it is not a sufficient indicator of poverty. For instance, as mentioned previously, 2100 calories as a minimum standard may be correct for some people but not for others, depending on age, gender and a variety of factors such as whether a person lives in a rural area or the city (since urban dwellers tend to be more sedentary and need fewer calories). Caloric intake likewise does not address actual *nutrition*: a person might get his 2100 calories, but those calories may not provide all the nutrients he needs. In terms of conceptualizing wellbeing, too, we have to recognize that for most people a good life does not presume just basic calories, but some variety and quality of food. Interestingly, as people get richer, they spend less of their incomes on food, though they can get enough food but still remain poor within the context of their society. The fact that food poverty lines can be manipulated for political reasons – to determine who gets what – means that access to food, while an important potential indicator of poverty, is ideally considered in conjunction with other indicators.

---

has a powerful effect in generating awareness and concern among wider publics for the problems of extreme poverty. As an easily comprehensible, stark indicator of deprivation, income measures such as the 1.90 a day line serve a useful purpose.

Income data also factor into measurements of inequality. Wealth or income inequality is an indicator of relative deprivation. Measuring income inequality can therefore provide a valuable perspective on poverty in a country. Amartya Sen notes that the absolute deprivation of capabilities typically depends on relative deprivation of incomes, and Andy Sumner reminds us that to understand poverty we must ask the question 'Who gets what?' (Sen 2006, Sumner 2012). The most prominent measurement of income inequality, known as the Gini coefficient (or index), helps answer that question. This measure computes the statistical distribution of wealth in a country. It ranges theoretically from 0 (where all income would be completely equally distributed) to 100 (where a single person would control all income). In practice, values typically range from around 25 to around 65 (see Table 3.2). The United States has a Gini score of 41, for example, Canada 32.6 and Mexico 48.1. There are a number of variations to the Gini coefficient – such as whether it is calculated from before-tax or after-tax numbers – as well as

Table 3.1 List of countries by GDP (PPP) per capita

World rank	Country	PPP $	World rank	Country	PPP $
1	Qatar	132,099	176	Madagascar	1,462
2	Luxembourg	98,987	177	Eritrea	1,297
3	Singapore	85,253	178	Guinea	1,214
4	Brunei	79,587	179	Mozambique	1,186
5	Kuwait	70,166	180	Malawi	1,124
6	Norway	68,430	181	Niger	1,080
7	United Arab Emirates	67,617	182	Liberia	873
8	San Marino	63,104	183	Burundi	818
9	Switzerland	58,551	184	Democratic Republic of Congo	770
10	United States	55,805	185	Central African Republic	630

Source: International Monetary Fund data (2015)

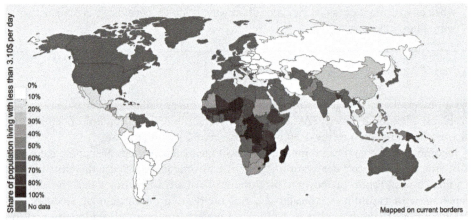

Share of population living with less than 3.10$ per day, 2013

Since some observations for 2013 are not available the map displays the closest available data (2008 to 2013).

Our World in Data

Share of population living with less than 3.10$ per day

0%
10%
20%
30%
40%
50%
60%
70%
80%
100%
No data

Mapped on current borders

Data source: Poverty – Below 3.10$ per day (2011 PPPs)   OurWorldInData.org/world-poverty/ • CC BY-SA

Note: Incomes per day are adjusted for inflation over time and for price differences between countries and expressed in 2011 PPP international dollars.

Figure 3.1 Countries by percentage of population living under USD 3.10 PPP per day

alternative inequality measures, such as the Atkinson index or the Theil index. But the Gini index is the most widely used.

There are many critiques of the 1.90 a day poverty line and other income measures that anyone studying poverty must keep in mind. Income measures often fail to account for the impact of public services such as access to clean water or health care on individuals' wellbeing. Further, such measures say almost nothing about how income gets used. Do people spend their income on things that actually improve their wellbeing? Or does the money get spent on drugs/alcohol, frivolous items or other things not necessary for survival? At the household level, is the income spent to benefit family members equitably, or do women, the elderly or the young get short shrift? Do some individuals, such as the elderly or the sick, actually need disproportionately *more* income in order to achieve the same wellbeing as younger or healthier people (Alkire and Santos 2009)? Income measures in general do a superficial job of capturing deprivations across a range of dimensions whether housing, literacy, life expectancy or political empowerment. In fact, it is certainly possible that a person or a household could be rich in income but poor in other dimensions (Bourguignon and Chakravarty 2003).

There are also many questions about how the data for PPP are generated that weaken overall confidence in its adequacy as a measure. For instance, all governments do not gather the data from which PPP numbers are derived using the same methodology, nor do some governments regularly update those data. Sometimes the prices that go into governments' calculations of the data include things largely irrelevant to poor people, such as real estate values. The basic formulae by which global PPP comparisons are calculated have also been changed several times, which means that PPP statistics from 1995 might not be strictly comparable with the numbers from 2010. The outcome of this range of methodological controversies is that estimates of the number of people in poverty can swing wildly. For instance, when calculation methods were changed, estimates for the percentage of the population below the poverty line in sub-Saharan Africa in 1993 jumped from 39 to 49 per cent. For Latin America, it declined from 23.5 to 15 per cent (Deaton 2001). Similarly, depending on the calculation method used, estimates of China's GDP per capita in 1990 ranged from USD 1300 to USD 2695 (Reddy and Pogge 2010). The Gini index also receives a range of criticisms, many of them based on technical mathematical issues (see i.a. Cowell 2011).

Table 3.2 List of highest and lowest countries by Gini coefficient

Country	Gini (%)	Country	Gini (%)
Denmark	24	Seychelles	65.8
Sweden	25	Comoros	64.3
Norway	25.8	Namibia	63.9
Austria	26	South Africa	63.1
Czech Republic	26	Botswana	61
Slovakia	26	Haiti	59.2
Ukraine	26.4	Angola	58.6
Belarus	26.5	Honduras	57.0
Finland	26.9	Central African Republic	56.3
Afghanistan	27.8	Bolivia	56.3

Source: World Bank data (2014)

What to make of these problems of cross-country comparisons of monetary measures? First, one has to acknowledge that they are always going to be approximations. More precise numbers can come from income data relevant strictly to the national level (i.e. per capita incomes in a given country). Nonetheless, it is still valuable to be able to compare income levels between countries. Second, do not forget that income measures are unidimensional rather than multidimensional; they capture only one potential aspect of poverty, namely monetary deprivation. The USD 1.90 a day and 3.10 a day poverty lines do have many potential flaws in their technical calculations as well as with their empirical validity: in many very poor countries which are alleged statistically to have a population living below 1.90 a day, according to facts on the ground, people with such a low income would actually die. Still, defenders of the 1.90 a day line argue for its power as an 'umbrella concept' identifying extreme poverty (Johnston 2010). And though critics say that PPP numbers are too crude a measure to provide much detail on the lives of poor people, as a rough but useful approximation it will doubtless continue to be cited.

Box 3.2 Just how many poor people are there in the world?

The disputes over poverty lines, national accounts versus household consumption surveys, and the USD 1.90 a day measure may seem abstruse to non-economists. But disagreements over how to measure poverty do translate to genuinely important results. Take for example the question of the total number of people worldwide considered extremely poor, living below the World Bank's earlier extreme poverty lines. According to the Bank's 2004 calculations, in 2001 there were 1.101 billion people living below the USD 1 a day line (which was more precisely USD 1.08). Later in 2004, a revision in those calculations using new data gave an estimate of 1.089 billion, so some 12 million people were suddenly no longer poor. Then in 2008, new estimates were made for poverty in 2005 using an adjusted USD 1.25 a day line which found 1.4 billion people living below the line. So now there were some 300 million more poor people than at the last estimate. According to a 2012 analysis, 22 per cent of the world's population in 2008 lived below the USD 1.25 line, which amounts to 1.289 billion people (Chen and Ravallion 2008, 2012).

The World Bank continually revises its numbers, but other researchers have attacked the World Bank's statistics for being wildly inaccurate. One of the most vociferous critics has been Surjit Bhalla, who claims that with more accurate calculations there were actually only 770 million people below the USD 1.08 line in 2001, and 456 million below that same line in 2005. On the basis of these numbers, Bhalla says that the Millennium Development Goal of reducing extreme poverty below 15 per cent of the world's population was met already in 2005, 10 years before the deadline. (Bhalla 2009) On the opposite end of the spectrum, Robert Wade argues that because of a litany of problems such as unreliability of data sources and changes in calculation methods that make the data from different years non-comparable, the World Bank actually *under*estimates the number of people in poverty (Wade 2004). Despite many valid criticisms of its methodology, the World Bank's statistics generally set the standard and are considered 'official', and we rely on them throughout this book.

Measuring capability poverty

Though monetary measurements may be somewhat simplistic, they have an obvious advantage in that they are relatively easy to calculate and understand. They do provide one useful lens for measuring poverty. Capability measurements, on the other hand, offer a more nuanced picture of poverty and wellbeing, but are typically more difficult to calculate. Capability measures are more nuanced because they seek to gauge the actual requirements necessary for an individual to live a life that she has reason to value. They thereby offer a more multidimensional conception of quality of life than income alone. They can also be more attentive than monetary measures to certain qualitative aspects of wellbeing. For instance, women educated through a literacy programme in Pakistan might not see a boost in incomes or other quantitative metrics, but they may report a major boost in feelings of self-esteem, empowerment and autonomy (Alkire 2002). Even where such positive outcomes can be hard to quantify, they are vital for conceptualizing what development means and how poverty reduction can be achieved.

The difficulties with capability measurements are both conceptual and methodological. Conceptually, a major challenge is that researchers seeking to measure the elementary requirements for wellbeing must first determine what those requirements are. This relates back to the question of what the basic capabilities are, which is subject to dispute and societal variation. An additional conceptual and methodological difficulty is how to define metrics for capabilities: after all, how can one measure 'freedoms', or the 'freedom to choose' that the capabilities approach holds as the standard for an acceptable life? Moreover, how can you measure achieved capabilities, i.e. functionings? There is also the difficulty that different people will require different inputs (such as resources or commodities) to achieve the same level of functionings. Remember that age, health status, characteristics of the physical environment, cultural norms and societal features such as hierarchies and political arrangements can all impact an individual's ability to convert opportunities to functionings. Even when valid indicators are identified to measure capabilities, data collection can be very complicated, especially in the poorest countries. Sometimes household surveys provide data on education, child mortality and access to clean water, but since the capabilities approach emphasizes *individuals'* freedoms, those household statistics must sometimes be converted to apply to individuals. Also, because most statistics relevant to capabilities tend to change very slowly (such as adult literacy rates), it can be hard to track trends either of improvement or of decline.

Despite such concerns, there are a number of indicators that provide useful information on capability deprivation and quality of life for people around the world. Health measures are some of the most powerful. One reason is that studies have shown that health measures are not highly correlated with incomes, which means that they capture aspects of wellbeing that monetary measures miss (Sahn and Younger 2010). The information that goes into the health measures is often more reliable than that derived from consumption surveys, since health measures are typically done at the individual level, and they use nearly universal units such as kilograms. Thus measuring a child's weight and height relative to others her age provides a fairly uncomplicated insight into that child's healthy physical development. Educational attainment is another oft-used indicator of functionings. The idea is that schooling empowers people through knowledge applicable to the kind of life they want to live, and that the capability to get educated can be measured through functioning outcomes such as literacy rates.

Table 3.3 Examples of human development indicators

Some key health indicators	Some key education indicators
Rates of child malnutrition	Net enrolment in primary education and secondary education
Infant mortality rate; under age 5 mortality rate	Proportion of pupils in grade 1 who reach grade 5
Adult mortality rate	Adult literacy rate
Maternal mortality rate	Learning outcomes measurements such as passing rates on standardized tests
HIV/AIDS prevalence	Mean years of schooling (adults)
Proportion of population at risk of malaria; death rates associated with malaria	Expected years of schooling (children)
Prevalence of tuberculosis; death rates associated with tuberculosis	Ratio of girls to boys in primary, secondary, and tertiary education
Percentage of population without access to an improved water source	Government expenditure on education as a percentage of GDP
Percentage of population without access to improved sanitation facilities	

A capability understanding of poverty has inspired several measures that combine multiple indicators into a broader 'index measure'. These index measures include the Human Development Index (HDI), several gender-related index measures and the Multidimensional Poverty Index. Researchers at the United Nations Development Programme devised the HDI to combine both economic and social indicators relevant to 'the enlargement of people's choices', and to enable cross-country comparisons (UNDP 2007). The HDI seeks to measure a society's overall attainment of wellbeing. It is composed of measures of life expectancy at birth, a 'knowledge' indicator measuring mean years of schooling and expected years of schooling, and Gross National Income per capita in USD PPP. See Table 3.3.

The Gender-related Development Index (GDI), the Gender Inequality Index (GII) and the Global Gender Gap Index (GGGI) have been designed to capture important aspects left out of the HDI. The GDI is composed of indicators comparing men and women in terms of life expectancy, education and earned income. The GII measures the loss of achievement due to gender inequality in the dimensions of health, empowerment and labour market participation. The Global Gender Gap Index measures gender-based disparities in access to resources and opportunities. It incorporates indicators for women's health and survival, plus others such as the ratio of female participation in the labour force and the ratio of women with seats in parliament. Figure 3.2 shows countries' Gender Inequality Index scores. There are also other indexes compiled from some of the same data, such as the inequality-adjusted HDI. Part of the appeal of these index measures is that by combining a number of indicators, they provide a more cohesive picture of human development that can be easily understood by policymakers and the public.

Inevitably, the very idea of combining indicators in such an index is considered problematic by some writers. One reason is that the indicators are often highly correlated with each other. So for example, unless the methodology is careful, an illiterate individual with a life expectancy of less than 40 years might be doubly counted, distorting the measurement (Bibi 2005). The respective weights of the indicators (i.e. their importance in the overall index calculation) have also been called arbitrary, and it has been charged that too many other indicators of human development are left out. The HDI does not address areas potentially relevant to basic capabilities such as political freedoms, justice and equity, personal security, ecology and sustainability, or other fundamental human rights (Streeten 1998). There may be some danger, too, that by enshrining health and education indicators in these indexes, health and education improperly come to define human development to the exclusion of other dimensions, represented for instance by the list of basic capabilities in the Introduction. So once again these index measures should only be taken as approximations: they provide a compelling but partial view on poverty and human development at the national – but not the individual – level.

Table 3.4 List of countries by Human Development Index score

Overall HDI rank	Country	HDI score	Overall HDI rank	Country	HDI score
1	Norway	.944	179	Mali	.419
2	Australia	.935	180	Mozambique	.416
3	Switzerland	.930	181	Sierra Leone	.413
4	Denmark	.923	182	Guinea	.411
5	Netherlands	.922	183	Burkina Faso	.402
6	Germany	.916	184	Burundi	.400
6 (tie)	Ireland	.916	185	Chad	.392
8	United States	.915	186	Eritrea	.391
9	Canada	.913	187	Central African Republic	.350
9 (tie)	New Zealand	.913	188	Niger	.348

Source: United Nations Development Program data (2015)

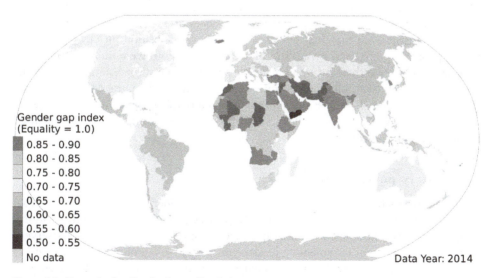

Figure 3.2 Countries by Gender Inequality Index score

In response to some of the difficulties with measuring capability poverty, and the limitations of other index measures, a relatively new, very promising Multidimensional Poverty Index (MPI) has been developed, principally by the scholars Sabina Alkire and James Foster. This measure is focused intentionally on poverty – not development or empowerment or income – and it includes indicators to gauge multiple, simultaneous deprivations. As Alkire and Foster have written, 'When poor people describe their situation [. . .], part of their description often narrates the multiplicity of disadvantages that batter their lives at once. Malnutrition is coupled with a lack of work, water has to be fetched from an area with regular violence, or there are poor services and low incomes' (Alkire and Foster 2011: 13). The Multidimensional Poverty Index also draws explicitly on the capabilities approach: indicators reflect functionings, and so low scores on the indicators are analogous to states of 'unfreedom' (Alkire and Santos 2013). Another advantage of the MPI is that it allows much finer-grained analysis than the HDI or the Human Poverty Index (which was used before the MPI). For instance, the data computed into the MPI make it possible to identify *who* is poor by individuals or groups, *where* poor people are by region or locality, *how* they are poor by which deprivations they suffer from, and *how intense* their poverty is by the number of deprivations.

The MPI's indicators allow for cross-country comparison as well as country-specific modifications. The breakdown of poverty dimensions and indicators is shown in Figure 3.3. A person is defined as multidimensionally poor if he or she is deprived in one-third of these weighted indicators (Alkire and Sumner 2013). A list of countries with the severest multidimensional poverty is presented in Table 3.4. The weights and poverty thresholds can also be adjusted for applications to specific countries. For instance, Mexico has begun adapting the MPI to identify and measure poverty for its own national policies. In Mexico's application, deprivations in one of several indicators help define a person as multidimensionally poor, including access to health care, access to social security, basic services in homes, and housing quality. For access to social security, a person falls below the poverty threshold if she does not receive medical services through a public, voluntary or family network. For basic services, the poverty threshold is lacking access to piped or fresh water, public drainage services or public electricity. An analysis of 2010 data concluded that 46.2 per cent of Mexico's population (in other words, 52 million people out of a total population of about 112 million) were multidimensionally poor, and on average these 52 million people suffered from deprivations in 2.5 of the indicators (OPHI 2013). Like previous measures we have studied, the MPI is not sufficient in itself. Because its usage is still expanding, and it is still working out methodological issues of calculation and data collection, the MPI is best used as a complement to income and other measures.

Participatory poverty assessments

The final approach to measuring poverty we will consider differs significantly from the preceding ones in that it does not rely primarily on statistics for cross-national comparisons. Also important is that this approach is not predicated on external observers' ostensibly objective measurements, but depends instead on groups of (usually poor) people defining poverty within the context of their own community. The goal is to understand how poor people themselves would subjectively measure poverty. Known

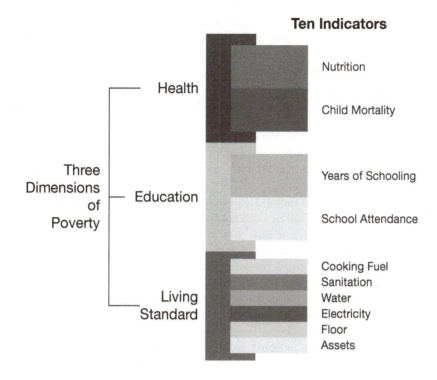

Figure 3.3 Components of the Multidimensional Poverty Index.
Source: Oxford Poverty and Human Development Initiative.

Table 3.5 Top ten countries by highest Multidimensional Poverty Index score

Country	MPI score	% Population in multidimensional poverty	Intensity of deprivation (average % of weighted deprivations)
Niger	.605	89.3	67.7
Ethiopia	.564	87.3	64.6
South Sudan	.557	91.1	61.2
Chad	.554	87.2	63.5
Burkina Faso	.535	84.0	63.7
Somalia	.514	81.2	63.3
Sierra Leone	.464	81.0	57.3
Guinea-Bissau	.462	77.5	59.6
Guinea	.459	75.1	61.1
Mali	.457	77.7	58.9

Source: Oxford Poverty and Human Development Initiative (2015), /www.ophi.org.uk/multidimensional-poverty-index/mpi-2015/

as participatory poverty assessments (PPAs; or sometimes participatory rural appraisals), the participatory aspect is that a group of people gather together to talk about definitions of poverty, how to identify need, and who is deprived in what ways. PPAs can play a vital role in the capability approach by providing information about the capabilities or freedoms that individuals deem 'fundamental', and what their minimum thresholds would be for an adequate life. Besides giving outsiders an insight into the community's definitions of poverty, these participatory assessments often fulfil other functions, such as promoting self-determination, empowerment and group cooperation (Laderchi 2001). By helping to highlight the specific concerns or priorities of poor people, PPAs can serve as an important policy tool for governmental or NGO programmes. Evidence also suggests that PPAs often do not identify the same people as poor as monetary measures.

Of course, like any other way of measuring poverty, these PPAs have certain limitations. Because they are qualitative research, the results of PPAs can be difficult to use in comparisons of development from one society to another, or to quantify for econometric analyses. Also, researchers have found that sometimes such participatory assessments can be skewed when the participants think they are more likely to receive some commodity (whether food, health care or something else) as a result. For instance, it can happen that more people claim they are poor in the hopes of getting help. People are essentially always biased in regard to their own situation. Though subjective reports are part of the rationale of PPAs, they nearly always involve some post-hoc evaluation or synthesis by an external researcher. The external researchers' work must be designed very carefully to avoid methodological problems in the data gathering, and ethical pitfalls in the relationship with the community. There is no guarantee, either, that the actual participants in these assessments are the most representative of poverty in the community; it is certainly possible that the most marginalized people are excluded (Norton *et al.* 2001).

Regardless, PPAs are valuable for providing a 'grassroots' picture of poverty that can be different from that provided by the other measures. For instance, results from various PPAs have revealed that income is often not people's primary concern but other considerations such as security and self-respect are. People value a wide variety of things that are probably impossible to capture via monetary measures. These things include freedom to choose jobs and livelihoods; freedom from persecution, humiliation, violence and exploitation; the ability to participate in decision making; and preservation of and ability to participate in traditional cultural values (Streeten 1998). In Clark and Qizilbash's research in South Africa, people in poor communities identified these ten 'essentials of life', in rank order of importance: housing/shelter, food, clean water, work/jobs, money/income, clothes, education/schools, health and health care, electricity/energy, and safety/security (Clark and Qizilbash 2005). A PPA in Laos documented villagers' tribulations with crises such as crop losses from bad weather, pests or land degradation. Those crises tended to cause food shortages, and human crises such as illness, alcoholism or death, which led to labour shortages and reduced income. The PPA also identified political/legal problems leading to the unsustainable exploitation of environmental resources, which in turn harmed people's security in other ways (Action Aid 2006). The World Bank's *Consultations with the Poor* series was a monumental project of PPAs interviewing 20,000 people in 200 communities in 23 countries. A very small selection of findings from the project is presented in the box below.

Box 3.3 Findings from the World Bank's *Consultations with the Poor* PPAs

From their roughly 20,000 interviews, the World Bank team synthesized five interconnected dimensions of wellbeing that poor people identified.

- *Material wellbeing*. Defined by a person in Ecuador as 'A livelihood that will let you live.'
- *Physical wellbeing*. An older man in Egypt described deprivation in this area: 'My children were hungry and I told them the rice is cooking, until they fell asleep from hunger.'
- *Freedom of action and choice*. A poor woman in Brazil defined freedom in this way: 'The rich [person] is the one who says: 'I am going to do it' and does it. The poor, in contrast, do not fulfill their wishes or develop their capacities.'
- *Security*. For a person in Russia, security meant 'the absence of constant fear.'
- *Social wellbeing*. 'It is neither leprosy nor poverty which kills the leper, but loneliness', said a person in Ghana.

The World Bank team also identified five consistent, cross-cutting problems that trapped people in poverty: corruption, violence, powerlessness, weakness and bare subsistence. A person in Bulgaria claimed that 'corruption is virtually everywhere', and another in Uzbekistan complained that 'the police have become the rich people's stick used against common people.' People decried violence in society and in the household: 'Women are beaten at the house for any reason that may include failure to prepare lunch or dinner for the husband', said a respondent in Ethiopia. The lack of security also applied to basic living conditions. A woman in Brazil lamented that 'the sewage runs in your front door, and when it rains, the water floods into the house and [. . .] the waste brings some bugs, here we have rats, cockroaches, spiders, and even snakes and scorpions.' The PPAs showed that poor people around the world routinely felt themselves ignored by both government and NGOs. This powerlessness defined poverty for an old man in Nigeria: 'If you want to do something and have no power to do it, it is poverty.'

Source: Narayan *et al.* (1999)

How much overlap is there between these measures?

Having surveyed a broad range of different measurements of poverty, and their respective advantages and disadvantages, a natural question would be to ask how the measurements relate to each other. Specifically, do they identify the same people as poor? It would be nice, for the sake of simplicity, if the answer were 'yes', but in fact the picture is mixed, and ultimately there are many ways that the different measures fail to overlap. Several studies have concluded that monetary and human development measures sometimes overlap, but often do not. (see Stewart *et al.* 2007, Bourguignon *et al.* 2008) At the national level, for example, a country might make major strides in eliminating health-related aspects of poverty such as malaria prevalence, yet have no income growth, and hence still be counted as poor according to monetary measures. At the individual level, consider again the example that opened this chapter: Aneni in Zimbabwe would not be considered income poor, but she does suffer from serious deprivations in health and education, and she lacks some fundamental rights of autonomy in her own household. So is she truly poor? One approach, known as the 'union' approach, would say that if she has deprivations in *any* dimension – either income, or health, or education, or rights, for instance – then yes, she is poor. But another approach, the intersection approach, would say that she is poor if she has deprivations in *all* dimensions, so income *and* health, and education, and rights (Atkinson 2003). The problem is that these two approaches may not identify the same people as poor. As one example, a study found that 97 per cent of India's population was poor according to the union approach, but according to the intersection approach, only 0.1 per cent of the population was poor (Alkire and Seth 2009).

This is not to say there is never overlap between measures; sometimes there is, but it can be weak. The weak overlap leads to surprising cases such as that of Nicaragua, which achieved a relatively favourable score of 18 on the Human Poverty Index, but where 80 per cent of the population was living below the old USD 2 a day line. South Africa had the opposite problem, with a relatively high HPI of 31.7 but with only 23.8 per cent of the population living on less than USD 2 a day. Further demonstrating how different data sources can complicate analysis, one study found that 11 per cent of the population of South Africa was income poor, and 11 per cent were poor according to the MPI – but only 3 per cent of the population was poor by both measures. Clearly, there are mismatches between these data and indicators (Alkire and Sumner 2013). Cuba is another classic example of a country with a GDP per capita of USD 7,274 – below the world average – but with relatively strong health and education numbers, giving it an HDI score in 2015 of .769, which was classified as 'high' and above the world average. Comparing countries such as Saudi Arabia and Uruguay also complicates definitions of wellbeing: Saudi Arabia has a higher GDP per capita than Uruguay, but Uruguay scores much higher on human development indicators such as adult literacy, life expectancy, child mortality, and political rights (Alkire and Deneulin 2009).

Conclusion

Given the intimidating complexity of arriving at accurate measurements for individuals' income in many developing countries, as well as the dizzying profusion of different ways to measure poverty, what is the wisest way forward? Recall the vital underlying goals of measuring poverty: to identify people who are in need, to ascertain in what areas they are deprived, and then to track the progress of policies to help them. The simple fact is that no single global poverty line is going to give a reliable picture of poverty around the world. The circumstances of poverty are ultimately too country and society specific to allow for single measures in which we can have much confidence. Similarly, an index of a variety of poverty measures will not provide a complete picture. Not all deprivations are relevant in all situations. Remember also one of our fundamental tenets, which is that poverty is multidimensional.

Therefore, it is smartest to consult a number of different measures of poverty, with reference to specific societies, to examine deprivation using several indicators. The measures should embrace multiple dimensions, whether income, health, education and empowerment, or employment status, housing quality, personal safety and subjective measures of wellbeing. The measures should include both quantitative and qualitative data – statistics, but ideally also interviews, participatory analyses and ethnographies. Also, a more comprehensive analysis will not be restricted to poverty, but will also examine indicators for inequality (such as the Gini index and the Gender Inequality Index) and quality of life (such as the Human Development Index). You cannot expect that different measures will produce one cohesive answer. And you must not forget that these measures are relevant to people's lives. Measurement is but one part of the process of understanding the social, political, economic and cultural reasons why people are poor, and understanding should lead to action. The ultimate purpose of measuring poverty is to identify the people who need help, and then to find ways to alleviate their suffering.

This multidimensional view of poverty, the need to consult a variety of measures, and the use of such measures to drive pro-poor policies informs both the Millennium Development Goals (MDGs), which applied from 2000–15, and the Sustainable Development Goals, which apply for 2015–30. The MDGs embraced eight broad goals that were measured by a series of indicators. Goal 1 was to 'eradicate extreme poverty and hunger', goal 2 was to 'achieve universal primary education', and goal 3 was to 'promote gender equality', for example. This development push fell short of many of its targets, but still achieved respectable progress. In 1990, 47 per cent of the world's population lived on less than USD 1.25 a day. In 2015, that number was 14 per cent. The proportion of undernourished people fell over that timeframe from 23.3 to 12.9 per cent, though that result did not meet the target of halving the proportion of people suffering from hunger. Similarly, major gains were made in education – the net enrolment rate in primary education rose from 83 per cent in 2000 to 91 per cent in 2015 – but still fell short of the goal of universal primary enrolment. Child and maternal mortality both fell by half, and in gender empowerment, the proportion of women in parliament almost doubled. However, results in those areas fell short of targets. Some targets were achieved, such as halving the incidence and mortality from malaria and halving the proportion of people without access to safe drinking water (United Nations 2015).

The Sustainable Development Goals (SDGs) encompass 17 goals, 169 targets and 300-some indicators – see a condensed list below. The SDGs were designed in part to respond to some of the criticisms of the MDGs. For example, the MDGs did not specifically mention human rights, and in practice they were goals only for developing countries, not for the high-income countries. The SDGs are supposed to promote a holistic process of truly global development for all countries. Nonetheless, the SDGs are prone to some of the same criticisms as the earlier set of goals. The number of indicators can seem like a laundry list, and some of the information required may be difficult to come by. Some of the health goals for example, including maternal mortality and disease prevalence, may not have consistently reliable data, especially for the poorest countries. As with the MDGs, it is also debatable how many of the SDGs can realistically be achieved. What happens if goals are not met, and what is the point of such exercises if there is no real accountability attached to the targets? These debates are worth considering. But as a relatively coherent, internationally valorized and highly visible attempt to agree upon definitions and measurements of poverty, deprivation and wellbeing, the Sustainable Development Goals have established reference points that will remain influential for years to come.

Box 3.4 Sustainable Development Goals and selected targets

Goal 1: End poverty in all its forms everywhere

- By 2030, eradicate extreme poverty for all people everywhere, currently measured as people living on less than USD 1.25 a day
- By 2030, reduce at least by half the proportion of men, women and children of all ages living in poverty in all its dimensions according to national definitions

Goal 2: End hunger, achieve food security and improved nutrition and promote sustainable agriculture

- By 2030, end hunger and ensure access by all people, in particular the poor and people in vulnerable situations, including infants, to safe, nutritious and sufficient food all year round
- By 2030, end all forms of malnutrition, including achieving, by 2025, the internationally agreed targets on stunting and wasting in children under 5 years of age, and address the nutritional needs of adolescent girls, pregnant and lactating women and older persons

Goal 3: Ensure healthy lives and promote wellbeing for all at all ages

- By 2030, reduce the global maternal mortality ratio to less than 70 per 100,000 live births
- By 2030, end preventable deaths of newborns and children under 5 years of age, with all countries aiming to reduce neonatal mortality to at least as low as 12 per 1000 live births and under-5 mortality to at least as low as 25 per 1000 live births

Goal 4: Ensure inclusive and quality education for all and promote lifelong learning

- By 2030, ensure that all girls and boys complete free, equitable and quality primary and secondary education leading to relevant and Goal-4 effective learning outcomes
- By 2030, ensure that all girls and boys have access to quality early childhood development, care and preprimary education so that they are ready for primary education

Goal 5: Achieve gender equality and empower all women and girls

- End all forms of discrimination against all women and girls everywhere
- Eliminate all forms of violence against all women and girls in the public and private spheres, including trafficking and sexual and other types of exploitation

Goal 6: Ensure access to water and sanitation for all

- By 2030, achieve universal and equitable access to safe and affordable drinking water for all
- By 2030, achieve access to adequate and equitable sanitation and hygiene for all and end open defecation, paying special attention to the needs of women and girls and those in vulnerable situations

Goal 7: Ensure access to affordable, reliable, sustainable and modern energy for all

- By 2030, increase substantially the share of renewable energy in the global energy mix
- By 2030, double the global rate of improvement in energy efficiency

Goal 8: Promote inclusive and sustainable economic growth, employment and decent work for all

- Sustain per capita economic growth in accordance with national circumstances and, in particular, at least 7 per cent gross domestic product growth per annum in the least developed countries
- Achieve higher levels of economic productivity through diversification, technological upgrading and innovation, including a focus on high-value added and labour-intensive sectors

Goal 9: Build resilient infrastructure, promote sustainable industrialization and foster innovation

- Promote inclusive and sustainable industrialization and, by 2030, significantly raise industry's share of employment and gross domestic product, in line with national circumstances, and double its share in least developed countries
- Increase the access of small-scale industrial and other enterprises, in particular in developing countries, to financial services, including affordable credit, and their integration into value chains and markets

Goal 10: Reduce inequality within and among countries

- By 2030, progressively achieve and sustain income growth of the bottom 40 per cent of the population at a rate higher than the national average
- By 2030, empower and promote the social, economic and political inclusion of all, irrespective of age, sex, disability, race, ethnicity, origin, religion or economic or other status

Goal 11: Make cities inclusive, safe, resilient and sustainable

- By 2030, ensure access for all to adequate, safe and affordable housing and basic services and upgrade slums
- By 2030, provide access to safe, affordable, accessible and sustainable transport systems for all, improving road safety, notably by expanding public transport,

with special attention to the needs of those in vulnerable situations, women, children, persons with disabilities and older persons

Goal 12: Ensure sustainable production and consumption patterns

- By 2030, achieve the sustainable management and efficient use of natural resources
- By 2030, halve per capita global food waste at the retail and consumer levels and reduce food losses along production and supply chains, including post-harvest losses

Goal 13: Take urgent action to combat climate change and its impacts

- Integrate climate change measures into national policies, strategies and planning
- Improve education, awareness-raising and human and institutional capacity on climate change mitigation, adaptation, impact reduction and early warning

Goal 14: Conserve and sustainably use the world's oceans, seas and marine resources

- By 2025, prevent and significantly reduce marine pollution of all kinds, in particular from land-based activities, including marine debris and nutrient pollution
- By 2020, sustainably manage and protect marine and coastal ecosystems to avoid significant adverse impacts, including by strengthening their resilience, and take action for their restoration in order to achieve healthy and productive oceans

Goal 15: Sustainably manage forests, combat desertification, halt and reverse land degradation, halt biodiversity loss

- By 2020, ensure the conservation, restoration and sustainable use of terrestrial and inland freshwater ecosystems and their services, in particular forests, wetlands, mountains and drylands, in line with obligations under international agreements
- By 2020, promote the implementation of sustainable management of all types of forests, halt deforestation, restore degraded forests and substantially increase afforestation and reforestation globally

Goal 16: Promote just, peaceful and inclusive societies

- Significantly reduce all forms of violence and related death rates everywhere
- End abuse, exploitation, trafficking and all forms of violence against and torture of children

Goal 17: Revitalize the global partnership for sustainable development

- Developed countries to implement fully their official development assistance commitments, including the commitment by many developed countries to achieve the target of 0.7 per cent of ODA/GNI to developing countries and 0.15 to 0.20 per cent of ODA/GNI to least developed countries.

• Assist developing countries in attaining long-term debt sustainability through coordinated policies aimed at fostering debt financing, debt relief and debt restructuring, as appropriate, and address the external debt of highly indebted poor countries to reduce debt distress

Explore the Sustainable Development Goals at the UN's dedicated website: www.un.org/sustainabledevelopment/sustainable-development-goals/

Discussion questions

1 Are there basic capabilities essential to a definition of poverty that have been left out of this discussion? If so, what are they? How should they be measured?

2 Use the internet to explore indicators of poverty, inequality and wellbeing. What can you learn about individual countries, trends among countries, trends over time and relationships between different indicators?

    a Nationmaster.com offers a wealth of country-level statistical data and is relatively easy to use.

    b The World Bank's eAtlas of Global Development is a powerful tool for mapping and graphing data.

    c Gapminder.org may seem complicated at first, but you can investigate a wide variety of discrete indicators and the relationships between them, as well as statistical trends and videos.

    d Ourworldindata.org/worldpoverty has many useful infographics.

    e Explore the Social Progress Index (www.socialprogressimperative.org). How is 'social progress' defined? What is the range of indicators? Examine how several individual countries perform according to this measurement. How does the Index as a whole relate to the capabilities approach?

3 Envision a participatory poverty assessment for your society. How would you define what constitutes 'poverty'? How would you identify who is poor and not poor? What is 'deprivation' in your society, and how can you measure it?

4 Examine the full list of Sustainable Development Goals and their measurements online. Is there anything missing from the SDGs, in your view? What do you think are the most important of the 17 goals?

5 If measures such as the SDGs and the HDI have major flaws, then what is the point of using them? What do you see as the advantages and disadvantages of such measures?

Further reading

Banerjee, Abhijit V. and Esther Duflo. 'The economic lives of the poor', *The Journal of Economic Perspectives*, 21.1 (Winter 2007): 141–167.

Edin, Kathryn J. and H. Luke Shaefer. 2015. *$2.00 a Day: Living on almost nothing in America.* New York, NY: Mariner Books.

Grusky, David B., and Ravi Kanbur, eds. 2006. *Poverty and Inequality*. Stanford, CA: Stanford University Press.

Oxford Poverty and Human Development Initiative. 'Measuring multidimensional poverty: insights from around the world', briefing paper, June 2013.

Saith, Ruhi. 'Capabilities: the concept and its operationalisation', Queen Elizabeth House Working Paper 66, February 2001.

Works cited

Action Aid. Participatory Poverty Assessment, Attapeu Province, Lao PDR. Mekong Wetlands Project, 2006.

Alkire, Sabina. 2002. *Valuing Freedoms: Sen's capabilities approach and poverty reduction*. Oxford: Oxford University Press.

Alkire, Sabina and Séverine Deneulin. 'A Normative Framework for Development', in Séverine Deneulin and Lila Shahani, eds. 2009. *An Introduction to the Human Development and Capability Approach*. London: Earthscan.

Alkire, Sabina and James Foster. 'Understandings and misunderstandings of multidimensional poverty measurement', *Journal of Economic Inequality*, 9 (2011): 289–314.

Alkire, Sabina and Maria Emma Santos. 'A multidimensional approach: poverty measurement & beyond', *Social Indicators Research*, 112 (2013): 239–257.

Alkire, Sabina and Maria Emma Santos. 'Poverty and Inequality Measurement', in Séverine Deneulin and Lila Shahani, eds. 2009. *An Introduction to the Human Development and Capability Approach*. London: Earthscan.

Alkire, Sabina and Suman Seth. 'Determining BPL status: some methodological improvements', *Indian Journal of Human Development*, 2.2 (2009): 407–424.

Alkire, Sabina and Andy Sumner. 'Multidimensional poverty and the post-2015 MDGs', Oxford Poverty & Human Development Initiative brief, February 2013.

Anand, Sudhir, Paul Segal and Joseph Stiglitz. 'Introduction', in Sudhir Anand, Paul Segal and Joseph Stiglitz, eds. 2010. *Debates on the Measurement of Global Poverty*. Oxford: Oxford University Press.

Atkinson, A.B. 'Multidimensional deprivation: contrasting social welfare and counting approaches', *Journal of Economic Inequality*, 1 (2003): 51–65.

Bhalla, Surjit S. 'Raising the standard: the war on global poverty', unpublished working paper, March 2009.

Bibi, Sami. 'Measuring poverty in a multidimensional perspective: a review of literature', Poverty and Economic Policy working paper, November 2005.

Bourguignon, François *et al.* 'Millennium Development Goals at midpoint: where do we stand, and where do we need to go?' European Report on Development, September 2008.

Bourguignon, François and Satya R. Chakravarty. 'The measurement of multidimensional poverty', *Journal of Economic Inequality*, 1.1 (2003): 25–49.

Chen, Shaohua, and Martin Ravallion. 'An update of the World Bank's estimates of consumption poverty in the developing world.' World Bank research paper, March 2012.

Chen, Shaohua and Martin Ravallion. 'The developing world is poorer than we thought, but no less successful in the fight against poverty.' World Bank research paper, August 2008.

Clark, David A. and Mozaffar Qizilbash. 'Core poverty, basic capabilities and vagueness: an application to the South African context', Global Poverty Research Group paper GRPG-WPS-026, July 2005.

Cowell, Frank A. 2011. *Measuring Inequality*. Oxford: Oxford University Press.

Deaton, Angus. 'Measuring Poverty in a Growing World (or Measuring Growth in a Poor World)', in Sudhir Anand, Paul Segal and Joseph Stiglitz, eds. 2010. *Debates on the Measurement of Global Poverty*. Oxford: Oxford University Press.

Deaton, Angus. 'Measuring poverty', Paper for the Research Program in Development Studies, Princeton University, 2004.

Deaton, Angus. 'Counting the world's poor: problems and possible solutions', *The World Bank Research Observer*, 16.2 (2001): 125–147.

Johnston, Robert. 'Poverty or Income Distribution: Which Do We Want to Measure?', in Sudhir Anand, Paul Segal and Joseph Stiglitz, eds. 2010. *Debates on the Measurement of Global Poverty*. Oxford: Oxford University Press.

Laderchi, Caterina. 'Participatory methods in the analysis of poverty: a critical review', QEH Working Paper QEHWPS62, January 2001.

Narayan, Deepa, Robert Chambers, Meera Shah and Patti Petesch. *Global synthesis: Consultations with the poor*. Washington, DC: World Bank Poverty Group, 1999.

Norton, Andy with Bella Bird, Karen Crock, Margaret Kakande and Carrie Turk. 2001. *Participatory Poverty Assessment: An introduction to theory and practice*. London: Overseas Development Institute.

Oxford Poverty and Human Development Initiative. 'Measuring multidimensional poverty: insights from around the world', briefing paper, June 2013.

Ravallion, Martin. 'The Debate on Globalization, Poverty, and Inequality: Why Measurement Matters', in Sudhir Anand, Paul Segal and Joseph Stiglitz, eds. 2010. *Debates on the Measurement of Global Poverty*. Oxford: Oxford University Press.

Reddy, Sanjay G. and Thomas Pogge. 'How Not to Count the Poor', in Sudhir Anand, Paul Segal and Joseph Stiglitz, eds. 2010. *Debates on the Measurement of Global Poverty*. Oxford: Oxford University Press.

Sahn, David E. and Stephen D. Younger. 'Living Standards in Africa', in Sudhir Anand, Paul Segal and Joseph Stiglitz, eds. 2010. *Debates on the Measurement of Global Poverty*. Oxford: Oxford University Press.

Sen, Amartya. 'Conceptualizing and Measuring Poverty', in David B. Grusky and Ravi Kanbur, eds. 2006. *Poverty and Inequality*. Stanford, CA: Stanford University Press.

Stewart, Frances, Ruhi Saith and Barbara Harriss-White, eds. 2007. *Defining Poverty in the Developing World*. New York, NY: Palgrave Macmillan.

Streeten, Paul. 'Beyond the six veils: conceptualizing and measuring poverty', *Journal of International Affairs*, 52.1 (1998): 1–31.

Sumner, Andy. 'Where do the world's poor live? A new update', Institute for Development Studies Working Paper No. 393, June 2012.

Szekely, Miguel, Nora Lustig, José Antonio Mejía and Martin Cumpa. 'Do we know how much poverty there is?' Inter-American Development Bank Research Working Paper No. 437, December 2000.

United Nations. 2015. *The Millennium Development Goals Report 2015*. New York, NY: United Nations.

United Nations Development Programme. 2007. *Measuring Human Development: A primer*. New York, NY: United Nations.

Wade, Robert H. 'Is globalization reducing poverty and inequality?' *World Development*, 32.4 (2004): 567–589.

4   Health and poverty

Paula E. Brentlinger

*Paula Brentlinger is a Clinical Assistant Professor
in the Department of Global Health, University of Washington*

Key questions

- Considering 'health' as a central capability, what are some important links between poverty, ill health and capabilities?
- How does poverty affect the prevention, diagnosis and treatment of disease? Does poverty affect all diseases in the same way?
- What are the similarities and differences between poorer and wealthier populations with regard to the prevention and treatment of illness?
- How is the capabilities approach reflected in national and international health policies and in international law?
- How are health, poverty and capabilities linked in your own community (positively or negatively)?
- Can individuals secure their health-related capabilities alone, or must there be a contribution of the community or government?

Introduction

Just as there are many definitions of 'poverty', there are many definitions of 'health'.

The Preamble to the Constitution of the World Health Organization (WHO) defines health as 'a state of complete physical, mental and social well-being and not merely the absence of disease or infirmity'. Though some have criticized WHO for leaning too far towards a utilitarian definition of health, by seeming to conflate health with happiness (Saracci 1997), and others have observed that interpretation of 'well-being' will vary markedly across cultures and social classes (Susser 1974), WHO's is now a standard definition. It does not include the term 'capabilities', but its conceptual overlap with capabilities theory is substantial. For example, Martha Nussbaum's list of ten central capabilities includes 'Bodily Health', and her description of bodily health focuses on 'good health' and explicitly addresses the importance of nutrition, housing and reproductive health, not just 'the absence of disease' (Nussbaum 2003).

Relationships that involve health, poverty, capabilities, opportunities, human rights and freedoms are complex. Briefly, if we conceptualize capabilities as the freedom and opportunity for a person 'to be and to do' what is of value to that person, it is not hard to imagine that physical and/or mental suffering and dysfunction might constrict a person's freedoms and opportunities, and that deficits of freedoms or opportunities might impede a person's ability to prevent or obtain treatment for specific diseases.

In this chapter, we will explore aspects of three diseases or medical conditions (maternal mortality [caused by eclampsia], Hepatitis C and malaria) to illustrate important principles, and to illuminate similarities and differences between the capabilities approach and other methods of analysing and addressing health problems. The first discussion, on maternal mortality, will be the longest, and will serve as our introduction to most of the concepts that will also appear in later discussions. The three health problems that will be addressed have been chosen because they illustrate different concepts and challenges, and different ways in which health may influence human capabilities and human capabilities may also influence bodily health.

Maternal mortality

Vignette 4.1: Maternal mortality (eclampsia)

In the late twentieth century, there were armed conflicts in nearly every country in the Central American isthmus, from Panama to southern Mexico. In the particular place where a pregnant woman named Rosa Maria lived, a low-level conflict had gone on for years. (Note that Rosa Maria is not her real name; the details of all of the vignettes in this chapter have been altered to protect personal privacy.) Rosa Maria and her family lived in a mountainous rural area where they grew corn, beans and a few vegetables, and raised chickens and pigs. They bartered for most of their needs and lived almost entirely outside the cash economy. They spoke an indigenous language with no written form. They had no electricity, telephone or piped water; their water was drawn from the river.

This was not the family's home village – the fighting had driven them from their original village. The conflict had polarized the region. Nearly every village was aligned with one of the two warring factions; the dominant faction drove the minority members out. A few villages were almost physically split, with supporters of the different factions living on opposite sides of a street or other dividing line.

Rosa Maria and her family were aligned with one faction, but the other faction controlled most of the local hospitals. Rosa Maria planned to deliver her baby at home with the village midwife, because it would be less expensive than going to the single hospital that she trusted, and also because if her labour was rapid, or if it started at night (when it was dangerous to travel) she didn't think that she would be able to get to the hospital. Also, Rosa Maria and the local midwife spoke the same indigenous language, which almost no one spoke at the hospital. The midwife had never been formally trained in pregnancy and delivery care, and there was no clinic, hospital or higher-level health worker in the village.

In the pregnancy's seventh month, Rosa Maria noticed that her ankles were swelling, but neither she nor the midwife worried about this until the swelling worsened. It extended halfway to her knees, and she developed headaches. She didn't have a fever, but she took some malaria tablets that her husband bought from a neighbour. The headaches got worse. Then, during the worst headache she had ever had, she fell unconscious to the dirt floor of her house. Her family found her there, convulsing. The midwife did not know what to do. Rosa Maria's husband rounded up some relatives and neighbours, and they put Rosa Maria into a rope hammock and started walking to the hospital they trusted.

Eight hours later, they arrived. Rosa Maria was still unconscious and still having seizures. The doctor on duty quickly found that Rosa Maria's face, hands and legs were very swollen, and her blood pressure was dangerously high. Rosa

Maria almost certainly had a condition called eclampsia, which occurs only in pregnancy and threatens the life of both mother and baby. At that point, though, the foetal heartbeat could still be heard and seemed normal. Rosa Maria's convulsions were quickly stopped with medications, and an intravenous line was placed to provide a steady drip of medication to prevent further attacks. The blood pressure was soon controlled, but Rosa Maria did not wake up. Immediate delivery of the baby would have been best for both Rosa Maria and the baby, because delivery stops the disease process in the mother. But Rosa Maria was not yet in labour, and the small rural hospital had no surgeon to perform a caesarean section, and no specialists in the care of premature newborns. The nearest hospital with a surgeon and a higher-level nursery was about two hours away, down a road that was closed by the fighting.

After long conversations, the family and the hospital opted to try to get Rosa Maria through the military roadblocks by ambulance. There was no telephone link between the two hospitals, and the decision to transport was made based on desperation and faith. And the plan worked, insofar as Rosa Maria and her unborn baby were still alive on arrival to the referral hospital, and the driver made it back safely. Because of the communications difficulties in this conflict zone, the health workers who arranged for Rosa Maria's transfer to the referral hospital were never able to find out whether the higher-level hospital had been able to perform a caesarean section, but they eventually learned that neither mother nor infant had survived.

This story, with a few variations, could have come from any of many war zones in the region. Rosa Maria's story ended in what is called 'maternal mortality'. The definition of maternal mortality (per the International Statistical Classification of Diseases, 10th revision [ICD-10]) is: 'The death of a woman while pregnant or within 42 days of termination of pregnancy, irrespective of the duration and site of the pregnancy, from any cause related to or aggravated by the pregnancy or its management but not from accidental or incidental causes' (World Health Organization, 2014b). If a woman dies during pregnancy or childbirth, it is sometimes, but not always, possible to save her infant. The story of Rosa Maria's death ended with the loss of the infant (foetal or neonatal mortality) as well. How might we analyse this story of poverty and ill health?

Analysis of disease (eclampsia) and its treatment in one patient

We will start with a disease-focused medical review, focusing on the diagnosis and treatment of the patient and her specific illness(es). Rosa Maria clearly did not enjoy 'the absence of disease', and her primary medical problem was almost certainly eclampsia, as noted above. Although eclampsia is one of the most dangerous complications of pregnancy, recognition and treatment in an earlier stage (pre-eclampsia) offers an opportunity to control the mother's high blood pressure and prevent seizures, and early delivery of the baby, if necessary, can occur in a planned way, with attention to the safety of both mother and infant. In the vignette above, the untrained midwife did not recognize the signs or symptoms of pre-eclampsia and did not even know how to measure Rosa Maria's blood pressure. Thus, Rosa Maria did not receive proper medical attention until her condition had become life-threatening, with loss of consciousness and convulsions. The definitive treatment of eclampsia – early delivery of the baby –

Box 4.1 Disease-focused analysis: Rosa Maria and eclampsia

- *What was the most probable medical diagnosis?* Pre-eclampsia with evolution to eclampsia and both maternal and foetal (or neonatal) death.
- *What medical errors led to adverse outcomes?* Failure to identify signs and symptoms of pre-eclampsia (midwife), late initiation of treatment for pre-eclampsia and eclampsia (midwife and hospital[s]).

---

was not available at the hospital she chose, and it is unclear whether it was ever achieved. A physician (medical doctor) reviewing this case would conclude that it was a case of treatable maternal morbidity (sickness), culminating in avoidable direct maternal and foetal or neonatal mortality (death) because of failure to identify and treat a life-threatening condition before severe complications developed. A conscientious physician would also have concluded that it was a terrible tragedy, and that something should be done about it.

A public health analysis of eclampsia

A disease-focused analysis does not reflect the complexity of this story. A public health analysis would go further. One definition of public health, from the CDC Foundation, is 'Public Health is the science of protecting and improving the health of families and communities through promotion of healthy lifestyles, research for disease and injury prevention and detection and control of infectious disease. Overall, public health is concerned with protecting the health of entire populations' (CDC Foundation 2016). Public health analyses commonly begin with an estimate of the size of a problem – in this case, eclampsia – for the entire population of pregnant women in the country (or state, region, province or planet).

WHO has estimated the burden of maternal mortality on the global level (Say *et al.* 2014). Per WHO's calculations, there were 2,443,000 maternal deaths worldwide between 2003 and 2009, and 343,000 (14.0 per cent) of them were caused by 'hypertensive disorders', a category that includes eclampsia and other conditions causing very high blood pressure in the mother. Hypertensive disorders caused approximately 22.1 per cent of maternal deaths in Latin America and the Caribbean (the region in which Rosa Maria lived). WHO has concluded that 99 per cent of maternal deaths worldwide occur in resource-constrained countries. In the worst-affected region, sub-Saharan Africa, one of every 38 women is likely to die of pregnancy-related causes (World Health Organization, 2014b). Examining these metrics, it is hard to deny that maternal mortality caused by eclampsia and/or other conditions is a significant problem in the world, especially when we recall that the death of a pregnant or post-partum woman often implies death for the foetus or newborn as well, and orphanhood for older siblings.

Having identified an important problem at the level of the population (global or smaller units), a public health analysis would go on to identify gaps in capacity for prevention, recognition and treatment of eclampsia at different levels of the population and the health system. With pre-eclampsia and eclampsia, the focus is on identifying

---

Box 4.2 Public health analysis step 1: How big is the problem of eclampsia-related mortality, and where is it concentrated?

- *How many women die of eclampsia or pre-eclampsia?* Tens of thousands per year.
- *Where are they?* Everywhere, but primarily in the poorer countries and in Latin America.

---

women with early signs and symptoms, and then providing treatment to slow progression of pre-eclampsia to eclampsia, with early delivery if required. Because pre-eclampsia can progress quickly, rapid diagnosis and rapid initiation of effective treatment are the highest priorities. For this reason, one commonly used scheme for analysis of factors contributing to maternal mortality focuses on 'three delays': delay in recognizing and seeking care for a pregnancy complication, delay in arrival at a health-care facility, and delay in receiving appropriate treatment after arrival at the appropriate health facility (Thaddeus and Maine 1994). The delays are identified based on a review of cases of maternal mortality. Analysing Rosa Maria's case using the 'three delays' approach, we can easily see that all three delays occurred.

A full regional maternal mortality review would be far more complex than what is described above (Averting Maternal Death and Disability Program, 2010). For example, a thorough analysis would look beyond the specific situation of just one patient and would address broader questions, such as: How many health workers in the region were trained to identify pre-eclampsia and eclampsia? Where were they located relative

---

Box 4.3 Public health analysis step 2: Review of an eclampsia-related maternal mortality case (identifying the three delays)

Based on Rosa Maria's story:

- *Delay 1: Recognition of the problem.* No one was trained or able to recognize the signs and symptoms of pre-eclampsia in Rosa Maria's village.
- *Delay 2: Transport.* Rosa Maria and her family were hesitant to use the nearest hospital because of cultural and political barriers. Also, they lacked passable roads, telecommunications, and vehicles. Travel was risky because of the armed conflict.
- *Delay 3: Treatment.* Initial transport did not get Rosa Maria to a hospital that was able to provide adequate emergency obstetrical care. Although Rosa Maria's first-choice hospital was able to control her seizures and reduce her high blood pressure, it had no surgeon (to perform a caesarean section) or premature-infant care, and she had to be transferred elsewhere (a second transport delay).

to populations of women of child-bearing age? Which health facilities could lower blood pressure, stop convulsions, perform a caesarean section, and care for a premature infant? Were affordable ambulance services available?

A capabilities analysis: eclampsia

Now, let us analyse Rosa Maria's case from the perspective of capabilities. Was her illness caused by a deprivation of capabilities or freedoms? Did her illness deprive her of any capabilities or freedoms?

Before and during her illness, Rosa Maria suffered a deprivation of multiple capabilities within Nussbaum's list of the 'central capabilities'. (See Chapter 1 for complete definitions of central capabilities.) Some of these deprivations are listed below, but the reader may be able to identify others.

a   Bodily health: Because of her pre-eclampsia and eclampsia, Rosa Maria was not able to enjoy good reproductive or other health.
b   Bodily integrity: Because of the armed conflict, Rosa Maria was not able to move from place to place freely and without fear.
c   Senses, imagination, and thought: Rosa Maria was not able to read and had never had the opportunity to attend school.
d   Affiliation: Because Rosa Maria belonged to a particular minority ethnic group, she worried that she would not be treated with dignity at the hospital.
e   Control over one's environment: Rosa Maria's family had been forced out of their original village by the armed conflict.

Rosa Maria's illness also deprived her of the most central of the capabilities – 'Life'.

An alternative summary would be that Rosa Maria's life circumstances deprived her of the freedom and opportunities necessary to obtain timely, life-saving medical treatment for her pre-eclampsia and eclampsia, and the consequences of her eclampsia then deprived her of all other freedoms and opportunities. We will return to the role of capabilities later in this discussion.

The role of poverty (eclampsia)

Let us look briefly at Rosa Maria's story and its association with core definitions of poverty (described in earlier chapters of this book). Pre-eclampsia and eclampsia may occur in pregnant women in any country or economic circumstance. But the availability of diagnosis and treatment is not so evenly distributed.

Poverty of money: The family had almost no cash with which to purchase a vehicle, pay for fuel and maintenance, or hire a driver to take Rosa Maria to her preferred hospital. Her preferred hospital did not have enough money to pay for round-the-clock emergency surgery coverage or the construction of an intensive care nursery for sick or very premature babies. The family almost certainly became even poorer because of Rosa Maria's illness, because of the time they spent away from their fields and what they must have paid to get home from the second hospital.

Poverty of income at the village level: In Rosa Maria's village of displaced indigenous persons, no one was wealthy enough to own a car or truck, and so no neighbour could have done her the favour of driving her to the hospital.

Insofar as the loss (or deprivation) of capabilities can be regarded as a poverty of freedoms, Rosa Maria and her family were impoverished in both capabilities and freedoms.

Yet another layer of discussion

From the perspectives of medicine, public health and capabilities, we can affirm that many things went wrong in Rosa Maria's life and in the course of her pregnancy and her medical care, and that several kinds of poverty and deprivation were implicated. But our analyses are not over until we address an even more complex question: What is to be done to prevent future tragedies of this kind, and how are we to decide where to start? Who had the obligation (or duty) to treat Rosa Maria's pregnancy complications and prevent her death, or to protect other pregnant women in the future? These may be regarded as human rights questions, not just medical ones, and both international law and health activism have created important standards and precedents for problem-solving in the setting of health-related capabilities deprivation.

Martha Nussbaum has emphasized that the relationship between human rights and the central capabilities is very close (Nussbaum 2011). She holds that human rights exist whether or not they are codified in constitutions or legal codes, and that human rights discussions touch on 'an especially urgent set of functions' (Nussbaum 2000).

Our discussion of relevant human rights will begin by invoking international humanitarian law, which (among other aims) seeks to protect civilians from the consequences of armed conflict. Legal language referring specifically to the protection of civilians was developed in the aftermath of the Second World War and the conflict in Vietnam. For example, the 1977 'Protocols additional to the Geneva Conventions of 12 August 1949', states, in its 'basic rule and field of application' section (Part IV, Section 1, Chapter 1, Article 48) that 'the Parties to the conflict shall at all times distinguish between the civilian population and combatants and between civilian objects and military objectives and accordingly shall direct their operations only against military objectives' (Diplomatic Conference on the Reaffirmation and Development of International Humanitarian Law Applicable in Armed Conflicts 1977). The concept of 'medical neutrality' has been developed to define and promote the health rights of those affected by war. Physicians for Human Rights, for example, has defined medical neutrality as 'the principle of noninterference with medical services in times of armed conflict' (Geiger and Cook-Deegan 1993, Averting Maternal Death and Disability Program 2010, Physicians for Human Rights undated).

In Rosa Maria's story, though, the conflict-related aspects are intertwined with other factors that affected her country and village more generally, even before the fighting began. So, in addition to the Geneva Conventions, we will look closely at the International Covenant on Social, Economic, and Cultural Rights (ICESCR) (United Nations 1966).

ICESCR's Article 12 recognized 'the right of everyone to the enjoyment of the highest attainable standard of physical and mental health'. The United Nations Committee on Economic, Social, and Cultural Rights' General Comment 14 provided practical definitions of the components of the human right to health (as defined by ICESCR), defined governmental duties and obligations in regard to the right to health, and defined mechanisms for securing health rights. It also acknowledged the close links between poverty and health (Committee on Economic Social and Cultural Rights 2000). The resulting definitions of the core components of the right to health (abbreviated for our purposes) are:

(a) Availability. Functioning public health and health-care facilities, goods and services, as well as programmes, have to be available in sufficient quantity within the State party. . . . They will include . . . the underlying determinants of health, such as safe and potable drinking water . . .

(b) Accessibility. Health facilities, goods and services have to be accessible to everyone without discrimination, within the jurisdiction of the State party. Accessibility has . . . overlapping dimensions:

- Non-discrimination: health facilities, goods and services must be accessible to all, especially the most vulnerable or marginalized sections of the population, in law and in fact, without discrimination on any of the prohibited grounds.
- Physical accessibility: health facilities, goods and services must be within safe physical reach for all sections of the population, especially vulnerable or marginalized groups, such as ethnic minorities and indigenous populations, women . . .
- Economic accessibility (affordability): health facilities, goods and services must be affordable for all, including socially disadvantaged groups. Equity demands that poorer households should not be disproportionately burdened with health expenses as compared to richer households . . .

(c) Acceptability. All health facilities, goods and services must be respectful of medical ethics and culturally appropriate, i.e. respectful of the culture of individuals, minorities, peoples and communities . . .

(d) Quality. As well as being culturally acceptable, health facilities, goods and services must also be scientifically and medically appropriate and of good quality . . .

There is much more to ICESCR and General Comment 14, but let us stop to compare Rosa Maria's situation to that of the healthy person and functioning health services envisioned above.

Functioning health-care facilities were not available 'in sufficient quantity' where Rosa Maria lived, nor were they 'accessible to everyone without discrimination'. The local hospitals (with one exception) also failed the 'acceptability' test, because they did not provide culturally appropriate services for members of her ethnic group. Both the midwife and the first hospital failed the 'quality' test – the midwife because she did not know how to recognize or treat danger signs in pregnancy, and the hospital because it did not have adequate capacity for treatment of obstetrical emergencies. The language of ICESCR and General Comment 14 provide us with the terms we need to describe the principles that were violated in Rosa Maria's case.

Later sections of General Comment 14 defined the core obligations of states parties (countries that have adopted the ICESCR) with regard to health services. Although many of the core obligations are relevant to Rosa Maria's situation, we will only give key excerpts below:

14 The provision for the reduction of the stillbirth rate and of infant mortality and for the healthy development of the child (art. 12.2 (a)) [. . .] may be understood as requiring measures to improve child and maternal health [. . .]

including emergency obstetric services and access to information, as well as to resources necessary to act on that information.

18   By virtue of article 2.2 and article 3, the Covenant proscribes any discrimination in access to health care and underlying determinants of health, as well as to means and entitlements for their procurement, on the grounds of race, colour, sex, language, religion, political or other opinion, national or social origin [. . .] even in times of severe resource constraints, the vulnerable members of society must be protected by the adoption of relatively low-cost targeted programmes.

19   With respect to the right to health, equality of access to health care and health services has to be emphasized. States have a special obligation to provide those who do not have sufficient means with the necessary health insurance and health-care facilities, and to prevent any discrimination . . .

Upon reading the excerpts above, it becomes clear that the State party (the national government of the country where Rosa Maria lived) had the duty, under the Covenant (which it had endorsed), to see that she had access to emergency obstetrical care (EmOC) as well as access to the information she needed in order to make use of EmOC.

Per General Comment 14, states parties that have not yet fully realized the right to health for their citizens are obliged to make specific plans for the 'progressive realization' of those rights, and the plans must have measurable benchmarks. The core obligations of states parties include:

(f) To adopt and implement a national public health strategy and plan of action, on the basis of epidemiological evidence, addressing the health concerns of the whole population; the strategy and plan of action shall be devised, and periodically reviewed, on the basis of a participatory and transparent process; they shall include methods, such as right to health indicators and benchmarks, by which progress can be closely monitored; the process by which the strategy and plan of action are devised, as well as their content, shall give particular attention to all vulnerable or marginalized groups.

After ICESCR, ongoing advocacy for maternal mortality reduction resulted in even more specific definitions of related duties and rights. The United Nations High Commissioner for Human Rights' 'Technical guidance on the application of a human-rights based approach to the implementation of policies and programmes to reduce preventable maternal mortality and morbidity' (United Nations General Assembly. Human Rights Council 2012) gave detailed guidance on planning, budgeting, implementation, monitoring, review, oversight, and on the use of a 'human rights approach' to analyse maternal mortality:

Example of identified problem: women arriving late or failing to seek emergency obstetric care

56   The first step is to analyse the cause of delays and failure to seek care. A human rights-based approach places responsibility on the State for ensuring available, accessible, acceptable and quality facilities, goods and services to address life-threatening delays. Delays in the decision to seek care or opting out of the

health system entirely are treated not as idiosyncratic, personal choices or immutable cultural preferences but as human rights failures. [. . .]

57 The second step is to identify responsibility for each specific factor leading to delays or failure to seek care . . .

58 The third step is to suggest and prioritize actions by different duty-bearers required for each factor causing the problem . . .

The High Commissioner's technical guidance also inserts another remarkable element in the approach to problem-solving – the active participation of civil society in overseeing each country's efforts to reduce maternal mortality: 'Social accountability calls for civil society and public participation at all levels of decision-making regarding sexual and reproductive health, and throughout the project cycle.' This human-rights-based approach has also been described and amplified by Fukuda-Parr, Freedman and Yamin, among others (Freedman 2001, Fukuda-Parr 2009, Yamin, 2013).

Within the context of maternal mortality reduction, the creation of legal definitions of the right to health (in both wartime and peacetime) has led in turn to creation of standards by which governmental efforts to secure health rights might be developed and evaluated. Real-life examples of health-rights approaches to maternal mortality reduction have begun to appear. In Mexico, for example, national efforts to reduce maternal mortality as part of Mexico's effort to achieve the Millennium Development Goals (MDGs) have been monitored and evaluated over time by the Observatory of Maternal Mortality in Mexico (Observatorio de Mortalidad Materna en Mexico, undated).

Elsewhere in Latin America and other regions, less formally organized groups of citizens have developed their own approaches to prevention and management of pregnancy-related health problems (Smith *et al.* 2015). In its chapter 'Community solutions to make birth safer', the book *Health Actions for Women* describes community-level actions such as forming an emergency health committee, organizing emergency transportation, creating an emergency loan fund, establishing safe motherhood houses, ensuring the safety of blood donation, and creating community medicine kits (Smith *et al.* 2015). Imagine how Rosa Maria's story might have ended if her community had established an emergency health committee and an emergency transportation plan!

At this point the reader may wonder whether we have strayed too far from the capabilities approach. Amartya Sen himself maintained that, while the capabilities approach was not designed specifically for policy making, the capabilities approach could be instrumental in the analyses that support policy decisions (Sen 2009).

Summary

So, let us now revisit the problem of maternal mortality in light of the preceding comments, emphasizing the complementary contributions of medicine, public health, human rights, and capabilities. The science of medicine has identified risk factors, signs, symptoms and means of treatment of pre-eclampsia and eclampsia (in the context of EmOC); with this knowledge, we can declare that Rosa Maria's death was almost certainly preventable. The science of public health enables us to know how the problem of eclampsia is distributed within and among populations, and what might be done to identify and treat it in groups of pregnant women, not just in individuals. The capabilities approach shows us that deprivation of Rosa Maria's capabilities contributed to her death, and had repercussions for the capabilities of her family.

A human rights analysis based on the laws of war reveals the contributory role of armed conflict in Rosa Maria's suffering, and a human rights analysis based on ICESCR not only permits us to describe the health-system and societal characteristics that would best support diagnosis and treatment of her obstetrical emergency, it identifies the individuals and entities assigned the duty or obligation of preventing maternal mortality, and offers guidance for national or sub-national groups of citizens who wish to define a pathway towards attainment of the relevant human capabilities. Efforts to monitor and reduce maternal mortality in Latin America and elsewhere are illustrative of a pathway – a form of 'public discussion', as Amartya Sen might have put it – by which citizens might collectively identify what they value (with respect to 'being and doing'), and define the steps they wish to take to secure the associated rights and capabilities for themselves and their neighbours.

All of these approaches have their own implications for poverty, whether defined as material resources or freedoms: the various poverties affecting both Rosa Maria and the local health system rendered medical error and the terrible outcome of maternal mortality more likely. Medical, public health, human rights and capabilities approaches can be used together to clarify difficult health questions and their interconnectedness with different kinds of poverty. Below, we will address two other health conditions – Hepatitis C and malaria – that illustrate other aspects of the complementarity of these approaches.

Hepatitis C

Vignette 4.2: Hepatitis C

The vignette below describes someone we will call George (again, details of the case of this real person have been changed). George was born in the 1960s, in a developed country. In his teens, he injected drugs, including heroin, with friends. They often shared needles, because clean needles were scarce and expensive. This practice did not seem unsafe to them at the time. Eventually, George developed a bloodstream infection caused by bacteria, almost certainly caused by using a contaminated needle, and he had to be hospitalized. He was so sick that he had to stay in the intensive care unit; his blood count dropped so much that he required multiple blood transfusions. He recovered, but his nearly fatal illness scared him so much that he stopped using drugs. He graduated from high school, went on to college and became a social worker. He did his best to live a healthy life, and felt fine.

Then, in his forties, George felt unusually tired, and went for a medical check-up. His doctor told him that his liver function was not normal. Because George's earlier transfusions had been given before there was any known way to test blood for chronic viral infections, the doctor tested for three important viruses. George's HIV and Hepatitis B tests were negative (normal), but he tested positive for Hepatitis C antibodies (showing that he had been exposed to Hepatitis C at some point), and follow-up tests confirmed that his Hepatitis C infection was still active and had caused significant scarring in his liver. Although George felt fine aside from the fatigue, his doctor recommended Hepatitis C treatment, because of the liver scarring and the high level of virus detected. The treatment involved multiple medications that had to be taken for 6 months. On this treatment George felt exhausted, his blood count dropped so much that he required more transfusions, and he became so depressed that he could barely go to work. He dropped out of treatment before finishing, and soon lost his job and his health insurance. Once off the medications his blood count normalized and his depression resolved, and he felt reasonably good aside from fatigue. But the fatigue was better than it had been, because he had taken his doctor's advice and started to avoid alcohol (to prevent further damage to his liver) and to exercise more.

George found a new job, with new health insurance. He didn't want to think about the Hepatitis C ever again but his wife kept urging him to get checked. He went to a liver specialist. The specialist informed George that his liver function tests and liver scarring both looked worse than before. But there was also good news – new drugs were available for Hepatitis C treatment, and they were much better than the old ones. They had very few side effects, no injections were required, treatment could be completed in 12 weeks rather than 6 months, and there was a greater than 90 per cent chance of eliminating the virus permanently. If the virus was eliminated, George's liver would probably recover, and he would be much less likely to develop liver failure or liver cancer in the future. There was only one problem: George's insurance would not cover the USD 85,000 cost of treatment. George and his family did not have that kind of money.

Then, the liver specialist's clinic received enough donated medications (from a drug company) to provide immediate hepatitis treatment for 15 patients. They hoped to have even more donated medication in the future, but for now they could only select 15 of their sickest patients for free treatment. Would George like to have his name entered in a lottery for free hepatitis C treatment? George thought that this was a really strange way to make treatment decisions, but his doctor explained that a group of the sickest Hepatitis C patients in her clinic had decided that a lottery would be the fairest way of deciding who would be treated first. George's family convinced him to participate because his children were young, and the specialist had told him that he was very close to liver failure. George was one of the lottery winners. By this stage in his life he had avoided drugs and alcohol for years and had a lot of support from family and friends; he never missed a dose of his Hepatitis C medications and finished his treatment with no important side effects. Ultimately, he was declared to have been cured.

George and his family felt very, very lucky. Then, when George found out that one of his old high-school friends also had Hepatitis C complicated by liver cancer, he felt terrible because his friend had not had the same chance at treatment. George is now volunteering with a non-profit organization that is trying to make Hepatitis C drugs more available to those who need them, and he has a big poster with Hepatitis C information hanging in his social-work office.

The illness often called 'Hepatitis C' is caused by the Hepatitis C virus, which was not identified until the late 1980s (Webster *et al.* 2015). The Hepatitis C virus infects and inflames the human liver and may cause death from its various complications (liver failure, liver cancer, bleeding from the intestinal tract etc.), which usually do not occur until years or even decades after the initial infection. Hepatitis C is usually passed from person to person through contact with contaminated blood – dirty needles used in health-care facilities or for illegal drug use, unscreened blood transfusions, and (much less commonly) sexual activity or the birth of an infant to an infected mother. At the time of infection, there are often no symptoms, and so diagnosis is usually delayed. Although some people's immune systems resolve the infection without any treatment, most of those infected are infected for life. The earliest treatments for Hepatitis C caused many side effects and failed to cure many patients (Webster *et al.* 2015). In the present century, treatments involving combinations of several medications finally succeeded in curing more than half of patients, and cure rates of over 90 per cent have now been achieved with combinations of well-tolerated but expensive medications that must be taken every day for at least 8 weeks (Webster *et al.* 2015).

As above, we will look at George's case from several complementary perspectives, but we will try not to repeat what has already been said about Rosa Maria's illness.

Analysis of disease (Hepatitis C) and its treatment in one patient

George's case was different from Rosa Maria's. When he first became infected with Hepatitis C, there was no way to diagnose or treat the disease. For many years he had no symptoms. When he finally developed fatigue and sought medical care, his Hepatitis C was diagnosed promptly and treatment was begun – but he could not tolerate the side effects. He was re-treated with much better medications shortly after those medications became available, and he was cured.

In George's case, medical errors did not really contribute to his problem. We can't even argue that there was a failure to screen his early blood transfusions for Hepatitis C, because no test for the virus existed at the time. Here, we need a different perspective on George's illness.

Public health analysis

Is George's case isolated, or are there others who share or shared his diagnosis and his difficulty in accessing treatment? According to WHO, between 130 million and 150 million people had chronic Hepatitis C infection by 2015, about 500,000 people die every year of complications of this disease, and the most affected regions are Africa,

---

Box 4.4 Disease-focused analysis: George and Hepatitis C

- *What was the medical diagnosis?* Chronic Hepatitis C infection, with evolution to liver damage and impending liver failure.
- *What medical errors led to adverse outcomes?* In this case, the final outcome was good and there were no significant medical errors. Diagnosis and initial treatment were delayed by the absence of symptoms, reliable lab tests and safe/effective medications. His first treatment failed because of uncontrollable side effects, and because it was not very effective, not because of medical error. George had his second round of treatment just as the first really effective, well-tolerated treatments for Hepatitis C became available, and his treatment was successful. His doctors acted as quickly and correctly as the available science (which was still evolving) and the fortuitous medication donation permitted.

Box 4.5 Public health analysis step 1: How big is the problem of Hepatitis C, and where is it concentrated?

- *How many individuals with Hepatitis C?* More than one hundred million. About 500,000 die each year.
- *Where are they?* Everywhere, but primarily in Africa and Asia.

Central Asia and East Asia. So, as in the case of maternal mortality, the resulting deaths are in the hundreds of thousands, and the problem is worse in the poorer parts of the world (World Health Organization 2015a).

The second step in our public health analysis is to identify gaps in prevention, diagnosis, and treatment of Hepatitis C. WHO, the Centers for Disease Control and Prevention (CDC) in the United States, and other agencies have considered these problems in detail within the past decade. WHO's recommendations for prevention now include 'provision of clean injection supplies' to those who inject drugs, and testing of the blood supply for hepatitis (World Health Organization 2015a). The American Association for the Study of Liver Disease (AASLD) now recommends that all patients with chronic Hepatitis C be offered effective treatment as soon as they are diagnosed (www.aasld.org).

In George's case, the most likely source of his infection was through injection of heroin, but he could also have been infected by contaminated needles or transfusions during his hospitalization. Because the hospitalization was caused by complications of heroin use, the best prevention for George's infection would have been avoidance of heroin injection in either scenario. However, had he had regular access to clean needles, his heroin addiction would have been less dangerous to his health.

Box 4.6 Public health analysis step 2: Gaps and delays in prevention and in George's care

- *Prevention*: If there were existing drug-abuse prevention programmes when George was an adolescent, they failed to prevent his heroin use or to educate him about blood-borne infections. When he had his original blood transfusions, no test was yet available to screen the transfused blood for Hepatitis C.
- *Diagnosis*: The delay in George's diagnosis was caused by the absence of a blood test and by the absence of symptoms during the earlier years of his chronic infection. Indeed, the Hepatitis C virus had not yet been discovered when he was young.
- *Treatment*: When George was initially infected, there was no treatment for Hepatitis C. His first attempt to be treated failed, because the available drugs caused intolerable side effects. Fortunately, he returned to medical care just as safe, effective drugs became available, and he was able to access the extremely expensive regimen because of the unusual circumstance of the lottery.

This is a different analysis from that of Rosa Maria's case. In the case of eclampsia, the best means of diagnosis and treatment were defined decades ago, although there have been refinements over time. Adequate treatment was theoretically available near Rosa Maria's village, but it was not available to her for reasons related to her poverty, her ethnicity and her status as an internally displaced person. In George's case, Hepatitis C had not even been discovered when he became infected, and good methods for diagnosis and treatment of his illness were not discovered until he had been infected for years.

Capabilities analysis

What is there to be said about George's Hepatitis C and capabilities that has not already been said earlier, in the discussion of eclampsia? George was fortunate in that his illness was cured before it caused death or disability, and after his cure he was in a good position 'to be and to do' what he valued. But there are two other aspects of the capabilities approach that bear exploring here: 'agency' and 'entitlements'.

Amartya Sen has written extensively about agency and capabilities. He has noted that a person's 'agency freedom' may support a person's efforts to help others, not just serve more individual desires (Sen 2009). In Rosa Maria's story the utter deprivation of her capabilities also deprived her of agency (although her neighbours and family used their own agency to try to save her). But George's story is different. His goals and values went beyond mere short-term happiness or wellbeing. He gave up both heroin and alcohol (both of which he had originally used because of the feeling of happiness that they initially provided) to pursue other goals that he valued more: to feel healthy, to finish his education and to care for his family. He sought treatment for Hepatitis C a second time, in spite of his fears of medication toxicities, for similar reasons. His fellow Hepatitis C patients used their agency freedom to support what they deemed 'fair' distribution of expensive drugs, not just to fight for their own individual advantages. Finally, George became an activist for increased access to Hepatitis C treatment for others, such as his school friend.

George's later role as an activist is also relevant to the issue of entitlements. Martha Nussbaum has stated clearly that her list of central capabilities can also be viewed as a list of freedoms to which human beings are entitled by virtue of being human. 'Entitlement' in this descriptive sense does not mean entitlement to money or objects or other tangible things, often referred to as the 'normative' meaning of entitlement. Rather, Nussbaum states that the 'central capabilities are fundamental entitlements inherent in the very idea of minimum social justice, or a life worthy of human dignity' (Nussbaum 2011). These entitlements, though fundamental in theory, must be 'secured' in order to be usable in practice. In the case of George's Hepatitis C, had he not had access to high-quality treatment, he would have progressively lost a multitude of central capabilities as his disease advanced to liver failure and/or liver cancer and death. But he was spared these bad outcomes because he was fortunate enough to win a lottery – not because society had made any arrangements to secure the entitlement of 'bodily health' from risks conferred by Hepatitis C. The other 130 to 150 million Hepatitis C infected citizens of Earth will not, for the most part, enjoy such lucky circumstances. George became an activist to secure the relevant entitlements for others.

The role of poverty (Hepatitis C)

As in the case of eclampsia, Hepatitis C has multiple associations with different kinds of poverty. Hepatitis C causes monetary and income poverty and poverty of capabilities in those who are too ill to work. Lack of money or income or freedoms or opportunities at the individual or health-systems level may increase the likelihood of Hepatitis C infection (through unsafe injection and transfusion practices, for example) and decrease the likelihood of early diagnosis and effective treatment.

Human rights analysis (Hepatitis C)

We will now revisit the question of effective Hepatitis C treatment in terms of General Comment 14's requirements for availability, accessibility, acceptability and quality. For our purposes, effective treatment is defined as treatment with an established, well-studied combination of direct-acting antiviral drugs known to result in high likelihood of disappearance of the Hepatitis C virus from the blood and liver, provided for a period of time that is known to be long enough to yield high cure rates, and administered in a setting that permits proper support for patients and monitoring of response to treatment.

Because the best medications were so expensive, George's chance of receiving adequate treatment for his Hepatitis C did not originally seem much greater than it might have

---

Box 4.7 Effective Hepatitis C treatment and ICESCR

- *Availability*: Not really available outside the research setting until about 2014, because the most effective drugs had not yet been developed or adequately tested.
- *Accessibility* (1): Non-discrimination. George did not encounter discrimination, except any inherent discrimination described below under 'economic accessibility.'
- *Accessibility* (2): Physical accessibility. George had physical access to a health facility with a liver specialist, laboratory and pharmacy capacity.
- *Accessibility* (3): Economic accessibility. Between his first and second rounds of Hepatitis C treatment, George had no health insurance, and could not have afforded to see a specialist or pay for Hepatitis C treatment. When he obtained his new health insurance, he was able to see a specialist without economic hardship but his insurance would not pay for the medications, and he could not afford to pay this price out of his own pocket. The very unusual lottery saved him from the severe accessibility constraints that affect many (if not most) Hepatitis C patients. (Note: since George was treated, access to Hepatitis C drugs has improved in certain settings, because of manufacturers' assistance programmes, liberalized insurer policies and price negotiations.)
- *Quality*: The quality of treatment initially available to George was poor. When he was re-treated, the treatment was of high quality because new medication regimens had been developed.

been had he been a resident of a much poorer country. What are the duties and obligations of the countries in which Hepatitis C is present? Is there a process parallel to that defined for maternal mortality reduction? Hepatitis C is not mentioned directly in ICESCR or General Comment 14, but there is a clear intent to support control of important infectious diseases, such as AIDS and malaria. Discussions of inequity in access to Hepatitis C treatment were not as heated when treatments were very toxic and cure rates were low. With the recent development and approval of treatments that are more effective and much less toxic, but very expensive (more than USD 1000 per tablet at times), the debate has become much more active, and links between Hepatitis C treatment access and human rights concerns have become more explicit.

In mid-2015, WHO added five of the newest, most effective Hepatitis C medications to its Model List of Essential Medicines (World Health Organization 2015b). Cheaper, generic versions of the newer standard regimens are now expected to become available in poorer countries. A greater than 90 per cent reduction in Hepatitis C drug prices has been negotiated to support treatment in Egypt, where large numbers of persons were infected with contaminated medical syringes (World Health Organization 2014a). Humanitarian organizations such as Médecins sans Frontières (MSF) have engaged in advocacy for increased availability of effective Hepatitis C treatment (Médecins Sans Frontières, undated).

This is an interesting variant on the concept of 'progressive realization of the right to health' as described in General Comment 14. Originally, 'progressive realization' was described primarily as a catch-up process for countries that were very resource-constrained and were unable to adopt existing, effective health measures overnight. Rapid advances in the science of Hepatitis C diagnosis and treatment have forced another kind of progressive realization, driven by the imperative to keep up with development of new diagnostics and new medications, rather than by the catch-up model.

Summary

In contrast to Rosa Maria's story, George's story had a happy ending. The different outcomes were driven by different forces. Before her illness, Rosa Maria did not enjoy the same opportunities or freedoms that George did, because of the armed conflict, her ethnicity, and the extreme poverty of her family, her community and the local health system. Her illness started abruptly, and she needed to obtain effective treatment within hours or days in order to survive, so there was little time for her health strategy to evolve. She was so ill that she really could not exercise agency. Some time after her death, human rights law and policy with regard to maternal mortality were expanded, and civil society (in some countries) took on this cause in a way that might have saved Rosa Maria's life had it occurred earlier. Indeed, in the country where Rosa Maria died, free ambulance transport and free treatment for obstetrical emergencies are now guaranteed by law.

In contrast, George lived in a wealthier society, and it took decades for his Hepatitis C to progress to near-failure of his liver. During that period, medical science made immense progress – the Hepatitis C virus was identified, laboratory tests were developed, and newly discovered treatment regimens had few side effects and usually resulted in cure. George had a college education and health insurance and access to a liver specialist. He had the remarkably good fortune to win a treatment lottery. Because of his successful treatment, he preserved important freedoms and opportunities, and exercised his agency not just to preserve his own health but to advocate for the health of others. His post-treatment advocacy approach was influenced by previous health-rights endeavours in support of maternal mortality reduction and HIV/AIDS treatment expansion (Ford *et al.* 2012), among other causes, and may, in the future, help create the normative entitlement of 'effective Hepatitis C treatment' to support others' descriptive entitlements to 'bodily health'. Thus, the concepts of medicine, public health, capabilities and human rights are relevant to both cases, but in different ways.

Malaria

Vignette 4.3: Malaria

Luz's mother lived near a broad African river that flooded over and over; the floodwaters were paradise for mosquitoes. When the waters were high, local residents travelled to health centres by canoe (they paddled right down the middle of flooded streets), but Ministry of Health vehicles could not transit the roads, so medications and other supplies were not re-stocked, ambulances were unavailable and the centres lacked staff. Insecticide-treated bednets (ITNs, designed to repel and kill the mosquitoes that bit at night) could be bought in some of the local shops, but Luz's mother could not afford to buy one. Some ITNs were given away for free in the health centres, but only to pregnant women who were infected with HIV. Luz's mother became pregnant during the rainy season, and had malaria twice before Luz was born. In both instances, a Ministry of Health-trained community health worker based in her village diagnosed the malaria with a finger-prick test, and then dispensed malaria tablets. The tablets were provided free by the Ministry of Health, and seemed to work both times. The community health worker did not provide prenatal care, though, and Luz's mother was unable to get to the district health centre for even a single prenatal visit. Luz was eventually born at home. She was a month early and was tiny, just over 4 pounds, but she survived.

At first, Luz was usually swaddled in clothes or rags and the mosquitoes could not reach her. When she grew bigger, her older sister took her outside to play. Luz was bitten by mosquitoes many times. She developed a fever and became listless; she would not look at her mother, she would not eat or breast-feed; she seemed pale. The community health worker diagnosed malaria. Luz was too sick to swallow malaria tablets, and the community health worker did not have any other way to administer the needed medication. So Luz's father pedalled his ancient bicycle to the health centre; her mother rode behind, holding Luz. The health centre nurse pricked Luz's finger again, and informed Luz's parents that she had a dangerously low blood count in addition to malaria. The nurse gave Luz an injection of an antimalarial drug and called the doctor to admit Luz to the small hospital ward for further treatment. Luz, somewhat amazingly, survived and went back home.

At about that time, a non-profit aid agency started a programme to improve child development in the district. They came to the family house and evaluated Luz. Luz had not learned to roll over or crawl or walk at the usual times for her age group, and she had only learned about half the expected number of words. Her height and weight were also much too low for her age (now 17 months).

> *The project provided Luz and her family with ITNs, iron and vitamin supplements, and a high-energy nut-based food supplement. A volunteer came to visit once a week and showed Luz's parents and older sister how to make homemade toys and play educational games with Luz. Bit by bit, Luz started to grow more quickly; she became physically stronger and more active, and she started to learn new words at a much faster pace.*

Malaria is not just one disease, nor does it have just a single cause or consequence, and we will not be able to describe malaria in all of the detail it deserves (for those who are interested in learning more we would recommend starting with the most recent edition of WHO's annual World Malaria Report: World Health Organization Global Malaria Programme 2014). But we will describe some of basic facts here.

Four protozoans of the *Plasmodium* family (P. falciparum, P. vivax, P. malariae and P. ovale) cause nearly all malaria disease in humans; the most lethal of the four is P. falciparum. Malaria is almost exclusively transmitted to humans through the bites of infected mosquitoes. Malaria infection can evolve in several different ways: (a) uncomplicated malaria (primarily featuring fevers, chills, and aching); (b) severe malaria (with seizures, coma, profound anaemia, and/or other possibly fatal complications); (c) chronic 'asymptomatic' malaria (malaria parasites live in the bloodstream but the human host doesn't feel ill); (d) relapsing malaria (like acute malaria, except that after the first episode, some malaria parasites remain in the host's liver, where they cause no symptoms until, at an unpredictable later date, they re-emerge and fever and other symptoms recur); and (e) placental malaria (the malaria parasite sequesters in the pregnant woman's placenta, where it may impair foetal growth and/or cause premature labour or pregnancy loss).

With prompt diagnosis and effective treatment, most adults and children recover fully from malaria episodes. But when malaria is severe, consequences may include death or permanent disability. 'Asymptomatic' (without symptoms) and recurrent malaria may cause chronic anaemia, undernutrition and (for children) delays in both cognitive and motor development. Malaria in pregnancy may cause pregnancy loss (miscarriage), premature birth and/or low birth weight.

Analysis of disease and treatment in one patient: malaria

As before, we will start by looking only at issues of medical diagnosis and treatment. But this analysis will be a bit different from the medical analyses of the two previous vignettes, because we have to consider episodes of malaria both in Luz's mother and in Luz.

Our narrow analysis of diagnosis and treatment of acute symptomatic malaria (in Luz and in her mother) is not able to tell us whether Luz's problems were really avoidable or not. As before, we will go on to a more public health-focused analysis.

Public health analysis

In 2013, WHO estimated that there were 198 million cases of malaria worldwide, resulting in 584,000 deaths. According to the World Malaria Report (World Health Organization Global Malaria Programme 2014), the burden of malaria disease is largely

---

Box 4.8 Disease-focused analysis: Luz and malaria

- *What was the medical diagnosis?* (A) In Luz's mother, two episodes of acute malaria with symptoms, probably associated with placental malaria. (B) In Luz herself, one episode of acute malaria, with symptoms.
- *What medical errors led to adverse outcomes?* In this two-person case, there were no significant medical errors related to diagnosis or treatment of symptomatic malaria. Both Luz and her mother recovered physically from their episodes of acute symptomatic malaria.

---

determined by geography and age: approximately 90 per cent of malaria deaths occur in Africa, and 78 per cent of all malaria deaths occur in children under 5 years of age. Other factors that increase risk of malaria include pregnancy (before the initiation of effective preventive measures, about one in four pregnant women in sub-Saharan Africa tested positive for the presence of malaria parasites in her blood at the time of delivery: Desai *et al.* 2007) and HIV infection (persons with advanced HIV infection are about 2.5 times more likely to have malaria-related fever than HIV-infected persons with intact immune systems: French *et al.* 2001). Estimates of the number of children who survive but suffer from the consequences of malaria-related low birth weight and neurodevelopmental delay are less precise.

Once again, we are examining a problem that takes hundreds of thousands of lives every year, although this particular problem has many known solutions, some of them known for over a century. Malaria was a major health problem in Europe and the United States of America as recently as the early twentieth century. One economist estimated that the infant death rate from malaria in the USA in 1850 was not significantly different from the infant death rate from malaria in the ten most malaria-affected African countries in 2008: 93 deaths of infants under 1 year of age per 1000 live births in the USA, vs. 99 in the ten African countries (Hong 2011). Wealthier countries – such as the USA and Italy – defeated their malaria epidemics decades ago, through reduction of human contact with mosquitoes and through population-wide distribution of antimalarial tablets.

Box 4.9 Public health analysis step 1: How big is the problem and where is it concentrated?

- *How many people fall ill with malaria?* Hundreds of millions per year, with over half a million deaths.
- *Where are they?* Primarily in sub-Saharan Africa. Within sub-Saharan Africa, young children, pregnant women and persons living with HIV infection are at higher risk.

Current options for malaria prevention include spraying of larvicides or insecticides to kill mosquitoes, use of ITNs to prevent mosquito bites at night, and (for special populations, such as pregnant women and travellers) periodic use of malaria medications to prevent malaria infection and/or to treat malaria infection that has not become symptomatic (Desai *et al.* 2007, World Health Organization, 2014c). HIV-infected persons can prevent malaria by taking daily doses of co-trimoxazole, a common antibiotic that also helps prevent certain other AIDS-related infections (French *et al.* 2001, Church *et al.* 2015). Malaria vaccine development is now making progress (RTSS Clinical Trials Partnership 2015).

Malaria is not only preventable, it is treatable if effective medications are given promptly. In contrast to the high cost of treating Hepatitis C (as of this writing), malaria can be treated much more cheaply. Non-profit groups such as the Medicines for Malaria Venture (MMV) and the Drugs for Neglected Diseases initiative (DNDi) have contributed to the discovery, development and/or delivery of effective, affordable antimalarial drugs (Drugs for Neglected Diseases initiative 2015, Medicines for Malaria Venture 2015). The national malaria control programmes of many countries now guarantee free malaria treatment for their citizens. However, where national health systems are weak, the sick may have to buy antimalarial drugs over the counter. Antimalarial medication may still be unaffordable to the most vulnerable families. For example, in one region of Ethiopia, the private sector price for a three-day course of malaria treatment was reported to be equivalent to or higher than 'about a week's wages' (SIAPS – Ethiopia PMI/AMDM Program 2014).

Large international initiatives (for example the Roll Back Malaria Partnership and the President's Malaria Initiative, among others) have systematically helped malaria-affected countries to implement the most effective measures for mass malaria control. WHO estimated that annual malaria cases dropped from 227 million in 2000 to 198 million in 2013, and that malaria deaths declined from 882,000 to 584,000. Indeed, by the end of 2015, over 50 countries were likely to succeed in reducing malaria death rates by 75 per cent over their year 2000 levels (World Health Organization, 2014c).

So, let us look at Luz's situation again (see Box 4.10).

It is clear that the local malaria control programme was not able to protect Luz or her mother from this illness. Although both survived their episodes of malaria, the consequences for Luz have been alarming.

Capabilities

What is the association between malaria and Luz's capabilities? Here, we will focus on the special way that the capabilities approach regards children. Martha Nussbaum, in particular, has written about this issue extensively. She (with Rosalind Dixon and others) has emphasized two aspects of capabilities that are different for children: their 'special vulnerability' and 'the special cost-effectiveness of protecting children's rights' (Nussbaum and Dixon 2012). Briefly, and perhaps too simplistically, the special vulnerability of children is a result of the long period of dependency (more than a decade) that characterizes human development. The special cost-effectiveness principle arises from the fact that if a child is deprived of the opportunity of fully developing the central capabilities that must underpin his or her ability to be, to do, and to live the adult life that he or she values, this period of dependency is prolonged and the

---

Box 4.10 Public health analysis step 2: Gaps and delays in prevention and in Luz's care

- *Prevention*: During pregnancy, Luz's mother should have been given antimalarial medication to prevent malaria (intermittent preventive treatment of malaria in pregnancy, or IPTp), but she had no prenatal care. Luz's premature birth and low birthweight were probably caused by her mother's malaria. The household should have used ITNs, but they were not available or affordable. The family's house was apparently never sprayed against mosquitoes.
- *Diagnosis*: When Luz and her mother felt sick, they were promptly checked for malaria, using modern rapid tests. But Luz's mother also probably had malaria without symptoms during her pregnancy, and it was not diagnosed or treated. Earlier diagnosis and/or IPTp might have prevented Luz's premature birth and low birth weight. Luz's anaemia was diagnosed during her malaria hospitalization, but was not followed up afterward. Her developmental delay (very likely caused by long-standing anaemia) was not diagnosed until an aid agency started a programme in her district.
- *Treatment*: Once Luz's mother was diagnosed with malaria, she was treated with a medication that appeared to work promptly. But there was a delay in providing effective medications for Luz herself, because the village health worker did not have medications that would work for a child too sick to swallow. Luz's anaemia treatment was probably delayed (she may have been born with anaemia because of her mother's malaria infection), as was the therapy for her developmental delay.

---

cost (to the family and the society) of providing needed services is therefore increased. Nussbaum and Dixon mention, for example, that if inexpensive antiretroviral medications are given to an HIV-infected woman during pregnancy and labour and the post-partum period, the resulting avoidance of HIV infection in the exposed baby may 'prevent a spiraling need for state intervention to protect more and more capabilities' (Nussbaum and Dixon 2012).

Although other factors, such as malnutrition or anaemia in her mother, may have contributed to Luz's premature delivery and underweight, malaria was certainly a major contributor to this problem. Prematurity and low birth weight are important causes of capability deprivation in children. In 2010, for example, approximately 15 million babies were born at least 3 weeks early, only 13 million survived, and about 900,000 babies were thought to have some degree of neurodevelopmental impairment (Blencowe *et al.* 2013), and also had elevated risks of infections and heart or lung diseases.

In addition to premature birth and low birth weight, Luz suffered from symptomatic malaria at a very young age. Both symptomatic and asymptomatic malaria have been shown to affect child development. In one study in Zanzibar, children who had had more episodes of malaria were slower to start walking, slower to develop language, and were fussier and less active than children who had no or fewer episodes of malaria (Olney *et al.* 2013). In Sri Lanka, the mean mathematics test score for a child who had not had malaria might be 69.4 per cent, vs. 37.6 per cent for a child who had had at least six episodes (Fernando *et al.* 2003).

Is Luz doomed to a lifetime of dependency and capabilities deprivation? We don't know yet. As the vignette ends, she is 17 months old. To be effective, interventions to address developmental delay should usually start during the first 2 or 3 years of life, to take advantage of a period of active brain development (Engle *et al.* 2007, Doyle *et al.* 2009). The most effective programmes combine multiple interventions – for example, nutritional supplementation, prevention of infections (such as malaria and diarrhoea), and psychosocial stimulation. The aid agency that has just come to Luz's district appears to understand these principles and it is possible that, with their help, Luz will continue to catch up.

The role of poverty

As in the preceding vignettes, the role of poverty is pervasive here. Monetary poverty affected both Luz's family and the local health system, as reflected in the family's difficulty in procuring ITNs, prenatal care, IPTp and treatment for Luz. Income poverty affected the family and the whole region, because the combination of frequent flooding and constant exposure to malaria greatly reduced the productivity of individuals (such as Luz's father) and the society as a whole. Malaney, Spielberg and Sachs (2004) have observed that malaria is a cause of income poverty. One may infer that effective malaria control measures may therefore relieve poverty, and this has been demonstrated. Famously, two decades of intensive malaria control programmes in Zambia (then known as Northern Rhodesia) are thought to have prevented approximately 14,000 deaths and nearly a million work-shift losses, and increased national copper-mining revenue (Utzinger *et al.* 2002).

Human rights

Luz's family had difficulty preventing and treating malaria because of problems with availability, accessibility and other core elements of the right to health as defined in ICESCR and related documents (discussed in previous vignettes). As in the case of the capabilities approach, human rights law also recognizes that children require special protections. The Convention on the Rights of the Child affirms, in Article 24, that children also have the right 'to the enjoyment of the highest attainable standard of health'; Article 27 recognizes children's right 'to a standard of living adequate for the child's physical, mental, spiritual, moral and social development', and both articles describe the states parties' obligation to assist families in the securing of these rights (United Nations 1990). In their paper on children and capabilities, Nussbaum and Dixon outline the congruences between the Convention on the Rights of the Child and the capabilities approach.

Summary: malaria

How can we merge the perspectives of medicine, public health, capabilities and human rights to understand this vignette about malaria and poverty, and to compare its implications to those of the two preceding vignettes? To start with the disease perspective, malaria has been recognized for centuries. The first effective treatment (quinine) has been known for over 400 years, though the causative parasites were not identified until the late nineteenth century. Malaria has caused widespread disease and disability almost worldwide, including in the United States and Europe. Public health approaches to malaria control have existed for over 100 years, but have become much more effective and systematized in the era of the Millennium Development Goals, and the burden of malaria is now dropping.

Where malaria is still widespread, it poses a significant threat to human capabilities. Because pregnant women and children are particularly vulnerable to malaria, because malaria in a pregnant woman may affect infant health, and because malaria may result in slowing of neurocognitive development in early life, the capabilities of children are more severely affected by malaria. Malaria's adverse effect on the capabilities of children is most likely to occur when they are still unable to live independently and before they can develop effective agency. Both the capabilities approach and human rights law have recognized that the great dependence and vulnerability of children, and the dire consequences of interruption of normal child development, impose greater duties on families and on society. Thus malaria may cause the greatest poverty of freedoms and opportunities in its youngest victims; and poverty of freedoms and opportunities may also impede effective prevention and treatment of malaria. With regard to other kinds of poverty: malaria is most rampant in poorer communities, and rampant malaria exacerbates income and monetary poverty. For all of these reasons, intensified efforts to control malaria worldwide may help decrease world poverty, by all of its definitions.

Poverty reduction and health: some major debates

Within the past few decades, global policies on maternal mortality, Hepatitis C and malaria have all changed in response to new scientific discoveries and to activism. The relevant scientific discoveries have included identification of new diseases (Hepatitis C), development of newer and better medications (Hepatitis C and malaria), development of better preventive interventions (malaria) and improved descriptions of the actual burden of suffering and of the potential impact of combinations of preventive and curative interventions on that burden of suffering (all three conditions). Many relevant recent and active debates revolve around issues of equity, fairness, rights and responsibilities. The implications for human capabilities are seldom articulated but may seem obvious to those of you who have read this far. Ongoing debates and open questions that are relevant to these concerns include the following.

Malaria: The burden of malaria is greatest in countries with fewer resources. Multiple interventions are now available for the effective prevention and treatment of malaria, but countries with the highest malaria burdens can't afford to pay for them without external assistance. If combined intelligently and applied across all malarial regions, currently available interventions might even result in the elimination of malaria worldwide (Newby *et al.* 2016). How might the countries, regions and sub-populations of the world organize themselves to achieve malaria elimination?

Maternal mortality: In the vignette above, we described a case of avoidable maternal (and foetal or neonatal) mortality that occurred in a poor country. But maternal mortality is not confined to poor countries. In the USA, not only does maternal mortality still occur, the rates are steadily rising (Centers for Disease Control and Prevention 2016). Why might maternal mortality rates increase where resources are thought to be abundant?

Hepatitis C: In addition to debates over drug prices and availability (described above), other debates revolve around safe injection practices for heroin and other drug users. In the United States, a recent outbreak driven by needle-sharing among drug users resulted in a cluster of over 150 new cases of HIV infection in a single county in southern Indiana; over 80 per cent of the HIV-infected were also infected with Hepatitis C. Needle-exchange programmes were illegal in Indiana when this occurred. Public health experts have called for legalization and improvement of needle-exchange programmes in order to stop the spread of both HIV and Hepatitis C; but this issue has not yet been settled as of this writing, even though unsafe injections have been linked to a near-explosion in Hepatitis C cases in the region in recent years (Strathdee and Beyrer 2015). What is your opinion?

Conclusion

This chapter has not addressed all of the most important issues related to health and poverty. For example, we have not analysed problems related to mental health, global warming or income inequality. But close examination of maternal mortality, Hepatitis C and malaria should provide an opportunity to understand the multiplicity of pathways that connect health and poverty and capabilities and rights, both for individual human beings and across populations. Many of these pathways are bidirectional; poverty is a threat to good health, and ill health contributes to poverty. But, when sound science and the right-to-health framework are combined, effective medical and public health measures can preserve or increase human capabilities, and alleviate many kinds of poverty.

Discussion questions

1   What role did poverty play in causing the maternal mortality, Hepatitis C and malaria cases described above? Describe and compare the three cases.
2   Did maternal mortality, Hepatitis C or malaria worsen the poverty of those described in the vignettes? Describe and compare the three cases.
3   If Rosa Maria had lived in George's city, or if George had lived in Luz's village, how might their capabilities have been different both before and after their illnesses?
4   Describe an important health problem in your own community, and its association with poverty (any definition) and capabilities. Alternatively, can you think of a way in which illness or treatment of illness has affected your own capabilities, or those of your friends or family?
5   Identify a health-related law or programme that is controversial right now in your community or country. Debate its role in increasing or reducing illness, poverty and capabilities development.

Further reading

Alkire, Sabina, and Lincoln Chen. 'Global health and moral values', *The Lancet*, 364.9439 (2004): 1069–1074.
The Center for Global Development's 'Millions Saved' series of success stories in global health: http://millionssaved.cgdev.org/
Dodd, Rebecca, and Lise Munck. 2001. *Dying for Change: Poor people's experience of health and ill-health*. World Health Organization.

Fox, Ashley M., and Benjamin Meier. 'Health as freedom: addressing social determinants of global health inequities through the human right to development', *Bioethics*, 23.2 (2009): 112–122.
Walraven, Gijs. 2013. *Health and Poverty: Global health problems and solutions*. London: Routledge.

Works cited

Averting Maternal Death and Disability Program. 2010. Needs Assessments of Emergency Obstetric and Newborn Care. New York, NY: Columbia University.
Blencowe, H., Lee, A. C. C., Cousens, S., Bahalim, A., Narwal, R., Zhong, R., Chou, D., Say, L., Modi, N., Katz, J., Vos, T., Marlow, N. and Lawn, J. E. 'Preterm birth-associated neurodevelopmental impairment estimates at regional and global levels for 2010', *Pediatric Research*, 74 (2013): 17–34.
CDC Foundation. 2016. What is Public Health?
Centers for Disease Control and Prevention. 2016. *Pregnancy Mortality Surveillance System* [Online]. Available: www.cdc.gov/reproductivehealth/maternalinfanthealth/pmss.html [Accessed 14 November 2016].
Church, J. A., Fitzgerald, F., Walker, A. S., Gibb, D. M. and Prendergast, A. J. 'The expanding role of co-trimoxazole in developing countries', *The Lancet Infectious Diseases*, 15 (2015): 327–339.
Committee on Economic Social and Cultural Rights. 2000. Substantive issues arising in the implementation of the International Covenant on Economic, Social and Cultural Rights. General Comment No. 14. The right to the highest attainable standard of health (article 12 of the International Covenant on Economic, Social, and Cultural Rights). *In:* United Nations (ed.) *E/C.12/2000/4*.
Desai, M., Ter Kuile, F. O., Nosten, F., Mcgready, R., Asamoaa, K., Brabin, B. and Newman, R. D. 'Epidemiology and burden of malaria in pregnancy', *The Lancet Infectious Diseases*, 7 (2007): 93–104.
Diplomatic Conference on the Reaffirmation and Development of International Humanitarian Law Applicable in Armed Conflicts. 1977. *Protocols additional to the Geneva Conventions of 12 August 1949*. Geneva: International Committee of the Red Cross.
Doyle, O., Harmon, C. P., Heckman, J. J. and Tremblay, R. E. 'Investing in early human development: timing and economic efficiency', *Economics & Human Biology*, 7 (2009): 1–6.
Drugs for Neglected Diseases Initiative. 2015. *2014 Annual Report. Partnerships to Bridge Innovation and Access*. Geneva: Drugs for Neglected Diseases initiative.
Engle, P. L., Black, M. M., Behrman, J. R., Carbral De Mello, M., Gertler, P. J., Kapiriri, L., Martorell, R., Young, M. E. and The International Child Development Steering Group. 'Strategies to avoid the loss of development potential in more than 200 million children in the developing world', *The Lancet*, 369 (2007): 229–242.
Fernando, S., Gunawardena, D., Bandara, M., De Silva, D., Carter, R., Mendis, K. and Wickremasinghe, A. 'The impact of repeated malaria attacks on the school performance of children', *American Journal of Tropical Medicine* and *Hygiene*, 69 (2003): 582–588.
Ford, N., Singh, K., Cooke, G. S., Mills, E. J., Von Schoen-Angerer, T., Kamarulzaman, A. and Du Cros, P. 'Expanding access to treatment for hepatitis C in resource-limited settings: lessons from HIV/AIDs', *Clinical Infectious Diseases*, 54.10 (2012): 1465–1472.
Freedman, L. P. 'Averting maternal death and disability. Using human rights in maternal mortality programs: from analysis to strategy', *International Journal of Gynecology & Obstetrics*, 75 (2001): 51–60.
French, N., Nakiyingi, J., Lugada, E., Watera, C., Whitworth, J. and Gilks, C. F. 'Increasing rates of malarial fever with deteriorating immune status in HIV-1-infected Ugandan adults', *AIDS*, 15 (2001): 899–906.
Fukuda-Parr, S. 'Human Rights and Human Development', in K. Basu and R. Kanbur, eds. 2009. *Arguments for a Better World. Essays in Honor of Amartya Sen*. Oxford: Oxford University Press.
Geiger, H. and Cook-Deegan, R. 'The role of physicians in conflicts and humanitarian crises. Case studies from the field missions of Physicians for Human Rights', *JAMA*, 270 (1993): 616–620.

Hong, S. C. 'Malaria and economic productivity: a longitudinal analysis of the American case', *Journal of Economic History*, 71 (2011): 654–671.

Malaney, P., Spielman, A. and Sachs, J. 'The malaria gap', *American Journal of Tropical Medicine and Hygiene*, 71 (2004): 141–146.

Médecins Sans Frontières. undated. *Strategies to secure access to generic hepatitis C medicines* [Online]. Available: www.msfaccess.org/content/strategies-secure-access-generic-hepatitis-c-medicines [Accessed 13 November 2016].

Medicines For Malaria Venture. 2015. *Annual Report 2014*. Geneva: Medicines for Malaria Venture.

Newby, G., Bennett, A., Larson, E., Cotter, C., Shretta, R., Phillips, A. A. and Feachem, R. G. A. 'The path to eradication: a progress report on the malaria-eliminating countries', *The Lancet*, 387 (2016): 1775–1784.

Nussbaum, M. C. 2000. *Women and Human Development. The Capabilities Approach*. New York, NY: Cambridge University Press.

Nussbaum, M. C. 'Capabilities as fundamental entitlements: Sen and social justice', *Feminist Economics*, 9 (2003): 33–59.

Nussbaum, M. C. 'Capabilities, entitlements, rights: supplementation and critique', *Journal of Human Development and Capabilities*, 12 (2011): 23–37.

Nussbaum, M. C. and Dixon, R. 2012. 'Children's rights and a capabilities approach: the question of special priority.' Chicago, IL: University of Chicago Law School.

Observatorio de Mortalidad Materna en Mexico. Undated. Available: www.omm.org.mx [Accessed 13 November 2016].

Olney, D., Kariger, P., Stoltzfus, R., Khalfan, S., Ali, N., Tielsch, J., Sazawal, S., Black, R. E., Allen, L. and Pollitt, E. 'Developmental effects of micronutrient supplementation and malaria in Zanzibari children', *Early Human Development*, 89 (2013): 667–674.

Physicians For Human Rights. Undated. *The Principle of Medical Neutrality* [Online]. Available: http://physiciansforhumanrights.org/issues/persecution-of-health-workers/medical-neutrality/ [Accessed 13 November 2016].

RTSS Clinical Trials Partnership. 'Efficacy and safety of RTSS/AS01 malaria vaccine with or without a booster dose in infants and children in Africa: final results of a phase 3, individually randomised, controlled trial', *The Lancet*, 386 (2015): 4–10.

Saracci, R. 'The World Health Organisation needs to reconsider its definition of health', *British Medical Journal*, 314 (1997), 1409.

Say, L., Chou, D., Gemmill, A., Tuncalp, O., Moller, A.-B., Daniels, J., Gulmezoglu, A. M., Temmerman, M. and Alkema, L. 'Global causes of maternal death: a WHO systematic analysis', *The Lancet Global Health*, 2 (2014): e323–333.

Sen, A. 2009. *The Idea of Justice*. Cambridge, MA: The Belknap Press of Harvard University Press.

SIAPS – ETHIOPIA PMI/AMDM Program. 2014. Technical report: availability, price, and affordability of artemisinin-based combination therapies (ACTs) and other antimalarial drugs in Oromia regional state of Ethiopia: implications on universal access to malarial treatments, June 2014. Arlington, VA: Management Sciences for Health.

Smith, M., Shannon, S. and Vickery, K. 2015. *Health Actions for Women. Practical Strategies to Mobilize for Change*. Berkeley, CA: Hesperian Health Guides.

Strathdee, S. A. and Beyrer, C. 'Threading the needle – how to stop the HIV outbreak in rural Indiana', *New England Journal of Medicine*, 373 (2015): 397–399.

Susser, M. 'Ethical components in the definition of health', *International Journal of Health Services*, 4 (1974): 539–548.

Thaddeus, S. and Maine, D. 'Too far to walk: maternal mortality in context', *Social Science and Medicine*, 38 (1994): 1091–1110.

United Nations. 1966. 'International Covenant on Economic, Social, and Cultural Rights', in United Nations (ed.). New York, NY: United Nations.

United Nations, ed. 1990. Convention on the Rights of the Child. New York, NY: United Nations.

United Nations General Assembly. Human Rights Council. 2012. Technical guidance on the application of a human rights-based approach to the implementation of policies and programmes to reduce preventable maternal morbidity and mortality. Report of the Office of the United Nations High Commissioner for Human Rights. New York, NY: United Nations.

Utzinger, J., Tozan, Y., Doumani, F. and Singer, B. H. 'The economic payoffs of integrated malaria control in the Zambian copperbelt between 1930 and 1950', *Tropical Medicine and International Health*, 7 (2002): 657–677.

Webster, D. P., Klenerman, P. and Dusheiko, G. M. 'Hepatitis C', *The Lancet*, 385 (2015): 1124–1135.

World Health Organization. 2014a. *Egypt steps up efforts against Hepatitis C* [Online]. Available: www.who.int/features/2014/egypt-campaign-hepatitisc/en/ [Accessed 13 November 2016].

World Health Organization. 2014b. Trends in maternal mortality: 1990 to 2013. Estimates by WHO, UNICEF, UNFPA, The World Bank and the United Nations Population Division. Geneva: World Health Organization.

World Health Organization. 2014c. WHO Global Malaria Programme. World Malaria Report 2014. Geneva: World Health Organization.

World Health Organization. 2015a. Hepatitis C. Fact sheet no. 164. Updated July 2015. Geneva: World Health Organization.

World Health Organization. 2015b. *WHO moves to improve access to lifesaving medicines for hepatitis C, drug-resistant TB and cancers.* [Online]. Available: www.who.int/mediacentre/news/releases/2015/new-essential-medicines-list/en/ [Accessed 13 November 2016].

Yamin, A. E. 'From ideals to tools: applying human rights to maternal health', *PLoS Medicine*, 10 (2013).

5 Geographical and spatial poverty

Benjamin Curtis

Key questions

- Why are tropical areas of the planet more likely to be poor than the temperate areas?
- Why are landlocked and mountainous places more likely to be poor?
- What does remoteness have to do with poverty, and how can integration promote human and economic development?
- What is the connection between spatial poverty and capabilities?
- What polices can counteract the geographical and spatial aspects of poverty?

Introduction

Look at the map of the world distribution of gross domestic product per capita by country, shown in Figure 5.1. Two things immediately stand out: many of the world's poorest countries are clustered in a band around the equator, while the world's richest countries tend to fall in the higher latitudes, whether in the Northern or the Southern hemispheres. Likewise, a map of countries by their Human Development Index score shows that nearly all the highest-scoring countries are located outside of the planet's tropical zone (Figure 5.2).

A mere glance at a map is of course not enough to ascertain whether location on the globe has anything to do with the level of economic or human development. Dig deeper, though, and a number of surprising facts present themselves. Consider this: of the 30 countries in the world with the highest GDP PPP per capita, only three – Hong Kong, Brunei and Singapore – lie completely within the tropics. According to one analysis, tropical countries have on average a third of the income of countries located in the temperate zone. Astoundingly, a small group of countries in the temperate zone, encompassing only 8 per cent of the planet's total land and 22 per cent of the total population, account for approximately 52 per cent of the world's GNP. Life expectancies for people living in tropical countries are also 7 years below those for people in temperate countries, even when factoring out the effects of overall income level and female education (Hausmann 2001).

The relationship between geography and poverty doesn't just pertain to the tropics. There are a number of other spatial factors that impact a person's poverty status – in fact, the 2009 World Development Report declared that 'Place is the most important correlate of a person's welfare' (WDR 2009: 1). This chapter will examine several of the most important characteristics of places that are detrimental to human and economic development at the country, regional, local and individual level. Some characteristics – the prevalence of disease in certain places, a lack of agricultural endowments such as

GDP per capita, 2014

GDP per capita is adjusted for price changes over time and between countries. It is expressed in 2011 international dollars. Since some observations for 2014 are not available the map displays the closest available data (2013 to 2014).

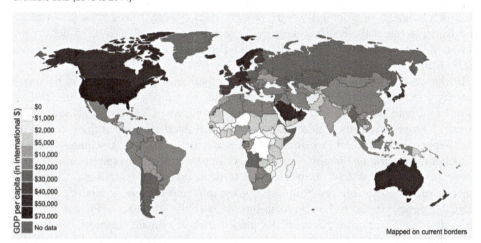

Figure 5.1 Countries by GDP per capita

Human Development Index, 2014

The Human Development Index (HDI) is a summary measure of average achievement in key dimensions of human development: a long and healthy life, being knowledgeable and having a decent standard of living. The HDI is the geometric mean of normalized indices for each of the three dimensions.

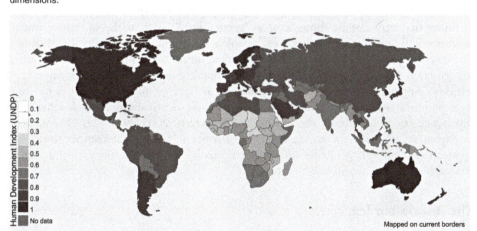

Figure 5.2 Countries by Human Development Index score

soil quality and rainfall, a remote or rugged location – have *direct* poverty effects by influencing individuals' health, food security, livelihoods and political rights. Other characteristics – such as the longer-term impact between environmental geography and institutions – can have *indirect* poverty effects (Nunn and Puga 2012). Taken together, such disadvantages of place can create poverty traps. Simply put, certain geographical and spatial factors make it more likely that a person is poor and make it harder for that person to escape poverty (see i.a. Jalan and Ravallion 1997, Ravallion and Wodon 1999, Minot *et al.* 2006).

In this chapter, we will explore how geographical and spatial factors can become a poverty trap, and we will survey policy responses to remedy such problems. But we must begin with definitions: what is the distinction between 'geographical' and 'spatial' poverty? There is actually a great deal of conceptual overlap between these two terms. Geography can be studied in many different ways; as an academic discipline, there are branches of physical geography, economic geography, cultural geography and political geography, to name a few. As we use the term in this chapter, though, 'geography' has two main applications: environmental geography and relative geography. Environmental geography refers to how humans interact with the attributes of the natural world characterizing a particular place on the planet, such as climate, latitude, biodiversity, the extent of rivers and coastline, and topographical features such as mountains and plains. These environmental attributes, as we will see, can have a variety of both beneficial and detrimental effects on a society's human and economic development. Relative geography, as its name implies, has to do with how certain geographical units – such as countries and their markets, but also regions within a country – relate to each other. The easiest way of thinking about relative geography is to conceive of it as 'neighbour geography'. Just as in any city or town, the neighbours who live next to you can impact your wellbeing. In explaining poverty, the relative geography between neighbouring countries can have a significant effect.

The term 'spatial' can subsume those environmental and relative factors but also adds in other characteristics such as the distribution of infrastructure and public services (Kanbur and Venables 2005). The idea of spatial poverty incorporates a greater attention to things that may not be thought of as 'geographical', such as the locational impact of institutions, politics and culture on people's economic or capability deprivations. The importance of spatial considerations is that severe and chronic poverty is often concentrated in particular places rather than being evenly distributed throughout a territory. Applying a spatial framework also sheds light on inequality, and why some areas within a country can remain mired in multiple deprivations even as other areas experience strong economic growth (Chronic Poverty 2005: 26). This chapter takes an expansive approach to analyse the characteristics of places that contribute to such deprivations, and will generally use the term 'spatial poverty' to embrace the various geographical, political and other factors.

The disease burden

To begin with, one environmental characteristic of certain places can have a very powerful impact on poverty, namely conditions in which diseases and parasites flourish. Places with warmer temperatures, in particular, provide the perfect breeding grounds for parasites such as the malaria virus. The problem of health and poverty is treated in a separate chapter, so at present our goal is simply to demonstrate that this burden does

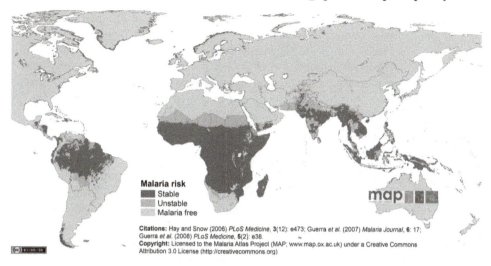

Figure 5.3 World malaria risk

have a pronounced geographic connection. Look at Figure 5.3, showing the areas of the planet with the highest malaria incidence. It shows that tropical regions above all are plagued by malaria. Malaria is not the only debilitating affliction in such regions; it is merely the most studied. There are multiple reasons for the higher disease burden in the tropics. Besides the climate and biological conditions that lend themselves to disease in the tropics, these areas also often suffer from poor food production, which in turn leads to poor nutrition. If a person is undernourished, she is also more susceptible to disease. Further, poverty itself makes it harder for people to resist diseases, because they are more likely to be illiterate and lack access to adequate medical care and sanitation. Studies have shown that when income is factored out of the equation, infant mortality and life expectancy are worse in the tropics than in temperate zones (Sachs 2001). It is on average simply less healthy to live in a tropical area.

The disease burden of such areas can increase poverty in a variety of ways. First, there are several direct, human effects. These effects often reduce a person's capabilities. For instance, if a person is unhealthy, he is less likely to be able to work productively to support himself or his family. Diseases can reduce not only physical capacity but cognitive capacity as well, whether by stunting a person's brain development or simply because it's harder to attend school if you're sick. Additionally, in places with high rates of disease-related mortality, fertility rates are likely to be higher, which can result in more mouths to feed with continually limited resources, thus depressing household incomes. As discussed in Chapter 4 on health and poverty, if you are sick, you are more likely to be poor, and if you are poor you are more likely to be sick. Disease negatively impacts quality of life and thereby makes people more capability poor. It also obviously reduces a person's chance to earn an adequate income.

There are a number of additional, indirect economic effects of the disease burden. Foreign investment to highly disease-prone regions may be reduced because the labour force is less productive or more costly. Other forms of trade can also be disrupted by disease outbreaks. Tourists, certainly, can be scared away by epidemics such as Ebola or typhoid fever. Serious economic damages have been calculated from the costs of a cholera outbreak in Peru in 1991 (USD 800 million lost because of a ban on seafood exports) and a plague outbreak in India (USD 2 billion in work stoppages and other disruptions) (see Hausmann 2001, Carstensen and Grundlach 2006). Sadly, the high disease burden in tropical regions, especially in Africa, amounts to a poverty trap: countries that most urgently need treatment and public health measures against rampant malaria are often too poor to afford them, but untreated malaria is one reason those countries are poor.

Agricultural and natural resource endowments

The next element in spatial and geographical poverty might be summed up as the quality of the land on which a person lives. Certain parts of the world have less fertile land and a dearth of natural resources, which can negatively impact human and economic development. Many people in developing countries live from agriculture, and where the land is not particularly fertile, that limits a family's livelihoods and subsistence potential. These problems affect many: 500 million people in the developing world live in arid areas with very limited irrigation, and some 400 million live on lands with poor soils (Chronic Poverty 2005: 31). At the country level, territory that is primarily desert, and lacks exportable natural resources such as minerals or oil, can limit the potential for economic growth. It is true that the natural resource 'curse' can undermine development and democracy, as we discuss in Chapter 7 on institutions. Yet having no natural resources can also be bad. One example is coal: relatively few tropical countries have significant reserves of coal, which may have negatively impacted their potential for energy production to provide power for people and the economy.

Deficient agricultural endowments can increase poverty in four main ways: (1) via the prevalence of pests and parasites; (2) soil quality; (3) water availability; and (4) lower plant growth rates. The problem of pests and parasites is related to the disease burden. But whereas the disease burden exacerbates poverty through its effects on humans, pests and parasites can also harm crops or livestock. Again, tropical areas in particular suffer from the warm conditions that foster rampant growth of pests, and those pests can wipe out plants or animals that people depend on for food or trade. The contrast is with locations in higher latitudes, and particularly those areas that experience a winter frost. Frost tends to kill pests and parasites, so they are less likely to damage agriculture in temperate areas. Winter frost plays a role in soil quality as well. In areas with winter frost, soil tends to build up for long periods of time, thereby becoming richer and more fertile. In tropical areas, soil often does not build up but is instead washed away by the heavy rains common to this climate zone. Moreover, due to the unique nature of tropical climatic conditions, most of the rich minerals exist not in soils but in the plant biomass above the ground. If those plants are cleared to make way for a farmer's field, their minerals are often lost rather than returning to the soil. The problem of poor soils is not exclusively a tropical condition: agriculture is more difficult anywhere with unfertile soil, and some tropical areas are highly productive.

The problem of water availability refers above all to irrigation for crops. The optimal condition for agricultural production is a fairly steady supply of precipitation throughout the year. Areas that are especially arid, or where precipitation is very heavy in certain months but very light in others, make agriculture more difficult. In some areas in the tropics, for instance, there is a particular rainy season of the year, during which intense downpours occur most days. Not only do such downpours have the effect of eroding soils, but they can also flood fields and make storage and accumulation of grains more problematic. In the months of the dry season, conversely, precipitation can be too sparse. Some parts of the world are more prone to drought or wild fluctuations from year to year in the amount of precipitation. In rugged, mountainous areas, both soil erosion and irrigation can make agriculture overall less productive. Finally, all of the above factors can affect plant growth rates. In the tropics, the intense, short downpours can be too much for plants to absorb, and the typical high temperatures mean that the excess water often evaporates quickly. Thus water can actually be scarce in some tropical areas. It has also been claimed that warm days and warm nights are worse for crop growth than the warm days and cool nights more characteristic of temperate zones (Sachs 2001). In any case, it is clear that some crops such as cotton just grow better in temperate areas.

Again, these problems are not all unique to the tropics, and it can be difficult for a person to earn a livelihood anywhere with poor soils or insufficient precipitation. However, these various disadvantages of agricultural endowments do tend to coalesce in certain areas, contributing to spatial poverty. Much of Africa suffers from several of these problems, such as the prevalence of pests and parasites, soil insufficiencies, and feast-or-famine with water availability. To understand how these conditions impact individuals' lives, imagine a small subsistence farm in the landlocked West African country of Burkina Faso. The northern part of the country belongs to the Sahel, the semi-arid transition zone between the Sahara desert and the savannas farther south. The modest mud houses are surrounded by small fields of reddish soil, acacia trees and grassland. Here most of the local villages literally live for the rainy season: with few other sources of irrigation, families depend on the approximately 50 days a year when it rains. When the rains come, in August for example, the precipitation is usually short and intense.

Farmers in this part of Burkina Faso have to contend not only with soil erosion from such rainstorms, but also with expanding desertification and the many droughts that have plagued their region over the past several decades. Farmers who wanted to leave behind these problems of poor soils and drought have often migrated to the more verdant south of the country. Even there, though, they have to avoid settling near a river – despite its promise of better soil and ample water – because in such areas their cattle would be prey to the tsetse fly, and the farmers themselves would be more likely to come into contact with the parasite that causes onchocerciasis, otherwise known as African river blindness. Though this latter affliction has been greatly reduced in recent decades, the combination of problems such as these in Burkina Faso helps explain why agricultural productivity throughout Africa tends to be low in comparison to other parts of the developing world. The environmental disadvantages of much of sub-Saharan Africa, and tropical areas in particular, are an important reason that agriculture in these regions can be some 30 to 50 per cent less productive than agriculture in temperate zones, even when controlling for the impact of tractors, fertilizer and irrigation (see Gallup *et al.* 1999, Forum for Agricultural Research in Africa 2006).

Remoteness and integration

The idea of remoteness incorporates a number of features that can exacerbate poverty, while integration is generally held to promote economic and human development. Remoteness means being located far from markets, political centres or public services

Box 5.1 Challenges of farming in semi-arid areas, by Andrew Gorvetzian

When I first met Naidu, he smiled and immediately asked, 'When are you coming to my farm?' We exchanged telephone numbers and he explained how he believed in organic farming not only because it was more sustainable, but also because of how it offered a fulfilling lifestyle. By no means would a small farmer gain extraordinary wealth, but organic farming offered a lifestyle that provided many positive outcomes. His goal in life was to share this knowledge with as many people as possible.

On the day we went to his farm, I immediately saw that Naidu's farm was a veritable paradise among the barren and rocky land that surrounded it. The semi-arid climate and sandy soils of this region of India's Telangana state require a lot of work to become viable farmland. Naidu's 30 years of hard toil in such conditions were clear when I saw his huge trees that swayed lazily in the breeze. The 12 acres before us were covered in not just trees, but crops and flowers in which 15 varieties of dragonflies and butterflies lived. In the nearby field, four workers hunched over the rows of newly planted mango trees, working the earth with well-worn tools to usher the creeping irrigation water down the rows. Naidu showed me around the farm, pointing out tomatoes, brinjal, wheat, mangoes, papayas, bitter gourd, banana, Bird of Paradise flowers, tamarind, coconut, coffee beans, black pepper, allspice, teakwood trees, a honeycomb, and more. I gaped in wonder.

Visiting Naidu's farm offered the chance to witness the potential of organic farming practices for small farmers in the face of so many obstacles. Naidu's farm is an oasis, yet the details of his daily routine are hardly anyone's idea of paradise. The Telangana state government can only provide 3 hours of power per day and 1 hour of water, a severe constraining factor for small farmers in a semi-arid environment. Naidu owns no vehicle yet transports thousands of pounds of produce per year using public transit on overcrowded buses. Climate change compounds these constraints as weather patterns become increasingly erratic. Yet he and his workers persevere, without complaint, despite these obstacles. To witness the effort behind the beauty of Naidu's farm revealed a glimpse into the daily struggles a farmer faces. It also engenders an appreciation for the scope of the challenges that agriculture faces in India, where virtually all small and marginal farmers are living at or below the USD 2 a day threshold.

Glaring problems are not solved with easy solutions, but rather hard work and creative solutions. Naidu has been able to create a beautiful and successful farm using organic techniques, including a focus on maintaining biodiversity through cultivating many different crop types. This diversity of crops, trees, flowers and herbs creates a healthy ecosystem that eliminates the need for expensive and harmful chemical fertilizers and pesticides. For many small farmers in India, maintaining biodiversity on farms is a potential key for reducing reliance upon expensive chemical inputs that can reduce soil fertility with no guarantee of higher yields.

However, the ability to cultivate biodiversity is coming under threat from restrictive intellectual property rights used by large agricultural corporations. These corporations identify and develop lucrative varieties and traits and then restrict others from accessing those seeds without paying large royalties. Furthermore, farmers may have to return to the market to buy seeds from year to year, because the patents do not allow farmers to re-sow their seeds. The problems are exacerbated by a lack of institutional credit available to provide small farmers with loans to buy such inputs. This forces them to rely on middlemen who are providers of both loans and physical inputs, ensnaring small farmers in debt traps from which escape is almost impossible. These practices have led to an alarming reduction in the diversity of seeds available to farmers who are strapped for cash, threatening biodiversity that is so crucial to sustainable farming systems. When you're living on only USD 2 a day, it can be very hard to afford seeds at market prices.

The Open Source Seed Initiative seeks to protect the rights of farmers and plant breeders to have access to seeds whose use is not restricted by patents. With an open source framework, farmers and breeders would have access to seeds in a protected open access commons, to which entry is guaranteed to those who promise to share openly the varieties that are developed from sources within the protected commons. This framework seeks to avoid the restrictions of agricultural patents and foster an ethic of sharing of seeds between farmers and breeders with legal protection against proprietary forces. Through open access plant breeding, many are hoping that resilient and locally adapted seed can withstand the challenges of climate change and inefficient governments.

Naidu's farm was visible proof of the ability of organic farming to maintain a healthy ecosystem that provides biodiversity and productive fields while also providing a more secure stream of income. With innovative solutions like the Open Source Seed Initiative, the development and improvement of diverse varieties of crops that can withstand the challenges of agriculture in India becomes more feasible. The socioeconomic dimension of poverty is obvious, but what is not so obvious is the ecological aspect. With creative initiatives such as open source seed, perhaps both of these dimensions of poverty can be alleviated for small farmers in India.

such as health care and education. There are three typical situations that can make a household, region or country more remote: being landlocked, or otherwise far from the sea or navigable rivers; being mountainous, or having rugged terrain such as jungle; and being surrounded by poor neighbouring countries. Remoteness and isolation can be the product of both physical distance (measured as miles/kilometres or travel time) and socio-cultural distance (if a group of people comes from a culture that is different from the dominant culture). Numerous studies have shown that physical remoteness is associated with higher rates of poverty (Jalan and Ravallion 2002, Chomitz 2007). As one example of socio-cultural distance, minority ethnic groups in Vietnam are more likely to live in remote villages and rugged areas, and are more likely to suffer from poverty (Epprecht *et al.* 2011). In general, people living in remote areas are more likely to have insecure economic livelihoods, poor quality housing, very limited access to banking and credit, less productive land, and nutrition deficits (Bird *et al.* 2002). These problems of remoteness and integration affect a very large number of people: some 1.8 billion according to one analysis (Chronic Poverty 2005).

Remote areas' difficulties with transportation can exacerbate both economic and capability poverty. Mountainous terrain means that building infrastructure such as roads or rail lines is significantly more expensive than in flat topography, and therefore mountainous places particularly in the developing world are more likely to have deficient transportation infrastructure and to be remote from markets. Studies consistently find that low access to roads or other transportation infrastructure is associated with higher rates of poverty. In Tanzania, for example, households located within 100 metres of a gravel road passable 12 months of the year, with bus service, had incomes a third higher than the rural average (Bird *et al.* 2010: 5). Even where roads exist, they can be of poor quality, which limits the mobility of people and goods. Bad roads mean that it can take hours to travel relatively short distances, making people and villages more isolated. Bad roads also drive up transport costs, which can make travel unaffordable for people, reducing their access to markets and public services. Higher transport costs hinder economic development by making it more difficult for goods to reach distant markets. Thus being landlocked can raise shipping costs as much as 50 per cent over shipping costs for coastal countries (Henderson *et al.* 2001).

People living in remote areas also typically have less access to public goods such as clean water, sanitation and health care. One study found that rural areas in over 90 per cent of countries had reduced access to sanitation and clean water, and 100 per cent of rural areas had less access to primary health care (IFAD 2000). The quality of services such as health care and education in remote areas also tends to be worse, in part because it can be harder to attract experienced medical professionals or teachers to those areas. This is another aspect of the relationship between spatial factors and institutions: remote areas may well suffer from neglect by government officials, and/or the costs of bringing public services to those areas may be prohibitive. The potentially beneficial effects of pro-poor policies may thus not reach poor people in the remotest areas.

Another public good that can be in shorter supply in remote areas is security from crime and conflict. Though it is not always the case, there are numerous examples from around the world (such as Madagascar, India, Zimbabwe and Sri Lanka) where crime rates were higher in rural and other areas more distant from law enforcement (see Fafchamps and Moser 2003). Besides remoteness, spatial factors also play a role in crime and security through regional inequalities, especially where these overlap with ethnic cleavages. For example, if an ethnic group is concentrated in a particular region, and the group's members share a sense of grievance about unequal political or economic opportunities compared to another group or within the state as a whole, tensions can erupt into armed conflict (Østby *et al.* 2009, Buhaug *et al.* 2011). Areas with rugged geography such as mountains or tropical jungles can also be associated with a higher risk of terrorism and illegal activities such as drug production and trafficking (Abadie 2004). And once conflict has broken out, geographical factors complicate conflict resolution. It is more difficult for the central state to root out criminal activity and violent rebel groups in remote and rugged areas.

The deleterious political dimensions of remoteness combine to isolate regions or people from centres of decision making and influence. In this way, integration problems due to geography can increase capability poverty by marginalizing people economically, politically and even socially. People remote from political and economic centres may be more likely to suffer from exclusion that prevents them from fully exercising their rights or maximizing their economic livelihoods. As but one example, consider the case of villagers from minority ethnic groups in Cambodia's far northeastern province of Ratanakiri. Jeremy Ironside (2009) has documented how these villagers' relative remoteness from the capital has made them neglected and often powerless. Villages in this province consistently have worse health indicators such as malnutrition and infant mortality, and some are too far from schools for their children to get an education. Villagers in the region were rarely consulted on Cambodia's development projects, such as road building or policies to convert local agriculture to cash crops that may be less traditional, such as cashews. There is even evidence of open discrimination by individuals and government officials from the Khmer majority, since in some cases minority villages have lost their communal land to expropriation or illegal sales by outsiders.

There are a number of very specific economic aspects of remoteness as well (see i.a. Bosker and Garretsen 2012). Countries that are poorly connected with world markets will have difficulty developing the industries that would help them integrate to those markets, and which would in turn help them become more prosperous. Paul Krugman and Anthony Venables (1995) have shown how agglomeration effects accrue to places that are able to integrate into producing for world markets. What this means is that companies will choose to locate near each other in somewhere like Vietnam, even if wages are higher there than in Tanzania, because moving to where wages are lowest can impose additional costs through the transportation and other difficulties of being farther from world markets. Therefore, assembly and manufacturing jobs have 'agglomerated' in certain Asian countries, often bypassing low-wage but less integrated Africa, at least for now. It has also been shown that being landlocked can reduce a country's growth rate by 0.6 per cent compared to a country that is not landlocked (cited in Hausmann 2001: 46). Coastal areas, and/or those with good transportation infrastructure, in general have a better chance of consistent economic development, while landlocked, poorly integrated and remote areas are more likely to remain poor.

The problem of neighbours

In addition to difficult terrain and a landlocked location, neighbouring countries also can have an impact on poverty status. This is the issue of *relative geography* mentioned at the beginning of the chapter. Countries' economies and politics have an identifiable impact on nearby countries. In terms of economies, a country that is surrounded by poor countries is itself more likely to be poor. This happens for several reasons. First, take the example of a landlocked country such as Chad. For this country to reach international markets, it must depend on the transportation infrastructure of the countries that surround it, including Sudan, Cameroon and Nigeria. Unfortunately, these are poor countries with seriously deficient transportation systems and histories of occasional conflict. Thus even if Chad had a reasonably well-functioning economy and stable politics, it would still be a 'hostage to its neighbours' (in a phrase from Collier 2008) because it would have to depend on other poor countries to reach the sea. As Limão and Venables (2001) have explained, being landlocked is not a death sentence. Switzerland and Austria are landlocked and rich, for instance, but they can depend on rich neighbours with excellent infrastructure – such as Germany – to reach wider markets. As one interesting example of Africa's disadvantages, an analysis by Redding and Venables (2004) concluded that Zimbabwe's GDP per capita would be 24 per cent higher if it had a seacoast, and 80 per cent higher if it were located in central Europe.

Paul Collier's research (2008) has added another aspect to how neighbours can be a problem. The difficulty isn't solely with infrastructure; countries also must depend on their neighbours as markets for their own goods. Switzerland and Austria have rich neighbours with big markets, such as Germany, Italy and France, and that has helped Switzerland and Austria grow rich themselves. Unfortunately for Chad, neighbours such as Sudan, Cameroon and the Central African Republic are poor countries with small markets. All of these countries have weak economic growth, which makes it much harder for Chad to develop a thriving economy. Weak regional economies, and country borders, also inhibit labour migration that can help pull people out of poverty. In the case of Mexico, the huge, high-wage economy of the United States provides an abundant source of jobs to Mexicans who come north looking for work, and who often send part of their wages home. Chad does not benefit from that kind of regional magnet economy. In sum, being landlocked and having to cross borders can impose high costs on a country's potential economic development.

Political problems associated with neighbours can also have distinct, though related, negative effects. The essence of this problem is that countries must deal with each other to coordinate their efforts on issues such as infrastructure, particularly if they are landlocked. Chad, even if it had the resources to build a fast rail line to reach the sea, cannot easily do so: it would have to work with the governments of Cameroon or Sudan in order to build any such link. In Switzerland's case, such a hurdle is not so high, since Italy and Germany have stable governments. Chad, though, lives in a 'bad neighbourhood'. Sudan and the Central African Republic have experienced bouts of serious instability and conflict. This is where the relative geography of neighbours is an especially serious problem.

Political instability in one country can impose all kinds of costs on a neighbouring country, such as causing the second country to increase military expenditures, or cope with refugees fleeing conflict, or bring waves of disease from mass population movements. Further, the 'bad neighbourhood effect' can result in one country financing rebels in the second country. Alternatively, investors can be scared off because they associate (rightly or wrongly) the first country's corrupt institutions with the institutions in the second country (Bosker and Garretsen 2009). All these setbacks mean that a landlocked country in Africa has much more serious impediments to its economic growth than does a landlocked country in Europe. And unfortunately, sub-Saharan Africa has an unusually large number of landlocked countries.

In fact, all of the above problems of remoteness and integration plague sub-Saharan Africa especially (though not exclusively). Studies have repeatedly found that sub-Saharan Africa's geography helps account for the lower levels of trade both on world markets and even among African countries, when compared to the levels for Asian or Latin American countries (see i.a. Limão and Venables 2001, Faye *et al.* 2004). Especially compared to some Asian countries, many African countries, because of their geography, have been hindered in exploiting their low labour costs to break into the market for assembling goods. The assembly of such goods, such as clothing or electronics, is something that has helped reduce poverty in a number of Asian countries such as Taiwan, Vietnam or China. However, the Asian countries that have managed to use their low labour costs to their advantage all benefited from coastal locations. The geographical locations of these countries, in contrast to many African countries, meant that their transport costs were relatively low and integration into the world economy was relatively easy. Sub-Saharan Africa's number of landlocked countries also means more borders between countries, which makes shipping goods across borders more expensive because of tolls and customs fees. None of these difficulties are insurmountable, but they require particular policies to help overcome sub-Saharan Africa's geographical disadvantages.

Geography and institutions

How geography can impact poverty through institutions is explained more fully in Chapter 7, but here we will briefly treat a few important points as well as a scholarly debate. Deficient institutions and governance often have a spatial dimension strongly associated with poverty. Areas where very poor people are concentrated tend to have a weaker civil society, less responsive government and less involvement by NGOs (Chronic Poverty 2005: 33). Those concentrations of poverty may even arise as a *result* of state institutions and government. Areas that are politically marginalized typically have less government investment in projects for human and economic development. The reasons for that neglect can include a high proportion of people from a minority ethnic group living in an area, an area being a stronghold of an opposition political party, and distance from the capital or other centres of political power. It is thus possible that institutional neglect can actually make a place more remote, less integrated, and therefore poorer – though it can be difficult to isolate such factors' causal contribution to spatial poverty (Burke and Jayne 2010).

The scholarly debate concerns the relative importance of geography or institutions for explaining human and economic development. Writers such as Acemoglu, Johnson and Robinson (2001) have claimed that geography exerts only an *indirect* influence on economic development by helping shape the kind of institutions that arose in a given territory. Acemoglu *et al.* claim that certain geographical factors induced European settlers to create either (a) 'extractive institutions' that subjugated local populations and concentrated power and wealth in a small minority, or (b) more egalitarian, democratic institutions that fostered more widely shared prosperity. The key geographical factors were the disease burden (principally the incidence of malaria), the prevalence of natural endowments such as good soils and/or mineral wealth, and indigenous population densities sufficient to provide a large pool of labour. Where the disease burden was high, where there were abundant minerals such as gold and where there was a large indigenous population, Europeans set up extractive institutions.

This thesis attempts to explain specifically how the geographical endowments in much of Latin America helped shape the undemocratic governance of colonialism. In Latin America, and eventually in Africa, Europeans created a social and political structure designed to protect the interests of the small, wealthy landowning class from the interests of the larger population. The contrast is with places such as North America, Australia or New Zealand, which had low disease burdens and low indigenous population densities. More Europeans settled there, land ownership was broader based, and a more egalitarian rule of law was implemented. In short, institutions created under certain geographical conditions depended on undemocratic power concentration, while those created under other conditions were for the most part democratic.

The position held by Acemoglu *et al.*, Rodrik *et al.* (2002) and Easterly and Levine (2003), that geography affects economic growth only through its impact on institutions, has been widely criticized. One target of criticism is the way that these scholars have conducted their econometric analyses of the relative effects of geography and institutions. Critics of these analyses say that the causal relationships between geography, income levels and institutions are extremely difficult to separate. For example, geography does impact institutions and institutions impact income levels, but geography also impacts income and institutions can also impact geographical attributes (good governments can eradicate malaria, for example). Moreover, geographical disadvantages encompass a number of different potential effects on poverty, as we have seen. Though malaria and the disease burden are an important one, there are the additional factors of soil quality, precipitation, landlocked location and potentially even such long-term influences as biodiversity and diffusion of technologies. These latter factors are typically glossed over by many of the strongest proponents of the institutions thesis.

It is important to remember that geography's effect on institutions presupposes direct effects on human health, environmental stability and the productivity of economic systems (Sachs 2003). In terms of relative geography, evidence suggests that a country surrounded by neighbours with good institutions is more likely to trade with them and the rest of the world (Bosker and Garretsen 2009). There are also many different aspects of institutions. For example, markets are an institution that can be debilitated by spatial/geographical factors. Where terrain is difficult, individuals' access to markets can be impaired by a lack of adequate roads or otherwise high transportation costs. Where population densities are low, similarly, markets may be underdeveloped and access reduced. It may therefore be difficult for people to earn money by selling what they produce, or to trade for desired goods. Such conditions can contribute to income poverty as well as capability poverty, since deficient access to markets can limit the capability to earn a livelihood. Though the debate over the relative importance of geography or institutions for explaining poverty has not been definitively settled, in a sense the debate does not need to be resolved. Both spatial/geographical factors and institutions explain poverty levels, and they both affect each other.

Spatial poverty and capabilities

Spatial/geographical factors can impact capabilities in a variety of ways, some obvious and some less so. To begin with, remoteness and isolation can deprive people of basic capabilities in health and education. The reason is that people living in remote and isolated places may have less access to health services and school opportunities. Reduced access to other public services can also undermine capabilities: lack of clean water and sanitation can be bad for a person's health, and lack of electricity can limit a person's ability to read and study at night, among many other possible effects. Peripheral areas, particularly isolated ones with minority ethnic groups, also can suffer from deprivations in political capabilities. People in peripheral areas may not be able to make their voices heard to distant policy makers. The deprivations here can be the result of both neglect (when political elites ignore people in remote or isolated places) and discrimination (when political elites purposefully deprive people of their rights). Such discrimination can lead to exclusion along a variety of dimensions (cultural, economic, political), which cripples both people's capabilities and functionings. To the extent that remote areas suffer from increased criminality or conflict, capabilities in basic personal security also suffer. Living in fear from banditry, terrorism or other forms of crime can sharply reduce a person's quality of life.

Digging deeper, we see that spatial/geographical factors can weaken capabilities in a number of other ways as well. Having adequate food security and nutrition is a basic human entitlement, but this can be hard to achieve in places with low agricultural productivity due to poor soils. A place prone to famine can be seriously detrimental to a person's basic capabilities. Having adequate shelter is also typically considered a basic capability, in part for its influence on health and security. Some places make having adequate shelter much more difficult. A dwelling in a place prone to floods, landslides, epidemics, heavy pollution or a host of other problems may well violate the right to adequate shelter. People who are forced to live in such places typically suffer from multiple overlapping deprivations. If they have to live in marginal areas, they are very likely victims of discrimination, with few economic and educational opportunities, unable to exercise political rights and possibly afflicted with health problems as a result of their dwelling's location.

Remoteness and isolation in themselves can potentially deprive people of basic capabilities. Remember that the capabilities approach prioritizes 'the actual freedom of choice a person has over alternative lives that he or she can live.' (Sen 1990: 114) Living in an isolated area can reduce a person's freedom of choice. Depending on how severe the remoteness and lack of integration, a person may have reduced choice over her profession, over where she lives, over how and when she participates in her society, in short, over the life that she wants. For example, one of Nussbaum's basic capabilities is access to information (Nussbaum 2011). The idea is that everyone should have the ability to learn from a variety of sources that he or she chooses, so that choice is not unfairly restricted either by governments or other external circumstances. Living in a remote area, however, can restrict a person's access to information. Remote and rural areas in the developing world often lack access to landline telephones, television and the internet. Media sources may also be limited, with inadequate access to newspapers or radio stations, or perhaps monopoly control over the supply of news (whether by a government or a single, dominant media outlet). In areas where the access to information is restricted, the free flow of ideas is also limited, which amounts to a deprivation in both capabilities and functionings.

The capabilities approach primarily focuses on the individual as the main unit of analysis, i.e. what can this person be and do? The rationale is that individuals' lives are the proper focus for our moral concern. However, the geographical disadvantages discussed in this chapter also point to the relevance of what are known as *collective capabilities* (see i.a. Thorp *et al.* 2005, Ballet *et al.* 2007, Alkire 2008, Murphy 2014). These are the capabilities that adhere to groups. Those groups could be village councils, women's clubs, unions, minority ethnic groups or other kinds of communities. Groups can have a major impact on an individual's capabilities because groups help constitute what people value. For instance, a group's cultural norms of what is 'good' influence what an individual wants for herself. Moreover, an individual's opportunity to attain what she values often depends on a group. The possibility to act together with others who share similar values gives rise to a collective agency that can benefit both the individual and the group (Evans 2002, Ibrahim 2006). Individual and collective capabilities are part of broader social structures and relationships, and the particular dynamic of concentrated spatial poverty demonstrates this interrelationship.

The disease burden, deficient agricultural endowments and remoteness have distinct place-based natures, which means that everyone living in such a place is potentially negatively affected. This is the concentration effect of spatial poverty: in an area with geographical disadvantages, what individuals and groups can achieve can be seriously limited. *Both* the individual's capabilities and the group's suffer. Refer again to the example of the villagers in the Cambodian province of Ratanakiri, cited earlier. These villagers are so remote from centres of power that they are often neglected or ignored by political authorities. The village itself suffers from worse outcomes in health and education, and both individually and collectively the villagers are discriminated against by members of the majority Khmer ethnic group. This is a concentration of disadvantage that undermines the group's freedoms, not just the individual's. It is a good illustration of how what an individual can be and do often depends on the collectivity's opportunities.

Strengthening the group's opportunities thus can help expand the individual's opportunities, since they are often mutually interdependent. The reason the group can be important for expanding the individual's capabilities is because of the possibility of collective action. Individuals almost always have to organize in order to make broader societal change. Collective action is a vital organizational strategy to bargain, to share resources, to increase economic opportunities, to use democratic structures to press one's interests. Acting together, individuals can often achieve more than by acting alone. Acting together will also likely have more success at changing *un*democratic power structures and righting injustices. Collective action in this sense supports not just an individual's self-interest (to realize individual capabilities and functionings), but helps achieve a social good that can expand the group's capabilities and functionings as well.

The idea of collective capabilities is especially relevant for people living in poverty, who typically must organize in order to improve their situation since individual action is much less likely to lead to change for the group beyond the individual. The concentration of multiple, overlapping geographical disadvantages makes individual efforts at escaping poverty much more difficult. Think of the villagers of Ratanakiri: one individual might improve her situation by leaving the village, but even if she expands her capabilities that way, what she could be and do might still be limited if she is obviously from a minority group and hence could be subject to discrimination. Thus because her capabilities depend in part on her collective membership, collective action is ultimately a more robust way of combating her individual and group-based capability deprivations.

It must be said that not all groups support an individual's capabilities, since some groups are exclusionary or repressive. Sen himself is also dubious that groups per se have capabilities beyond the sum total of individual capabilities (Davis 2015). Whether collective capabilities add that much to our understanding of an individual's freedoms is a question worth debating – and there are a number of other applications of the capabilities approach to spatial poverty that likewise merit discussion. Often the question comes down to whether a capability should count as 'basic', such that its deprivation equates to poverty. One example is with mobility. As we have seen, remote and rugged areas have weaker road networks and higher transportation costs, hence people in such areas in the developing world often have less mobility. Is this a problem? What would be the basic level of mobility to which everyone is entitled, so that we could ascertain when there is a fundamental capability deprivation in this area? Similarly, Nussbaum cites sociability and affiliation as aspects of basic capabilities. Here the idea is that people should have the freedom to choose their social relations, affiliating with the individuals and groups they want. However, isolation in some remote mountain village may limit a person's capabilities and functionings in this regard. If your social relations are limited to people from your own kinship group in your far-flung village, is that a fundamental capability deprivation? Finally, what should be the standard for basic capabilities in market access and earning a livelihood? Again, as we have seen, people in remote areas often have reduced access to markets and reduced choices for their livelihoods. In such geographical and spatial conditions, people's freedoms are definitely constrained, but it may be debatable as to whether those limitations constitute poverty.

The difficult geography discussed in this chapter thus does not automatically translate to capability deprivations. Obviously, it is possible to live in a far-flung, rugged, tropical place and still enjoy the full range of basic capabilities. The challenge with difficult

Box 5.2 Technology and geography

Jeffrey Sachs (2001) has advanced a thesis about the relationship between technological development and geography that has implications for economic growth in the long, medium and short terms. In both the long and medium terms, Sachs has theorized that economies in temperate zones developed more effective technologies especially in the areas of health, agriculture and the military. Their faster technological development took place in part because of the higher population densities in temperate zone countries prior to the twentieth century. Higher population densities fostered the conditions that gave rise to more knowledge production and subsequently greater economic and technological growth. So the long-term influence of geographical factors on technological development is that certain places supported higher populations that made more technological advances possible. In the medium term, Sachs' argument also brings in the idea of diffusion. The technologies that were developed in temperate zone countries were often very specific to temperate climates and therefore could not be easily diffused to tropical climates. The technological diffusion *within* temperate zone countries contributed to faster economic growth among those countries, while the difficulty of diffusion *across* climate zones meant that tropical countries benefited less from technological advances developed in the temperate parts of the globe.

A concrete example is with agricultural technology. Over the centuries, and even the past few decades, agricultural productivity has improved among temperate zone countries because of the application of technology to such things as better seeds, pest-resilient crops and mechanized harvesting. Some of these technological developments cannot diffuse to tropical countries because different crops are grown there, or because governments or individuals in low-income countries lack the funds or the expertise to adopt the advances. Another concrete example involves health technology. Temperate countries typically suffer less from certain diseases than do tropical countries, and suffer from different diseases; the disease burden for tropical countries is both greater and somewhat divergent. Economies in the temperate zone have developed the technology to combat or eradicate the most common diseases there, such as smallpox or polio. Meanwhile, diseases and parasites endemic to the tropical zone, whether malaria or others such as schistosomiasis, are neglected by researchers because they are not as big a problem to populations in temperate areas.

Where short-term dynamics enter the picture most strongly is that countries in the tropical zones, because they are more likely to be poor, often lack the resources to invest in the research and development necessary to achieve the technological advances specifically targeted to help people in the tropics. Most of the world's R&D happens in the rich, temperate economies, and therefore that R&D usually focuses on the needs of those societies. Some technological advances fail to diffuse to the tropics, and because markets and other resources for innovation tend to be weaker in tropical countries, these countries continue to lag in both economic growth and the accompanying technological development. Sachs also hypothesizes that since urbanization and the transition to lower rates of population growth – both of which can promote more technological development – likewise tend to lag in tropical countries, those countries fall further behind. Finally, because these countries have fallen behind in the long and medium terms, it has been easier for technologically advanced rich countries to dominate them politically and militarily, such as during the colonial era or in contemporary globalization. Such domination usually reinforces poor countries' relative backwardness. Note that though this theory of the relationship between geography and technology is both plausible and supported by some evidence, it remains unproven, as Sachs himself acknowledges.

geography is that it can make it harder to enjoy that full range. Recall Sen's insistence that a person's freedom must include some perspective on the quality, quantity and diversity of her opportunities (Sen 1985, 1983). At its root, the problem of disadvantageous geography is that it often limits opportunities. It is not impossible to have adequate basic nutrition from farming in an arid place, but it is much harder. It is not impossible to gain an adequate education when living in a remote mountain village, but it is much harder. It is not impossible to earn a sustainable livelihood as a trader when you live far from roads, but it is much harder. Geographical factors can disadvantage a person's agency, i.e. her actual freedom to make valuable choices for herself. People who live in areas with difficult geography are often already marginalized: if given a real choice, few would elect to live in the malarial swamp distant from roads, electricity and health clinics. Therefore, individuals and groups who live with the geographical disadvantages that undermine basic capabilities may have already been deprived of the freedom to choose to live somewhere *without* those geographical disadvantages.

Policy solutions

A key lesson from this chapter is that poverty can not only be caused or worsened by spatial/geographical factors, but also that poor people can be concentrated in certain areas, which then deserve more attention for policies to reduce poverty. One of the difficult aspects of spatial effects and poverty, however, is that those effects are often overlapping. This means that the deprivations associated with living in a certain area can be multiple and reinforcing. Some places, for example, have few roads, a high disease burden, poor soils, weak market opportunities and deficient access to public services such as health clinics or sanitation. With such multiple disadvantages, it can be very difficult for an individual, family or community to escape poverty. Hence policies to alleviate aspects of poverty associated with spatial factors should themselves be multifaceted to address the various deprivations. Altering geography might seem a Herculean task. In order to help poor people afflicted with spatial disadvantages, is it necessary to level mountains, make dry places rain, and give landlocked places access to the sea?

Certainly major investments can be required to overcome spatial and geographical disadvantages. But there are also smaller-scale policies that can help. We will first consider projects focused primarily on benefiting households and regions, and then turn to country-level policies. To begin with, extending access to public services for remote areas is a common and essential approach to reducing spatial poverty. Doing so can support both individual and collective capabilities. Rural areas in developing countries around the world tend to have less access to clean water and sanitation. Similarly, building roads in rural areas should improve potential mobility for people and goods. One difficulty with such policies is that costs to expand public goods in remote areas are often high. Building roads through mountainous areas is very expensive, and extending the reach of water, sanitation, electricity or health services may bring remote areas onto the grid but may not serve many people in areas where population densities are low. Inadequate access to public services is not just a problem for rural areas, however. Remember that poverty can be spatially concentrated in urban areas too: slums or other marginalized settlements may often be deprived of clean water or sanitation.

Regionally targeted development programmes have been tried in a number of countries. Ghana, for instance, has devoted special attention to creating successful secondary schools in the more remote and impoverished northern part of the country. Indonesia has promoted special instructional programmes to help remote villages. In China, breakneck economic growth has led to enormous income disparities between the richer eastern coastal regions and the poorer interior provinces. Several programmes for the poorer areas have attempted to ameliorate these disparities, such as subsidized loans for households and enterprises, food-for-work programmes, and grants to governments to spur investment in disadvantaged areas (Higgins, Bird and Harris 2010). For places with deficient agricultural endowments there are a number of strategies. Increasing farmers' access to fertilizers can improve soil health. Irrigation projects such as pumps, wells, and large- or small-scale dams can help areas where managing water for agriculture is a problem (Sachs 2004). As noted in Box 5.1, providing farmers with specially bred seeds is another way of increasing productivity. These programmes all have the potential to support basic capabilities, such as through educational access or agricultural projects to strengthen livelihoods.

Because the disease burden disproportionately affects some places and is severely detrimental to basic capabilities, it is a particular focus for policies to promote human development. Though international efforts to combat malaria are perhaps the most prominent example, there are programmes for other parasites and diseases endemic to tropical areas. Such programmes can involve aspects of infrastructure to improve a population's health status, such as building delivery systems for clean water or sanitary sewage systems. One such project that involved providing safe water, larvicide and health education has helped drastically reduce the toll of guinea worm disease. Cases of this disease fell from 3.5 million people infected in 1986 to fewer than 11,000 20 years later (see Levine 2004). Reducing the disease burden is often linked to technological assistance to lessen developing countries' gap with the rich world, particularly with vaccines. Strategies to improve health in places with a high disease burden are essential not only to help people live lives that they value, but also to fight economic poverty by reducing disease's toll on productivity.

Policies to address the spatial dimensions of poverty should also take into account collective capabilities, since minority groups can disproportionately suffer from remoteness, exclusion and attendant deprivations. Because some groups can be more deprived than others, there is a strong argument that they deserve additional resources from poverty reduction policies. Such an approach might target regions where people from minority groups are concentrated, and/or target minority group households even in a region where most people are from another group and better off. The idea is to reduce inequalities not just between regions but between people, and to promote social inclusion of people who may often be discriminated against or disproportionately disadvantaged in some other way. One example is a programme in Laos that relocated entire ethnic minority villages in an effort to improve their access to markets and the range of public services. While this strategy may bring some benefits, it also shows some of the difficulties of trying to help minority groups suffering from multiple deprivations, since moving entire villages raises questions about coerced displacement and disruption of the villagers' cultural traditions and distinctness (Bechstedt *et al.* 2007). Besides steps to improve people's economic wellbeing and reduce capability deprivations, policies for social inclusion can also have as a goal promoting cross-cultural understanding and tolerance among groups through programmes of multilingual education (Epprecht *et al.* 2011). Such programmes can decrease cultural distance between groups, and value minority groups' cultures.

Increasing trade can play a vital role in reducing income poverty at both the household and the country levels. As we have seen, remoteness from markets can be associated with reduced opportunities for an economic livelihood and a lack of integration into the world economy. There are a number of ways to reduce remoteness, increase integration and foster more trade for poor countries. The first is to lower trade barriers by reducing tariffs and trade quotas. Establishing free trade zones and reforming customs and border protocols can help increase trade for landlocked countries whose goods must often traverse multiple borders to reach world markets. With reduced customs restrictions, the hope is that trade between neighbours will improve, bringing 'spillover effects' of economic growth that can raise people's incomes. Another strategy for increasing trade is Paul Collier's suggestion that a country can become a 'haven' in a particular regional sector. The idea is that a country can strive to have noticeably better, more transparent policies in one industry such as finance, thereby becoming the centre of finance for its region (Collier 2008). Free trade does not always benefit the poor, but as a general principle, most economists would agree that increasing poor countries' participation in world markets has overall positive outcomes (see i.a. Buys *et al.* 2006, World Bank 2007, IMF 2007).

Investing in infrastructure is another policy strategy relevant both to overcoming various spatial disadvantages as well as promoting trade. Better transportation infrastructure – whether roads, rail lines or port facilities – can make trade easier and more cost effective. A key goal is to improve access to the coast for landlocked countries. For Chad, improving transportation links to the sea via Cameroon could be an important boost to the economy of both countries, again through spillover effects. Part of what makes such infrastructure improvements difficult, though, is that they typically do depend on the cooperation and coordination between neighbouring countries. Nonetheless, such regionally focused projects should be a priority for their potential to benefit several countries at once.

If we examine the opposite side of the coin from spatial/geographic *dis*advantages, we can see which spatial/geographic factors are actually beneficial for economic growth. Contemporary thinking on this question has echoed and provided empirical support for the theories that Adam Smith proposed in his epochal work *The Wealth of Nations* in 1776. As Smith said, countries that have good harbours on the seacoast, or that have sea-navigable rivers, are more likely to be prosperous. In our terms, those countries are likely to be less remote from world markets, and may find it easier to integrate into those markets. In fact, Bloom, Canning and Sevilla (2003) have found that the percentage of a country's land that is within 100 kilometres of the coast is a good predictor of that country's income level. The other key variables in Bloom *et al.*'s analysis are measurements of a country's maximum average monthly temperature, average monthly rainfall, and the distribution of rainfall over the months of the year. They claim that these four variables account for 60 per cent of cross–country comparisons of income per capita. There are a few other factors that are also associated with higher incomes. These include a low average elevation (thereby obviating the problem of difficult, mountainous terrain), and neighbouring countries with good institutions and sizeable markets.

The good news is that the international aid community has acknowledged the need to help countries address geographical disadvantages. Infrastructure projects such as

---

Box 5.3 Where are the world's poor?

A spatial and geographical perspective on poverty is also useful for understanding where, at the global level, most poor people live. The answer is not what you might expect. Most poor people do not live in the so-called 'Bottom Billion' countries. In fact, 72 per cent of the world's poor live in middle-income countries. Moreover, 80 per cent of the world's poorest people (those living below the threshold of USD 1.25 a day) live in just ten countries: India, China, Nigeria, Bangladesh, the Democratic Republic of the Congo, Indonesia, Pakistan, Tanzania, the Philippines and Kenya. Four hundred million poor people live in fragile states, and 45 per cent of those states are classified as middle income. Two-thirds of the poor in Africa live in fragile states. Using the Multidimensional Poverty Index measure, we find that 62.4 per cent of the world's most deprived people live in South Asia, and 36.4 per cent live in sub-Saharan Africa. This means that only 1.2 per cent of the world's most deprived live elsewhere. The fact that more poor people live in middle-income countries challenges the idea that development policies should focus primarily on low-income countries.

This picture of where the world's poor live has changed dramatically in the past 20 years, since previously 93 per cent of poor people lived in low-income countries. Economic growth in China and India is one explanation for the change. Nonetheless, it is important to remember that though middle-income countries may have the largest numbers of poor people, low-income countries still tend to have higher proportions of the population that is poor, as well as more severe poverty overall. We must also always be attentive to the distribution of poor people within countries. Growth in China and India may have lifted many people's incomes, but many other people are being left behind. There can be a strong spatial dimension here: in India the overwhelming majority of poor people are concentrated in a few regions. This is important because it highlights very unequal distributions of prosperity. Several Indian states have attained middle-income status, but many others remain low income, and the latter account for two-thirds of India's total number of poor people. In sum, the weight of the world's poverty is highly concentrated by population in relatively few countries, and within those countries, some regions have disproportionately more poor people and more severe poverty.

Sources: Kanbur and Sumner 2012, Sumner 2012, Alkire *et al.* 2013

building dams, power plants, airports and telephone networks, as well as roads, rail lines and ports, have been an objective for several decades. Countries such as Rwanda have benefited from assistance to construct a fibre optic network to improve communications within the country and the rest of the world, reducing this landlocked country's remoteness. The Philippines has received aid to improve port facilities and thereby boost trade, and Sri Lanka has been assisted with building expressways to improve transportation, as two further examples. Likewise, programmes to develop vaccines for diseases prevalent in the developing world are receiving increasing attention. For instance, countries such as Canada, Norway and Italy, along with private donors such as the Gates Foundation, have committed more than a billion dollars to incentivize the development of vaccines for malaria, polio, rotavirus and meningitis.

Conclusion

Imagine that you live in a rural area of Papua New Guinea. You most likely live in a rugged place: over half of that country is mountainous or hilly. Like most rural people in the country, you live on and partly from the land. However, the land you live on is not very good. It is steep, with bad soil, has heavy rainfall and is prone to flooding; in fact, nearly 60 per cent of the land in Papua New Guinea is considered to be 'low' or 'very low' in quality (Allen *et al*. 2005). With land like that, it's no wonder you would have trouble growing enough food for yourself and your family. You therefore probably suffer from health problems due to protein and other nutrient deficiencies, and your children's growth will be stunted. Why not just buy better food? Living in such an area, you certainly wouldn't be able to earn much of a living from agriculture, but there are few other jobs.

Even if you owned enough land that you had surplus crops to sell, your income would likely be limited by the very bad roads, which make it difficult to get your crops to market. The infrastructure throughout much of Papua New Guinea is compromised not only by mountain ranges but also by big rivers and swamps. Mobility is not easy in this country. That means that if you need any serious health care, you probably have a long journey, if you can afford it at all. To top it off, parts of the country have significant risk of earthquakes and volcanoes, which means that your house, your livelihood and indeed your life are less secure (Allen *et al*. 2001). If you lived in such a place, then, you would find it much harder to earn a respectable income. Your opportunities to choose a different life for yourself would also most likely be limited. In such a place, you would see first-hand how spatial and geographical disadvantages can worsen capability poverty by limiting opportunities in health, education, political rights and livelihoods.

These overlapping disadvantages affect not just you but many others in your community. Economic opportunities in a locality or a region may be limited because transportation of goods is more expensive in landlocked or rugged terrain than it is along the coast. Likewise, a high disease burden typically reduces worker productivity, potentially impairing your own ability to earn money as well as economic growth for your whole region. These factors amplify each other and add up over time, so that a country that is landlocked, with a high disease burden and poor soils, will almost certainly have lower growth rates historically than a country without these disadvantages. This is why geographical difficulties have been termed a 'tax on development' (Woods 2004). Think of it this way: economic growth has been like a race. The countries with more difficult spatial and geographic conditions do not start out the race even with other countries, and they have more hurdles to jump. Because productivity, technological innovation and economic growth have mutually reinforcing effects, those countries that start out ahead have also found it easier to lengthen their lead on the geographically disadvantaged countries.

Does this mean that spatial and geographic problems condemn some countries or people to poverty forever? Absolutely not – there is no geographical determinism. Being landlocked, mountainous, remote, tropical, or with a high disease burden does not preclude human flourishing. Such features are only some of the many that can contribute to poverty. And while spatial disadvantages can overlap and worsen poverty, they are only part of an explanation for why individuals are poor. It is easy to think of places that share some of these disadvantages but that are nonetheless prosperous, such as landlocked Switzerland or tropical zone Singapore. Moreover, quite a few countries outside the temperate zone have made great strides in malaria eradication, including Paraguay, Costa Rica and Malaysia. Geographical disadvantages can be overcome, such as by supporting basic capabilities in health and education, promoting market opportunities through access and integration, and reforming state institutions to make them more effective. Thus bad geography is not a death sentence, but it does require both intellectual and policy attention so that vulnerable individuals and groups do not become trapped by spatial deprivations.

Discussion questions

1 How do geographical disadvantages negatively impact individual and collective capabilities? How should programmes to combat those disadvantages understand the relationship between individual and collective capabilities?
2 In what ways can geographical and spatial factors be a poverty trap?
3 What are the dangers of assuming a 'geographical determinism'?
4 What are the limits of geographical/spatial explanations? What can they *not* explain in terms of why places or people are poor? Do geographical/spatial factors do a better job of explaining why some places get rich and why some places remain poor?
5 What would you judge to be the most effective and realistic ways of ameliorating the geographical disadvantages that can exacerbate poverty?
6 Some development experts, as in the 2009 World Development Report, have said that spatial inequalities are inevitable, and that economic growth will always be uneven. According to this perspective, the key to economic development is to promote population density, urbanization and infrastructure projects in the areas that are most economically promising and suffer least from geographical disadvantages. Critics of this perspective say that it will only promote further divergence and inequality of opportunities. What do you think?
7 Explore this site: www.worldmapper.org/index.html. Though sometimes the data are not the most recent, what can you learn about the global spatial distribution of various indicators related to poverty and inequality?

Further reading

Bird, Kate, Kate Higgins and Dan Harris, 'Spatial poverty traps: an overview.' Overseas Development Institute Working Paper 321, December 2010.

Diamond, Jared. 2005. *Guns, Germs, and Steel: The fates of human societies*. New York, NY: W.W. Norton.

Kanbur, Ravi, and Anthony J. Venables, eds. 2005. *Spatial Inequality and Development*. Oxford: Oxford University Press.

Sachs, Jeffrey D., Andrew D. Mellinger and John L. Gallup, 'The Geography of Poverty and Wealth.' *Scientific American*, (March 2001): 70–75.

Woods, Dwayne. 'Bringing Geography Back In: Civilizations, Wealth, and Poverty.' *International Studies Review*, 5 (2003): 343–354.

Works cited

Abadie, Alberto. 'Poverty, Political Freedom, and the Roots of Terrorism', National Bureau of Economic Research Working Paper No. 10859, October 2004.

Acemoglu, Daron, Simon Johnson and James A. Robinson. 'The colonial origins of comparative development: an empirical investigation.' *American Economic Review*, 91.5 (2001): 1369–1401.

Alkire, S. 'Using the Capability Approach: Prospective and Evaluative Analyses', in: Comim, Flavio, Mozaffar Qizilbash and Sabina Alkire, eds. 2008. *The Capability Approach: Concepts, measures and application*. Cambridge, UK: Cambridge University Press.

Alkire, Sabina, José Manuel Roche, Suman Seth and Andy Sumner. 'Where do the world's poorest live? A Multidimensional approach to the bottom billion', manuscript, May 2013.

Allen, Bryant, R. Michael Bourke and John Gibson. 'Poor rural places in Papua New Guinea.' *Asia Pacific Viewpoint*, 46.2 (2005): 201–217.

Allen, Bryant, R. Michael Bourke and Luke Hanson. 'Dimensions of PNG village agriculture', in *Food security for Papua New Guinea: Proceedings of the Papua New Guinea food and nutrition 2000 conference*. Australian Centre for International Agricultural Research, Canberra. 2001.

Ballet, Jérôme, Jean-Luc Dubois and François-Régis Mahieu. 'Responsibility for each other's freedom: agency as the source of collective capability.' *Journal of Human Development*, 8.2 (2007): 185–201.

Bechstedt, Hans-Dieter, V. Gilbos and O. Souksavat. 'Impact of Public Expenditures on Ethnic groups and Women–Lao PDR, Phase 2.' Poverty and Social Impact Assessment (PSIA) Final Report. Part 1 (2007).

Bird, Kate, Andy McKay and Isaac Shinyekwa. 'Isolation and poverty: the relationship between spatially differentiated access to goods and services and poverty.' Overseas Development Institute Working Paper 322, December 2010.

Bird, Kate, David Hulme, Karen Moore and Andrew Shepherd. 'Chronic poverty and remote rural areas.' Chronic Poverty Research Centre Working Paper 13 (2002).

Bloom, David E., David Canning and Jaypee Sevilla. 'Geography and poverty traps.' *Journal of Economic Growth*, 8.4 (2003): 355–378.

Bosker, Maarten, and Harry Garretsen. 'Economic geography and economic development in Sub-Saharan Africa.' *The World Bank Economic Review*, 26.3 (2012): 443–485.

Bosker, Maarten, and Harry Garretsen. 'Economic development and the geography of institutions.' *Journal of Economic Geography*, 9 (2009): 295–328.

Buhaug, Halvard, *et al.* 'It's the local economy, stupid! Geographic wealth dispersion and conflict outbreak location.' *Journal of Conflict Resolution*, 55.5 (2011): 814–840.

Burke, William J., and Thom S. Jayne. 'Spatial disadvantages or spatial poverty traps: Household evidence from rural Kenya.' Overseas Development Institute Working Paper 327, December 2010.

Buys, Piet, Uwe Deichmann and David Wheeler. *Road network upgrading and overland trade expansion in Sub-Saharan Africa*. Vol. 4097. Washington, DC: World Bank, 2006.

Carstensen, Kai, and Erich Gundlach. 'The Primacy of Institutions Reconsidered: Direct Income Effect of Malaria Presence.' *The World Bank Economic Review*, 20.3 (2006): 309–339.

Chomitz, Kenneth. *At Loggerheads? Agricultural Expansion, Poverty Reduction, and Environment in the Tropical Forests*. Washington, DC: World Bank, 2007.

Chronic Poverty Research Center. *The Chronic Poverty Report 2004–05*, Chapter 3: 'Where do chronically poor people live?' Manchester, UK, 2005.

Collier, Paul. 2008. *The Bottom Billion: Why the poorest countries are failing and what can be done about it*. New York, NY: Oxford University Press.

Davis, John B. 'Agency and the Process Aspect of Capability Development: Individual Capabilities, Collective Capabilities, and Collective Intentions.' (July 1, 2015). *Filosofía de la Economía*, forthcoming. Available at SSRN: http://ssrn.com/abstract=2625673

Easterly, William, and Ross Levine. 'Tropics, germs, and crops: how endowments influence economic development.' *Journal of Monetary Economics*, 50.1 (2003): 3–39.

Epprecht, Michael, Daniel Müller and Nicholas Minot. 'How remote are Vietnam's ethnic minorities? An analysis of spatial patterns of poverty and inequality.' *The Annals of Regional Science*, 46.2 (2011): 349–368.

Evans, Peter. 'Collective capabilities, culture, and Amartya Sen's *Development as Freedom*.' *Studies in Comparative International Development*, 37.2 (2002): 54–60.

Fafchamps, Marcel, and Christine Moser. 'Crime, isolation and law enforcement.' *Journal of African Economies* 12.4 (2003): 625–671.

Faye, Michael, John W. McArthur, Jeffrey Sachs and Thomas Snow. 'The challenges facing landlocked developing countries.' *Journal of Human Development*, 5.1 (2004): 31–68.

Forum for Agricultural Research in Africa. *Framework for African Agricultural Productivity*. Accra, Ghana, June 2006.

Gallup, John Luke, Jeffrey D. Sachs and Andrew Mellinger. 'Geography and Economic Development.' Center for International Development Working Paper No. 1, March 1999.

Hausmannn, Ricardo. 'Prisoners of geography.' *Foreign Policy*, 122.1 (2001): 44–53.

Henderson, J. Vernon, Zmarak Shalizi and Anthony J. Venables. 'Geography and development.' *Journal of Economic Geography* 1 (2001): 81–105.

Higgins, Kate, Kate Bird and Dan Harris. 'Policy responses to the spatial dimensions of poverty.' Overseas Development Institute Working Paper 328, December 2010.

Ibrahim, Solava S. 'From individual to collective capabilities: the capability approach as a conceptual framework for self-help.' *Journal of Human Development*, 7.3 (2006): 397–416.

International Fund for Agricultural Development (IFAD). *Annual Report 2000: Working with the rural poor*. Rome: IFAD, 2000.

International Monetary Fund. 'Regional Economic Outlook: Sub-Saharan Africa.' Washington, DC, 2007.

Ironside, Jeremy. 'Development – in whose name? Cambodia's economic development and its indigenous communities – from self-reliance to uncertainty', in Peter J. Hammer, ed. *Living on the Margins: Minorities and borderlines in Cambodia and Southeast Asia*. Detroit, MI: Wayne State University, Center for Khmer Studies, 2009.

Jalan, Jyotsna and Martin Ravallion. 'Geographic poverty traps? A micro model of consumption growth in rural China.' *Journal of Applied Econometrics*, 17 (2002): 329–346.

Jalan, Jyotsna and Martin Ravallion. 'Spatial Poverty Traps.' Policy Research Working Paper 1862. Washington, DC: World Bank, December 1997.

Kanbur, Ravi, and Andy Sumner. 'Poor countries or poor people? Development assistance and the new geography of global poverty.' *Journal of International Development*, 24.6 (2012): 686–695.

Kanbur, Ravi, and Anthony J. Venables, eds. *Spatial Inequality and Development*. Oxford: Oxford University Press, 2005.

Krugman, Paul and Anthony J. Venables. 'Globalization and the Inequality of Nations.' *The Quarterly Journal of Economics*, 110.4 (1995): 857–880.

Levine, Ruth, ed. *Millions Saved: Proven successes in global health*. Vol. 3. No. 3. Peterson Institute, 2004.

Limão, Nuno, and Anthony J. Venables. 'Infrastructure, geographical disadvantage, transport costs, and trade.' *The World Bank Economic Review*, 15.3 (2001): 451–479.

Minot, Nicholas, Bob Baulch and Michael Epprecht. *Poverty and Inequality in Vietnam: Spatial patterns and geographic determinants*. Washington, DC: International Food Policy Research Institute, 2006.

Murphy, Michael. 'Self-determination as a collective capability: the case of indigenous peoples.' *Journal of Human Development and Capabilities*, 15.4 (2014): 320–334.

Nunn, Nathan, and Diego Puga. 'Ruggedness: the blessing of bad geography in Africa.' *Review of Economics and Statistics*, 94.1 (2012): 20–36.

Nussbaum, Martha. 2011. *Creating Capabilities: The human development approach*. Boston, MA: Harvard University Press.

Østby, Gudrun, Ragnhild Nordås and Jan Ketil Rød. 'Regional inequalities and civil conflict in sub-Saharan Africa.' *International Studies Quarterly*, 53.2 (2009): 301–324.

Ravallion, Martin, and Quentin Wodon. 'Poor areas, or only poor people?' *Journal of Regional Science*, 39.4 (1999): 689–711.

Redding, Stephen, and Anthony J. Venables. 'Economic geography and international inequality.' *Journal of international Economics*, 62.1 (2004): 53–82.

Rodrik, Dani, Francesco Trebbi and Arvind Subramanian. 'Institutions rule: the primacy of institutions over integration and geography in economic development.' International Monetary Fund, 2002.

Sachs, Jeffrey. 'Institutions Don't Rule: Direct Effects of Geography on Per Capita Income', National Bureau of Economic Research Working Paper No. 9490, February 2003.

Sachs, Jeffrey. 'Tropical Underdevelopment.' NBER Working Paper No. 8119. National Bureau of Economic Research, Cambridge, MA, 2001.

Sachs, Jeffrey, *et al.* 'Ending Africa's poverty trap.' *Brookings papers on economic activity*, 1 (2004): 117–240.

Sen, Amartya. 'Justice: means versus freedoms.' *Philosophy and Public Affairs*, 19 (1990): 111–121.

Sen, Amartya. 'A sociological approach to the measurement of poverty: a reply to Professor Peter Townsend.' *Oxford Economic Papers*, New Series, 37.4 (1985): 669–676.

Sen, Amartya. 'Poor, relatively speaking.' *Oxford Economic Papers*, New Series, 35.2 (1983): 153–169.

Sumner, Andy. 'Where Do the World's Poor Live? A New Update.' Institute for Development Studies Working Paper No. 393, June 2012.

Thorp, Rosemary, Frances Stewart and Amrik Heyer. 'When and how far is group formation a route out of chronic poverty?' *World Development*, 33.6 (2005): 907–920.

Woods, Dwayne. 'Latitude or rectitude: geographical or institutional determinants of development.' *Third World Quarterly* 25.8 (2004): 1405.

World Bank. *Accelerating Development Outcomes in Africa-Progress and Change in the Africa Action Plan*. Washington, DC, 2007.

World Development Report. *Reshaping Economic Geography*. Washington, DC: World Bank, 2009.

6 Gender and poverty

Serena Cosgrove

Key questions

- What are the relationships between gender roles, poverty and capabilities?
- Why has there been a move to discuss 'gender' and not just 'women'? What are some of the reasons for talking about 'men and masculinities'?
- Why do some economists say that 'beyond moral reasons, it makes economic sense to empower women'?
- What are examples of gender-related programming that can reduce poverty?

Vignette 6.1

Gladis is a young indigenous woman from Sololá, Guatemala (see Figure 6.1). In Central America, Guatemala still experiences high levels of violence even though the 30-year civil war ended in 1996. Guatemala enjoys a fairly high level of economic development at the aggregate level, but income inequality and poverty are severe for the country's majority Maya, comprised of over 20 different indigenous groups, most with their own languages. From an early age Gladis observed that her women relatives and women in her community suffered a lot, often in silence. Women were expected to have as many children as they could. Women were expected to do all the unpaid domestic work but simultaneously had to generate income because even if male partners or other relatives had income, it was often not enough to ensure the family could eat. According to Gladis, their culture says that men are better, that men are the only ones who have the right to study. Women only serve to work, to cook. Gladis saw how her women family members also did so much for their communities: active in church events, charity and service activities, and always stepped up to take care of the community when there was a crisis due to drought, bad weather or political crisis. Women work around the clock and seldom get to have fun or time off.

Gladis began to ask why women suffer so much. Why is it women's role to work so hard and suffer so much? How could it be that her culture dictates that women must suffer? Then Gladis had a flash of insight: culture isn't something that exists outside of us. We re-create culture through our actions. The point isn't to continue suffering but to transform these oppressive practices. So, Gladis began to talk to other young women in her community about their dreams. They wanted to study; they wanted to become professionals and serve their communities in new and more impactful ways. They wanted to be social workers, teachers, nurses and lawyers. They wanted to choose when they would marry and have children. They wanted to know about their legal rights, and they wanted to know more about their bodies because many didn't know how women actually get pregnant or why they have their periods.

These conversations led Gladis and this group of young women to form an organization. First, they sought out mentors from women's organizations to teach them the topics they wanted to know. Then they developed training materials to take to the schools where they teach girls and boys about the rights of young

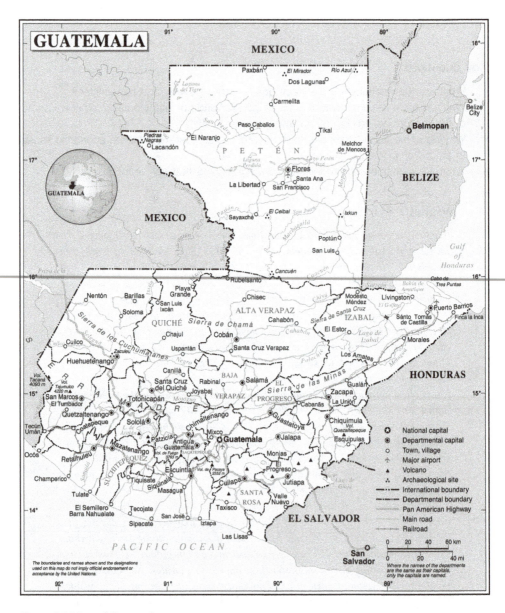

Figure 6.1 Map of Guatemala
Source: Map No. 3834 Rev. 3 UNITED NATIONS May 2004

women and men; and they teach basic sexual education. In this process, Gladis and her young women's group have begun to transform their own lives and the lives of others. They are transforming the very cultural limitations put on them. Through conversations with their elders, they're in active conversation about what aspects of their culture are vital for the community, such as values and practices around the importance of nature, community and family and speaking their own language. Today, Gladis continues to run this organization and each year a new cohort of young women take up teaching in the schools. Gladis is now in the second year of law school, working towards her career goal of defending women's and indigenous rights. Gladis not only found a way to start her college studies, but she decided to bring along other young women in her community, showing them that change is possible.

Introduction

Like Gladis, who is young, poor and indigenous, many women around the world face poverty and discrimination because they are women, but like Gladis, many women are deciding to do something about their marginalization and poverty by working with other women to create change. Many experts, international development practitioners and women's rights advocates support women's empowerment and leadership, agreeing that women and girls are the solution to not just their own poverty but global poverty. They argue that if women have equal access to education and opportunities, they will increase the economic and social development of themselves, their families and their countries. Because women are discriminated against in most societies in one way or another, transforming these inequalities can take many forms, such as striving to provide women and girls with equal access to food, education and health care; creating income-generating opportunities for women; or promoting women's civic and political participation. Women and girls are discriminated against in societies around the world due to culturally accepted hierarchies that preference men over women. Where discrimination against women is the highest, violence against women is exemplified by high levels of domestic abuse, honour killings, rape, molestation, sexual harassment, mass rape, feminicide – the systematic targeting and assassination of women – and increased rates of selective abortion of female foetuses and female infanticide.

Inequalities between men and women mean that women and girls are more vulnerable to poverty, illiteracy and ill health than men and boys. However, these oppressive gender roles limit women and girls as well as men and boys, though often in different ways. While women are expected to carry out caretaking roles at home, men are expected to enact fairly rigid masculinity and provider roles. Long-term change will require changes for all genders; men and women – as well as those who may not identify with a particular gender or transgender individuals – will have to participate in new ways of relating if more equitable conditions are to be achieved. The advantages that men are accorded in society mean that women – and often gender non-conforming people and transgender people – face discrimination and exclusion. Given the expectations on women to take care of children and the elderly, their poverty means they have fewer resources to take care of their children and others who depend upon them. The number of people affected by a woman's poverty is exponential if you count her dependants and extended family members who rely upon her to take care of them. If women are discriminated against in a society, it can also mean they have difficulty accessing needed services for their sexual and reproductive health; this can lead to unwanted pregnancy, maternal mortality and child morbidity. Also due to poverty and women's low position in society, sometimes parents are compelled to sell their daughters to pay for food or debts for the rest of the family: this contributes to increasing levels of enslavement and human trafficking.

In the agencies of the United Nations, in the programmes of many international and local non-governmental organizations, and among many of the world's governments, there is a call to invest in women and girls by supporting programmes for women to access leadership positions, increased educational and vocational opportunities, and skill development. Yet, the international development research, advocacy efforts and policy papers also point to how women and girls are targets for discrimination: 35 per cent of women worldwide suffer from domestic violence (WHO 2013), over 100 million women are missing due to sex ratio imbalances caused by parents choosing abortion when they learned the sex of the child (Sen 1990, 1999, Sev'er 2011), they are trafficked into brothels and the sex trade, and women are often the poorest of the poor (see Klasen 2004, Chant 2006).

The goal of this chapter is to explore the connection between women's *and* men's roles in society and how this connects to poverty, but it is also very important to understand the ways in which women are simultaneously key contributors to their communities, not just at home but within their communities and across the countries where they live. Often women are the ones to volunteer on community development projects or set up soup kitchens and lead advocacy efforts during economic or political crisis (Cosgrove 2010). They are involved in many aspects of daily human surviving and thriving because of their culturally ascribed roles as caretakers. In this chapter, I examine women's vulnerability to poverty and the multidimensionality of this phenomenon. Women aren't just more likely to earn less income than men; they're also more likely to suffer diminished capabilities and functionings. Unpacking the connection between gender and poverty will lead to an analysis of how women's agency, empowerment and incorporation into development can benefit all in countries around the world.

Gender and poverty

Since the 1990s, many international development agencies and experts have claimed that 70 per cent of the world's poor are women and children (see Klasen 2004, Chant 2006) due to systemic discrimination and violence against women. Though the actual statistic is debated, there is a consensus – corroborated by UNIFEM and other international development agencies – that women often face greater deprivation than men in regards to income and economic participation, education, certain health-related issues, and political representation. In fact, women are often over-utilized and required to work at home and outside the home to compensate for family deprivation during economic and political crises (Chant 2006). Furthermore, the deficiency of data on these topics indicates that governments, researchers and international agencies need to increase their measurement of development indicators by gender as well as measuring the gaps and costs that women's inequality generates. (Klasen 2004, Chant 2006) The fact that this has not happened yet indicates that gender blindness – not seeing how the differences between men and women can adversely affect women – endures when it comes to measurement and assessment. As shown in Box 6.2, women and girls experience greater deprivation and lack of opportunities compared to men and boys across a range of indicators. Interestingly, these findings are not just corroborated by quantitative studies but also by qualitative, ethnographic studies and investigative journalism.

The causes of women's and girls' discrimination and vulnerability can be found in the inequalities that preference men's opportunities, access to resources, and decision-making abilities over women's. To understand why this happens and identify ways to address this problem, we have to look at the differences between men and women and examine the gendered messages that reinforce difference. Gender – akin to other social constructs of difference such as ethnicity and race – is defined as the culturally ascribed roles for masculine and feminine behaviour (Russo 2006, Cosgrove 2010). Though gender roles for appropriate masculine and feminine behaviour are often linked to biological sexual differences, this definition has been expanding in recent years to include people who don't identify with the gender binary of men and women, and identify as gender non-conforming, a-gender, gender queer or as transgender, meaning that their gender identity differs from the sex they were assigned at birth. Furthermore, there are societies in around the world with more than two genders, showing the gender binary is not universal. Even so, dominant gender roles in many cultures around the world continue to impose a gender binary on people, which includes all the messages, expectations and sanctioning behaviours that convey what it means to be a man and a woman in a given society. Gender responds to expectations for how individual men and women should act, which in turn become customary modes of behaviour that inform everyday life and relations between people. These expectations are 'built into the major social organizations of society, such as the economy, ideology, the family, and politics, and is also an entity in and of itself' (Lorber 1994: 1). These messages are perpetuated by social, economic and political institutions – including the media, the family, schools and other institutions – and thereby socialized, internalized, and reproduced by members of a particular culture or social group.

Gender isn't egalitarian because it grants preferential treatment to men over women in most cultures around the world. Gender includes the social relations between men and women, in which women are subordinated to men (Moser 1993: 3) and have less power, privilege and resources than men (Russo 2006). In patriarchal cultures where fathers and male relatives exercise power over women, women are not allowed to make basic decisions that affect their lives. This means that often they don't get to choose how to spend income they earn; they don't get to choose whether they get to continue school or have to get married; and they don't get to decide when and if they will have children. Because gender means different levels of access, the term 'gender hierarchy' has been coined to refer to situations in which masculinity is synonymous with 'social power and control over labour, resources, and products are associated with masculinity' (Gailey 1988: 32). Structures of subordination translate into men having more tacitly accepted power at home and in the community as well as access to formal positions of power than women. This means that often women simultaneously don't have access to power or the opportunity to make decisions that affect their lives or those for whom they are responsible. In many countries, women – whether married or not – often have limited control when it comes to their own health care, large purchases, daily purchases, and even what food to cook (UNIFEM 2008). To sum up, gender means that often women are denied access to basic capabilities, assets and income opportunities necessary for their wellbeing and agency: gender inequalities mean increased risk of poverty for people who are disadvantaged due to their gender identity, such as women, girls, transgender people and the family members who depend upon them for their own wellbeing. Obviously, gender is not the sole factor that explains differences between the experiences of certain women and men, because their lives are not determined just by gender roles but by other forms of difference as well.

As an analytical tool, looking at a situation from a gender perspective encourages a more comprehensive understanding of a given social reality by allowing us to look at how it affects women, how it affects gender-nonconforming people and how it affects men. Since gender defines appropriate masculine and feminine behaviour, using a gender perspective facilitates understanding how women and men experience particular realities in different ways, be it at an individual, family, community or institutional level. If gender roles mean that men have more power than women, then looking at how women and men have different experiences will reveal the power differential and provide a lens into understanding discrimination and marginalization. Examining social reality from the perspective of women allows the observer to trace how women are affected or accommodate this treatment, but it also provides the opportunity to examine how women resist or try to change these patterns.

Gender and capabilities

Many who write on the capabilities approach pay particular attention to how forms of social and economic difference such as gender, sexuality, race and class, among others, can lead to diminished capabilities and functionings of individuals. Access to important capabilities such as education, health and income, but also political participation, is often less for women due to gender messages that preference men over women, but importantly, women's functionings are also limited: though they might have the legal entitlement, women are often stymied in how much they can realize their capabilities (functionings) due to discrimination and gender-based violence (Robeyns 2003). Though a woman may be legally entitled to go to school or work, she may live in a society in which a father or a husband makes this decision for her. Amartya Sen argues that women's wellbeing and their agency – exercising their roles as members of a society and participants in economic, social and political actions – are both important, mutually reinforcing capabilities; women's wellbeing is always at risk if their agency is being systematically limited due to sexism (Sen 1999). As philosophers have continued to interrogate Sen's reluctance to suggest a definitive list of capabilities, Robeyns (2003) raises the important concern that, depending on the capability, women may appear more advantaged than men; for example, in many societies around the world, women live longer lives than men. A commitment to addressing gender inequality thus necessarily entails a careful review of which capabilities are essential so that women's inequality doesn't get invisibilized. In parts of the world where women's discrimination is the strongest, the male–female sex ratios at birth are uneven. There are more boys born than girls. This is due to the selective abortion of female foetuses. Obviously, this is the deprivation of life that does not affect males. When women are systematically denied sufficient food and health care as children because their families prioritize the health of male children, women's entitlements to health are being denied. The same limitations are placed on women's and girls' capabilities and functioning when male children's education is given priority over theirs.

Other academics influenced by the capabilities approach have studied how accepted gendered expectations become habitual – accepted as normal by many, including women themselves. (Klasen 2004, Khader 2011) This explains why many women may not even be aware they are discriminated against and don't find their situations problematic: they have had no other experience of how life might be. These 'adaptive preferences' mean that women have adapted their outlooks to their circumstances and don't question that men receive better treatment than they do in their societies. Adaptive preferences, according to Serene Khader, are 'formed in response to unjust social arrangements that are incompatible with a person's basic wellbeing' (2012: 303) and thereby limit that person's capabilities and functionings. Careful distinction needs to be applied here: just because a person may not recognize that they're disadvantaged due to these preferences does not mean that the person lacks agency or has been brainwashed, because there is a lot of research about how women negotiate, challenge and subvert limitations that are placed on their behaviour. Many capabilities proponents argue that the discrimination and gender bias women face have to be addressed by more than a call for cultural change, which can take generations, but has to be led by governments and state institutions which can protect women's rights and foment opportunities for them. For this reason, many programmes focus on the accountability of governments to enforce laws and protect women's rights. This is also why there is a push to get more women into political leadership positions and security forces: more women in these roles will mean that it's that much easier to increase women's inclusion.

Gender discrimination

There are hidden aspects of the discrimination that women face such as having to work a double day – income generation and family responsibilities (Klasen 2004) – or a triple day – income generation, unpaid care work (UNIFEM 2005) and community activism

---

Box 6.1 Unpaid care work

The term 'unpaid care work' is used to refer to the provision of services within households for other household and community members. It avoids the ambiguities of other terms, including 'domestic labour', which can refer both to unpaid care work and the work of paid domestic workers; 'unpaid labour', which can refer to unpaid care work as well as unpaid work in the family business; 'reproductive work', which can refer to unpaid care work as well as giving birth and breastfeeding; and 'home work', which can refer to paid work done in the home on subcontract basis from an employer. Each word in the term 'unpaid care work' is important:

- 'UNPAID' means that the person doing the activity does not receive a wage for it.
- 'CARE' means that the activity serves people and their wellbeing.
- 'WORK' means that the activity has a cost in terms of time and energy and arises out of a social or contractual obligation, such as marriage or less formal social relationships.

(Summarized from UNIFEM 2005)

(see Chant 2006: 206–207, 214, Cosgrove 2010: 10–11). This *triple burden* (Craske 2003: 67) means that women from poor communities are often working around the clock to guarantee their families' survival. Women's triple work day – comprised of unpaid care work (family and domestic care), income generation and community development responsibilities – is a useful analytical lens for bringing attention to how hard women are working, but it does divide women's activities into separate categories. Many women, for example, carry out their responsibilities simultaneously or in an interspersed manner rather than separately ... taking care of children while selling at the market or participating in income-generating activities as part of a community development project. This multi-layered, simultaneous and dense set of activities includes taking care of family members, generating income and even leading a group of people to achieve a certain goal.

In addition to working around the clock because of the gendered expectations that inform their lives, women also face gender discrimination in the workplaces of their societies. Women make up the majority of those who generate their income in the informal sector, earning income as marketers, itinerant saleswomen and service providers (childcare, cleaning, cooking, etc.) without receiving benefits or state protections. When women do get formal sector jobs, they comprise the majority of manufacturing and service sector jobs where employees earn less than in other sectors. Women predominate in sectors that are associated with women's caretaking roles in the family, working in fields such as education, nursing and social work which often are remunerated less than occupations where men predominate. Though exact ratios are debated, there is agreement that when women do enter the labour force in sectors where men predominate, they are paid less than men.

These economic and employment discrepancies are perpetuated by legal frameworks and political institutions that allow the discrepancies to continue. Though the rates of women in ministerial positions and legislatures are on the rise, men still predominate, with notable exceptions like Rwanda (67 per cent women legislators) and parity of women in a couple of European countries (UNIFEM 2008). The discrimination and exclusion of women continues, in part, because there is still an education gap for women and girls as well as for vocational training and education for women. If women can't get educations, then they can't get jobs and improve their lives. The status quo of gender discrimination gets reinforced by widely held beliefs that women are different from men when it comes to doing certain things, and women exist to serve their families and their men. These cultural constructs – ideas that are reproduced by groups of people – can change, but this takes time and sustained effort. Today, many of you reading this text may have been raised by mothers and fathers who both worked, or you've been raised by your dads, or you've been given role models that reinforce non-traditional gender roles. But for many girls and young women in the developing world or in less-resourced families in the developed world, they don't have a lot of freedom to challenge oppressive gender roles: this can lead to their discrimination, but also limits their agency or ability to chart their actions, life choices and goals. As you continue reading this chapter, think about what life might be like for a young woman from a country ranked low in terms of human development: will she even be able to go to school? Will she have to get married young and drop out of school if she was able to go to school? Will she be able to work outside of the house when she's an adult?

In addition to the gender discrimination and subordination that can restrict women and girls in their livelihoods, there is another factor of gender subordination that affects

Box 6.2 Women and the economy

Introduction

Expanding women's participation in the workforce isn't just something that shows off a company's commitment to diversity. It has powerful, positive and measureable results. Academics, policy makers and business leaders assert that long-term economic growth requires the expanded participation of women in the workforce. 'Greater representation of women in senior leadership positions within governments and financial institutions is vital not only to find solutions to the current economic turmoil, but to stave off such crises in the future', says Klaus Schwab, Founder and Executive Chairman of the World Economic Forum.

Economic force

The economic benefits of investing in women are self-evident when you consider that women reinvest 90 per cent of their income in their families and communities compared to men who reinvest only 30 to 40 per cent.

Occupational and wage disparities

Despite their obvious potential, women do not enjoy the full benefits of participation in the workforce. In 2005, women accounted for roughly 40 per cent of the world's economically active population. But in most developing countries, women in the labour force work longer hours than men, earn significantly less when doing so, and spend more time on unpaid tasks such as household work.

Critical mass

'From supporting micro-enterprise in the Global South to assuring gender parity in the executive suite, investing in women is the smartest economic venture that the corporate world can undertake', says The White House Project's Marie Wilson. 'Decades of research have proven that adding women to the leadership mix not only begets creative solutions and a focus on long-term results, but also higher profits. Advancing women is more than a powerful tool for advancing communities alone; it is also a critical tool for advancing the bottom line.'

(Summarized from Ernst and Young 2009)

women and girls worldwide. Gender-based violence has been defined as 'any act that results in, or is likely to result in physical, sexual, or psychological harm or suffering to women, including threats of such acts, coercion or arbitrary deprivation of liberty, whether occurring in public or private life' (Russo and Pirlott 2006: 181). As a result of the pervasive nature of this phenomenon, one in three women worldwide will face abuse or sexual violence in her lifetime. This is not a problem just for women in the developing or developed worlds: many women in most societies face threats of violence at home or out in the world. For instance, in the United States one in four women will be raped while at college, according to a Department of Justice report (Sampson 2002: 2). Also in the United States, 25 per cent of women will be affected by domestic violence in their families. The situation is also very serious for women in the developing world. In addition to high rates of risk of sexual assault and domestic violence, gender-based violence also manifests itself in such actions as female gender mutilation and high rates of abortion of girls while in utero compared to boys. In his work on capabilities, Amartya Sen was one of the first to use the term 'missing women' in which he quantified how selective abortions were leading to increased rates of births of males in places in the world where boy children are preferred over girls.

Another gender-based practice that leads to acts of violence enacted on women's bodies is female genital mutilation (FGM). This coming of age practice involves the full or partial removal of girls' external genitalia. Ending FGM will not be achieved solely by decrying its practitioners as barbaric, nor will the behaviours simply be changed because the law changes to make it illegal in a particular country. Though legal frameworks and the implementation of laws are very important, there must be buy-in from local communities. Long-term change resides in supporting the efforts of local leaders and communities to create new cultural forms to replace the old ones. In many societies, FGM emerged as a cultural practice acknowledging women were of the age to marry; the practice also served to control women's sexuality and assure their fidelity, but today, it may not be as relevant to lines of succession and property rights as it may once have been. FGM is performed on girls by traditional circumcisers, often older women; in countries where FGM is practised, it is a rite of passage for girls, a form of employment for those who practise the ritual, and women are expected to have this when they marry. Stopping FGM will require addressing all these aspects through the formation of new cultural practices for girls' rite of passage into adulthood, income generation for the women who perform the operation, and cultural change from societies where women aren't considered marriageable without it. For this reason, transforming harmful culture practices requires a long-term view and must have a bottom-up approach; change is seldom accepted and acted upon just because another country or institution says something should be done differently.

Box 6.3 Missing women

To get an idea of the numbers of people involved in the ratios of women to men, we can estimate the number of 'missing women' in a country, say, China or India, by calculating the number of extra women who would have been in China or India if these countries had the same ratio of women to men as calculated in areas of the world in which they receive similar care. In China alone this amounts to 50 million 'missing women', taking 1.05 as the benchmark ratio. When that number is added to those in South Asia, West Asia and North Africa, a great many more than 100 million women are 'missing'. These numbers tell us, quietly, a terrible story of inequality and neglect leading to the excess mortality of women.

(Sen 1990 and 1999)

Not all members of groups separated by difference such as gender, race, ethnicity or class are discriminated against equally. Because the category 'women' refers to so many different kinds of human beings from an immense diversity of cultural, ethnic, religious and social class backgrounds, researchers, development practitioners and we, as well, need to be cognizant of these differences and not make claims that all women are alike. As all women are not alike, all people who find themselves in a particular racial category are not alike either: some will have advantages through education, socioeconomic status and gender that others do not. Rather, actions and choices are informed by gender and other forms of social difference such as sexual orientation, life events and circumstances, race, ethnicity, education, socioeconomic class, ability and political activism. This is why *intersectionality* – or the effects of combined forms of social difference – needs to be taken into account: some women – like Gladis mentioned at the beginning of this chapter – hold multiple stigmatizing identities (young, woman and indigenous, for example) and face even more discrimination than other women in their societies (Russo 2006).

What happens when multiple forms of social difference intersect? What kinds of different opportunities do poor white women have compared to African Americans in the United States, for instance? 'The social experience of being white, poor, and female, for instance, cannot be meaningfully separated into the distinct categories of race, socioeconomic status, and gender. The social context of affluence is not the same experience for African Americans as it is for whites, being unmarried is not the same social experience for men as it is for women' (Roxburgh 2009: 359). When multiple forms of difference intersect to place someone at a disadvantaged position, the results can lead to extreme limitations of capabilities and functionings, suffering and oppression. Rural indigenous women in Guatemala, like Gladis and the women with whom she works, are discriminated against by the broader Guatemalan society and the government, but also by their own families. Often these women comprise the poorest of the poor, and they have to contend with gender discrimination within their families and communities as well. They are discriminated against because they are indigenous and because they are young women. This phenomenon can be seen in numerous countries around the world; the most vulnerable sectors of society are also most often those with the least participation, representation and opportunities to change their situations. This is why it is so important to support the efforts of people themselves when they do become aware of their rights and seek fair redress for their situations or opportunities for education, health care and advancement.

Gender and development

Vignette 6.2

Many experts, peacebuilders and women's rights activists claim that the Democratic Republic of the Congo is the worst place to be a woman (Figure 6.2). In Congo the civil war of the 1990s and ensuing regional war led to the extensive practice of sexual assault by army soldiers and rebel groups who were ordered to rape and sexually assault women, girls, boys and some men to prove local leaders could not protect their own. It is in the cities – as well as displaced people's camps and marginalized urban communities – where people have arrived fleeing violence in the countryside that sexual assault, molestation and sexual harassment are still

Figure 6.2 Map of Democratic Republic of the Congo
Source: Map No. 4007 Rev. 11 UNITED NATIONS May 2016

on the rise. *Young women – often minors – are raped or coerced into having sex in exchange for food or household goods and then find themselves pregnant. Traditional values that reinforce sex only in the context of marriage are used against these young women by their families, communities and institutions, and they are shunned, ostracized from society and forced to deal with their situations on their own as best they can.*

At a local non-governmental organization in Goma, a city in eastern Congo, young mothers come together for vocational training and training in human and women's rights. In turn, these women take what they've learned and visit schools, displaced people's camps and other institutions to talk with girls, boys, young women and young men about health, hygiene and birth control. These young women, who have been shunned by their own families and societies, find empowerment through trying to change the very circumstances that have led to their ill treatment. Marie said, 'The camp where we went to make our presentations is calling us to come back and teach others.' Others echoed her sentiments: 'Many people don't know about these subjects and are thirsty for knowledge', 'I went to the school and got permission to talk with the students about family planning', 'I have kept track of who I've talked with; each of us talks with 90 people every month', 'It is very important for us to work to bring awareness to as many people as possible given how important the messages are that we have to share.' These young women have decided that education and knowledge are the way to transform the way young women are treated, and they're raising awareness about these issues. (Adapted from Cosgrove 2016)

This example from the Democratic Republic of the Congo depicts how a group of teen mothers are educating other teens about gender-based violence, women's health and other related topics in Democratic Republic of the Congo. Not only are these girls trying to help other girls not get pregnant, they are working with young men to transform their ideas about women. Even more, these women are giving workshops in local schools and other public institutions and demanding that their government actually enforce the laws which exist on paper to protect women's rights. Even though gender-based violence and gender inequality are deeply rooted and pernicious, there is so much that can be done to transform the problems. Women's non-governmental organizations like the one that provided the Congolese teen mothers with training and support can help address the challenges that women face. At the national and international levels, social movements in the form of women's movements and other like-minded organizations, such as self-help groups and community associations, coordinate actions, advocate for change and even carry out projects together. International non-governmental organizations can provide funding, capacity strengthening and project implementation at the local and national levels as well as advocacy at the international level. The United Nations has a number of different agencies that target women's development: UNIFEM, OSAGI, DAW, INSTRAW and the new agency: UN Agency for Gender Equality and the Empowerment of Women (Visvanathan 2011). All of these organizations are important and can make a difference. But, it is important never to let governments off the hook: they are obliged to protect the rights of their citizens and guarantee the implementation of these rights. Women themselves can organize and demand change and increased accountability from government through voting, lobbying, civic engagement and getting the word out using the media: this is called vertical accountability (UNIFEM 2008), in which women and others committed to women's equality and empowerment work through local NGOs and social movements to leverage change in national and international government institutions. The branches of government – legislative, executive and judicial – can seek to pass laws and then guarantee their implementation through the facilitation of resources, training and sensitization, and programming. This is called horizontal accountability (UNIFEM 2008) as it involves change and coordination among governmental offices and agencies.

At an international level, international agencies and non-governmental organizations can provide funding and facilitate training to support locally led programmes that empower and train women leaders and the organizations they run. International efforts can support the capacity building of public sector efforts to address these problems. Together, international efforts and government programming – such as affirmative action policies in employment and education, quotas for women's political participation, and access to credit for business loans – can promote women's increased participation, income generation and leadership opportunities.

At the international level, development efforts have evolved over the past decades in how they have targeted women and gender inequality. In the 1960s and 1970s, as social scientists began to carry out research about women's discrimination and how it contributed to poverty, new programming was designed to address the situation.

The Women in Development agenda was created to ensure women also benefited from modernization and development efforts (Rai 2011). The focus was on supporting women's participation in society through women's income generation projects, for example, but not on transforming gender relations between men and women. Women in Development proponents advocated for legal and economic reform, believing that unjust gender relations would change automatically as women become income earners. Though many of these projects were successful in the short term, increased income does not mean that women have control over the income or increased agency in society.

Critiques of the Women in Development approach led international agencies, particularly the agencies of the United Nations, to focus on gender relations (Rai 2011). Development efforts that focus on gender – women and men – are often referred to as 'gender and development' initiatives and include a broad range of local, national and international strategies aimed at transforming oppressive gender roles and increasing women's agency and participation, not just wellbeing. These efforts focused on the gender differences and expectations for women at home and in the labour force, access to and control over resources, and the material and social rewards that men and women receive in different contexts (Rai 2011). 'There is now an international consensus that "men are both part of the problem and part of the solution" for achieving gender justice and equality' (Wanner and Wadham 2015: 28). Men – who are often in a position to facilitate access for women, be it at home, in the workplace or in society at large – need to be included in gender-sensitive development efforts – particularly training and consciousness-raising efforts – for a number of reasons: (1) when men and boys know about (and have sensitivity towards) women's rights, they are in a position to advocate for women's rights, and (2) men's privileged position in society means they have more access to positions of power; so if they see themselves as partners in women's empowerment, they can help change the structural and institutional barriers to women's advancement.

Pressure is being applied to international development efforts, especially gender and development programmes, to include men in gender-sensitization efforts and development programming as well (Wanner and Wadham 2015). Empowering women and not training men as well can lead to dire consequences for women who go home armed with knowledge about their rights but with few other resources to protect themselves against violence. Supporting women in productive projects without opportunities for men can reinforce messages that men are failures and not good providers. This lack of programming can reinforce gender messages that women can do it all. In fact, there is some concern that because of economic crises and uneven economic development, there is actually a crisis of masculinity in which men – unable to fulfil their role as providers – have lost self-esteem and decreased their abilities to help their families (Chant 2006, Cosgrove 2010). For all of these reasons, it is important to work with men and women, girls and boys, as well as all sectors of society, to ensure the basic capabilities and functionings of women as well as those of men are fulfilled.

'Gender and development' efforts also received criticism because they focused on gender relations as separate from other development priorities. This led to gender mainstreaming, in which international agencies and even governments are expected to integrate a gender perspective into all policies and programming (Prugl and Lustgarten 2006). The UN Economic and Social Council described it as 'the process of assessing the implication for women and men of any planned action, including legislation, policies or programmes, in any area and at all levels' (cited in Prugl and Lustgarten 2006). Though many agree that it is important to carry out gender analysis in institutions, not just in target communities, mainstreaming has led to assumptions that a gender perspective is now cross-cutting. The problem is that there is uneven implementation of mainstreaming efforts across institutions due to differences in funding, leadership, training, cultural views and commitment. Where once there may have been a gender office in a particular agency, now there have been trainings of staff and the gender experts have been spread across the organizations.

These different approaches have attempted to include women and address unequal gender relations. There have been many achievements: the Women in Development approach brought attention to women as economic agents who needed opportunities and assets to generate income; 'gender and development' efforts moved the focus from women to gender relations between men and women, arguing that gender roles for both men and women needed to change; and finally gender mainstreaming has attempted to make gender something all employees in all development agencies take into account when carrying out their work. Furthermore, academic research and impact assessments about the effectiveness of programming targeting women or transforming unequal gender relations have led to a robust literature in which quantitative and qualitative research is being used to improve programming. From the randomized control trials of the Massachusetts Institute of Technology's Poverty Action Lab in which the impact of microcredit or health projects on poor women are investigated to in-depth impact assessments over time in communities, there are more data about what works and doesn't work, which can lead to improved efficiency and effectiveness of programming. However, given the complexity of transforming gender relations and cultural messages that limit women, it is also important to work with institutions such as the media, the business sector and political leaders to reinforce new messages. These changes, in turn, must be supported by changes in legal frameworks, individual laws, enforcement, and resource allocation so that they protect women and their capabilities, on one hand, and help level the playing field so women can occupy leadership positions as well as gaining access. These cultural and political transformations will only be sustained if there are economic changes so that women can participate in the labour force, so that they receive equitable reimbursement for their work, aren't consigned to the informal sector, and have local opportunities so they aren't pushed to leave their own countries.

Conclusion

When women gain knowledge about their rights, receive an education so they can read and write, and obtain the tools to generate income, they are able to employ themselves and support their families and meet their obligations towards their children and families. Women invest 90 per cent of their earnings back into their families while men only bring home 40 per cent (Ernst and Young 2009). It makes good sense to invest in women's empowerment, but it also makes good sense to invest in increasing men's awareness of how their decisions and their privilege affect their partners and children. Long-term change for women requires transforming gender roles so men and women can share family responsibilities and feel that they have agency in their lives, communities and societies. This can happen through the efforts of women themselves to achieve change, education and training of both genders, the support of governments and international agencies, and long-term sustained cultural change.

This chapter began with the story of Gladis, a young indigenous woman in Guatemala, who has grown up seeing that women's lot in life is suffering. Indigenous women in Guatemala face discrimination for their ethnicity, thereby limiting their economic, educational and social opportunities. Women have little control over their bodies and sexuality, leading to high rates of teenage pregnancy and vulnerability to sexual violence. We read about a similar dynamic for poor young women in Democratic Republic of the Congo. In both cases, we read about young women advocating for change; they are not just waiting for governments and organizations to assure their protection. The empowerment of women is best exemplified by women who believe their lives can be different and organize together to achieve that change.

Discussion questions

1   How would you compare and contrast the challenges and opportunities that women have in the developing world and the developed world? Girls? Transgender people?
2   For many years, international development efforts focused on women's empowerment rather than focusing on gender relations. What are the pros and cons of each approach?
3   Gender relations that lead to discrimination against women often have their roots in cultural, historical, economic and political institutions that have evolved over long periods of time. Whose responsibility is it to address this unfair treatment? Governments? International organizations? Women's organizations? Women themselves? Women and men? Justify your answer.
4   Gender activity: Get out a piece of paper and write a line down the middle of the page. On the left side write down characteristics of what it means to be a good man in the place where you're from. On the right side, write down what it means to be a good woman. Then, next to each point, describe where that message comes from: media/TV, family, school etc. Then reflect on how you embody or challenge the messages you receive. If culture is one of the reasons women have less power than men, we can choose to transform some of the elements we manifest through our genders.

Further reading

Adichie, Chimamanda Ngozi. 2015. *We Should All Be Feminists.* New York City, NY: Anchor Books.

Adichie, Chimamanda Ngozi. 2003. *Purple Hibiscus: A novel.* New York City, NY: Anchor Books.

Bulawayo, NoViolet. 2013. *We Need New Names.* London: Chatto & Windus.

Coleman, Isobel. 2010. *Paradise beneath her Feet: How women are transforming the Middle East.* New York City, NY: Random House.

Cosgrove, Serena. 2010. *Leadership from the Margins: Women and civil society organizations in Argentina, Chile, and El Salvador.* New Brunswick, NJ: Rutgers University Press.

Danticat, Edwidge. 1994. *Breath, Eyes, Memory.* New York, NY: Vintage Books.

Ehrenreich, Barbara and Arlie Russell Hochschild, eds. 2004. *Global Woman: Nannies, maids, and sex workers in the new economy.* New York City, NY: Henry Holt.

Kristof, Nicholas and Sheryl WuDunn. 2009. *Half the Sky: Turning oppression in opportunity for women worldwide.* New York, NY: Random House.

Menchu, Rigoberta. 1984. *I, Rigoberta Menchu: An Indian woman in Guatemala.* New York City, NY: Verso.

Works cited

Chant, Sylvia. 'Rethinking the 'Feminization of Poverty' in relation to aggregate gender indices', *Journal of Human Development*, 7.2 (2006): 201–220.

Coleman, Isobel. 'The payoff from women's rights.' *Foreign Affairs*, 83.3 (2004): 80–95.

Cosgrove, Serena. 2016. 'The Absent State: Teen Mothers and New Patriarchal Forms of Gender Subordination in Democratic Republic of Congo', in Sanford, Victoria, Katerina Stefatos and Cecilia Salvi, eds. *The State and Gender Violence*. New Brunswick, NJ: Rutgers University Press.

Cosgrove, Serena. 2010. *Leadership from the Margins: Women and civil society organizations in Argentina, Chile, and El Salvador*. New Brunswick, NJ: Rutgers University Press.

Ernst and Young. 2009. Groundbreakers: Using the strength of women to rebuild the world economy. (Accessed 29 October 2016: www.vitalvoices.org/sites/default/files/uploads/Ground breakers.pdf)

Gailey, Christine. 1988. 'Evolutionary Perspectives on Gender Hierarchy', in Hess, B. and M. Ferree, eds. *Analyzing Gender*, 32–67. London: Sage.

Khader, Serene. 'Must theorising about adaptive preferences deny women's agency?' *Journal of Applied Philosophy*, 29.4 (2012): 302–317.

Khader, Serene. 2011. *Adaptive Preferences and Women's Empowerment*. New York, NY: Oxford University Press.

Klasen, Stephan. 2004. *Gender-Related Indicators of Well-Being*. Discussion Papers/Universität Göttingen, Ibero-Amerika-Institut für Wirtschaftsforschung, No. 102. (Accessed 26 April 2015: www.econstor. eu/handle/10419/23863)

Lorber, Judith. 1994. *Paradoxes of Gender*. New Haven, CT: Yale University Press.

Moser, Caroline O. N. 1993. *Gender Planning and Development: Theory, practice and training*. New York, NY: Routledge.

Prugl, Elisabeth, and Audrey Lustgarten. 2006. 'Mainstreaming Gender in International Organizations', in Jaquette, Jane S. and Gale Summerfield, eds. *Women and Gender Equity in Development Theory and Practice: Institutions, resources, and mobilization*. Durham, NC: Duke University Press.

Rai, Shirin M. 2011. 'Gender and Development: Theoretical perspectives', in *The Women, Gender and Development Reader* (2nd edn). London: Zed Books.

Robeyns, Ingrid. 'Sen's capability approach and gender inequality: selecting relevant capabilities', *Feminist Economics*, 9.2–3 (2003): 61–92.

Roxburgh, Susan. 'Untangling inequalities: gender, race, and socioeconomic differences in depression.' *Sociological Forum*, 24.2 (2009): 357–381.

Russo, Nancy Felipe, and Angela Pirlott. 'Gender-based violence.' *Annals of the New York Academy of Sciences*, 1087.1 (2006): 178–205.

Sampson, Rana. 2002. *Acquaintance Rape of College Students*. Problem-Oriented Guides for Police Series 17. US Department of Justice Office of Community Oriented Policing Services. (Accessed 26 April 2015: www.cops.usdoj.gov/pdf/e03021472.pdf)

Sen, Amartya. 1999. *Development as Freedom*. New York, NY: Anchor Books.

Sen, Amartya. 1990. 'More than 100 Million Women are Missing', *New York Review of Books*. (Accessed 26 April 2015: www.nybooks.com/articles/archives/1990/dec/20/more-than-100-million-women-are-missing/)

Sev'er, Aysan. 2011. 'Discarded daughters: The Patriarchal Grip, Dowry Deaths, Sex Ration Imbalances and Foeticide in India', in Visvanathan, Nalini, Lynn Duggan, Nan Wiegersma and Laurie Nisonoff, eds. *The Women, Gender and Development Reader* (2nd edn). London: Zed Books.

United Nations Development Fund for Women (UNIFEM). 2008. 'Progess of the world's women 2008/2009: Who answers to women? Gender and Accountability.' (Accessed 8 April 2017: www.unifem.org/progress/2008/media/POWW08_Report_Full_Text.pdf)

United Nations Development Fund for Women (UNIFEM). 2005. 'Progress of the world's women: Women, work, and poverty.' (Accessed 8 April 2017: https://www.un-ngls.org/orf/women-2005.pdf)

Visvanathan, Nalini, Lynn Duggan, Nan Wiegersma and Laurie Nisonoff, eds. 2011. *The Women, Gender and Development Reader* (2nd edn). London: Zed Books.

Wanner, Thomas, and Ben Wadham. 'Men and masculinities in international development: "men-streaming" gender and development?' *Development Policy Review*, 33.1 (2015): 15–32.

World Health Organization. 2013. 'Global and regional estimates of violence against women: prevalence and health effects of intimate partner violence and nonpartner sexual violence.' (Accessed 29 October 2016: http://apps.who.int/iris/bitstream/10665/85239/1/9789241564625_eng.pdf)

7 State institutions, governance and poverty

Benjamin Curtis

Key questions

- What do we mean by 'governance' and 'institutions'?
- How do governance and institutions contribute to poverty?
- Why do bad or inadequate governance/institutions happen?
- What can be done to promote better governance and institutions to benefit human development?

Vignette 7.1

As we drove up to the intersection, an electronic sign indicated that there were four seconds left before the traffic lights would turn. We slowed, the light turned to yellow, and we stopped. A traffic cop stood on one of the corners and nodded at us pleasantly. Our driver nodded back and said to us, 'You don't have to fear the police. You can always ask them a question or ask for help if you need it.' For many of us raised in high-income countries, this anecdote seems so commonplace as not to warrant recounting, much less inclusion in a book on causes and solutions to global poverty. But this event did not occur in some comfortable, affluent suburb in the rich world – it occurred in Rwanda, where in 1994 the extremist Hutu government, militias and paramilitary groups perpetrated a genocide that killed around 850,000 Tutsis and moderate Hutus.

The government that took power after the genocide was headed by President Paul Kagame, the leader of the rebel forces that fought the Hutu extremists. Though much of what state institutions provide – laws, law enforcement, courts, public services and infrastructure – had been destroyed during the genocide, President Kagame vowed to rebuild the country and make it an example of the type of development and prosperity African countries can achieve. From utter calamity in 1994, Rwanda has made significant progress, in 2015 ranking 163 out of 188 countries on the Human Development Index and 44 out of 168 on the Corruption Perceptions Index. Needless to say, Rwanda is still a poor country, but it is definitely not a failed state. From functioning traffic lights to police who can be trusted, our research trip to Rwanda operated quite smoothly. Even when leaving the capital to drive to the border with the Democratic Republic of the Congo, we were happy to find good, paved roads that reached out across the country. When work was being done on the road, highway workers organized the traffic so everyone could get to their destination promptly and in an orderly fashion.

This picture changed dramatically when we walked across the border to the Congolese city of Goma. With one million inhabitants, Goma is the largest city in the Eastern Congo, a region ravaged by war since 1994. Our all-wheel drive vehicle rocked and bucked as it attempted to make its way around the city, traversing potholed roads strewn with volcanic rock that had not been cleared since the 2002 eruption of nearby Mount Nyiragongo. Here there were no functioning traffic lights, but there were a few traffic police in evidence. Mostly, they acted as human traffic lights, waving one line of vehicles through an intersection at a time. In other cases, they stood on the side of the road, motioning drivers around particularly deep potholes. As we commented on the more chaotic traffic situation in Goma, our driver said, 'Don't trust the police or the soldiers.' And both times we were stopped during our trip there, soldiers asked for bribes even though we had all vehicle papers in order and had committed no traffic infractions.

Given how poor the Congo is (with a very low HDI score), you might assume that the government has prioritized health, education, security and poverty over such things as road maintenance and traffic police. But that would assume there is a functioning government with adequate resources to fund its priorities. In fact, doctors, teachers and other state employees often seek employment outside of their regular jobs because the government is seldom able to pay them. It has not been government police that have managed to improve the security situation around Goma, but rather the peace-enforcing troops of the United Nations. When we visited camps outside of Goma for people displaced by the conflict, we were overwhelmed by the poverty and need of the people living there. Without access to any form of housing that would be considered dignified, families sleep on the rocky ground under tattered tarps. Disease, malnutrition, violence and unemployment keep these families dependent on handouts from UN agencies and international non-governmental organizations. After a long day visiting community leaders in the camps, we drove back into the city and invited our hosts out to dinner. They declined, saying, 'It's best you be in for the night by 6pm because it's just not safe once it's dark.'

Introduction

What a difference a border can make. But what is the difference, precisely? This anecdote comparing Rwanda with the Eastern Congo reveals a lot about the relationship between state institutions, governance and poverty. When institutions and governance function reasonably well, as in Rwanda, people's wellbeing can be demonstrably improved. When institutions and governance do not function well, as in the Congo, then governments cannot pay their employees, they cannot control their territories, uphold laws or prevent violence, citizens lack basic services and democratic public institutions that respond to their needs, and people may fear for their very lives. In the worst case, when institutions completely collapse, a society risks falling into anarchy, as in Rwanda in 1994 or Somalia more recently, and human development is tragically compromised.

Over the course of the past several decades, state institutions and governance have increasingly been recognized as crucial for good development outcomes. The World Bank and many other international bodies have enshrined 'good governance' as a programmatic goal for promoting economic growth. But there are still some major uncertainties about the relationship between institutions, governance and poverty. Those uncertainties can perhaps best be summed up by this question: Do countries get rich because they have good institutions, or do they have good institutions because they get rich? This chapter will explore answers to that question, explaining what 'institutions' are, how they relate to poverty and how they can be improved for the purposes of poverty reduction.

Definitions and measures

The scholarly literature offers many different attempts to define institutions, and a consistent criticism of the institutional approach to studying poverty and development is that these definitions are too vague or multifarious (see i.a. Hydén and Court 2002, Williams and Siddique 2008, Van Doeveren 2011, Gisselquist 2012, Sáez 2012). Douglass North provides probably the most commonly-cited definition of institutions as 'the rules of the game in society, or the humanly devised constraints that shape human interaction' (North 1990: 3). What does this mean? Institutions are sets of formal and informal rules that determine how humans behave in society. Informal rules include norms, traditions, religion or culture most broadly; their relationship to poverty is discussed in Chapter 6 on gender. The present chapter is primarily concerned with formal institutions such as laws, the judiciary, the bureaucracy and electoral systems, in other words, state institutions. These state institutions are what provide basic services such as education, health care and other forms of infrastructure, including roads and electricity, as well as law enforcement and protection of public order. They also, as per the North definition, shape human interaction: laws obviously help determine how we behave in society, and institutions such as the judicial system or the representative assemblies of government deeply impact how society functions. So for example, property rights are an institution, as are the laws laying out business regulation, or who can run for political office.

Governance can be thought of as a specific aspect of institutions, which is why these two concepts are combined in this chapter. 'Governance' is also subject to a dizzying variety of definitions, but its key components include: how citizens and groups express their interests and exercise their rights; how officials are selected; how policies are formulated and implemented; and how public services are managed. Governance thus refers not only to how governments are elected by and respond to citizens, but also to how public policies are designed and carried out. So governance encompasses *what* is done (i.e. specific policies) but also *how* it is done (i.e. the processes for making policies). Governance grows out of institutions such as the constitution, the electoral system, the bureaucracy and other administrative systems that manage a country's affairs. If institutions are the 'rules of the game', then governance can be thought of as 'how the game is played', i.e. how those formal state institutions are used in practice (Williamson 2000). Governance (and political elites) can also change institutions, such as by passing laws that then become 'the rules'.

More concretely, institutions such as the constitution, the courts and bureaucratic/ administrative offices can all determine how elections are run or what economic policies are adopted, and governance is the actual running of elections and the implementation of economic policies. Think of state institutions as structures, and governance as the particular policies implemented within those structures. In the United States, the Internal Revenue Service is an institution, but actual tax policies are examples of governance. Likewise in, say, Algeria, the Ministry of Education is a governmental institution, but the policies it adopts and services it provides depend upon the governance, namely the interaction of citizens, political elites and various other factors. Hence governance can determine the extent to which people have access to institutions and the services they provide; for example, policies relating to school fees affect whether poor families can send their children to school. Decisions on where to locate medical clinics influence whether poor families have access to health care. Henceforth, to avoid unwieldy language, most of the time when 'institutions' are mentioned in this chapter the concept of governance will be included, unless otherwise noted.

These basic definitions of institutions and governance have generally avoided normative claims, i.e. what state institutions and governance *should* be. Such normative prescriptions for institutions are commonplace, however. The United Nations has proposed that 'good' institutions operate according to these principles: equity, transparency, participation, responsiveness, efficiency, accountability and the rule of law (United Nations 2012). The idea is that good institutions treat everyone equitably, are reliably transparent, promote citizen participation and are both responsive and accountable to those citizens. Further, good institutions operate efficiently and according to the rule of law.

Similarly, as soon as one examines the typical indicators or measures used to evaluate governance quality, normative assumptions enter. A number of different evaluative schemes exist, such as the Polity Project or the Quality of Government Institute; two data sets more accessible to non-specialists are Freedom House's Freedom in the World Survey, or the World Bank's Worldwide Governance Indicators (WGI). The World Bank's system, while often criticized, is also highly influential, so this chapter draws heavily from it (for critiques see i.a. Apaza 2009, Hickey 2012, Fukuyama 2013). The WGI defines governance as 'the traditions and institutions by which authority in a country is exercised. This includes (a) the process by which governments are selected, monitored and replaced; (b) the capacity of the government to effectively formulate and implement sound policies; and (c) and the respect of citizens and the state for the institutions that govern economic and social interactions among them' (Kauffman *et al.* 2010: 4). Six different indicators each relate to one of these three areas (see Box 7.1).

Voice and accountability, because they relate to freedom of expression and assembly, involve basic freedoms without which a government may be unresponsive to citizens. Moreover, a denial of these basic freedoms is also an infringement of an individual's basic capabilities, as we will discuss later. Political stability and the absence of violence is fairly self-explanatory, since problems in these areas impact basic human security (see Chapter 8 on conflict). Government effectiveness attempts to gauge how well a government fulfils the requirements of providing basic services for human development such as education and health. One element of this indicator, the quality of the civil service, has major influence on the quality of government services. Regulatory quality is another compound of measures related to 'market-unfriendly policies' such as price controls and excessive government regulations on business.

Rule of law refers to a collection of concepts such as security of property rights, contract enforcement and incidence of crime. The rationale for this indicator is that such legal guarantees are essential to protect not only rights but also investments and the incentive for economic gain. For example, if property rights are not protected, such that political elites can come along at any time and expropriate a businesswoman's enterprise that she built up over years, then the individual drive for economic development will be undermined. The control of corruption is generally measured by *perceptions* of corruption in a given country (since actual corruption is usually illegal,

---

Box 7.1 The World Bank's worldwide governance indicators

(a)   The process by which governments are selected, monitored and replaced:

1   **Voice and Accountability:** capturing perceptions of the extent to which a country's citizens are able to participate in selecting their government, as well as freedom of expression, freedom of association and a free media.

2   **Political Stability and Absence of Violence/Terrorism:** capturing perceptions of the likelihood that the government will be destabilized or overthrown by unconstitutional or violent means, including politically-motivated violence and terrorism.

(b)   The capacity of the government to effectively formulate and implement sound policies:

3   **Government Effectiveness:** capturing perceptions of the quality of public services, the quality of the civil service and the degree of its independence from political pressures, the quality of policy formulation and implementation, and the credibility of the government's commitment to such policies.

4   **Regulatory Quality:** capturing perceptions of the ability of the government to formulate and implement sound policies and regulations that permit and promote private sector development.

(c)   The respect of citizens and the state for the institutions that govern economic and social interactions among them:

5   **Rule of Law:** capturing perceptions of the extent to which agents have confidence in and abide by the rules of society, and in particular the quality of contract enforcement, property rights, the police and the courts, as well as the likelihood of crime and violence.

6   **Control of Corruption:** capturing perceptions of the extent to which public power is exercised for private gain, including both petty and grand forms of corruption, as well as 'capture' of the state by elites and private interests.

Source: Kauffman, Kraay and Mastruzzi (2010)

---

and hence often hidden). Corruption's definition of 'the exercise of public power for private gain' can refer to government officials engaging in graft, embezzlement, or taking bribes in order to enrich themselves. Though corruption exists to varying degrees in almost every society, where it is frequent it represents a breakdown of law that amounts to a fundamental failure of both institutions and governance. Tables 7.1, 7.2 and 7.3 give lists of the countries that rank best and worst on several of these indicators.

How institutions impact poverty and development

When state institutions break down or do not operate well, they make people's lives worse. Think of the example of the Congo and Rwanda at the beginning of this chapter: local government did very little for the displaced people in the camps outside

Table 7.1 Countries ranked according to Voice and Accountability score

Best	Worst
Norway	Turkmenistan
Sweden	Somalia
Switzerland	North Korea
Netherlands	Eritrea
Finland	Equatorial Guinea
New Zealand	Uzbekistan
Denmark	Syria
Luxembourg	Saudi Arabia
Germany	Laos
Canada	Iran

Table 7.2 Countries ranked according to Government Effectiveness score

Best	Worst
Singapore	Somalia
Switzerland	South Sudan
Finland	Haiti
New Zealand	Central African Republic
Hong Kong	Comoros
Netherlands	North Korea
Japan	Libya
Norway	Eritrea
Denmark	Sudan
Sweden	DR Congo

Table 7.3 Countries ranked according to Rule of Law score

Best	Worst
Finland	Somalia
Denmark	Venezuela
Norway	South Sudan
New Zealand	Central African Republic
Switzerland	North Korea
Sweden	Afghanistan
Netherlands	Libya
Austria	Eritrea
Australia	DR Congo
Luxembourg	Zimbabwe

Source: World Bank World Governance Indicators, 2014 data

Box 7.2 Corruption and poverty in Nigeria

Nigeria has a regrettable but well-founded reputation for high levels of corruption; the country ranked 136 out of 168 in Transparency International's 2015 Perceptions of Corruption Index. Many Nigerians can tell a story of extortion at the hands of a police officer. At traffic checkpoints, police routinely demand bribes for invented reasons. There are even reports of police simply pulling guns on people and demanding money, which is robbery as much as corruption. Police officers have admitted to targeting women sellers at markets because they are so vulnerable: they have to sell in order to make a living, so they will pay anything to stop the police from arresting them. Sometimes when the women don't have money, the police demand sex as payment. Resistance to such techniques can be costly in many ways. Police regularly round up a group of people for detention, which forces the people to pay for their freedom. One man in such a roundup described what happened when he refused to pay: 'Two of them started to beat me. They used their guns to hit me on my face and body. [. . .] The police said I was an armed robber and that they would kill me.' When police officers demand even a small bribe equivalent to a few US dollars, it can represent a frighteningly large sum to a poor person. The poor are also less likely to have the knowledge, time, money or personal connections to use the legal system for redress against corrupt officials. Judges and lawyers in Nigeria have confirmed that often anyone who brings a criminal complaint must first pay to have that complaint investigated. Corruption cases such as these fundamentally compromise the rule of law, and constitute a human rights abuse. There are also very high crimes: embezzlement at upper levels of government is unfortunately common. According to one estimate, in the 40 years after 1960, USD 380 billion was lost to graft and mismanagement. As a single example, a governor of one of Nigeria's oil-producing states was convicted of stealing USD 55 million, though he was later (controversially) pardoned. The theft of such large sums of money prevents the funds from potentially being spent on projects that would benefit the public. Corruption also seriously undermines the equitable distribution of economic development and its benefits.

Sources: Human Rights Watch (2011, 2010); US State Department (2012)

Goma, so it was up to international institutions to provide relief. Or refer to the case of Nigeria: official corruption results in persecution and human rights abuses against the disempowered in particular. These examples suggest that institutions can have a profound impact on both economic and human development. The theory behind the Worldwide Governance Indicators is that good institutions make economic growth possible. Good institutions protect property rights, which bolsters peoples' incentives to work for gain. When people work hard and are rewarded appropriately for their labour, then their incomes should rise. There are some serious methodological difficulties that complicate teasing out how much good institutions contribute to economic growth, and how much economic growth leads to good institutions. Therefore, though there are many studies claiming that good institutions promote economic growth, there are also many that deny a clear relationship. (see i.a. Glaeser *et al.* 2004, Rodrik *et al.* 2004, Perera and Lee 2013)

Nonetheless, there are several specific aspects of institutions/governance that have been reliably shown to boost economic growth. Those aspects can include protecting property rights, providing adequate security and upholding the law in general. Corruption, for example, has often been highlighted as impeding economic growth and exacerbating poverty (see Méon and Sekkat 2005, Herrera *et al.* 2007, Tebaldi and Mohan 2010) Tebaldi and Mohan call institutions a 'deep factor' impacting prosperity and poverty, i.e. a factor with both long- and short-term implications that can influence various other causes of poverty. For example, meritocratic bureaucracies have been associated with economic growth, and higher levels of corruption deter economic growth. Similarly, countries with more stable governance and institutions have also been found to have experienced more growth (Soubbotina and Sheram 2000). Countries with better institutions as measured by the World Bank's indicators also do better in terms of health outcomes such as lower infant mortality, education outcomes such as higher literacy rates, and food security (Sacks and Levi 2010, UNDP 2011).

Evidence is strong overall that better institutions can limit poverty (Chong and Calderón 2000). They do so in part by determining who benefits from economic growth, which in turn helps determine who exercises political power (Rodrik 2000, Bastiaensen *et al.* 2005). Some institutional arrangements such as tax policies allow political elites disproportionately to capture the benefits of economic growth. This is the problem whereby, say, the top one per cent of the population receives 40 per cent of economic gains, as has happened in the United States in recent years. Institutions and governance can thereby produce income inequality, but income inequality can also reinforce weak or bad institutions (Chong and Gradstein 2007). 'Bad' institutions means that they are used consciously by political elites to reinforce inequality, or otherwise where institutions intentionally disadvantage the poor. 'Weak' institutions disadvantage the poor not through intention but by being inadequate through lack of funds, competency, planning, etc.

Institutional failures can come about through intentional and unintentional means (Rotberg 2003). Sometimes people in power (whether in political office, or with major economic or political influence) use institutions and governance to pursue policies that actually create poverty. For example, Omar al-Bashir, the president of Sudan, was charged by the International Criminal Court with waging genocide in Darfur for his own political ends. Elites in many lands' colonial regimes structured institutions so that rights and economic benefits accrued to very small segments of the population. Institutional arrangements that allow political elites to neglect public services to the poor, or in which government is so weak that it cannot provide those services, are another way that institutions contribute to poverty. In intentional cases, institutions, governance and politics are all designed to benefit certain groups or individuals while disadvantaging others. Unintentional institutional deficiencies can arise in concert with institutional ones, but sometimes separately. Inadequate basic services such as clean water or sanitation are not always the outcome of insidious elites. Sometimes governments and people in power have the will to provide such services, but they simply do not have the means. Likewise, weak legal systems, lack of security for life and property, and inequitable economic development can exist despite efforts against them; institutional change, as we will see, can be very difficult. It is not uncommon that countries may adopt policies with the intention of aiding the poor, but the country's institutions are too weak to implement those policies effectively. There is a poverty trap here: bad or weak institutions can make poverty worse, but poverty also can make institutions worse (Bowles 2006).

Institutions and capabilities

Whatever their exact relationship with economic growth, state institutions' impact on poverty must also be considered from the capability perspective. We will consider four main areas in which institutions can either diminish or expand human freedom: (1) basic human security; (2) basic public services; (3) economic development with equity; and (4) basic civil rights such as political participation and free speech. Failures and inadequacies of institutions in these areas create capability and income poverty. They limit what people are able to do and to be; they unjustly constrain the choices people are able to make to live a life that they have reason to value.

Basic human security refers to the most fundamental facts of daily safety. Are we afraid of being killed at any moment? Of someone stealing our property or otherwise hurting us? When we fear for the most elemental protection of our bodies and our lives, we are living in a kind of unfreedom, namely to live without constant fear. In a violent society such as that famously described by the seventeenth-century philosopher Thomas Hobbes – the 'war of all against all', where life is 'solitary, poor, nasty, brutish, and short' – institutions are so deficient that basic security is threatened. Such an unsafe society does not support human flourishing. Institutions to guarantee basic bodily and property security include a police force, laws that are clear and apply equally to everyone, and a court system that aids in the enforcement of those laws. Fragile and failed states such as the Democratic Republic of the Congo, and other states experiencing conflict such as Rwanda in 1994 or Syria more recently, often have serious deficiencies to meet this basic criterion of adequate human life.

Basic public services refers to clean water, sanitation, education, health care, and infrastructure such as roads. In some countries, government programmes supply needy people with housing, food subsidies, fuel such as kerosene, seeds for planting, relief during natural disasters, or pensions for widows and the disabled. Institutions impact capabilities by the provision of such public services. For instance, are people able to read and write? That often depends on whether there was a school in their community that they were able to attend. State institutions are vital here because private markets are less likely to supply these public goods, or at any rate unlikely to supply them in a way that would assure equitable access to the services for people who do not have the money to acquire them. Educational and health deficiencies exacerbate poverty, but institutions partly account for why those deficiencies exist, and who suffers the most from them.

The level at which a government should supply public services can vary and may be disputed – to how much health care are we entitled in order to meet 'basic' levels, for instance? Those basic minimum threshold levels can be societally specific. However, we can affirm that it is the job of state institutions to provide access to these services, especially for people who would not otherwise be able to afford them. There is a long and powerful tradition in ethical philosophy holding that one of the foremost jobs of government is to assist the poorest and neediest in a society. The reason is that without such governmental assistance, the poorest and neediest would continually fall below the minimum thresholds of an adequate human life. Government assistance is supposed to help them over the minimum threshold and ensure that they are not perpetually deprived and disadvantaged. Thus government must have some preference for the poor to assure the attainment of the minimum capabilities, otherwise it will fail to meet basic standards of justice. When institutions are so weak or bad that government cannot perform this function, then they help create or perpetuate poverty.

Institutions that promote economic development with equity will usually be attentive to this preference for the poor and the need to assure the attainment of basic capabilities. As we have seen, most scholars agree that certain institutional features are beneficial for economic development, including the aforementioned rule of law, low levels of corruption and bureaucratic effectiveness. When these features are not present – in other words, when you have a government in which corruption is rampant, that does not protect property rights, that does not provide roads and other infrastructure – the absence of such features can retard economic growth. On an individual, human level, state institutions impact capabilities by setting the rules of earning a livelihood. For instance, are people able to own land without fear of expropriation, and invest in that land to make it more productive and help support themselves or their family? This often depends upon legal frameworks that recognize rights and ensure equal enforcement of laws. Hence bad or weak institutions contribute to conditions in which people are likely to live in material and income poverty. Beyond this, however, institutional arrangements including laws, the electoral system and the judicial system can influence who benefits from economic growth, sometimes concentrating wealth and power in the hands of a small minority, as mentioned earlier. Such institutions thereby also disproportionately distribute and exacerbate poverty by disadvantaging people economically and politically.

The fourth area in which institutions can contribute to poverty is through basic civil rights. In accordance with the Universal Declaration of Human Rights, every human being is entitled to freedom of expression, of association and assembly, of religious exercise, and other fundamental rights guaranteeing political participation and freedom from unwarranted search and seizure. These rights equate to capabilities: we should all have the capability to reason for ourselves, to express our political opinions, to associate with the individuals or groups we choose, and to exercise some control over our political officials. Put simply, the absence of such rights and capabilities is a form of poverty, since we are all entitled to them as human beings. Institutions that infringe upon such rights therefore create or increase poverty. Regimes that arrest democratic protestors, for instance, or that crack down on speech criticizing the government, or that uphold discriminatory laws against people of particular minority groups whether religious, ethnic, or sexual, all exacerbate forms of poverty. There is a deeper issue beyond the authoritarian regimes that infringe upon civil rights freedoms, however. The absence of political participatory rights can mire people in poverty because without those rights, how are poor people going to articulate their political interests and hold leaders accountable?

It is clear that institutional deficiencies disproportionately disadvantage the poor. This is first of all because poor people are more likely to depend upon public goods that the state should provide (since they often cannot afford private schools, private health care, their own cars for transportation, etc.). When institutions are weak, then public goods are probably in short supply, and the possibilities for poverty reduction are seriously limited. A very common complaint of poor people is that public services do not reach them, or that they are denied access to existing public services. 'Poor people have no access to the police station, bank, government offices, and the judge of the village court', a villager in Bangladesh reported. 'The rich people dominate these institutions' (Narayan *et al.* 2000a: 200). A respondent from a participatory poverty assessment in Madagascar lamented, 'The state is simply absent from people's lives and strategies for securing their needs' (Narayan *et al.* 2000b: 67). 'Only God listens to us', a respondent in Egypt said (Narayan *et al.* 2000a: 200).

Poor people often rate state institutions very low on responsiveness, trust, accountability, respect, honesty and fairness. Indeed, research from the *Voices of the Poor* series found that poor people rate state institutions as overwhelmingly ineffective. (Narayan *et al.* 2000a) They reported that the services themselves were often shoddy: wells or other water schemes did not work, hospital care was substandard or unavailable, teachers did not show up for school, subsidies for farming did not arrive or did not help. 'We keep hearing about money that the government allocates for projects, and nothing happens on the ground', according to one respondent in South Africa (Narayan *et al.* 2000b: 67). Access problems are also very common. Poor people often complained that because of corruption and maltreatment on the part of government officials, they found their interaction with state institutions to be humiliating. Respondents said that they would rather not go to a police station to report a crime because the police would extort money from them; that hospital workers would ignore them, harass them, or demand bribes; or that when they went to government assistance offices, they were made to feel stupid and greedy for asking for help. In short, institutions sometimes fail poor people by robbing them of their dignity.

The importance of democracy in institutions and governance

The discussion of basic civil rights alludes to the relationship between democracy, institutions and governance. Is democracy essential for human development? Interestingly, it is not essential for *economic* development. Scholars dispute whether democratic government promotes stronger economic growth. Some studies have found correlations between GNP growth rates and various indicators of democracy (see Adelman 2006). Others have dismissed those findings, however – and there are certainly historical examples of authoritarian governments achieving significant economic growth, such as in South Korea, Taiwan, Singapore or China (see Gerring *et al.* 2011). It has even been claimed that democracy has no necessary association with the quality of government (Rothstein and Tannenberg 2015). Despite these contrary perspectives, democracy should still be an ideal for every society, for two reasons. The first is that poor people themselves often see undemocratic governance as contributing to their poverty (Leavy and Howard 2013). The second is that democratic practices are fundamental to the expansion of capabilities.

To avoid the imprecision of loose understandings of 'democracy', it must be defined. The key democratic practices, and their relation to capabilities and human development, build upon the notion of basic civil rights discussed earlier. Robert Dahl's influential criteria of democracy include free and fair elections in which officials are chosen, and inclusive suffrage in those elections so that the vast proportion of the adult population has the right to vote and to run for office. Further, democracy presumes freedom of expression, such as to criticize political officials without fear of punishment, and what in American terms is often referred to as freedom of assembly, i.e. the right to form independent associations or organizations, whether political parties, NGOs or interest

Table 7.4 Forms of democratic deficits

In formal constitutional and political arrangements	*In substance or practices of power*
• Poorly protected civil and political rights • Access to legal and administrative systems skewed against minorities, the unorganized, the poor • Lack of free and fair elections • Electoral systems that distort outcomes or disenfranchise minorities • Weak constitutional checks and balances • Rule of law absent or weak • Lack of governmental transparency • Weak democratic control of military, police, and intelligence bodies • Key decisions made by international bodies (IMF, World Bank, UN and its agencies, etc.) not by national governments	• Major societal inequities (on basis of class, gender, region, religion, ethnicity, etc.) • De facto disenfranchisement of the poor due to lack of resources and organization • Uncivil society: cultures of intolerance, lack of respect for difference • Violence, intimidation, especially against marginalized groups • Electorates offered little effective choice between alternative political programs • Few autonomous, effective, broadly-based civil society groups to challenge the government and vested interests • Political processes weakened and social capital destroyed through violent conflict • Patrimonial politics: government manipulation via patronage, ethnicity, etc. • Endemic corruption • Political processes suborned by elite economic and social interests • Judiciary weak or coopted • Weak opposition parties • Media lacking in independence • Hegemony of international firms

Source: Luckham et al. (2000: 24)

groups. Dahl also adds the component of 'alternative information', such that citizens have the right to sources of information that are not controlled by the government or any one political group (Dahl 2000). These various practices and arrangements help assure that citizens can challenge their government and other sources of power (such as large corporations), and that these sources of power remain accountable to citizens. Finally, democracy entails that citizens have legal means of redress against each other, against government and against corporations; this again is part of the equitable rule of law.

These features may seem obvious to anyone raised in a democracy. After all, what legitimate arguments could there be *against* individual liberties such as freedom of expression, association and equal legal rights? But it is not sufficient to take democracy for granted as a kind of assumed imperative. The capabilities approach explores more specifically why these rights and practices help bring people out of poverty. This goes beyond the mere idea of political freedoms and civil rights to which everyone is entitled. Certainly, as Sen proclaimed, development is about expanding the scope of human freedoms. So the denial of basic political freedoms is a kind of poverty. Deficits in democracy therefore lead to capability poverty. Such deficits can take many forms, as indicated in Table 7.4.

One way that people can be empowered, that poverty can be eliminated, is by eliminating these democratic deficits. Democratic institutions help assure that people have the agency to decide collectively about matters that concern their communities. Similarly, democratic processes enhance people's influence over decisions that may impact their capabilities (Drydyk 2005). In this way political participation cannot be reduced merely to elections. It needs to be both deeper and more expansive. The kind of democratic participation that the capabilities approach envisions promises that every adult should have a participatory role in discussions and deliberation (Alkire 2002, Crocker 2007). Reasoning, for both private and public matters, is one of Nussbaum's central capabilities. True democracy means that all individuals should be equipped so that they can realize the functionings of their rights to deliberation, discussion and political decision making. Education is one of the foremost ways that people can acquire the cognitive and communicative skills to realize these functionings (see Sen 2000, Deneulin 2009).

This commitment to democracy must operate in both high politics and 'deep politics' in order to expand people's capabilities. High politics refers to the state-level institutions such as electoral systems, representative government, and checks and balances. It can also refer to a 'high' level of civil society beyond that of the nation-state. Democratic politics that give people agency must apply to the institutions of governance at the state level, but should also operate above the state, at a supranational or global level. International institutions that ignore, discriminate, devalue or marginalize people or societies from the developing world can be perniciously undemocratic, just as dictators within a country can. Hence global civil society must have the same respect for agency, deliberation and participation as nation states. 'Deep politics' is a term used by Luckham *et al.* to denote the micro level of political interactions at a quotidian, often individual level (Luckham *et al.* 2000). Democratic deep politics embrace the rights, voice and agency of women, the poor and other marginalized groups to give them their due influence in institutions and on governance. Much as institutions created to entrench particular individuals' or groups' power are harmful to democratic government, so too are persistent inequities of power at the micro level, in homes, schools, markets, places of worship or local governmental offices. From the capabilities perspective, democratic politics affirms that all people are entitled to participate not just at the most visible levels of voting and freedom to speak out against rulers, but also with decision making and freedom of expression at the household, village and international levels.

Democracy is an elusive goal – even the vaunted democracies in the West such as the United States or Britain have to work at (and often fall short of) including marginalized and excluded groups, and equalizing political power. So in many regards democratic institutions and governance are an *aspiration*, but one that all societies should strive for in order to maximize human development. Democracy is the best way of respecting human dignity and providing a space wherein people can express their interests and decide collectively on the public good. Even in countries with relatively good institutions, democratic governance must battle against corruption, bureaucratic inefficiencies and unequal distributions of power. Indeed, democratic institutions are no guarantee of democratic politics, since political elites and/or wealthy people are adept at manipulating those institutions to serve their interests. Thus throughout the world poor people have difficulty driving pro-poor policies. Besides the way the wealthy are able to engineer policies that favour them, poor people face an additional hurdle in that they often lack the education, social capital and security that would enable them more effectively to mobilize so that the government is adequately responsive to their needs and interests. When it works as it should, however, democracy ensures that the poor have equitable access to and control over institutions that enhance capabilities such as schools and hospitals. By exercising that control, the capability to lead a life that one values is itself enhanced (Drydyk 2005).

What shapes institutions and governance?

The necessity of correcting institutional deficiencies points to the need to understand how institutions develop. Most simply, how do you get 'good' institutions rather than 'bad' ones? We will first examine the long-term factors that have shaped institutions, and then turn to the shorter-term ones. An influential explanation for the historical evolution of institutions centres on the impact of geography. There are two broad, intertwined strands here: first, how geography impacted where Europeans settled, and second, how geography impacted the institutions Europeans set up in those places where they settled. As elucidated by scholars such as Engerman and Sokoloff (1997 and 2003) and Acemoglu, Johnson and Robinson (2001 and 2004), this perspective holds that European colonial powers set up different kinds of institutions depending upon a territory's disease burden, resource endowments and level of human capital (which in these studies is usually taken to mean population density). These institutions typically supplanted or fused with whatever governance structures societies in Latin America, Africa and Asia had prior to colonialism.

To begin with, the influence of the disease burden is this: in places such as the tropics where incidence of malaria was higher, Europeans settled in smaller numbers than in temperate zones with a lower disease burden. In areas where Europeans settled in larger numbers, including what became the United States, Canada, Australia and New Zealand, they set up good institutions, the kind of institutions under which they wanted to live, namely those that protected property rights and ensured the rule of law. What kind of institutions did colonists set up in places where they settled more lightly? Acemoglu *et al.* call them 'extractive institutions', namely institutions that were designed to extract the wealth of the locality for the benefit of the upper classes.

Institutions became extractive where territories had good soils, mineral wealth and relatively high density of native populations. In such territories, European colonists sought to concentrate power and wealth into the hands of the elites who would derive most of the benefits of agriculture or mining, while the native peoples worked as slaves or tenant farmers with few rights. Examples are the Spanish colonies in Mexico and Peru, both of which had significant mineral wealth as well as high population densities. The Spanish colonists intended to harness this wealth for their own benefit, employing the native populations to work in mines or on large agricultural estates. Throughout Latin America and the Caribbean, imperial powers exploited native populations via labour systems such as plantations to harvest the kind of crops (such as sugar cane) that grew well in those warm, wet latitudes. These plantations were predicated on the existence of a relatively small number of landowners and a large number of peasant labourers or slaves.

This is a marked contrast to what became New England in North America, which had neither mineral wealth nor high indigenous population densities, and was not suitable for crops such as sugar cane. Instead, wheat and corn grew better in New England, which encouraged a settlement pattern of independent, small family farms, rather than the large estates owned by the elites where land was worked by tenant farmers, as in much of Latin America. There was therefore less intent to control and concentrate land and wealth, which influenced the kind of institutions that arose in North America. Moreover, as per Acemoglu *et al.*, the disease burden in much of North America was less than in the southern lands, and therefore Europeans set up the kinds of institutions that they actually wanted to live under, since they intended to settle these areas long-term and not just exploit their wealth in the shorter term.

The argument, then, is that these historical and geographical conditions led to the creation of fundamentally inegalitarian, undemocratic institutions in Latin America and the Caribbean (and later in Africa), where European colonists wanted primarily to control wealth. These institutions were designed to benefit a small, wealthy landowning class that held a disproportionately large share of political and economic power. In the United States and Canada, where more Europeans settled, a more egalitarian rule of law was implemented, leading to more democratic institutions designed to benefit larger proportions of the population. The inegalitarian institutions of Latin America not only concentrated political power, but also constricted governance. Their tax burdens disproportionately favoured the wealthy, such that the states raised a larger share of money from taxing the lower classes. However, the resources raised from taxing the less well off were rarely very great, which in turn hampered the development of local governments and the public services they provide. Human development was thereby impeded, and even economic development was less robust and its gains more restricted to the elites.

Another way that the deficient institutions implanted by Europeans may have retarded economic development, and thereby increased poverty, is by weakening the transition to an industrial economy. Engerman and Sokoloff (1997) have theorized that industrialization requires the participation of a broad spectrum of society to foster entrepreneurship and innovation. In countries with the highly concentrated power structures characteristic of extractive institutions, which in turn resulted in highly unequal distributions of wealth, such broad, entrepreneurial participation in the economy was much reduced. Critics of this analysis say that the causal relationships between geography, income levels and institutions are extremely difficult to separate. For example, geography does impact institutions, and institutions impact income levels, but geography also impacts income, and institutions can also impact geographical attributes (good governments can eradicate malaria, for example).

Nonetheless, the central takeaway from these accounts of institutional development is that historical conditions going back hundreds of years can exert a notable impact on the kinds of institutions that societies have today. Institutional arrangements exhibit a high degree of inertia and persistence. The historical legacy of undemocratic institutions has promoted both income and capability poverty by helping keep the rich, rich, and the poor, poor. This is not to say that institutions do not change. There are always historical junctures that produce relatively sudden changes, such as wars or revolutions, or even slower, gradual evolutions that alter institutional forms. Humans are constantly modifying societal institutions, in large and small ways. Still, unequal regimes set up 500 years ago have not only shaped countries' economic and human development since then, but continue to contribute to poverty today through inadequate access to civil rights, public services and basic security.

Several other short-term factors also contribute to bad or weak institutions and governance. The less pernicious ones include an inadequate tax base and a dearth of qualified civil servants. In especially poor countries, there may be relatively little taxable wealth, and hence fewer resources for governments to provide services to the population. For example, whatever Haiti's other institutional and governance problems, the society as a whole is so poor that it limits what funds a government could raise to build things such as hospitals, highways, schools and ports. A shortage of highly-trained and competent bureaucrats can also hamper government effectiveness. Any programme, municipality or region is not likely to be well administered if the people responsible have little experience or know-how. Sometimes weak governance in the developing world can be an outcome of a scarcity of qualified managers.

The more malign deficiencies relate to politics. As mentioned previously, it is not at all uncommon that institutions remain unequal, and governance inadequate, by intention. If political elites regard sharing power, protecting civil rights, promoting equitable economic development or ensuring widespread access to basic services as undermining their own powers or privileges, then concentrated power and wealth will persist. Perhaps the most famous example of elites insidiously manipulating governance – and one that links back to the above discussion of extractive institutions – is the 'resource curse'. Dependence on natural resources such as oil in countries like Venezuela, Nigeria, Chad or Iraq has had palpable negative impacts on institutions and governance. Scholars have shown that autocratic governments are more common in countries where the economy is dominated by natural resources: leaders try to control the resource revenues, clamping down on political competition to ensure that they do (see i.a. Ross 1999, Mehlum *et al.* 2006, Humphreys *et al.* 2007, Robinson *et al.* 2007). Obviously, dictatorships do not arise in every country where natural resources are important to a country's economy; Norway is a major oil producer, for instance, yet remains a sturdy democracy. But Norway already had strong institutions before its oil sector grew, unlike many developing countries.

Whether with oil, diamonds, copper, cocoa or some other commodity, revenues from natural resources are relatively easy for political elites to capture, compared to economic sectors based on manufacturing or services. State-owned oil companies are ripe for corruption and authoritarian control in a way that, say, the technology sector would not be. If a dictator attempted to capture Silicon Valley, he would kill the goose that laid the golden egg, whereas oil wells will probably keep pumping even if they are not managed in a perspicacious fashion. Besides how they lend themselves to authoritarian control, natural resource revenues can warp institutions and governance in another way as well. Such revenues reduce the need to tax, which weakens accountability for leaders. If your government is flush with money by selling diamonds from the mines you control, then you have less motivation to tax your population. Once you start taxing the population, you become more beholden to the citizenry. Hence natural resource revenues mean that leaders can derive money for government functions without a strong tie to citizens' consent through taxes. By attenuating the bond between government and populace, natural resource revenues can corrupt the institutions that are supposed to serve the people, again making government a preserve of the elite. In short, the resource curse incentivizes political elites to manipulate institutions in a way that serves the few rather than the many (Collier 2008).

Several final short-term factors further undermine institutions and governance. Political calculations and the resource curse can play another role through the corruption of bureaucratic administration. Bureaucracies in the developing world that are not staffed by qualified people are sometimes an intentional strategy of political elites. Too often, people in power give civil service jobs as a reward to supporters. This is the system of clients and patrons: patrons generate support by doling out rewards – often in the form of positions in government – at the local, regional or national level. The result is that a society's bureaucratic administration is not meritocratic and there truly to serve the society, but rather to serve the interests of the clients and the patrons. The resource curse acts here in that elites can use resource revenues to buy support through patronage (such as by paying for roads, subsidies for consumer products, or other giveaways) rather than through electoral competition. So not only does a society end up with an ineffective institution in the form of a bureaucracy that cannot adequately administer, it also is saddled with autocratic institutions that are less responsive to citizen interests and less respectful of citizen rights.

The resource curse can also impact capabilities by harming basic human security, since resource-rich countries are sometimes more prone to conflict. The Democratic Republic of the Congo is again a paradigmatic case: the unaccountable official government has long warred with various paramilitaries and other states such as Rwanda, the fighting spurred in part by a contest to control the Congo's rich resources in diamonds and minerals. As with the long-term influences on economic growth discussed above, economic development with equity is also damaged by the resource curse because countries that are heavily dependent on natural resources tend to have lower economic growth. When a developing country's economy depends heavily on oil, diamonds or minerals, it tends to lack productive investment in other economic sectors that could boost the country's competitiveness. Indeed, the resource curse has been shown to make other economic sectors less competitive, leaving the country even more dependent on the problematic natural resource. Low levels of economic development are usually associated with weak institutions, which in turn are associated with inadequate public services and civil rights, thereby contributing to poverty.

Critiques of the institutions/governance perspective

Though weak or bad institutions can certainly worsen poverty, it is important to remember that the precise relationships between particular institutions and economic development are not always clear. There are enough questions or criticisms of the institutions literature that caution is necessary in drawing too firm conclusions about how institutions impact economic development. Some scholars such as Sachs *et al.* (2004), for instance, say that bad governance is not really a powerful explanation for underdevelopment. Others have noted that many of the concepts, definitions and operationalization of variables in studies of institutions are vague at best and faulty at worst. The methodology of some studies that have claimed positive relationships between institutional quality and economic development have later been found problematic. Again, causality can be hard to isolate given that indicators such as rule of law, corruption, accountability, government effectiveness etc. are often intertwined. What is the relative impact of corruption versus faulty rule of law versus a lack of accountability in explaining poverty in, say, Myanmar? As yet there are few answers to that question.

Another caution is not to privilege Western models of institutions unduly. The typical definition of what constitutes 'good' institutions is derived primarily from the Western experience and examples. There is some justification for this practice, but one must not go too far and conclude that Western models in their idealized form are appropriate for every society around the world (see i.a. Unsworth 2010, Hickey 2012). For example, Ha-Joon Chang has launched a powerful critique of economists' fixation on property rights, alleging that this is an obsession too unquestioningly derived from Anglo-American examples, and that even the notion of 'property rights' itself is a bundle of many other institutional arrangements such as land law, tax law, contract law and intellectual property law (Chang 2005). The point is that what works in Western societies, which have grown to depend on formal institutions, may not work so well elsewhere, such as in much of sub-Saharan Africa where informal institutions may still predominate (Hydén

2007). One must beware of adopting a 'one size fits all' approach to institutions and governance, assuming that what works in one rich country will work everywhere.

Two things should be kept in mind about this dispute over the importance of institutions. The first is that the dispute above all concerns institutions' role in economic development. The problems of causality and conceptual application are severest there. Much more confidence can hold for the role of institutions in human development. Certainly there are potential causality problems here too, in that relationships between health, education, and other forms of measurable welfare likely operate in a feedback loop with institutional development. Nonetheless, good institutions are essential for the capability approach by virtue of protecting political rights and helping to assure the equitable distribution of other rights and resources in a society. Rights and principles of equity, as we have argued, are fundamental to protect basic capabilities, and therefore trying to build institutions that will protect those capabilities can be a worthwhile programme of poverty reduction. The second important thing to keep in mind from critiques of the institutions literature is that such critiques make policy prescriptions more difficult. Given that the impact of institutions on economic development is still questioned, what policies should countries in the global south implement to promote development? What do the cautions not to impose 'one size fits all' Western-derived institutions mean for trying to cultivate some of the benefits of such institutions in countries that currently lack them?

What works to get better institutions and governance

The preceding two questions are vital as we turn to the topic of policies to reduce poverty through institutional reform. The difficulties alluded to in these two questions remind us that easy, prescriptive lists of how developing countries must reform governance are unlikely to be helpful. Because there is no one right path for achieving good institutions, different contexts and societies demand an array of different responses – an array far too vast to cover in depth here. Rather than provide prescriptions for multiple different scenarios, this chapter will examine some general principles for governance reform, and zoom in on a few applications of specific reforms.

First off, reforms to improve governance and institutions are daunting in complexity. As Merilee Grindle has written,

> Getting good governance calls for improvements that touch virtually all aspects of the public sector – from institutions that set the rules of the game for economic and political interaction, to organizations that manage administrative systems and deliver goods and services to citizens, to human resources that staff government bureaucracies, to the interface of officials and citizens in political and bureaucratic arenas. Getting good governance at times implies changes in political organization, the representation of interests, and processes for public debate and policy decision-making.
>
> (Grindle 2002: 1)

Moreover, these reforms often have to take place in very poor countries, where institutions are deeply deficient, and/or in societies that are sometimes plagued by violent conflict and tremendous inequities. This means that the countries that most urgently need better institutions will have the most difficulties in carrying out reform.

Indeed, the bad news is that according to an analysis by Pritchett, Woolcock and Andrews (2010), many developing countries may *never* attain the high quality of institutions such as in Singapore. For instance, at the average rate with which countries improved their bureaucratic administration between 1985 and 2009, it would take Côte d'Ivoire 503 years, Paraguay 377 years and Cameroon 314 years to reach Singapore-level institutions. However, because many of these countries over this time period exhibited a *negative* rate of improvement (i.e. the quality of their bureaucratic administration actually worsened), if that rate continued then they simply could not reach Singapore's level. That discouraging conclusion applies also for the opportunity of almost all the countries in the survey to make progress along another dimension of institutional quality, lack of corruption: most of them will never attain Singapore's low levels.

There is some hope. But it requires a pragmatic acknowledgement that the ideal-type perfection of institutions may be a very, very distant goal for many countries. This has led Grindle to advocate for reforms aiming at 'good enough governance' (Grindle 2002, 2007a, 2011). Governance that is 'good enough' insists that reforms should 'fit' the particular society. The idea is to aim for realistic targets in particular areas of institutions and governance, not necessarily expecting to reach the standards of Singapore or Denmark. There can be a considerable variation in the specificities of adequate governance, even in the rich countries. So institutional reforms should build upon what works in the country context rather than try to import some foreign, possibly unworkable model (Carothers and de Gramont 2010).

Nonetheless, we can affirm one consistent principle, namely that reforms should favour poverty reduction and democracy. The overriding question is how institutions can expand human capabilities. They can do so by emphasizing equity (so that the most disadvantaged get special attention), participation and empowerment (so that people have the freedom to make their own choices to lead lives that they value). These values can be applied to four broad areas of institutional reform: administration, participation, decentralization and legal frameworks, most of which are interrelated in practice (Deolalikar *et al.* 2002).

Reforms to administration deal principally with improving the bureaucracy to make the state more efficient and effective. From the perspective of poverty reduction, the goal of administrative reforms is to help guarantee and improve the public services that poor people depend on. There are a number of ways this reform can be accomplished, including technical capacity building by training competent civil service workers. More competent people in administration should hopefully provide better public services. Making the bureaucracy more meritocratic (rather than a preserve of patronage) is an important step in the right direction. Of course, adequate fiscal resources are necessary to fund those services, which means that another critical institution is an effective and legitimate system of taxation. (If large numbers of people evade taxes, where is the money supposed to come from for schools, hospitals, roads and sanitation?) A more efficient state administration can also foster economic growth by reducing regulatory hindrances to private enterprise and increasing transparency, which can help reduce corruption. Part of the rationale for transparency is to improve the administration of public finances through strengthened protocols of auditing and monitoring budgets. Better budget management can make even scarce fiscal resources more efficient. A concrete example of an end goal is government ministries for education and health with more competent workers, better managed funding, and thus more beneficial services provided to the poor and non-poor alike. Those services then do a better job of supporting the development of people's capabilities through schooling and health care.

Reforms to participation involve ensuring regular, free and fair elections, guaranteeing freedom of expression and assembly, and the right to run for office. Assistance to poor or other non-dominant sectors of society to form political parties, interest groups or other means of articulating and advancing their interests can boost participation and enhance democracy. If institutions and governance incorporate broader citizen involvement, then they should be more responsive to citizens' needs and desires. Increased citizen engagement can make governments more transparent and accountable, which helps foster good governance. For the purposes of poverty reduction, such reforms should pay special attention to boosting participation and civic engagement for the poor and marginalized. Recall that part of the definition of poverty is the denial of the basic civil rights that political participation presumes. Thus institutional reforms to boost participation are a critical method for empowering the poor. When they are more civically engaged, poor people have more ability to influence policy, and thereby to support politicians and programmes that are working to reduce poverty (Holmes *et al.* 2000). At the level of basic capabilities, these institutional reforms support items from Nussbaum's list such as 'senses, imagination and thought', 'practical reason' and 'affiliation'.

All of these participatory reforms are also ways of strengthening civil society. A robust civil society will probably have more success in changing unequal structures of political power that reinforce bad institutions. Note, too, that this recommendation for institutional reform applies not just to national governments but also to international organizations and NGOs. Incorporating local participation should help ensure that poverty reduction programmes genuinely serve a community's needs, and that those programmes are accountable to the community.

The recommendation for decentralization refers to transferring governance when possible to local institutions and communities. The idea is that when policies are formed at a more local level, they may be more responsive to the needs of the community. Hence it is common that proposals for governance reform include measures to strengthen the capacity of local governments via technical and/or financial assistance, such as with training for managing budgets (Grindle 2002). Decentralization may also buttress institutional checks and balances between the branches of government, and promote accountability *between* the branches (and levels) of government. An example is with rules to assure budgetary transparency and oversight so that money designated to be spent on projects that will benefit the poor really gets spent on those projects. Stronger checks and balances (and decentralized institutions in general) help combat authoritarianism. Such reforms further support political participation and making government institutions responsive to citizens (Grindle 2007b). Again, if governments in developing countries are more responsive and accountable, that should help promote poverty reduction policies. Decentralization can support basic capabilities that enable an individual to control her environment, in this case by influencing the public authorities that shape policies and deliver services. Like all these recommendations, however, decentralization may not be appropriate in every case, since there could be some policies that are best formulated at the national level.

Finally, institutional reform of the legal framework refers to strengthening the rule of law and judicial systems. Improved legal institutions enhance law enforcement, help combat corruption and encourage investment and political/economic stability. A strong legal regime to guarantee order and basic public safety is a vital step towards alleviating one source of poverty, particularly in societies that have experienced conflict. The legal regime must protect bodily integrity and the basic capability to live a life of a normal human length, and it is also essential for ensuring economic development with equity. Reforms should therefore support the equitable protection of civil and human rights, in part by expanding the access that poor people have to the judicial system. Reformed legal frameworks contribute to strengthening checks and balances between levels of government as well. A concrete policy example in this area is land reform, which can involve making sure that poor people have secure title rights to their land, and instituting a system that resolves land disputes fairly (Deolalikar *et al.* 2002). The importance of land reform is that people who own and cultivate their land are more productive than tenant farmers, which leads to productivity growth and (ideally) poverty reduction.

Two specific facets of poverty reduction give an idea of how the above areas of institutional reform overlap. First, one of the indispensable functions state institutions must fulfil is to protect basic human security, whether from corruption, crime, violence or economic shocks. Security from corruption, crime and violence comes from fair, impartial and easily accessible law enforcement whether from police or courts, which depend on adequate legal frameworks as well as efficient government bodies to uphold the laws. Institutions that are more democratic, accountable and transparent may also help avoid the kind of violence engendered by domestic and international conflicts. Reforms to protect against economic shocks target the very high vulnerability of poor people to sudden changes in their physical or financial assets. Such reforms can include legal statutes to protect the property rights of poor people, social insurance to cushion the blow of job loss, and vocational training to build marketable skills. All of these programmes depend on basically functional governance and institutions.

Second, another essential aspect of reducing poverty is providing economic opportunities to the poor. Reforms can institute and enforce laws and rules to prevent discrimination against poor people in markets for land, labour and credit. Economic opportunities can also be enhanced by reducing red tape to lower hurdles to starting a business, instituting anti-monopoly laws to prevent harmful concentrations of market (and attendant political) power, and assuring access to loans for poor people – all of which require effective institutions (Holmes *et al.* 2000).

There are several final points to keep in mind when considering how governance reform can be made most effective for poverty reduction. To begin with, it is naïve to think that merely changing laws will improve how institutions work. Remember that a frequent reason why institutions do not serve the poor well is because of intent: elites manipulate institutions for their own benefit. Thus institutional reform that does not alter the underlying distribution of political power may produce few positive changes. As but one example, though African Americans were ostensibly given equal legal rights in the South after the American Civil War, the white, landowning elite still retained considerable political power, and many forms of discrimination remained in place (Baland *et al.* 2009). This is why land reform is often cited as a means of altering the distribution of political power, since by breaking up concentrated land ownership so that more people are owners, economic power is also redistributed. Reforming institutions is a politically contentious process because it typically contravenes the power of established elites and even long societal traditions. Reform must not only correct unequal balances of power, but also overcome the path dependency of history that can continue shaping whatever reforms are put in place. Reforming the inequitable institutions in much of Latin America, with their colonial origins, is one example.

Box 7.3 Strengthening independent judiciaries, by Alexander Ozkan

What is an independent judiciary, and why is it so often considered an important part of institutional reform? The United States Agency for International Development (USAID) claims that 'Judicial independence lies at the heart of a well-functioning judiciary and is the cornerstone of a democratic, market-based society based on the rule of law.' An independent judiciary is one where judges render impartial rulings, are not manipulated by politicians, have the power to regulate the government's behaviour, and interpret the constitution and laws from a neutral perspective. According to this definition, three main tenets must hold for a judiciary to be independent: insularity, impartiality and legitimacy. First, the judges must be insulated and protected from manipulation. Second, judges must be impartial and unbiased when making decisions. Third, the judiciary should have enough legitimacy and power to be respected by elites and the general population.

Studies have found that countries with established independent judiciaries have a number of benefits for human and economic development. Independent judiciaries can help prevent democracies from regressing into authoritarian regimes. They can help ensure a separation of powers and act as an essential check to the power of the executive branch of government. Independent judiciaries are also associated with stronger protection of citizens' political rights and rule of law, which in turn can promote economic growth. Thus independent judiciaries have an important role to play in protecting basic human security and basic civil rights, and in encouraging equitable economic development. However, a familiar problem arises in trying to ascertain causal relationships: it may be that independent judiciaries contribute relatively little to such benefits, and that other factors are more important.

Nevertheless, policies to create an independent judiciary are common in the developing world, even if many countries struggle with implementing the long list of suggested reforms. That list includes depoliticized appointment systems, objective criteria for career advancement, constitutionally codified powers of judicial review for the highest court, continuing legal education for judges and judicial staff, formal ethics codes and public access to judicial proceedings. Two of the most common policies to insulate judges from political interference are security of tenure and of salary. If politicians have the ability to punish judges for their decisions, either by means of job termination or by reducing their salaries, then judicial independence is compromised. To keep judges impartial, many developing countries forbid their judges from participating in political activity, or engaging in economic activity besides writing or teaching. The idea is that a judge who works in some way for the timber industry cannot be impartial when hearing a case on deforestation. Policies such as minimum education or professional requirements for judges, and publication of rulings, are designed to increase legitimacy as well as the public's access to the judiciary. While these reforms can strengthen a country's institutions in a variety of ways, as with many other such reforms, scholarship is not yet clear on how they should be optimally prioritized.

Sources: Larkins (1996), USAID (2002), Howard and Carey (2004), Sousa (2007), Gibler and Randazzo (2011)

Institutional reforms, like most projects for societal change, can take decades to show results. Scholars have yet to identify an agreed-upon protocol for how to reform institutions. Nonetheless, international donors have frequently decided on their own protocols despite the lack of conclusive answers about which reforms to prioritize, which can have the most benefits in reducing poverty, and the timeframe for results. This has led to sometimes lengthy checklists that developing countries must complete in order to satisfy donors, which in turn leads to countries promising too much and trying to accomplish too many reforms at once. What is clear, though, is that countries at different levels of institutional development should focus on different things. For example, in some fragile or collapsed states such as the Democratic Republic of the Congo or Somalia, institutional deficiencies are so severe that it makes sense to focus on protecting basic security and personal safety. In countries with an existing if weak institutional structure, such as Burkina Faso or Honduras, reforms can support the expansion of public services, reducing corruption, and formalized rules for political succession. In countries with more established institutions such as India, Thailand and Mexico, the focus can be on boosting participation, making administrative structures more efficient and encouraging government transparency, accountability and responsiveness (Grindle 2007a).

For many countries in the global south, it will take a complex constellation of factors, including technological change, economic growth and support from international bodies, to surmount the considerable hurdles to institutional reform. Remember that there is a poverty trap here. Poor societies typically have deficient institutions; one reason that governance is weak in places such as Niger or Nepal is because those places lack the financial and human capital to have good governance. Whatever the difficulties and debates surrounding institutions and governance, though, they should not obscure the fact that reducing poverty depends vitally (though not exclusively) on governance systems that do not undermine human capabilities, and that can carry out policies to *expand* capabilities. Amartya Sen reminds us that institutions are central to poverty reduction and, in particular, to the expansion of human freedoms: 'Our opportunities and prospects depend crucially on what institutions exist and how they function' (Sen 1999: 142).

Conclusion

For some scholars, state institutions are not a primary cause of poverty. Primary causes would be ill health, illiteracy and lack of an economic livelihood. However, institutional deficiencies help explain why those primary causes exist or persist. A major reason why people are illiterate is because the state does not provide the public service of education. Thus even if institutions and governance are a background cause of poverty, they are still a pervasive reason for why people are poor. Moreover, from the capabilities perspective, institutions can be a primary cause. One reason is that state institutions have a major responsibility for protecting basic personal security, providing essential public services, guaranteeing key rights of expression, speech and participation, and ensuring that economic benefits are fairly distributed. When they fail to do these things, institutions increase poverty.

A second, powerful reason is that institutions can rob people of the dignity to which they are entitled. 'Dysfunctional institutions do not just fail to deliver services', Narayan explains. 'They disempower – and even silence – the poor through patterns of humiliation,

Box 7.4 Examples of governance reform programmes

Mexico

A goal for many countries is to strengthen state capacity by hiring more highly-qualified people into the bureaucracy. An evaluation by the Poverty Action Lab confirmed that in Mexico, raising salaries attracted more talented people to enter the civil service. Higher pay could also induce them to live in less desirable locations where the government's effectiveness might otherwise be weaker.

Indonesia

Seeking to combat corruption, an initiative focused on the village governance level, specifically on the misuse of public funds to build local roads. Audits of government accounts were increased, actual incidents of corruption were more widely publicized when they were uncovered, and community members were more consistently invited to open meetings on corruption. These measures helped decrease the misuse of public funds and strengthened community–government engagement as well.

Ethiopia

The World Bank and other donors have pursued a programme called the Protection of Basic Services. Besides supporting services in health, water, agriculture, education and other areas, the programme sought to increase governmental accountability for those services. Donors wanted to avoid giving money to the repressive central government, so instead funding was decentralized to regional and district governments, which had to follow strict transparency regulations.

Peru

Natural resources account for a very large proportion of Peru's export economy, but the country has implemented measures to prevent corruption and ensure good governance of resource revenues. There are laws on transparency and access to information to strengthen monitoring and accountability. Peru also became the first Latin American country fully compliant with the Extractive Industries Transparency Initiative, which advances a global standard for resource governance.

Tajikistan

The Global Partnership for Social Accountability has overseen a programme to improve management and transparency of water service providers. Citizens (and particularly women) have been assisted to form oversight boards for those providers. The boards have made the providers more responsive to people's needs and boosted people's willingness to pay the fees for the water they use. This is an example of how civil society and state institutions can work together to improve public services and increase trust in government.

For more information, see the websites of the Poverty Action Lab (Indonesia, Mexico), the World Bank (Ethiopia), the Extractive Industries Transparency Initiative (Peru) and the Global Partnership for Social Accountability (Tajikistan).

exclusion and corruption. The process is further compounded by legal and other formal barriers that prevent the poor from trading or gaining access to benefits. Thus, those at society's margins are further excluded and alienated' (Narayan *et al.* 2000b: 85). When state institutions (or the government officials behind them) are disempowering and shaming people in this way, they are fundamentally impeding a person's right to live a life that she has reason to value.

Development practitioners have staked a lot on the proposition that building better institutions and reforming governance in poorer countries will improve people's lives. But is this priority properly placed? After all, we do not have a consensus on best practices to help a society move from weak or bad institutions to good ones. No rote formula exists that every country can follow to achieve optimal institutions. Nonetheless, while application must be context specific, the guiding goals should be to guarantee basic human capabilities, encompassing personal security, public services, participation and economic opportunities. Therefore, even if they are not a primary cause of poverty, a reason that institutions deserve significant attention when studying causes of and solutions to poverty is that they are human creations and so can be changed. Indeed, institutions are one of the means of responding to other causes of poverty that are not outcomes of human action. For instance, the inherent conditions associated with geography such as being landlocked or in an area with a high disease burden require institutions to address them. Without functioning institutions – whether an effective police force, adequate health and education programmes, democratic means of ensuring citizens' power and politicians' accountability, or legal systems that equitably protect individuals' economic gains – probably no society will be able to escape poverty.

Discussion questions

1   Give examples of state institutions that can impact poverty. What role do capabilities play?
2   Give examples of governance that either worsens or reduces poverty. What role do capabilities play?
3   How do the examples of governance reform programmes in Box 7.4 reduce poverty and/or support capabilities?
4   Investigate how countries score using the following measurement tools. What patterns do you see, if any? What stands out to you?

   a   The World Bank's Worldwide Governance Indicators. Pick a country and see how it scores according to the six indicators, and then compare countries by indicator.
   b   The Bertelsmann Transformation Index. This is a complex but informative tool to measure countries' institutions. What are the indicators, and how might they relate to poverty? Go to Country Reports, pick a country, and see how it scores.
   c   Transparency International's Corruption Perceptions Index
   d   The Fragile States Index
   e   Sustainable Governance Indicators

5   Examine Sustainable Development Goal number 16 ('Promote just, peaceful, and inclusive societies'). What does it have to do with institutions? What are the targets for this goal? How can you measure those targets?
6   What do you see as the pros and cons of the following proposal? Some analysts have suggested that foreigners be installed as the governing power in fragile states. Doing

so could break the common cycle of warlords capturing political power in such states, and instead allow democratic institutions to be built up.

7   Assume that a benevolent dictator takes over a developing country. He or she promotes peace, good governance, and economic and human development in the country. However, institutions are not democratic. Can this situation be justified? What do you see as the pros and cons?

Further reading

Acemoglu, Daron and James Robinson. 2013. *Why Nations Fail: The origins of power, prosperity, and poverty*. New York, NY: Crown Business.

Gisselquist, Rachel and Danielle Resnick. 'Aiding government effectiveness in developing countries.' *Public Administration and Development* 34.3 (2014): 141–148.

Grindle, Merilee S. 2010. *Good Governance: The inflation of an idea*. HKS Faculty Research Working Paper Series, RWP10–023, John F. Kennedy School of Government, Harvard University.

Hydén, Göran and Kenneth Mease. 2004. *Making Sense of Governance: Empirical evidence from sixteen developing countries*. Boulder, CO: Lynne Rienner.

Works cited

Acemoglu, Daron, Simon Johnson and James A. Robinson. 'Institutions as the Fundamental Cause of Long-Run Growth', NBER Working Paper 10481. Cambridge: National Bureau of Economic Research, 2004.

Acemoglu, Daron, Simon Johnson and James A. Robinson. 'The colonial origins of comparative development: an empirical investigation', *American Economic Review*, 91.5 (2001): 1369–1401.

Adelman, Irma. 'Democracy and Development', in David A. Clark, ed. 2006. *The Elgar Companion to Development Studies*. Cheltenham, UK: Edward Elgar.

Alkire, Sabina. 2002. *Valuing Freedoms: Sen's capability approach and poverty reduction*. Oxford: Oxford University Press.

Apaza, Carmen R. 'Measuring governance and corruption through the worldwide governance indicators: Critiques, responses, and ongoing scholarly discussion.' *PS: Political Science & Politics*, 42.01 (2009): 139–143.

Baland, Jean-Marie, Karl Ove Moene and James A. Robinson. 'Governance and Development', in Dani Rodrik and Mark Rosenzweig, eds. 2009. *Handbook of Development Economics*. Philadelphia, PA: Elsevier.

Bastiaensen, Johan, Tom De Herdt and Ben D'Exelle. 'Poverty reduction as a local institutional process.' *World Development*, 33.6 (2005): 979–993.

Bowles, Samuel. 'Institutional Poverty Traps', in Bowles, Samuel, Steven N. Durlauf and Karla Hoff, eds. 2006. *Poverty Traps*. Princeton, NJ: Princeton University Press.

Carothers, Thomas and Diane de Gramont. *Aiding Governance in Developing Countries*. Carnegie Endowment for International Peace, Washington, DC, November 2011.

Chang, Ha-Joon. 'Understanding the Relationship between Institutions and Economic Development: Some Key Theoretical Issues', paper presented at the WIDER Jubilee conference, June 2005.

Chong, Alberto, and César Calderón. 'Institutional quality and poverty measures in a cross-section of countries.' *Economics of Governance*, 1.2 (2000): 123–135.

Chong, Alberto, and Mark Gradstein. 'Inequality and Institutions.' *The Review of Economics and Statistics*, 89.3 (2007): 454–465.

Collier, Paul. 2008. *The Bottom Billion: Why the poorest countries are failing and what can be done about it*. New York, NY: Oxford University Press.

Crocker, David A. 'Deliberative participation in local development.' *Journal of Human Development*, 8.3 (2007): 431–455.

Dahl, Robert. 2000. *On Democracy*. New Haven, CT: Yale University Press.

Deneulin, Séverine. 'Democracy and Political Participation', in Séverine Deneulin and Lila Shahani, eds. 2009. *An Introduction to the Human Development and Capability Approach*. London: Earthscan.

Deolalikar, Anil B., Alex B. Brillantes Jr., Raghav Gaiha, Ernesto M. Pernia and Mary Racelis. 'Poverty Reduction and the Role of Institutions in Developing Asia.' ERD Working Paper No. 10. Asian Development Bank. May 2002.

Drydyk, Jay. 'When is development more democratic?' *Journal of Human Development*, 6.2 (2005): 247–267.

Engerman, Stanley L. and Kenneth L. Sokoloff. 'Institutions and Non-Institutional Explanations of Economic Differences', NBER Working Paper 9989. Cambridge: National Bureau of Economic Research, 2003.

Engerman, Stanley L. and Kenneth L. Sokoloff. 'Factor endowments, institutions and differential paths of growth among new world economies: a view from economic historians of the United States', in Stephen Haber, ed. 1997. *How Latin America Fell Behind*. Stanford, CA: Stanford University Press.

Fukuyama, Francis, 'What Is Governance?' Center for Global Development Working Paper 314, January 2013.

Gerring, John, Peter Kingstone, Matthew Lange and Aseema Sinha. 'Democracy, history, and economic performance: a case-study approach'. *World Development*, 39.10 (2011): 1735–1748.

Gibler, Douglas M. and Kirk A. Randazzo. 'Testing the effects of independent judiciaries on the likelihood of democratic backsliding.' *American Journal of Political Science*, 55.3 (2011): 696–709.

Gisselquist, Rachel. *Good governance as a concept, and why this matters for development policy*. WIDER Working Paper No. 2012/30, 2012.

Glaeser, Edward L., Rafael La Porta, Florencio Lopez-de-Silane and Andrei Shleifer. 'Do Institutions Cause Growth?' NBER Working Papers 10568. Cambridge: National Bureau of Economic Research.

Grindle, Merilee S. 'Governance reform: the new analytics of next steps.' *Governance*, 24.3 (2011): 415–418.

Grindle, Merilee S. 'Good enough governance revisited.' *Development Policy Review*, 25.5 (2007a): 553–574.

Grindle, Merilee S. 2007b. *Going Local: Decentralization, democratization, and the promise of good governance*. Princeton, NJ: Princeton University Press.

Grindle, Merilee S. 'Good Enough Governance: Poverty Reduction and Reform in Developing Countries', World Bank Poverty Reduction Paper, November 2002.

Herrera, Javier, Mireille Razafindrakoto and François Roubaud. 'Governance, democracy and poverty reduction: lessons drawn from household surveys in sub-Saharan Africa and Latin America.' *International Statistical Review*, 75.1 (2007): 70–95.

Hickey, Sam. 'Turning governance thinking upside-down? Insights from "the politics of what works".' *Third World Quarterly* 33.7 (2012): 1231–1247.

Holmes, M., S. Knack, N. Manning, R. Messick and J. Rinne. 'Governance and Poverty Reduction', World Bank, April 2000.

Howard, Robert M. and Henry F. Carey. 'Is an independent judiciary necessary for democracy?' *Judicature* 87.6 (2004): 284–290.

Human Rights Watch. 'Corruption on Trial? The Record of Nigeria's Economic and Financial Crimes Commission.' August 2011.

Human Rights Watch. 'Everyone's in on the Game: Corruption and Human Rights Abuses by the Nigeria Police Force.' August 2010.

Humphreys, Macartan, Jeffrey D. Sachs and Joseph E. Stiglitz, eds. 2007. *Escaping the Resource Curse*. New York, NY: Columbia University Press.

Hydén, Göran. 'Governance and poverty reduction in Africa.' PNAS 104.43 (2007): 16751–16756.

Hydén, Göran and Julius Court. 'Governance and Development', World Governance Survey Discussion Paper 1, United Nations University, August 2002.

Kaufman, Daniel, Aart Kraay and Massimo Mastruzzi. 'The Worldwide Governance Indicators: Methodology and Analytical Issues', World Bank Policy Research Working Paper 5430, September 2010.

Larkins, Christopher M. 'Judicial independence and democratization: a theoretical and conceptual analysis.' *The American Journal of Comparative Law*, 44.4 (1996): 605–626.

Leavy, Jennifer, Joanna Howard *et al.* 2013. *What Matters Most? Evidence from 84 Participatory Studies with Those Living with Extreme Poverty and Marginalisation*. Brighton, UK: Institute for Development Studies.

Luckham, Robin, Anne Marie Goetz, Mary Kaldor, Alison Ayers, Sunil Bastian, Emmanuel Gyimah-Boadi, Shireen Hassim and Zarko Puhovski. 'Democratic Institutions and Politics in Contexts of Inequality, Poverty, and Conflict: A Conceptual Framework.' Institute of Development Studies Working Paper 104. 2000.

Mehlum, Halvor, Karl Moene and Ragnar Torvik. 'Institutions and the resource curse.' *The Economic Journal*, 116.508 (2006): 1–20.

Méon, Pierre-Guillaume, and Khalid Sekkat. 'Does corruption grease or sand the wheels of growth?' *Public Choice* 122.1–2 (2005): 69–97.

Narayan, Deepa, Robert Chambers, Meera Kaul Shah and Patti Petesch. 2000a. *Voices of the Poor: Crying out for change*. New York, NY: Oxford University Press.

Narayan, Deepa, with Raj Patel, Kai Schafft, Anne Rademacher and Sarah Koch-Schulte. 2000b. *Voices of the Poor: Can anyone hear us?* New York, NY: Oxford University Press.

North, Douglass. 1990. *Institutions, Institutional Change and Economic Performance*. Cambridge: Cambridge University Press.

Perera, Liyanage Devangi H., and Grace HY Lee. 'Have economic growth and institutional quality contributed to poverty and inequality reduction in Asia?' *Journal of Asian Economics*, 27 (2013): 71–86.

Pritchett, Lant, Michael Woolcock and Matt Andrews. 'Capability Traps? The Mechanisms of Persistent Implementation Failure', Center for Global Development Working Paper 234, December 2010.

Robinson, James A., Ragnar Torvik and Thierry Verdier. 'Political foundations of the resource curse.' *Journal of Development Economics*, 79.2 (2006): 447–468.

Rodrik, Dani. 'Institutions for high-quality growth: what they are and how to acquire them.' *Studies in International Development*, 35.3 (2000): 3–31.

Rodrik, Dani, Arvind Subramanian and Francesco Trebbi. 'Institutions rule: the primacy of institutions over geography and integration in economic development.' *Journal of Economic Growth*, 9.2 (2004): 131–165.

Ross, Michael L. 'The political economy of the resource curse.' *World Politics*, 51.02 (1999): 297–322.

Rotberg, Robert, ed. 2003. *When States Fail: Causes and consequences*. Princeton, NJ: Princeton University Press.

Rothstein, Bo and Marcus Tannenberg. 2015. 'Making Development Work: The Quality of Government Approach', EBA Report 2015:07.

Sachs, Jeffrey, John W. McArthur, Guido Schmidt-Traub, Margaret Kruk, Chandrika Bahadur, Michael Faye and Gordon McCord. 'Ending Africa's Poverty Trap', *Brookings Papers on Economic Activity*, 2004(1), 117–240.

Sacks, Audrey, and Margaret Levi. 'Measuring government effectiveness and its consequences for social welfare in sub-Saharan African countries.' *Social Forces*, 88.5, (2010): 2325–2351.

Sen, Amartya. 'Democracy: the only way out of poverty.' *New Perspectives Quarterly*, 17.1 (2000): 28–30.

Sen, Amartya. 1999. *Development as Freedom*. New York, NY: Oxford University Press.

Soubbotina, Tatyana P. and Katherine Sheram. 2000. *Beyond Economic Growth: Meeting the challenges of global development*. Washington, DC: World Bank.

Sousa, Mariana. 'A Brief Overview of Judicial Reform in Latin America' in Eduardo Lora, ed. 2007. *The State of State Reform in Latin America*. New York, NY: The Inter-American Development Bank.

Tebaldi, Edinaldo and Ramesh Mohan. 'Institutions and poverty.' *Journal of Development Studies*, 46.6 (2010): 1047–1066.

United Nations Development Programme (UNDP). 2011. *Human Development Report 2011: Sustainability and Equity: A better future for all.* New York, NY: UNDP.

United Nations System Task Team on the Post-2015 UN Development Agenda. 'Governance and Development: Thematic Think Piece.' UNDESA, UNDP, UNESCO. May 2012.

United States Agency for International Development, Office of Democracy and Governance. 'Guidance for Promoting Judicial Independence and Impartiality', January 2002.

United States State Department, Bureau of Democracy, Human Rights, and Labor. *Country Reports on Human Rights Practices for 2012: Nigeria.* www.state.gov/j/drl/rls/hrrpt/humanrightsreport/index.htm?year=2012&dlid=204153. Accessed December 2013.

Unsworth, Sue. 2010. *An Upside Down View of Governance.* University of Sussex Institute of Development Studies.

Van Doeveren, Veerle. 'Rethinking good governance: identifying common principles.' *Public Integrity*, 13.4 (2011): 301–318.

Williams, Andrew, and Abu Siddique. 'The use (and abuse) of governance indicators in economics: a review.' *Economics of Governance*, 9.2 (2008): 131–175.

Williamson, Oliver E. 'The new institutional economics: taking stock, looking ahead.' *Journal of Economic Literature*, 38.3 (2000): 595–613.

8 Conflict and poverty

Serena Cosgrove

Key questions

- What is the relationship between poverty and armed conflict? How does poverty cause conflict and war, and how do conflict and war cause poverty?
- What are the effects of armed conflict on individuals, communities and countries?
- Why are war and conflict considered a trap?
- What strategies can promote reconstruction, recovery and reconciliation after a war?
- How do capabilities and human security apply to conflict and post-conflict situations?

Vignette 8.1

I came of age in a warzone. From 1986 to 1988 I worked with the ecumenical organization Witness for Peace, living in an active warzone in northern Nicaragua (Figure 8.1) where I was a witness to the war between the Sandinista Army – the Armed Forces of the Nicaraguan government – and the US-backed rebels – the Contras or counter-revolutionaries. What does it mean to be a witness? My role was to live with civilian communities located in the warzones and document the effects of the war on their lives. I took testimony from farmers whose crops, livestock, houses and barns had been destroyed by nearby fighting or looting. I visited civilians in clinics and field hospitals who had been injured by crossfire, attacks or land and anti-personnel mines. I accompanied women who had lost family members due to conflict or had to flee their homes for the resettlement community of San José de Bocay, the small town where I was based in the department of Jinotega.

While living in Bocay, I was approached by a group of women who wanted to form a sewing cooperative and learn a new skill that would occupy their time and help them generate income. They argued that my help was more important than documenting the war: 'Help us build something positive', they urged me. Mercedes, the town baker, was also a seamstress and agreed to teach the women if I could raise funds for the sewing machines and other materials. Even though I enjoyed starting to get to know the women as they met with Mercedes for classes, my focus was on finding three sewing machines, fabric, thread, zippers and buttons. This was not an easy feat when there were no sewing supplies in town, the roads to bigger towns were mined, and once I made it to a city, sewing supplies were limited due to the US trade embargo against Nicaragua. I took advantage of an annual trip home to the United States to talk about Nicaraguan farming women and how hard it is for them to generate income while a war is going on. I raised the money to purchase the machines. And slowly but surely the women began to sew: first for themselves and then family and community members as they mastered their new craft.

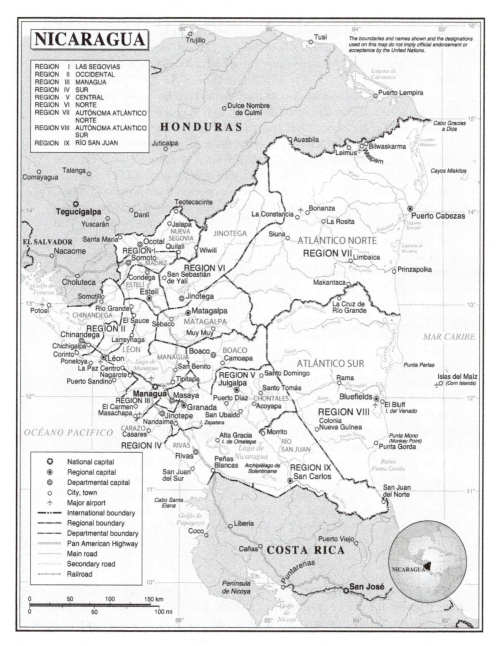

Figure 8.1 Map of Nicaragua

Source: Map No. 3932 Rev. 5 UNITED NATIONS November 2011

Each woman had strong motivation to learn to sew: Valeria and Eugenia wanted to have a way to generate income for when their boyfriends came back from fighting. Four other women were single moms – widowed by the war – and they desperately needed income for food for their children. And there was Violeta, whose husband was with the Contras, but she didn't talk too much about him given the town was held by the Sandinista army. She was 24 years old and had never been to school. A small woman, she had a permanent expression of dismay on her face: she was accustomed to bad news. Violeta had three children: a girl age 10 and two little boys. When the counter-revolution attacked the town of Bocay, her husband was killed in combat. Suddenly she was widowed, with three children to feed, with no pension because her husband had fought on the wrong side, and with no family in town to help her because they were spread out across the country having fled the fighting themselves. She lived in a makeshift house of bamboo with a dirt floor and no electricity or access to potable water. Her children were always hungry and frequently ill. When Violeta's husband died, the cooperative was just getting started, and the members were still learning, not generating income yet. Then Violeta's daughter, Jasmine, died of dehydration. Her health had been compromised by lack of food, preventable diseases, and diarrhoea. She just couldn't resist any more.

The members of the cooperative and I went to the wake the night before the funeral, all of us sensing that things would never be the same. As dusk fell, I watched Jasmine's body. She lay on the table with her one nice dress on, flowers tucked all around her, her hair plaited, her nostrils stuffed with cotton. Her skin looked yellow in the wavering light of the small kerosene lamps. The next day a group carried the little coffin to the cemetery. As the coffin disappeared into the ground, I looked up at the verdant mountains surrounding us; I listened to the river rushing by; I adjusted my glasses against the tropical sun. How could there be so much suffering and death in such a lush and beautiful place?

Soon after Jasmine's death, Violeta left Bocay for Managua, hoping relatives living in a shantytown in the capital would take her in. One by one the other women abandoned the cooperative: most of the group followed Violeta, leaving Bocay for other towns or cities away from the fighting. Valeria stayed in town but said her fiancé did not want her working outside the home. And then Mercedes, our teacher, told me she had stored away the sewing machines and our few remaining supplies in the health centre. She had decided to close the bakery and move south to Jinotega City where she had a small house on the edge of the city. 'It's just too dangerous and sad here', she told me guiltily. 'I have to think about my children.'

Introduction

War and other forms of armed conflict can be devastating for men, women and children, whether they're combatants or civilians. But as Violeta's story demonstrates, militarized violence and poverty intertwine in deep and complicated ways. Certainly conflict can cause or contribute to poverty. The turmoil in which Violeta lived made it harder for her to provide her daughter Jasmine with food and protect her from illness. Moreover, the fighting rendered very difficult any opportunity to learn new skills and earn a livelihood, and hence the sewing cooperative collapsed. These effects were writ large across the Nicaraguan countryside: villages scattered, people killed, bridges blown up, houses and schools and health clinics bombed. Thus conflict can destroy the economic and physical capital that a country needs to grow economically. However, what makes the poverty–conflict relationship so complicated is that poverty can also contribute to violence. There is a very strong correlation between low per capita incomes and a higher likelihood for civil war. But does this mean that poverty can *cause* violent conflict? If so, how frequent or powerful an explanation is poverty for why wars erupt? And if conflict causes poverty and poverty causes conflict, what are the ways out of this poverty trap?

The conflict–poverty nexus is not just complicated: it is common. According to a World Bank estimate, over two billion people routinely suffer from extreme violence. A third of all countries in the world have endured a civil war, and more than half the countries in Africa have experienced conflict in the last few decades. Oxfam (2007) calculated that Africa has lost more than 284 billion USD to armed conflict since 1990. More than a quarter of the world's population of people in extreme poverty live in fragile, conflict-ridden states. Those states account for one-third of children's deaths. UNICEF estimates that some 300,000 child soldiers are currently exploited in conflicts worldwide, six million children have been severely injured or disabled, and 20 million are living as refugees. As one final, sad fact, around 68 per cent of the global arms trade goes to developing countries (Grimmett 2012). Conflict, then, has been a major, all too frequent contributor to poverty.

These statistics are a reminder that wars are seldom waged solely between combatants (Kinsella 2011). Since the mid-twentieth century, there have been ten civilian deaths on average per single combatant death in conflicts around the world.[1] Though there is debate about the exact ratio because some conflicts with very high civilian casualties can skew the average, the point remains: it is generally agreed that over the past 60 years, it is more dangerous to be a civilian in a warzone than a soldier (Slim 2003). This is because armed groups – be they government forces (the army, the police, the national guard etc.), paramilitary groups affiliated with government forces, rebel groups and terrorists – intentionally target not only each other but also civilians. Street by street or community by community, warfare has affected many in the developing world, such as in Sierra Leone, Liberia, Guatemala, El Salvador and Vietnam. Terrorism similarly targets soldiers and non-combatants to kill, demoralize and destroy infrastructure and livelihoods needed by civilian populations for survival.

Militarized violence can be divided into the broad categories of intra- and inter-state conflicts. Intra-state conflicts are the most common: they are internal within a country's national borders, such as civil wars or coups. Civil wars are a specific phenomenon that entails a rebel group or multiple rebel groups fighting a central government for control over the country. Coups, on the other hand, involve actors within the state challenging each other for dominance, i.e., one faction of the army trying to wrest control from a president of other faction. Though internal conflicts are often distinguished by barbarism and intimacy due to proximity and familiarity (Kalyvas 2006), wars between countries extend the numbers of peoples affected directly and indirectly. These interstate conflicts can range from conflict between neighbouring states to world wars, and also include imperial and anticolonial wars (Dimah 2009). The scope of the suffering increases exponentially as additional countries – and their resources – are committed to the fighting and the spillover effects of traumatized refugees, political instability and economic stagnation spread to neighbouring countries not even participating in the fighting. Though there are useful distinctions to be drawn between these two broad categories, the dynamics behind intra- and interstate wars can be similar (Wimmer and Min 2006).

There are also other forms of violent conflict such as rampant crime, genocide and terrorism that are not necessarily captured by these two categories. 'Many current conflicts do not fit neatly into the traditional categories of international and non-international armed conflict' (Waszink 2011: 5). In reality, the differences can become blurry, and often an intra-state war can become an interstate war or vice versa.

Our purpose in this chapter is not to provide a precise typology of wars but rather to study the commonalities in how armed conflicts affect human lives. Conflicts, no matter the definition, often have similar impacts at the level of individuals, households and communities. This chapter takes a broad perspective on how militarized violence of various kinds damages human development. The objective is to untangle the complex relationships between conflict and poverty, and suggest how human development can be promoted even in conflict and post-conflict societies. The first section explores how poverty can cause conflict, while the second examines how conflict causes poverty at the macro level. The third section deepens the analysis by looking at conflict's micro-level impact on capabilities. The final section employs the human security framework to review some strategies to protect wellbeing during conflicts and to help societies rebuild once the fighting has stopped.

How poverty causes conflict

Poverty according to both economic and other definitions can and does cause conflict, though the dynamic is multifaceted and complex. This makes poverty eradication programmes an important component of peacemaking efforts. One of the most solid scholarly findings is that poverty conceived as low GDP per capita is a good predictor of when civil wars will erupt (Blattman and Miguel 2010). Slow economic growth rates, economic shocks, low crop yields due to drought or other causes, and vertical (between individuals) and horizontal (between groups) income inequality (Stewart 2016) can also spark conflict, since if people are poor enough the opportunity risks of violence will diminish, and conflict will appear a better survival strategy than extreme poverty. Economic motivations for war can sometimes be lumped under the term 'greed': the idea is that people start fighting in order to capture wealth through loot or plunder (Collier and Hoeffler 1998). However, this motivation does not apply just to poor people, since even those who are reasonably well off can be motivated by greed to seize assets. Warlords in various sub-Saharan African countries such as Liberia or Congo serve as an example: they may come from the elite, but they want to capture diamond mines or oil wells partly to enrich themselves.

Horizontal inequality – inequality among groups including ethnic, racial, political, religious and class dimensions – is argued by some theorists (Langer 2005 and Stewart 2000 and 2016) to contribute to creating inter-group conflict: as inequality and poverty increase for some groups in a society in comparison to other groups, so does the risk of conflict. Interestingly, horizontal inequality isn't just about income inequality between groups but also inequality across capabilities – political participation, access to health, education and other public services, and cultural entitlements – as well. Stewart (2000) argues that when groups mobilize violently, they do so out of group motivations, not just individual desires. Sometimes the mobilization occurs along ethnic lines, religious differences or class dissimilarities. In an analysis of the Ivory Coast, Langer (2005) proposes that ethnic inequalities at the level of societal elites combined with socio-economic inequalities at the level of the majority poor can combine in explosive ways.

Disenfranchised elites become leaders of poor people along ethnic lines protesting unequal treatment. It can be an interesting exercise to examine a war or conflict from the perspective of horizontal inequality indicators at the beginning of hostilities: to what extent were there differences between groups that were later used by group leaders to foment violence? Certainly, a number of examples used in this chapter lend themselves to this analysis.

'Grievance' is a related factor that can spark conflict. It means that people start fighting because of anger over historical injustices or inter-group inequalities (Buhaug *et al.* 2013). The poverty in this case can be relative deprivation in access to economic opportunities, political rights or other basic entitlements. Economic or political disparities between social classes or ethnic groups can become grievances that motivate leaders to form rebel groups, army officers to lead coups, or even collective violent responses from the population which lead to internal or regional wars. Where grievances overlap with ethnic fragmentation, some scholars claim that conflict is more likely (Gurr 1993, Stewart 2011). As but two examples: the Tamil Tigers in Sri Lanka and Basque separatists in Spain both launched campaigns of violence based on claims that as minority ethnic groups they were disadvantaged economically and politically.

While there is some empirical support for all of the above factors, there are also disputes over their relative impacts (Justino *et al.* 2013). Ethnic fragmentation by no means always leads to conflict. There are plenty of peaceful multi-ethnic societies such as Zambia or Indonesia. Likewise, effectively every society has some inequalities between people and groups, but that does not always mean that people are fighting. Though most civil wars occur in places with extreme poverty, not all extremely poor countries fall into conflict. These factors are all broad generalizations, but sometimes conflict can occur because of idiosyncratic reasons endogenous to that region or country such as a particularly despotic ruler or a drought, for example (Justino 2009 and 2010). Moreover, such generalizations at the societal level should be unpacked to examine the micro level of factors that spur individual decisions to fight. For instance, a person who has no job might join an armed group because it provides a kind of work. Or a person might have a job, but regard joining an armed group as providing a chance to earn more. Or a person might join an armed group as self-protection and the only way to protect family, especially if the government is seen as unable or unwilling to do so. Any of these motivations *could* impel someone to take up arms, but when they actually do will depend on individual cases.

There are of course other potential factors besides poverty associated with conflict. (Arnson and Zartman 2005, Levy and Thompson 2011, Demmers 2012) States' strategic interests, or weak states that aren't able to provide services, security or rule of law to all or parts of their territory, can be powerful explanations. Also with a role are neighbouring countries experiencing conflict, or mountainous territory where rebel groups can easily form and hide from the national government or international observers. Even where common motivators for conflict exist, when violence actually breaks out can be influenced by variables such as the level of technology and resources available to any armed group and/or the intensity and nature of a group's ideological beliefs (Justino 2011). The takeaway is that 'greed and grievance' and the factors they subsume (weak economic growth, income inequality, injustices of various kinds) *can* lead to conflict – but beyond these general principles, understanding how poverty sparks violence requires a more detailed examination of individual societies.

Box 8.1 Conflict in the Democratic Republic of the Congo, by Sophia Sanders

The Democratic Republic of the Congo (DRC) is Africa's largest country and host to the deadliest conflict in the continent's modern history. The Great African War began in 1996 and is also referred to as the First and Second Congo Wars. As the names suggest, the fighting was concentrated in one country; however, it engulfed much of sub-Saharan Africa, blurring the line between interstate war and intra-state conflict. The bloody and brutal fighting has killed over five million people (Stearns 2011:4) and displaced at least another two million. (Soderlund *et al.* 2013: xv) Wars are rarely fought over a single issue, resulting instead from an escalation of several factors. Congo is no different, but what has made its conflict so deadly and so prolonged are the staggering amounts of armed groups, variety of state actors supporting the various sides, and ever-shifting alliances. When compounded by high poverty, inequality, landlessness, a vicious colonial legacy and ineffective governance, Congo was and unfortunately continues to be little more than a staging ground for imported conflict.

The official start of the conflict can be traced back to the aftermath of the Rwandan genocide in 1994, though Congo was already an unstable and weak state, vulnerable to this spillover for a multitude of reasons. After the Tutsis succeeded in overthrowing the Hutu government and ending the Rwandan genocide, over two million Hutus fled into the eastern part of the DRC. (Prunier 2009) Hutu militiamen responsible for genocidal crimes formed new groups and the Congolese Tutsi population suddenly became the victims of escalating violence at the hands of these militias. Rwanda, looking to prevent the Hutus from establishing a stronghold so close to its borders, began to encourage and support Tutsi militias in eastern Congo. Eventually a Rwandan and Ugandan invasion of Congo sparked the First Congo War and led to the ousting of the Congolese government. However, the new government was just as incapable of stopping the violence in the east or disarming the many warring militias. This instability was once more intolerable to Rwanda and, with the support of Burundi and Uganda, it again invaded the DRC, beginning the Second Congo War. At the height of the conflict there were nine countries fighting each other on Congolese soil, including Angola, Chad, Namibia and Zimbabwe. Though the official war technically ended in 2002, eastern DRC remains plagued with armed conflict carried out by proxy militias supported by various regional countries, despite the most expensive and longest-running UN peacekeeping mission in history.

As the militias continue to vie for power and resources, civilians suffer deeply, with few options for escaping starvation, moving out of poverty, receiving an education or being sheltered from the violence. Young men are relatively easy to recruit to armed groups as most militias offer some food, wages and protection that the state does not. It is not a difficult decision to move from civilian to combatant when faced with unending starvation and destitution. This is just one example of how poverty and conflict reinforce each other in the Congo. Until these issues are addressed through effective governance, the Congolese of eastern DRC will continue to suffer in this vicious, self-perpetuating cycle.

It would be too simplistic to say that the Congo's recent wars are due only to the spillover of ethnic fragmentation, as this ignores historical factors that first crippled the country, making it so vulnerable to violence in the first place. Land inequality, colonial rule, illogically drawn borders, corrupt dictators and lack of public services have impeded economic and human development since the early 1900s and particularly after it gained independence in 1960. Issues of land inequality began under Belgian colonial rule when white settlers declared vacant land to be property of the colonial state. Congolese land owners were heavily taxed, often forced to give up their property. Once independent, DRC was ruled and robbed by a corrupt dictator who rewarded loyalty by giving away large swathes of land, further entrenching land inequality and food insecurity. Today, 'since the start of the Congolese war, land has turned from a 'source' of conflict into a 'resource' of conflict ... Rebel leaders ... have turned land into an asset to be distributed among their members. These practices are both based on inclusion and exclusion: those belonging to the ethnic network in control are granted free access to land; those not belonging to it become the main victims.' (Vlassenroot and Huggins, 2004: 2) Among the many tragic consequences of the continued violence (beyond the devastating loss of life) is that the largest country in the region, which has the capacity to feed the continent with its arable land, cannot even feed a majority of its own people.

Apart from land, perhaps Congo's greatest vulnerability is its abundance of natural resources including copper, diamonds, minerals, uranium and oil. These mineral and energy deposits have the potential to fuel significant economic growth and provide the Congolese with basic human services. Instead, the vast resources have been plundered and exploited to line the coffers of high-ranking government officials and militia groups who sell them to the highest bidder to fund their attacks. Many well-known US companies, such as Party City (the makers of My Little Pony toys among other household names) and Apple, have found conflict minerals from Congo in their supply chains. (Browning 2015) And while they profit from cheap access to these minerals, it is the Congolese who pay the real price. According to the United Nations World Food Programme, seven million Congolese face food insecurity, and the country has the highest rate of extreme poverty in the world, with 63 per cent of the population living on less than USD 1.25 a day (United Nations World Food Programme 2017). Is it the continuation of armed conflict that entrenches these conditions or is it the prevalence of these problems that make the country a magnet for conflict? Autesserre (2010) argues that regional wars – and the Congolese conflict exemplifies this – cannot be explained solely by regional or national narratives such as minerals or political elites but also has to include local tensions and stakeholders, what Kalyvas (2006) refers to as the macro-level, the meso-level and intra-community dynamics.

Sources: Vlassenroot and Huggins 2004, Prunier 2009, Soderlund *et al.* 2013, Browning 2015, United Nations World Food Programme 2017.

How conflict causes poverty at the macro level

Conflict can create or worsen poverty at both the macro and micro levels. 'Macro' in this case refers to effects that are society-wide, national or regional in scope. The 'micro' level centres on the individual but includes the household, the group and the local community. At the macro level we focus primarily on various forms of capital, while at the micro level we study conflict's effects on capabilities and functionings. We will also note both short-term and long-term effects. In reality, the macro and micro levels are difficult to separate: effects at the societal level can obviously have an impact at the individual level, and vice versa. Similarly, economic and capability poverty are deeply intertwined here as in many other areas.

To begin with, conflict can severely retard economic growth (Collier 1999, 2007). This is not surprising since fighting often destroys key infrastructure such as roads, bridges, markets and factories. War typically disrupts agriculture, industry and traditional crafts and skills. Through its economic effects, conflict can become a poverty trap, since it can exacerbate factors that lead to conflict in the first place, such as low incomes, stagnant economies, weak states and limited economic opportunities for youth (Blattman and Miguel 2010). A country that has had a civil war has roughly double the chance of relapsing into conflict (Collier *et al.* 2003). However, conflict is not *always* an economic poverty trap since, in the long run, war-torn countries' economies can rebound. There is some evidence that at least in the case of civil wars, countries can recover a significant portion of economic growth relatively quickly (Cerra *et al.* 2008).

Examining conflict's effects on different kinds of capital is a useful way of clarifying poverty relationships at the macro level. All of the kinds of capital we discuss can help support human wellbeing, so when they are destroyed, economic and human development are both undermined (Goodhand 2001). Physical capital includes the bridges, roads etc. mentioned above but also buildings and even people's houses – their destruction will obviously affect people in many ways. The loss of the materials and products that arrive on roads and are transported over bridges can lead to market shocks at a tremendous cost to economic growth and livelihoods. If products can't be imported and exported, business stagnates and markets shut down. Conflict can also destroy natural capital as people's access to environmental resources such as forests, fields, rivers and air is impaired by bombing, shooting, chemical weapons or land mines. If fields are mined, or fighting makes it unsafe to work them, then agricultural production plummets. Fearful of attack and displacement, farmers won't plant, which raises the risk of famine. As one example of how conflict can destroy natural capital, in the Vietnam War the United States dropped millions of litres of the defoliant Agent Orange on forests, creating vast swathes of barren territory.

Conflict can damage financial capital by destroying financial institutions and/or inhibiting access to investment, credit and markets. Foreign investors are extremely unlikely to invest in a country in conflict, and when violence erupts, capital often flees. For example, during Angola's civil war (1975–2002), capital flight in financial terms totalled upwards of USD 40 billion, one of the highest rates in Africa. Violence damages political capital by weakening states and the public goods they provide, by eroding the rule of law and democratic political processes (see Box 8.2). Schools and training programmes flounder as students and their families choose the immediacy of survival rather than attending classes and investing in the future. Health services are hindered as clinics and hospitals are destroyed and public health campaigns cancelled. Human

---

Box 8.2 Effects of conflict on the rule of law

1   Erosion of checks and balances on government powers
2   Increasing corruption
3   Decline in order and security
4   Violations of fundamental rights
5   Lack of open government
6   Inadequate regulatory enforcement
7   Inadequate access to civil justice
8   Ineffective criminal justice system

(Adapted from Haugen and Boutros 2014)

---

capital is thereby retarded as young people miss out on an education, or a population loses access to health care. Long-term, sustainable economic development and participative forms of governance are extremely difficult in war-affected areas because education, health services, other governmental services, local markets and local production cease or decrease when conflict occurs.

Conflict can also be particularly injurious to social capital (Aghajanian 2012). Social capital is a term that encompasses the vertical and horizontal relationships between people; these links help guarantee the survival of all members in the community. Most societies are hierarchically organized whether by social class, gender, ethnicity, roles in institutions important to the community, or traditional forms of leadership such as chiefs and local healers. This means that the people you know above and below you in your society's social hierarchy can help you to gain the necessary goods to provide for your family. Horizontal relationships can include peers, age mates and close siblings: these are important allies for survival. Social capital also includes the connections that an individual has with others placed in important institutions such as schools, government offices etc. The importance of social capital is not just one individual's connections but the extensive network of relationships that sustains a community.

In times of war, social capital suffers as families and communities are disrupted and separated, neighbours inform against neighbours, institutions cease to function and communities scatter (Ghobarah *et al.* 2003). After spending time in the Eastern Congo, Jones discusses how in wartime social capital dissolves, exemplified by how 'the durability of extended family ties, the allegiance of kinfolk, the pleasant give-and-take of hospitality ... all fade and fracture' (2010: 162). Trust is another factor necessary for human cooperation that can diminish during times of violent conflict. Given the fear, suffering and deprivation of war, the horizon of trust relationships can shrink. This, in turn, leads to the dissolution of social norms employed by the community for their survival, and the wealth of wisdom and knowledge that informs food production, marriage and the raising of children is eroded. Stearns comments that 'Mass violence does not just affect the families of the dead. It tears at the fabric of society and lodges in the minds of the witnesses and perpetrators alike' (2011: 261). The collapse of social capital, trust and mores further weakens poor communities' chances for survival.

Box 8.3 Case study on El Salvador and intra-state conflict

El Salvador, a small Central American country the size of Connecticut, exemplifies many of the challenges associated with intra-state conflicts (Figure 8.2). El Salvador experienced a civil war from 1980 to 1992, during which over 75,000 people were killed, 7000 were 'disappeared' and 500,000 civilians were internally displaced or became refugees fleeing to Honduras and other countries (see Cosgrove 2010, Silber 2010). The guerrillas proclaimed they were fighting to protect the civilian population that was being targeted by the repressive government. After the assassination of six Jesuit Catholic priests, their housekeeper and her daughter by the Salvadoran Army in November of 1989, towards the end of the war, international opinion turned against the Salvadoran government, and it found itself obliged to negotiate. In January 1992, the guerrillas (the Farabundo Martí National Liberation Front, known as the FMLN) and the Salvadoran government ended their armed conflict and agreed that the FMLN would become a legally inscribed political party. By 2009, the FMLN had won presidential elections, ending an 18-year run of presidents from the far-right. Sadly though, El Salvador is not a lot better off today than it was in 1980 when the civil war started. The FMLN negotiated a political settlement to the war and many commanders received government jobs or multiple turns in the National Assembly, but the majority of the country remains in poverty, with unemployment at 25 per cent. The minimum wage of USD 10 a day cannot meet the basic needs of a family of four. Gangs, whose membership increases as Salvadoran-American gang members are deported from the United States, have become the de facto leaders in many urban and rural communities where the government has little control. Today there are as many homicides as during the war, as organized crime and urban gangs fight for dominance in the arms and drug trades. Impunity still reigns as the police forces struggle to contain the violence and bring perpetrators to justice.

The Salvadoran case exemplifies a number of common themes that trap countries emerging from civil war in ongoing conflict. These challenges include the reintegration of displaced populations within the country and refugees outside the country; the reactivation of the economy and distributive policies that guarantee a basic living for all; the reconstruction of destroyed infrastructure; the demobilization, retraining and reintegration of combatants into civilian life; the purging of human rights abusers from the military, guerrillas and security forces; and the reconciliation of a country that has suffered so much death, torture and fear. El Salvador has high levels of violence past and present, impunity for human rights abuses committed during the war as well as violent acts perpetuated today, and high income inequality. As a result, the vast majority of Salvadorans are not able to enjoy their basic capabilities, including the ability to support themselves and their families, to access education and health services, to live in communities that are safe and secure, and to have a judicial system that enforces laws, investigates crimes, protects vulnerable groups and takes cases to court so that justice can be served (Cosgrove 2010, Silber 2010 and Lovato 2015).

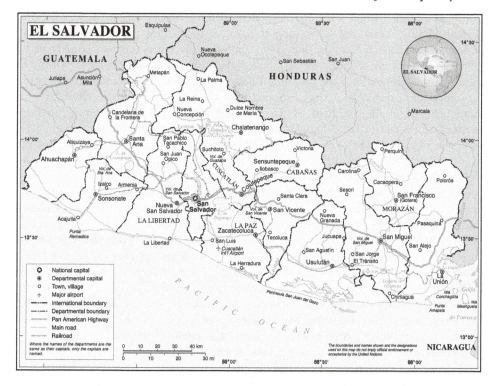

Figure 8.2 Map of El Salvador
Source: Map No. 3903 Rev. 3 UNITED NATIONS May 2004

How conflict causes poverty at the micro level

As important as they are, the macro-level effects of conflict are too general and abstract unless you drill down to the micro level to understand how mass violence actually impacts individuals, families and communities. War and conflict lead to unfreedom and poverty by limiting people's most central capabilities and functionings, particularly their entitlements to earn a living, to live free of fear, to receive an education and to live free of disease. Under the best of circumstances, the capabilities of poor people are vulnerable. Not only are their opportunities typically limited – which is one thing that defines poverty – but even the opportunities they do have may be insecure. Imagine that a poor woman does have the right to vote in her society, but on election day the road to the nearest polling place is blocked by a rebel group. She does not have the time or money to get to the polls any other way, so she has effectively lost the capability freedom to vote. Conflict is in many ways the *worst* of circumstances, which means that it pervasively threatens capabilities and functionings, and thereby creates and/or intensifies deprivation, inequality and suffering.

Violent conflict has short-term, long-term, direct and indirect consequences, all of which relate to both temporary and chronic poverty. Most broadly, violence involves coercion, often leading to states of unfreedom. Rebel groups, and even governmental forces, frequently maim children – including forced sterilization of boys and rape of girls and boys – and compel women, the elderly and children to feed and house their troops. When the troops move on, they often coerce civilians into joining them, either as new recruits, cooks and other support roles, or to provide combatants with wives or sexual services. Civilians are not given choices: they are ordered to comply or be killed. Sadly enough, such attacks on non-combatants are not just collateral damage to achieve a military goal but the purposeful destruction of civilian communities believed to support or harbour 'the enemy'. Sometimes, the troops do not take civilians with them but instead subject them to violence and torture to send a message to their enemies. These tactics mean unarmed civilians have few means of protecting themselves and little recourse to recovering what has been taken from them. This is one of the reasons why today's wars create so many internally displaced people and refugees who seek safety outside of the country.

Examining conflict's effects on several central capabilities from Nussbaum's list, some points are obvious (Nussbaum 2005). To begin with the capability of *life*, violence causes the premature death of over 500,000 people per year, roughly one person a minute.[2] Conflict also has massive effects on the capabilities of *bodily health* and *bodily integrity*. Soldiers and non-combatants alike sustain injuries: crippled or missing limbs, blindness, damaged internal organs. Conflict further impacts health through the spread of disease, famine and the destruction of public health services. People may not be able to go to the health centre for emergencies or check-ups because the actual building has been destroyed, or they fear the dangers that might lie on the way to the clinic. Illnesses that could have been easily prevented turn lethal. This phenomenon has many manifestations as infectious diseases proliferate: children already weakened by diarrhoea catch more fatal illnesses; regular complications of birth mean increased risk for mothers and infants; the flu becomes pneumonia; and cuts and abrasions get infected and turn gangrenous. Public health campaigns are cancelled: children don't get immunized and insect-treated bed nets don't get distributed. The disease burden increases as more people contract malaria, typhoid, tuberculosis and sexually transmitted diseases.

In fact, many civilian deaths in wartime are due to illness rather than combat. Malnutrition that people suffer during wartime can kill as well as have long-run and macro effects. For example, in both Zimbabwe and Burundi, children who were malnourished are shorter as adults, which can reduce their lifetime labour productivity (Alderman *et al.* 2006, Bundervoet *et al.* 2009). Bodily integrity is threatened also not just by injuries but through the mass sexual violence often practised against women and children. Those violations often seriously damage mental health as well, leading to depression, anxiety and despair. A common tactic in war is to attack mental health by sowing fear. Through violence against civilians, the objective is to demoralize enemy combatants and entire populations. Finally, bodily integrity in Nussbaum's formulation also involves the capability for mobility, which is restricted if it is too unsafe to move freely from place to place.

Violence also undercuts the capabilities for practical reason and affiliation. Education fits in here as one of the main ways every person can cultivate practical reason and expand her opportunities. When the public good of schools is destroyed, however, this basic support to human wellbeing collapses. Unfortunately, attacks on schools are a depressingly common tactic in conflict: they have been directly targeted in Nigeria, Afghanistan and Syria among many other places (Global Coalition 2014). Schools are also a vital community gathering point where children, parents and teachers interact and coordinate actions for the best of the children and the community. Education can also be interrupted when people have to flee fighting, or when it becomes too unsafe to travel to wherever the learning institution is located. A study in Tajikistan showed how girls whose homes were destroyed in that country's civil war were less likely to get a secondary education, reducing both wages and life chances in the long term (Shemyakina 2006). In terms of affiliation, if you live in a war zone, you may not be able to speak freely, or join any group you want (particularly if the local warlord views the group as dangerous), or participate in politics. War also often means that newspapers don't go to press, radio stations aren't on the air, and local people don't have reliable access to information about what is transpiring or how to avoid conflict. Access to information is an important entitlement so people can make informed decisions about how to maximize their options.

Losing the capabilities to free speech, political participation and affiliation relate to how conflict can cripple the basic capability of control over one's environment. This refers partly to environmental assets: in conflict, people might use such resources unsustainably because their urgent need for survival induces them to think with extremely short timeframes. For example, because people in Afghanistan have been so worried about immediate survival, they have in some places exploited scarce water and grazing land in such a way that degrades the long-term potential use of those assets (Goodhand 2001). Nussbaum includes employment under the heading of control over one's environment, and conflict can certainly damage livelihoods. Service providers such as masons, cobblers and seamstresses have to abandon their businesses and may no longer be able to generate an income. Farming families lose crops and animals. In Mozambique's 15-year-long civil war, people lost 80 per cent of their cattle, a key part of rural households' economic livelihood (Brück 1996).

Conflict's impact on capabilities also has a specific gendered dimension. High levels of sexual violence often happen in war zones. Commanders order soldiers to rape as a way of subjugating the local population, or soldiers carry out sexual violence as a part of pillage and looting. Since 1998, over 200,000 women have been raped in eastern Congo and a large part of the female population has experienced some form of sexual violence. (Stearns 2011) Women, girls and boys are raped often by multiple soldiers and by multiple objects being introduced into their bodies. Women, children and other vulnerable groups are sometimes forced to watch the torture and assault of their own family or community members. Mothers very well may have witnessed the deaths of their children. Orders to rape and pillage can also shape men's lasting habits, and so conflict can lead to the increased violent masculinization of society. Women's contributions to society are thereby minimized and their subjugation exaggerated, leading to an increased risk of physical, emotional and sexual abuse (Ghobarah *et al.* 2003). All of these gendered effects can seriously reduce women's freedom to live a life that they value.

The micro-level effects mentioned above are frequent realities for people living in war zones. They are often long-lasting: each of the above tragedies, when they don't lead to death, can lead to physical and/or emotional scarring. Soldiers and civilians alike suffer from the emotional and psychological effects of conflict, but for civilian populations the effects can be even more extreme because of sustained feelings of uncertainty and lack of control over many of life's basic decisions (Waszink 2011). The disruption of being forced from your home, the fear of getting caught in crossfire or falling into the hands of combatants who will treat you like the enemy, the hunger and thirst of not knowing where you'll get your next meal or find potable water, the grief of having lost family members and the trauma of having witnessed atrocities – all these conditions create stressors which can cause anxiety and panic attacks, insomnia, nightmares, flashbacks, antisocial behaviours, violent behaviours and increased susceptibility to abuse of drugs and alcohol. These symptoms often manifest themselves both during times of conflict and long after hostilities have ceased. Addressing the physical, psychological and social side effects of war is one of the biggest challenges countries face after fighting has ceased.

Conflict's micro-level effects on capabilities are intensely overlapping. When conflict directly harms capabilities in health, bodily integrity etc., it indirectly undermines capabilities in many other areas. This means that conflict seriously increases the vulnerability of capability freedom. One of the defining characteristics of poor people's vulnerability is that they may not be able to substitute one asset or capability for another (Dubois *et al.* 2007). If pests destroy the harvest you were planning to use to earn income and feed your family, then you might have no money and no food to survive. In the case of conflict, if fighting makes roads impassable (directly destroying the capability for mobility) then you might not be able to get your goods to market (indirectly destroying the capability to earn a livelihood). Conflict typically threatens poor people's survival strategies more fundamentally than do environmental or economic shocks (De Waal 1997). In times of war, it is often the most vulnerable people who will suffer disproportionately: women are raped, children go hungry, the elderly and disabled may be abandoned. By making it harder for poor people to cope, conflict renders their capabilities especially fragile.

That said, there are some surprising ways that conflict can actually expand opportunities (Justino 2011, 2013). For example, some people will take advantage of violence to begin looting assets. The turmoil of conflict can increase some groups' political empowerment and enjoyment of civil rights, particularly if they were formerly oppressed. It is also possible that population movements can have an upside for livelihoods and economic opportunities. Some individuals may find more freedom when they take up arms. For example, there is research about women as combatants and participants in violence against civilians. In Latin American civil wars, women participated as combatants in significant numbers in El Salvador and Cuba, which led to changing gender roles (Shayne 2004), and in Sierra Leone and Liberia, researchers such as Coulter (2008 and 2009) and Cohen (2013) document women's participation as combatants and perpetrators of sexual violence. Obviously, these effects are not always positive, and expanding one person's capabilities at the expense of another's is not moral. However, the point is that though conflict can exacerbate capability poverty in many ways, it can also have some unexpected (if perhaps rare) upsides. As one last example, some research has shown that experiences of violence made individuals' and groups' behaviour more altruistic and fair (Voors *et al.* 2012, Bauer *et al.* 2013).

Protecting people in conflict

Because of the many ways that conflict can harm basic capabilities, it is obviously essential to ask how those effects can be prevented or mitigated. There is a huge literature on humanitarian intervention, peacebuilding and post-conflict reconstruction (see i.a. Lambourne 2000, Zartman 2007, Weinstein 2007, Call and Cousens 2008, Addison and Brück 2009, Ware 2014). This chapter focuses primarily on how such interventions can preserve or restore human security and the fundamental entitlements to wellbeing that it presumes. Human security is a specific theoretical tradition that serves as a component to human development (Gasper and Truong 2005, Fukuda-Parr and Messineo 2012). According to one prominent definition, 'the objective of human security is to safeguard the vital core of all human lives from critical pervasive threats, in a way that is consistent with long-term human fulfillment' (Alkire 2003: 2). This refers not just to security from violence, but to any condition that can threaten an individual's ability to secure 'what is humanly central', which can be defined as fundamental freedoms (Gasper 2005: 222). The capabilities approach is foremost concerned with 'freedom to' (i.e. positive liberties, what an individual can be and do). In a complementary way, human security emphasizes 'freedom from' (i.e. negative liberties, what robs an individual of the basic components of a decent human life). The negative liberties include freedom from fear, want and indignity. Human security's perspective is multidimensional, encompassing threats to these freedoms that come from economic, food, health, environmental and other crises (Owen 2004). Violent conflict, as we have shown, can create crises in all these areas, threatening the essential components of wellbeing and compromising a person's right to live a life that she values.

What is the 'vital core' of human security that must be protected? Adapting Alkire's (2003) formulation, it is defined by a limited set of central capabilities necessary to basic survival, dignity and a livelihood. They are the capabilities essential so that people have security in shocks and emergencies. These capabilities embrace political and civil liberties as well as economic, social and cultural rights. However, much as in the question of what constitutes the universal central capabilities, Alkire shies away from offering a definitive, precise list for the vital core, insisting that its contents can be context specific, and should be elaborated in a democratic fashion. This is a sensible strategy because the actual operationalization of human security can depend on specific circumstances. In other words, in any given conflict situation, how do you know when central 'vital core' capabilities have been violated? Ideally, the people whose security is endangered should be consulted on their situation, which is one reason why operationalization is context dependent.

It is nonetheless essential to establish a few general parameters on which fundamental human entitlements must be prioritized for protection in an armed conflict. Johan Galtung, one of the founders of peace research, claims that human security entails the fulfilment of basic human rights that are in turn the fulfilment of basic human needs, which we can equate with capabilities in the vital core (Galtung 2005). Therefore, internationally valorized human rights guarantees suggest an outline for the vital core at the global level. Human security most broadly presumes a 'right to survive', and the Universal Declaration of Human Rights enumerates several guarantees relevant to that right. Article 3 of the UDHR states that 'everyone has the right to life, liberty, and security of person'. Article 5 states that 'no one shall be subjected to torture or to cruel, inhuman or degrading treatment or punishment.' Article 9 concerns freedom from arbitrary arrest or detention, and article 13 the freedom of movement. Additionally, the International Covenant on Economic, Social and Cultural Rights includes a right to adequate food in its article 11 and a right to physical and mental health in article 12. Hayden (2004) even goes so far as to assert that there should be a fundamental human right to peace. These guarantees are admittedly often abstract, so context is again vital to ascertain exactly what amounts to a violation of 'inhuman treatment' or freedom of movement.

For conflict situations, a legal framework has been elaborated for humanitarian treatment in war that makes abstract guarantees more specific. United Nations policies,

---

Box 8.4 International human rights organizations and the different offices of the United Nations that monitor human rights abuses in conflict-affected areas and provide services to affected populations

- International Red Cross
- Amnesty International
- Human Rights Watch
- Doctors without Borders
- International Rescue Committee (IRC)
- United Nations High Commissioner on Refugees (UNHCR)

---

the Geneva Conventions and the 1977 Additional Protocols comprise the key components of this legal framework that regulate behaviour in war. States, rebel groups, combatants and their commanders – regardless of whether they are actual signatories to particular treaties – are today bound by these rules on treatment of civilians, captured enemy soldiers, and the wounded. They are expected to implement a broad range of measures to protect civilians from conflict's effects. This means distinguishing between military objectives and risks to civilians, analysing the extent to which civilians may be affected by military objectives, and taking precautions to avoid undue impacts on civilians and civilian objects. Unfortunately the gap between international agreement and enforcement on the ground is often wide: these legal norms are routinely violated in actual conflict situations.

International humanitarian law provides both a legal justification and concrete policy areas relevant to human security. In practice, human security translates first of all to prevention and protection, namely to stop or mitigate threats to the vital core. It focuses mostly on shorter-term needs, such as peacekeeping in a conflict situation or humanitarian aid in a disaster. However, protecting the vital core is not sufficient for adequate human fulfilment, which is why human security must go along with human development. Human development is concerned with an individual's ability to flourish, with a long-term focus to ensure improvement in wellbeing over months and years. Both human security and human development are necessary to preserve and promote people's basic capabilities and help societies recover from conflict. Table 8.1 presents an overview of steps that societies in conflict need to undertake to further human security and human development.

Like any effort for poverty reduction, achieving success in protecting human security can be very difficult. Conflict situations have particularly complex and dangerous dynamics. When war ravages communities, people have to flee their homes and communities to seek refuge in other regions or countries. Large groups of refugees lead to enormous logistical and security concerns: how to guarantee the safety of and access to food, health and sanitation necessary to sustain the refugee populations? If active fighting is going on, this can make it difficult for humanitarian organizations to get support to refugees or other threatened people. Sometimes rebel groups set up check points and 'tax' organizations serving civilian populations, requisitioning supplies from

Table 8.1 Elements of human security protection and human development promotion

Public safety	Humanitarian relief	Rehabilitation and reconstruction	Reconciliation and coexistence	Governance and empowerment
Control armed elements (enforce cease-fire, disarm, demobilize)	Facilitate return of conflict-affected people to places of origin or new settlements (refugees and internally displaced)	Integrate conflict-affected people (refugees, internally displaced, former combatants)	End impunity (accountability, support and technical assistance so government offices can resume functions)	Establish rule of law (through judicial, legal, legislative institutions)
Protect civilians (rule of law, removing landmines and small arms)	Assure food security (adequate nutrition for the vulnerable)	Rebuild or rehabilitate infrastructure (roads, housing, power etc.)	Establish truth (through truth commissions set up tribunals, use traditional justice processes)	Initiate political reform (focus on democratic processes and institutions)
Build national security institutions (police, military, other security forces)	Ensure health security (access to basic health care for all)	Promote social protections (employment, education, shelter, health etc.)	Announce amnesties (immunity for lesser crimes, reparation for victims)	Strengthen civil society (through participation, accountability and funding)
Enforce external security (combat illegal trafficking in weapons, drugs and people)	Establish emergency safety net for people at risk (women, children, elderly, indigenous, disabled)	Dismantle war economy (fight criminal networks, re-establish markets)	Promote coexistence (rebuild social capital)	Promote access to information (through independent media and transparency)

Source: adapted from Ogata-Sen (2003)

aid workers for troops or profit. In her book about the contradictions of international humanitarian aid, Linda Polman (2010) shows how easily humanitarian workers get bullied or face obstacles to their work because of intimidation by military forces and armed groups. These tactics put humanitarian workers in an ethical bind: should they share goods with rebels in order to reach civilian populations or not? The ethical and practical dilemmas of protecting people during conflict are just the first part of the story – promoting human development in post-conflict societies comes with its own challenges.

Reconstruction, recovery and reconciliation

'War is not over when it's over': this is the title of Ann Jones' 2010 book on how war affects women and their children even after the formal fighting has ended. As high homicide rates in Guatemala and El Salvador demonstrate, post-conflict societies can often be as dangerous as wartime conditions for multiple reasons (Manz 2008, Silber 2010, Lovato 2015). These reasons include the fact that international attention formerly focused on the unfolding drama of the war turns instead to other parts of the world. Or state institutions, including the judicial system, may remain ineffectual or dominated by elite interests and cannot enforce the rule of law. A cessation in armed hostilities does not mean that the physical, cultural, health and education systems of a country are magically reinstated. In post-conflict periods, people's capabilities often remain deeply insecure. Just because warring parties have signed a cease-fire or even a peace accord, there is no guarantee that it will immediately be embraced by all. There is also the issue of impunity: how will the perpetrators of human rights abuses and destruction of infrastructure make reparations and be judged for their actions? And even if soldiers have demobilized for the time being, there is always the possibility that they will return to fighting or seek violent and/or illegal options for income generation.

For a post-conflict period to become a time of peace and reconstruction, a country must have an institutional commitment and necessary resources to address human rights abuses, return to a system of laws and civil behaviour, get government services back up and running, rebuild the infrastructure of the country, and activate the economy. It is no simple challenge to accomplish these tasks. Culturally sensitive treatments and economic development are needed for large segments of a population suffering various maladies associated with post-traumatic stress but who are also struggling to earn their livings after the fighting has ceased (Herman 1997). If neighbours have killed or denounced neighbours, if government forces have perpetrated human rights abuses against civilians, if rebel forces have participated in atrocities, then national programmes have to be implemented to hold abusers accountable and promote reconciliation. Disagreements have to be resolved legally, illegal activities have to be punished according to law, and those who commit crimes must be apprehended and held accountable for their crimes in court. This means that governmental offices and functionaries have to resume their work, or new staff has to be hired and trained. Police forces need training and support to carry out their jobs in an effective and lawful manner. Once the players are in place, the crimes of human rights abuses, torture and mistreatment of civilians have to be addressed and a plan for reconciliation implemented.

Peacekeeping efforts and commitments to transitional justice are based on the idea that long-term peace has to involve addressing the past violence and weakness of state institutions (Doyle and Sambanis 2000, Leebaw 2008). The overall objectives of transitional justice are promoting national reconciliation and conflict resolution, but to achieve this, transitional justice lawyers and advocates first must create the truth commissions and criminal tribunals to document what has happened during the war, gathering testimony from survivors and witnesses. Then they can assure that those guilty of the worst abuses are prosecuted. Transitional justice involves a tension: to what extent does the truth of what happened have to be clarified so a society can move on? Leebaw argues that 'in evaluating the political role of transitional justice institutions, more attention should be given to the ways in which their efforts to expose, remember and understand political violence are in tension with their role as tools for establishing stability and legitimating transitional compromises' (2008: 97). Part of the tension is that combatants may be reluctant to turn in their arms if they know that they will be held accountable for their actions, but civilians may be reluctant to trust peace if those who have perpetrated abuses against them don't have to face justice.

In the case of El Salvador, the Truth Commission was part of the United Nations peacekeeping efforts. It gathered testimony from survivors, officially documenting the atrocities of the war, while other UN agencies supported the creation and training of a new police force. When a population that has suffered extreme trauma in times of war has the opportunity to provide testimony to their suffering, the possibility of healing can emerge. Advocating for the importance of telling survivor stories, be it by civilians or former combatants, the psychiatrist Shay stresses 'that healing from trauma depends upon communalization of the trauma – being able safely to tell the story to someone who is listening and who can be trusted to retell it truthfully to others in the community' (1994: 4). Also, if not handled appropriately, survivors can be re-traumatized by having to share their story. Attention to survivors has to be culturally sensitive and integrated with physical and mental health services, community development and vocational training. Though telling one's story can be an important part of the reconciliation process, it remains incomplete if perpetrators are not punished in some form.

After the Rwandan genocide in which 850,000 Rwandans (mostly Tutsis and moderate Hutus) were killed in 1994, the new government instituted a country-wide programme called Gacaca Courts ('Justice among the Grass' Courts) in which local communities held outdoor tribunals based on traditional justice practices to hear the cases of violent perpetrators in the communities. The reinstatement of civil authorities and rule of law, a country-wide attempt to gather testimony of what happened, and some efforts of accountability are all vital for promoting healing, reconciliation and a resumption of normal life after conflict. Sadly enough, many fighting forces negotiate amnesty before ceasing hostilities, which creates challenges for justice to be served. There has to be recognition worldwide that the worst human rights perpetrators will be tried and punished for their abuses. However, those promoting peace and reconciliation activities often face funding and time limitations as well as the difficult balance between justice and reconciliation.

Reactivating the economy, creating productive options for all citizens and rebuilding destroyed infrastructure requires massive investments and sustained commitment from a variety of stakeholders, national and international. If citizens can't earn a living, they won't be able to heal and embrace peace. Citizens at all levels of society need to feel that they can generate enough income to support themselves and their families and achieve their goals. This requires training programmes, access to credit, and economic development that creates the necessary forward and backward linkages so that produce, products and goods created by people have markets. Income generation can also help empower women, but this often requires non-traditional vocational training programmes so that women can acquire higher-earning trades. Countries need integrated development plans in which local production feeds into national and international markets. Former combatants need training and support to reintegrate into civilian life.

The reconstruction of destroyed infrastructure will support economic development: road and bridge construction will facilitate transport, the re-establishment of electrical lines, sewer systems and potable water will provide the necessary inputs for industry and other types of businesses to resume production and support basic needs, and the rebuilding and staffing of schools, hospitals and health centres will support the basic capabilities and functionings necessary to human development. In areas of the country that were active war zones, entire communities have to be reconstructed, from housing to marketplaces. Governments have to prioritize the needs of the majority of the country, not solely the needs of political and economic elites.

Social norms – the habits of a people to guarantee the survival of the group – often get perverted in times of war. Belligerent forces have grown used to using violence to feed, clothe and take care of themselves, but former soldiers who have participated in violent practices during the conflict must abandon these practices during peace. Perversion and abuse may have been ordered or condoned by their commanders. Some may have

Box 8.5 Case study of post-conflict peacebuilding in Bosnia-Herzegovina

The war in Bosnia-Herzegovina (Figure 8.3) lasted from 1992 to 1995. More than two million people were displaced, approximately 100,000 people died and tens of thousands of women were raped. The Dayton Peace Accords put an end to the shooting, but created a political system that essentially institutionalized the ethnic cleansing committed by the three warring groups (Bosniaks, Serbs and Croats). Fashioning a stable country with an operational justice system in the post-conflict period has been extremely difficult, since political elites are barely accountable and can stoke up nationalist passions to remain in power. In some ways, Bosnia is a lesson in how *not* to conduct peacebuilding at the state level, though at the civil society level efforts have been more successful. Using the schema of peacebuilding proposed by Paffenholz and Spurk (2010), Bosnia has made progress in some areas while it lags in others. The first element in peacebuilding is *protection*, which refers to protecting people from the state and other armed actors. National, international and civil society actors should create safe zones, provide humanitarian aid and peacekeeping troops to ensure the vital core of human security. In Bosnia, international troops often failed their protection duties during the war. The saddest example is when UN peacekeeping forces stood idly by as Serbian extremists massacred 8000 Bosniak men and boys at Srebrenica in 1995. Since the war, though, a strong international presence has helped guarantee public safety and that most basic needs are met.

One essential element of protection in most post-conflict societies is disarmament, demobilization and reintegration (DDR). In Bosnia, 300,000 soldiers had to be demobilized after the war. A few state-level programmes to reintegrate former combatants into civilian society provided financial and job search assistance, vocational training and a basic civics course. However, a more profound effort has been made by the Centre for Nonviolent Action (CNA), a pioneering NGO that works to promote reconciliation among war veterans. As part of its work, CNA brings together men from the three nationalities in small groups so that they learn how to 'deal with the past'. Though they may have previously tried to kill each other, through CNA's method the men confront their prejudices, hate and fear associated with the other ethnic groups. They work to establish trust, which promotes emotional healing, which in turn can radiate out from the former soldiers to their families and communities. Kenan, one of CNA's peace trainers, lamented that many former soldiers are stuck in a feeling of victimization tied to their ethnic identity. But despite Bosnia's many divisions, he insisted that 'everyone wants the same version of peace.'

A second step in the peacebuilding process is *monitoring*, which involves tracking and reporting on human rights abuses. It is a critical part of democratization to hold governments accountable and promote rule of law. The Balkan Investigative Reporting Network (BIRN) conducts exemplary monitoring work in Bosnia. BIRN is an NGO that covers many issues relevant to peacebuilding, such as war crimes trials held both in Bosnia and at the International Criminal Tribunal for the former Yugoslavia (ICTY) in The Hague. BIRN and the ICTY form part of Bosnia's efforts for transitional justice. Daniel, one of BIRN's journalists, identified four pillars of transitional justice:

justice itself (e.g. bringing war criminals to trial), the right to truth, institutional reform and the right of reparations. In his view, Bosnia has focused mostly on the first of these, and has seriously neglected truth: the country never set up a truth commission to establish the facts of the war, for example. Institutional reform and reparations have also made little progress. Even justice itself, Daniel said, is 'failing spectacularly', since so few of the criminal cases have been prosecuted at the national level. The process is moving so slowly that many of the perpetrators will never be tried. Many have already died of old age, or will die within a decade.

Paffenholz and Spurk's peacebuilding schema also depends on *inter-group social cohesion*, which involves restoring social capital, trust, civic engagement and ties between groups. This has been an extremely fraught process in Bosnia. Where before the war Croats, Serbs and Bosniaks lived peacefully side-by-side, now they often live in ethnically homogeneous towns, interact relatively little with people from another ethnic group and have dramatically divergent views on what happened during the conflict. Intolerant attitudes are prevalent even among young people who did not experience the war. That is not surprising since in many parts of the country the school system has been divided: Croat children learn one version of history, Bosniak children another. Evidence from the leading Bosnian social psychologist Sabina Čehajić-Clancy shows that dehumanizing attitudes are still widespread. People from one ethnic group attribute less complex emotions to people from other groups, and continue to deny that people from their ethnic group have committed war crimes. As a result, Bosnia is a long way from reconciliation.

Nonetheless, some organizations are doing courageous work to promote inter-group social cohesion. One is the network of Nansen Dialogue Centres throughout the country. These centres often bring together young people from the different ethnicities for joint activities outside of their divided schools. According to Čehajić-Clancy's research, over time such inter-group contact can help people take the perspective of others. They learn to appreciate that multiple groups were both perpetrators and victims, and realize that all Bosnians still share much in common.

Sources: Kostic (2008), Moratti and Sabic-El-Rayess (2009), Paffenholz and Spurk (2010), Čehajić-Clancy (2012) and field research by the authors.

been coerced to participate in violent acts. Violence and sexual abuse can become normalized, so much so that men will continue wartime practices of rape into the post-conflict 'peace'. In peace and reconciliation processes, it is imperative that these practices be addressed and eradicated through the judicial system and often with the support of non-governmental organizations. Doing so will require effective state institutions, national media campaigns, the collaboration of leadership from local to national levels, the involvement of civil society organizations – especially women's organizations – and consequences for those who continue to use violence in this way (Cosgrove 2016). If authorities don't punish crime, they become complicit with criminals, creating a 'culture of impunity', a society in which the strong can continue to brutalize the weak (Jones 2010). To prevent such abuses post-conflict, it is extremely important that government institutions charged with implementing justice and protecting vulnerable groups receive sufficient capacity building and support to carry out their mandates.

Figure 8.3 Map of Bosnia–Herzegovina

Source: Map No. 3729 Rev. 6 UNITED NATIONS March 2007

Peacebuilding is a demanding process that requires cooperation, funding, sustained commitment and a new vision for society. To avoid a return to violence, people's basic capabilities and functionings have to be respected: there have to be opportunities for all to education, health, income generation and participation in the co-creation of the polity. State institutions and civil society organizations have to work together in the five areas of public safety, humanitarian relief, rehabilitation and reconstruction, reconciliation and coexistence, and governance and empowerment. Paul Lederach, who has worked as a mediator and peacebuilder around the world, writes, 'Transcending violence is forged by the capacity to generate, mobilize, and build the moral imagination' (2005: 5). This means envisioning a society where together the survivors – combatants and civilians alike – construct new opportunities and responsibilities for what it means to be a citizen and what it means to be a state accountable to its citizens.

Conclusion

Poverty and armed violence form a complex, vicious cycle. Both economic poverty and relative deprivation (including in areas relevant to capabilities, such as political rights) can spark conflict. And conflict, as we have shown, often creates or exacerbates many dimensions of poverty. Access to safety and security, education, health, generating income and freedom from discrimination are typically curtailed during periods of war. Economies are ruined, infrastructure destroyed, environmental assets degraded and institutions damaged. These losses can spread poverty as children who haven't received proper nutrition, education and access to health services may be affected for the rest of their lives. The most severe effects of war are often the least visible to the human eye – the spread of famine and disease, loss of social capital and traditions, psychological symptoms from trauma – and continue to be felt decades after the hostilities have ceased. This is why war is not over when it's over: poverty effects often persist long into the post-conflict period.

The way that poverty and violence can reinforce each other is one reason why this relationship is so complex. This is also why post-conflict peacebuilding is so very difficult, and rarely completely successful. Where some aspects of human security may be stronger – such as a reduction in violence and increased rule of law – other elements may be weak. Rwanda, for instance, has made strides in economic and human development, but it is considered by many to be an authoritarian state, lacking a robust civil society. In Bosnia, civil society, civil liberties and basic needs are more secure, but problems of impunity, truth and social cohesion fester. In El Salvador, basic human security is still seriously threatened. Though this picture can seem bleak, these societies and global society cannot give up on peacebuilding. Accountable governments, international coordination, citizen participation and economic and human development are all essential to promote reconstruction and reconciliation after periods of conflict.

Another part of the complexity is the blurred lines that conflict can create. Though civilians die at higher rates than combatants, sometimes civilians are complicit in the violence either through denunciations or support to one armed group or another. Though women are often disproportionately affected by war because of their cultural roles as mothers and caretakers, there are cases of women serving as combatants and even participating in human rights abuses in conflicts around the world. And though conflict does deepen poverty in all kinds of ways, it can sometimes reduce it, as new power structures rise, corrupt leaders are deposed and individuals find their opportunities expanded.

Finally, this complexity is why the poverty–conflict dynamic is such a major challenge for economic and human development. Besides the way violence can violate the essential components of a decent human life, it can have ripple effects around the globe. Chavet and Collier (2005) have estimated that fragile states prone to conflict can cost USD 100 billion, a number that is twice the annual budget for international development aid, a number that imposes costs on many people even far away from the conflict zone. Indeed, the danger from violence, the intertwining causes and effects, and the intense misery that the poverty–conflict dynamic can create make this one of the thorniest of all development challenges. The negative effects on human lives are severe, pervasive and all too common around the world. In order to help people secure their basic capabilities and live a valued life, however, this is a challenge those working for poverty reduction cannot shirk. A number of testimonials, memoirs and novels written by people who have lived through or researched war provide powerful, very human reminders of why this issue matters – see the list of further reading.

Discussion questions

1   In what ways does armed conflict contribute to poverty? In what ways does poverty contribute to armed conflict?
2   What are the relationships between capabilities, functionings and conflict?
3   What can happen to the culture – values, ways of living, habits, roles – of a people during and after a conflict?
4   What does it mean to say that 'war is not over when it's over'?
5   From the elements of protecting human security and promoting human development in Table 8.1, which seem the most important and why? How might you prioritize them in a conflict or post-conflict situation?
6   Imagine you are a humanitarian aid worker taking food and medicine to civilians in an area where there is frequent fighting between rebels and the national army. You get stopped at a military check point by one of the rebel groups. In order to let you on your way, they request half of your load, telling you it is a road tax. What would you do?

Notes

1   'Civilians have borne the brunt of modern warfare, with ten civilians dying for every soldier in wars fought since the mid-20th century, compared with nine soldiers killed for every civilian in World War I, according to a 2001 study by the International Committee of the Red Cross.' *New York Times*, 10/10/2010.
2   Geneva Declaration, Global Burden of Armed Violence 2015.

Further reading

Adichie, Chimamanda Ngozi. 2006. *Half of a Yellow Sun*. New York City, NY: Anchor Books.
Beah, Ishmael. 2007. *A Long Way Gone: Memoirs of a boy soldier*. New York City, NY: Sarah Crichton Books.
Cain, Kenneth, Heidi Postlewait and Andrew Thomson. 2006. *Emergency Sex (and Other Desperate Measures): True stories from a warzone*. London: Ebury Press.
Demick, Barbara. 2012. *Logavina Street: Life and death in a Sarajevo neighborhood*. New York, NY: Spiegel & Grau.

Gavilán Sánchez, Lurgio. 2015. *When Rains Become Floods*. Durham: Duke University Press.

Gourevitch, Philip. 1998. *We Wish to Inform You that Tomorrow We Will Be Killed with Our Families: Stories from Rwanda*. New York City, NY: Picador USA.

Households in Conflict Network research: www.hicn.org/

Marra, Anthony. 2013. *A Constellation of Vital Phenomena: A NOVEL*. New York, NY: Hogarth.

Menchu, Rigoberta. 1984. *I, Rigoberta Menchu: An Indian woman in Guatemala*. New York, NY: Verso.

Moore, Adam. 2013. *Peacebuilding in Practice: Local experience in two Bosnian towns*. Ithaca, NY: Cornell University Press.

Works cited

Addison, Tony and Tilman Brück, eds. 2009. *Making Peace Work: The challenges of social and economic reconstruction*. Houndmills, Basingstoke, UK: Palgrave Macmillan.

Aghajanian, Alia. 'Social Capital and Conflict.' Households in Conflict Network Working Paper 134, November 2012.

Alderman, Harold, John Hoddinott and Bill Kinsey. 'Long term consequences of early childhood malnutrition.' *Oxford Economic Papers*, 58.3 (2006): 450–474.

Alkire, Sabina. 'A Conceptual Framework for Human Security.' Center for Research on Inequality, Human Security, and Ethnicity, University of Oxford, 2003.

Arnson, Cynthia J., and I. William Zartman, eds. 2005. *Rethinking the Economics of War: The intersection of need, creed, and greed*. Baltimore, MD: Johns Hopkins University Press.

Autesserre, Séverine. 2010. *The Trouble with the Congo: Local violence and the failure of international peacebuilding*. New York City, NY: Cambridge University Press.

Bauer, Michal, Alessandra Cassar, Julie Chytilová and Joseph Henrich. 'War's enduring effects on the development of egalitarian motivations and in-group biases.' *Psychological Science*, 25.1 (2014): 47–57.

Blattman, Christopher, and Edward Miguel. 'Civil war'. *Journal of Economic Literature*, 48.1 (2010): 3–57.

Browning, Lynnley. 2015. 'Companies Struggle To Comply With Rules On Conflict Minerals.' *The New York Times*. (Accessed May 25, 2017: www.nytimes.com/2015/09/08/business/dealbook/companies-struggle-to-comply-with-conflict-minerals-rule.html?_r=0).

Brück, Tilman. 1996. *The economic effects of war*. Diss. University of Oxford.

Buhaug, Halvard, Lars-Erik Cederman and Kristian Skrede Gleditsch. 'Square pegs in round holes: inequalities, grievances, and civil war'. *International Studies Quarterly*, 58.2 (2013): 418–431.

Bundervoet, Tom, Philip Verwimp and Richard Akresh. 'Health and civil war in rural Burundi.' *Journal of Human Resources*, 44.2 (2009): 536–563.

Call, C. T. and E. M. Cousens. 'Ending wars and building peace: international responses to war-torn societies.' *International Studies Perspectives*, 9 (2008): 1–21.

Čehajić-Clancy, Sabina. 'Coming to Terms with the Past Marked by Collective Crimes: Collective Moral Responsibility and Reconciliation', in Olivera Simić, Zala Volčič and Catherine R. Philpot, eds. 2012. *Peace Psychology in the Balkans*. New York, NY: Springer.

Cerra, Valerie, Meenakshi Rishi and Sweta C. Saxena. 'Robbing the riches: capital flight, institutions and debt.' *The Journal of Development Studies*, 44.8 (2008): 1190–1213.

Chauvet, Lisa, and Paul Collier. 2005. 'Policy turnarounds in Fragile States.' Oxford: CSAE. (Accessed 8 April 2017: www.cgdev.org/doc/event%20docs/MADS/Chauvet%20and%20Collier%20-%20 Policy%20Turnarounds%20in%20Failing%20States.pdf)

Cohen, Dara Kay. 'Female combatants and the perpetration of violence wartime rape in the Sierra Leone civil war.' *World Politics*, 65.3 (2013): 383–415.

Collier, Paul. 2007. *The Bottom Billion: Why the poorest countries are failing and what can be done about it*. New York City, NY: Oxford University Press.

Collier, Paul. 'On the economic consequences of civil war.' *Oxford Economic Papers*, 51.1 (1999): 168–183.

Collier, Paul, and Anke Hoeffler. 'On economic causes of civil war.' *Oxford Economic Papers* 50.4 (1998): 563–573.

Collier, Paul, Lani Elliot, Håvard Hegre, Anke Hoeffler, Marta Reynal-Querol and Nicholas Sambanis. 2003. *Breaking the Conflict Trap. Civil War and Development Policy.* Oxford: Oxford University Press.

Cosgrove, Serena. 2016. 'The Absent State: An Analysis of Teen Mothers' Vulnerability in Goma, the Democratic Republic of the Congo', in Victoria Sanford, Katerina Stefatos and Cecilia M. Salvi, eds. *Gender Violence in Peace and War.* New Brunswick, NJ: Rutgers University Press.

Cosgrove, Serena. 2010. *Leadership from the Margins: Women and civil society organizations in Argentina, Chile, and El Salvador.* New Brunswick, NJ: Rutgers University Press.

Coulter, Chris. 2009. *Bush Wives and Girl Soldiers: Women's lives through war and peace in Sierra Leone.* Ithaca, NY: Cornell University Press.

Coulter, Chris. 'Female fighters in the Sierra Leone War: Challenging the assumptions?' *Feminist Review*, 88 (2008): 54–73.

Demmers, Jolle. 2012. *Theories of Violent Conflict: An introduction.* New York, NY: Routledge.

De Waal, Alexander. 1997. *Famine Crimes: Politics and the disaster relief industry in Africa.* Bloomington, IN: Indiana University Press.

Dimah, Agber. 'The roots of African conflicts: the causes and costs.' *Africa Today*, 55.4 (2009): 129–134.

Doyle, Michael W. and Nicholas Sambanis. 'International peacebuilding: a theoretical and quantitative analysis.' *The American Political Science Review*, 94.4 (2000): 779–801.

Dubois, Jean-Luc, Patricia Huyghebaert and Anne-Sophie Brouillet. 'Fragile States: An Analysis from the capability approach perspective.' Paper presented at the 'Ideas Changing History' Conference, September 2007.

Fukuda-Parr, Sakiko, and Carol Messineo. 'Human Security: A Critical Review of the Literature.' Centre for Research on Peace and Development (CRPD) Working Paper 11 (2012).

Galtung, Johan. 'Meeting Basic Needs: Peace and Development', in Felicia Huppert, Nick Baylis and Barry Keverne, eds. 2005. *The Science of Well-Being.* Oxford: Oxford University Press.

Gasper, Des. 'Securing humanity: situating 'human security' as concept and discourse.' *Journal of Human Development*, 6.2 (2005): 221–245.

Gasper, Des, and Thanh-Dam Truong. 'Deepening development ethics: from economism to human development to human security.' *The European Journal of Development Research*, 17.3 (2005): 372–384.

Ghobarah, Hazem Adam, Paul Huth and Bruce Russett. 'Civil wars kill and maim people long after the shooting stops.' *The American Political Science Review*, 97 (2003): 189–202.

Global Coalition to Protect Education from Attack. *Education under Attack 2014.* Report.

Goodhand, Jonathan. 'Violent Conflict, Poverty and Chronic Poverty', Chronic Poverty Research Center Working Paper 6, May 2001.

Grimmett, Richard. 2012. 'Conventional Arms Transfers to Developing Nations, 2004–2011.' *Congressional Research Service* 7-5700. www.crs.gov R42678.

Gurr, Ted R. 'Why minorities rebel: a global analysis of communal mobilization and conflict since 1945.' *International Political Science Review*, 14.2 (1993): 161–201.

Haugen, Gary A., and Victor Boutros. 2014. *The Locust Effect: Why the end of poverty requires the end of violence.* Oxford: Oxford University Press.

Hayden, Patrick. 'Constraining war: human security and the human right to peace.' *Human Rights Review*, 6.1 (2004): 35–55.

Herman, Judith. 1997. *Trauma and Recovery: The aftermath of violence – from domestic abuse to political terror.* New York City. NY: Basic Books.

Jones, Ann. 2010. *War Is Not Over When It's Over.* New York City, NY: Henry Holt.

Justino, Patricia. 'Research and Policy Implications from a Micro-Level Perspective on the Dynamics of Conflict, Violence and Development.' Households in Conflict Network Working Paper 139, January 2013.

Justino, Patricia. 'Poverty and Violent Conflict: A Micro-Level Perspective on the Causes and Duration of Warfare.' IDS Working Paper Vol. 2011 No. 385, December 2011.

Justino, Patricia. 2010. 'War and Poverty.' MICROCON Research Working Paper 32.

Justino, Patricia. 'Poverty and violent conflict: a micro-level perspective on the causes and duration of warfare.' *Journal of Peace Research*, 46.3 (2009): 315–333.

Justino, Patricia, Tilman Brück and Philip Verwimp, eds. 2013. *A Micro-Level Perspective on the Dynamics of Conflict, Violence, and Development*. Oxford: Oxford University Press.

Kalyvas, Stathis N. 2006. *The Logic of Violence in Civil War*. New York City, NY: Cambridge University Press.

Kinsella, Helen. 2011. *The Image before the Weapon: A critical history of the distinction between combatant and civilian*. Ithaca, NY: Cornell University Press.

Kostic, Roland. 'Nationbuilding as an instrument of peace? Exploring local attitudes towards international nationbuilding and reconciliation in Bosnia and Herzegovina.' *Civil Wars*, 10.4 (2008): 384–412.

Lambourne, Wendy. 'Post-conflict peacebuilding.' *Security Dialogue*, 31 (2000): 357–381.

Langer, Arnim. 'Horizontal inequalities and violent group mobilization in Côte d'Ivoire.' *Oxford Development Studies*, 33.1 (2005): 25–45.

Lederach, John Paul. 2005. *The Moral Imagination: The art and soul of building peace*. New York, NY: Oxford University Press.

Leebaw, Bronwyn Anne. 'The irreconcilable goals of transitional justice.' *Human Rights Quarterly*, 30.1 (2008): 95–118.

Levy, Jack S., and William R. Thompson. 2011. *Causes of War*. New York, NY: John Wiley & Sons.

Lovato, Roberto. 'El Salvador's gang violence: the continuation of civil war by other means.' *The Nation*, 8 June, 2015.

Manz, Beatriz. 'The continuum of violence in post-war Guatemala.' *Social Analysis*, 52.2 (2008): 151–164.

Moratti, Massimo, and Amra Sabic-El-Rayess. 'Transitional Justice and DDR: The Case of Bosnia and Herzegovina.' International Center for Transitional Justice Research Unit, June 2009.

Nussbaum, Martha C. 'Women's bodies: violence, security, capabilities.' *Journal of Human Development* 6.2 (2005): 167–183.

Owen, Taylor. 'Human security, conflict, critique and consensus: colloquium remarks and a proposal for a threshold-based definition.' *Security Dialogue*, 35.3 (2004): 373–387.

Oxfam Briefing Report 107, 'Africa's Missing Billions', August 2007.

Paffenholz, Thania, and Christopher Spurk. 'A Comprehensive Analytical Framework', in Thania Paffenholz, ed. 2010. *Civil Society and Peacebuilding: A critical assessment*. Boulder, CO: Lynne Rienner.

Polman, Linda. 2010. *The Crisis Caravan: What's wrong with humanitarian aid?* New York, NY: Metropolitan Books.

Prunier, Gérard. 2009. *Africa's World War: Congo, the Rwandan genocide, and the making of a continental catastrophe*. Oxford: Oxford University Press.

Shay, Jonathan. 1994. *Achilles in Vietnam: Combat trauma and the undoing of character*. New York, NY: Scribner.

Shayne, Julie. 2004. *The Revolution Question: Feminisms in El Salvador, Chile, and Cuba*. New Brunswick, NJ: Rutgers University Press.

Shemyakina, Olga. 2006. 'The Effect of Armed Conflict on Accumulation of Schooling: Results from Tajikistan.' Households in Conflict Network Working Paper 12.

Silber, Irina Carlota. 2010. *Every Day Revolutionaries: Gender, violence, and disillusionment in postwar El Salvador*. New Brunswick, NJ: Rutgers University Press.

Slim, Hugo. 'Why protect civilians? Innocence, immunity and enmity in war.' *International Affairs*, 79.3 (2003): 481–501.

Soderlund, W., E. Donald Briggs, Tom Pierre Najem and Blake Roberts. 2013. *Africa's Deadliest Conflict: Media coverage of the humanitarian disaster in the Congo and the United Nations response, 1997–2008*. Waterloo, ON: Wilfrid Laurier University Press.

Stearns, Jason. 2011. *Dancing in the Glory of Monsters: The collapse of the Congo and the Great War of Africa*. New York, NY: Public Affairs.

Stewart, Frances. 'Changing perspectives on inequality and development.', *Studies in Comparative International Development*, 51 (2016): 60–80.

Stewart, Frances. 2011. 'Religion versus Ethnicity as a Source of Mobilisation: Are There Differences?' in Yvan Guichaoua, ed. *Understanding Collective Political Violence*. Houndmills, Basingstoke, UK: Palgrave Macmillan.

Stewart, Frances. 'Crisis prevention: tackling horizontal inequalities.' *Oxford Development Studies*, 28.3 (2000): 245–262.

United Nations World Food Programme. 2017. 'Congo, Democratic Republic of.' World Food Programme USA (Accessed May 25, 2017: https://wfpusa.org/countries/congo-democratic-republic-of/).

Vlassenroot, Koen, and Chris Huggins. 'Land, migration and conflict in Eastern D.R. Congo.' *Eco-Conflicts, African Centre for Technology Studies*, 3.4 (2004): 1–4.

Voors, Maarten, Eleonora Nillesen, Philip Verwimp, Erwin Bulte, Robert Lensink and Daan van Soest. 'Violent conflict and behavior? Evidence from field experiments in Burundi.' *American Economic Review*, 102.2 (2012): 941–964.

Ware, Anthony, ed. 2014. *Development in Difficult Sociopolitical Contexts: Fragile, failed, pariah*. Houndmills, Basingstoke: Palgrave Macmillan.

Waszink, Camilla. 'Protection of Civilians under International Humanitarian Law: Trends and Challenges.' *NOREF Report*, August 2011. Norwegian Peacebuilding Resource Centre (NOREF).

Weinstein, Jeremy. 2007. *Inside Rebellion: The politics of insurgent violence*. Cambridge, UK: Cambridge University Press.

Wimmer, Andreas, and Brian Min. 'From empire to nation-state: explaining wars in the modern world, 1816–2001.' *American Sociological Review*, 71.6 (2006): 867–897.

Zartman, I. William, ed. 2007. *Peacemaking in International Conflict: Methods and techniques*. Washington, DC: US Institute of Peace Press.

9 Education as poverty reduction

Benjamin Curtis

Key questions

- Why are educational deficiencies a form of poverty?
- How are educational access and learning outcomes measured, and what parts of the world have the biggest deficiencies in these areas?
- What is the capabilities perspective on education and development?
- What policies and programmes help reduce education poverty by improving access and learning outcomes?

Introduction

A lack of an adequate education is one of the definitions of poverty. If a person is illiterate, he is almost certainly poor along one or more dimensions. He is quite probably poor according to economic measures: it is unlikely that a person lacking basic literacy or numeracy will have a livelihood that brings in a generous income. If a person lacks an education, he is also probably deprived along all sorts of other dimensions of wellbeing. He is more likely to have health infirmities, and less likely to be able to protect his political rights. Moreover, a deficient education is a kind of poverty trap. Families that are economically poor are less likely to send their children to school, which means the children may remain illiterate and innumerate, and hence poor. But even for children in the developing world who do manage to attend school, there are other ways that poverty can affect their education. Going to primary school in a low-income country is often a very different experience from that in a high-income country. The school may not have walls, or a roof, or toilets. Schools often lack many other resources that students in rich countries take for granted, such as textbooks, desks, paper and pencils. As a specific example, a World Bank study of Vietnam in the 1990s found that in one region, 39 per cent of primary school classrooms did not even have blackboards. In another such study, the average primary school class size in the Indian state of Tamil Nadu was 78 students (Glewwe and Kremer 2005).

A lack of an adequate education is a cause and definition of poverty – but education can also be an essential remedy for poverty. Thomas Awiapo's story is an excellent illustration of this complex interrelationship between education and poverty. Thomas grew up in the northern part of Ghana, in one of the country's poorest areas. Both of his parents died when he was a little boy, and two of his brothers died from malnutrition. Thomas had to find a way to survive, but he lacked marketable skills, almost any physical assets, and the maturity to figure out how to cope with his situation. Because he and his surviving brothers often did not have enough to eat, Thomas began attending a nearby school run by the Catholic Church, just because it offered a daily meal. At the outset, he would come for the food but not stay for the instruction. One of the teachers nonetheless gradually encouraged him to attend school regularly. Thomas came to find that he liked and was good at learning. He completed primary school, then secondary, and proved such an excellent student that he received a scholarship to attend university. His dedication and intelligence then secured him another scholarship, this time to attend graduate school in the United States. After he finished his Master's degree, Thomas returned to the northern region of Ghana to work in development. He became a global ambassador for Catholic Relief Services, and his experience demonstrates both how poverty can hinder access to education, and how education can be a way out of poverty.

This chapter explores the relationships between education and poverty, focusing on some of the most promising policies by which education can reduce poverty. It begins by surveying the common problems with educational access and learning outcomes in the developing world. After a consideration of the capabilities approach to education and development, the chapter then details several programmes that have proven effective for boosting access and outcomes. An understanding of the challenges and benefits of education in the global south is absolutely essential to grasp why, from the capabilities perspective, people are poor. This is also one of the biggest policy challenges in human development today. Some 85 per cent of the world's children – around two billion people in total – live in developing countries, and many of them are forced to deal with the problems of inadequate education nearly every day.

Fortunately, there is good news to report on education as a development priority. Between 1999 and 2008, the number of children of primary school age who were not attending school fell by nearly 40 million. As of 2014, 91 per cent of countries had achieved the goal of universal primary education for their populations (UNICEF Data on Primary Education). In the 60 years from 1950 to 2010, the average years of schooling for people in the developing world grew from 2.0 to 7.2 years (Beatty and Pritchett 2012). And the ratio of girls to boys in primary and secondary school has reached near parity; as recently 1991, only 84 girls were enrolled for every 100 boys (World Bank 2011). Nonetheless, much remains to be done to guarantee an adequate education to children everywhere, and to prevent educational deficiencies from being a persistent cause of poverty.

Problems with access

One of the persistent problems with education in developing countries is that of access, such that many children who should be in school are not. There are still some 58 million primary school-aged children out of school. Many of them live in the poorest countries, or in fragile states. In Eritrea, 65.8 per cent of primary-aged children are not in school, with Liberia at 59.1 per cent, South Sudan at 58.6, Djibouti at 41.7 and Côte d'Ivoire at 38.1 per cent. In Pakistan, 27.5 per cent of primary-aged children are not in school. For every 100 out-of-school children of primary age, 43 will never start school, 34 will start late and 23 have dropped out. These children also come disproportionately from the poorest families, or from areas suffering from conflict or natural disasters. On the whole, schooling levels are still lowest in sub-Saharan Africa; 29.6 million children – roughly half of the total number of out-of-school children worldwide – are in sub-Saharan Africa. In that region, approximately 13 per cent of children finish grade nine; in West and Central Africa, 59 per cent do not even complete grade five. And while increasing primary school enrolment has been the internationally valorized goal, secondary enrolment not surprisingly lags. Around 60 million children who should be in secondary school are not. Educational deficiencies are not just a concern for children: around 750 million adults worldwide lack basic literacy (UNESCO Institute of Statistics).

The single best predictor of children's school attendance is their parents' level of education: the more educated the parents, the more likely the kids are to get educated. What other reasons do children who are of school age not attend? The most common answers are financial costs, opportunity costs, life disruptions and systematic discrimination. In terms of financial costs, even though fees to attend primary school have been eliminated in many countries, families often still have to pay for uniforms, pencils, paper, books, or transportation to the school. Because such costs can add up to well over a hundred US dollars annually, some families simply cannot afford to send their children even to supposedly 'free' schools. Opportunity costs can also be high: sending a child to school often means that he cannot work to help support his family. Such was the situation of Ernesto, a shoe-shine boy I met in the town of Chichicastenango in Guatemala. Ernesto was about 12 years old, but he was far behind in his education because he so often missed school. His parents routinely expected him to walk the five miles into town to make money for the family. The more school Ernesto missed, the more likely it became that he would fail his classes and drop out. Sadly, having to earn an income for the short-term support of his family was depriving Ernesto of the opportunity to gain skills and develop capabilities that might improve his long-term chances for a prosperous and healthy life. To his credit, Ernesto was not unaware of this unfortunate compromise, but he had to obey his parents' wishes and contribute to his family's immediate survival.

Time spent in school can also take away from children's time doing essential household duties such as cleaning, cooking or tending to the familial fields. This problem particularly affects girls. Various disruptions in life also prevent children from attending school. Besides obvious shocks such as war and natural disasters, cyclical duties such as agricultural work can impede school attendance. In countries with pronounced wet and dry seasons, families can need children to help out in the fields during the rainy period. During the dry period, food and incomes can be sharply reduced, which not only hinders the family's ability to pay school costs, but also can lead to children's malnutrition, which hinders their progress if they do attend school. As Thomas's story illustrates, the death of parents is another life disruption that impacts school attendance, since children often have to fend for themselves. According to one study from the Central African Republic, school enrolment for children who had both parents living was almost twice that for children whose parents had died (Durston 2001).

Systematic discrimination inhibits school attendance for people from various groups. The most obvious is discrimination against girls (see i.a. Cameron 2012, Unterhalter 2012). The worst effects here are in Africa and South Asia, which make up three-quarters of the approximately 62 million girls not in primary or secondary school. In Niger, for example, 42.1 per cent of primary school-age girls and 81.8 per cent of lower secondary school-age girls were not in school (UNESCO Institute of Statistics). The same cultural norms that discriminate against girls getting an education can disadvantage people from minority groups; in fact, almost 70 per cent of the girls worldwide who are not in school are members of discriminated groups. This exclusion affects cultural minorities such as indigenous girls in Guatemala, only 26 per cent of whom complete primary school (compared to 62 per cent of non-indigenous Guatemalan girls) according to one study. Similarly, girls from hill tribes in rural Laos receive on average 2 years of school, compared to 5 years for girls from the majority ethnicity. (Lewis 2006) Such exclusion does not just affect women, of course. People from groups such as the Dalit in India, rural tribes in Pakistan, Berbers in the Middle East and North Africa, or the Roma in Eastern Europe often suffer from major educational disadvantages. Part of the problem is school curricula that do not accommodate them. Very often, members of these groups may find that teaching is not in the language they speak at home, but rather in the majority language. For example, the indigenous Guatemalan girls may be most comfortable in K'iche', and the fact that their schooling is in Spanish can pose problems for them. Similarly, it can happen that school systems throughout the developing world are designed by elites for elites. The education a child in rural Senegal receives may have little relevance to her if the curriculum centres on the lives of urban Senegalese.

Problems with learning outcomes

Enrolment rates are only one, narrow view of educational inadequacies that can be caused by and contribute to poverty. At least as serious are inadequate learning outcomes for the children who *do* attend school. For instance, in South Africa, which has impressive enrolment numbers by African standards, only 7 per cent of the students who completed grade nine passed basic literacy tests. In Ghana, only 5 per cent of students completing grade nine achieved basic literacy. The net rate of primary school enrolment in India is 90 per cent, but a study found that only 38 per cent of people could write their name correctly, and 12 per cent could not fluently read a paragraph from a second to third grade textbook (Kenny 2010). A flood of other data demonstrates that even when children are in school, too often they are failing to acquire basic skills. In Tanzania, of children who finished grade seven, only 21 per cent passed a benchmark language test and only 19 per cent passed the maths test (Levine 2005). In Pakistan, half of third graders could not answer the most basic multiplication questions. (World Bank 2011) In Peru, only about half of second graders could read anything. In Brazil and Botswana, two solidly middle-income countries, 66 and 63 per cent of people were found to be functionally illiterate (Hanushek and Wößmann 2007). On international tests that compare learning outcomes for a range of high- and middle-income countries, results showed that the average maths ability of Brazilian students would put them in the bottom two per cent of students in Denmark. The same tests found that in the Western Cape region of South Africa, only two out of 1000 sixth graders in predominantly black schools could pass a grade-level maths test. Forty per cent of Mexican students failed a reading test for 15 year olds that only 5 per cent of students in high-income countries failed (Kenny 2010).

The evidence is painfully clear that very many students in developing countries are not being well served by their school systems. One of the reasons for that failure – and a further element of the relationship between education and poverty – are the well-documented problems with teachers. Teachers are too often absent from work: in an influential study by Chaudhury *et al.* (2006), 11 per cent of teachers were absent on the average day in Peru, 16 per cent in Bangladesh, 20 per cent in Kenya, 25 per cent in India and 27 per cent in Uganda. In one monitoring study of teachers in the state of Andhra Pradesh in India, there was only a 28 per cent chance that a public school teacher was actually in class and actively teaching during the school day. Twenty-five per cent of teachers in the study were completely absent, and of those who did come to work, only about half were actually in their classrooms teaching. Teacher absence rates were generally higher in poorer areas of India (Muralidharan and Sundararaman 2013). Kenya showed broadly similar results (Glewwe *et al.* 2003).

Unfortunately, too many teachers in the developing world also lack adequate qualification for their jobs. They may lack knowledge: studies in Africa found that many primary school maths teachers were barely numerate, and that a majority of third grade teachers in South Africa could not pass a literacy test for sixth graders. (Kenny 2010) They may lack training: only 69 per cent of secondary school teachers in the developing world have adequate training, according to one study (Glewwe and Kremer 2005). In Mali, for example, the ratio of students to trained teachers is 92:1 (UNESCO 2014a). A result is that teachers may just not be very good at teaching. Though evidence is more anecdotal, according to various reports, teachers in the developing world too often treat learning as a matter of rote memorization, with teaching conceived as knowledge transmission from the authority figure to the passive students at their desks (See Barrett *et al.* 2007). Even given the frequently difficult teaching conditions in much of the developing world – classrooms filled with 40 or more students of widely varying abilities, and schools lacking many basic materials – typical assignments such as merely copying information from books or the blackboard is an unfortunate strategy to force on students, and few people learn optimally this way.

Education as a development strategy

These are not the sum total of all the problems of education in low-resource societies, nor are they an exhaustive list of reasons why such education is often inadequate. But they should give an unmistakable picture that many people in developing countries are not receiving the basic quality of education that we might wish for them. Why should everyone be entitled to a quality education? The answers are to some extent obvious – but they need to be empirically grounded, and linked to poverty reduction. To begin with, education has been recognized as a basic human right in the Universal Declaration of Human Rights. The reason it is a basic right is that an education is absolutely essential to so many things in human life, such as earning an income, enjoying decent health, thinking for oneself and participating fully as an autonomous adult and citizen. Education also has a particular connection to the rights of children. According to the Convention on the Rights of Children, young people have specific entitlements not only to education per se, but to aspects of a decent human life relevant to their educational process such as freedom of expression, freedom from child labour, and access to information (see UNICEF 2004).

Beyond the argument for education from basic rights, a great deal of research over the years has shown that education is associated with improved agricultural productivity, technological adaptation, higher wages, better nutrition, reduced female fertility and infant mortality. More educated people cope better with economic shocks (such as depressions or other crises) and environmental adversity (such as extreme weather events). A number of scholars have also claimed that having more educated people in a society tends to go along with more democracy, including higher rates of voting, improved governance and more tolerance for diversity (see e.g. Glaeser *et al.* 2007). One reason is that schooling helps educate people on their political rights and duties, empowering them as citizens.

The health benefits of education are particularly pronounced: it is incontrovertible that mothers who have more education are more likely to have healthier children, thanks to being aware of better basic health practices such as elementary hygiene and the necessity of vaccinations. They will also likely have fewer children. In fact, educating girls is one of the surest ways of combating various forms of poverty, since it means that girls usually have fewer children and take better care of the ones they do have. Admittedly, the causal relationships here can be murky. A greater number of educated girls alters norms about what girls are entitled to, but it is also partially a result of other cultural changes in society that are already empowering women. In any case, healthier children are more likely to stay in school, which leads to better learning outcomes (see UNESCO 2014b). Thus it is not always possible to say that education *causes* improved health outcomes and women's empowerment, but it is definitely part of a valuable feedback loop leading to progress in these areas.

Education has long been considered essential for creating 'human capital' that contributes to a society's economic growth. It does so by boosting people's skills and labour productivity. Education is also associated with the potential for economic innovation because it facilitates the acquisition of new technologies and other sorts of new knowledge (Hanushek and Wößmann 2007). At the individual level, education is clearly associated with higher earnings and more secure livelihoods. A minor debate in the scholarly literature has been fought by a few scholars who say that education mostly provides private returns, i.e. individual outcomes such as higher wages. These scholars claim that education makes only a negligible contribution to social returns, i.e. the 'spillover effects' that improve society as a whole. The preponderance of the scholarship, however, holds that education does benefit societies as well as individuals, through such things as reduced crime, reduced fertility and infant mortality, and improved economic productivity. The reason why this debate is relevant is that it raises the question of education's benefits beyond the economics-based human capital approach (Robeyns 2006).

Simply stated, regardless of economic benefits education is still indispensable because of its relationship to human capabilities. Besides helping people attain a livelihood and generate income, education builds many different skills and abilities – and this range of skills, habits, knowledge and general personal growth can empower people to live lives that they value. The positive economic effects associated with educational attainment are typically the easiest to measure. The other positive effects may be more difficult to quantify, such as empowering women and men to make decisions for themselves, to adopt more open-minded and reflective intellectual attitudes, to become more aware of the world and one's own rights, and to expand their opportunities. Such changes might not even lead to higher incomes. But they give individuals greater agency over their own lives. So though the human capital approach and its economic orientation have their merits, education is best conceived as expanding individuals' capabilities and hopefully helping them to realize their functionings (see Saito 2003, Chiappero-Martinetti and Sabadash 2014). In Amartya Sen's view, the capabilities approach is a vital supplement to human capital understandings of education, since the attainment of individual wellbeing and freedom will have indirect effects on economic production (Hart 2014).

Education is thus central to human development, both in the specialized sense of that term as a counterpart to economic development, and for the crucial meaning of development itself as growth, burgeoning, change. As a World Bank education report has noted, 'The human mind makes possible all other development achievements, from health advances to agricultural innovation to infrastructure construction and private sector growth.' And there is 'no better tool' for unleashing the potential of the human mind than education (World Bank 2011). Education promotes change and, ideally, improvement in human beings. This is one reason why education has a special relevance to the wellbeing of children: it helps young people develop their own capabilities, which then helps them develop into adults who can enjoy a full complement of capabilities and functionings (Comim *et al.* 2011). Education therefore *is* development, as Sen has remarked (Sen 1999). Conversely, lack of an adequate education *is* poverty.

Sen has pointed to three ways that education expands capabilities and can thereby reduce poverty. These three ways are grounded on ideas of what constitutes justice in regards to education. Through promoting literacy, education makes possible public debate and dialogue about social structures and politics, about the way society should be. Every person should be able to participate in that dialogue. Education also helps people to acquire the analytical and practical tools to make decisions for themselves, for their families and for their communities. Every person is entitled to make such decisions. Lastly, in Sen's framework, education has a special role in empowering marginalized and excluded people to both of the above functions. Once they are empowered in this way, they should hopefully gain leverage to reduce the conditions that contribute to their marginalization and exclusion (Unterhalter 2009). Furthermore, without an adequate education a person may be denied basic capabilities that Nussbaum (2011) has identified as fundamental to human life, including health (because of the relationships between education and better health), senses, imagination and thought (which in Nussbaum's formulation explicitly depend on intellectual training), practical reason (such as the ability to make decisions for oneself, which can be better informed through education), and control over one's environment (since education can be positively associated with political participation and democratic traditions of free speech).

Because education is central to development, it is critical to improve education especially for those people who experience the most serious deficiencies described earlier, and who therefore face the most serious threats to their basic capabilities. Children again deserve a special focus here since they are typically disproportionately represented among poor populations. Moreover, poor children often suffer from severe capability deprivations that can have long-lasting impacts on their own development and on the poverty status of their families (Biggeri and Mehrotra 2011). A difficult question when thinking about how to help such children is this: in applying the capabilities approach to poverty reduction through education, what is the minimum adequate threshold? In other words, what counts as the basic level of educational attainment and quality to which everyone is entitled? Millennium Development Goal number two specified universal primary enrolment by 2015. While considerable progress was made between 2000 and 2015 – with 50 million more children enrolled in primary school – the goal also fell short in several ways. The countries with the lowest primary enrolments when the goal was adopted stood absolutely no chance of achieving it in the time specified; they had too much ground to make up in too short a period. The MDG also paid very little attention to learning outcomes, to the quality of the primary education that everyone is entitled to receive. Thus too many children could complete grade six and yet remain functionally illiterate.

For the post-2015 development agenda, a number of educational objectives have been announced. They include ensuring that by 2030, every child will be able to complete early childhood, primary and secondary education; that all young people and adults are fully literate; and that education is adequately financed and governed, with transparency and community participation. These objectives include greater attention to learning outcomes, but also to equity for disadvantaged groups such as poor people and girls (see Sustainable Development Goal number 4).

The problem of assuring a minimum standard of education for everyone can be usefully conceived with the terminology of capabilities and functionings. The goal of universal primary enrolment envisions giving everyone the capability of going to school, though it says little about what capabilities come from being well educated. Moreover, it ignores the issue of how individuals can convert the capability of going to school to the functionings of actually using the capabilities that come from education. Different children will need different resources to be able to attend school, to be able to participate and understand, and then to complete learning successfully (Vaughan 2007). For example, if a child is hungry, or speaks a different language at home than at school, or fears for bodily safety at school because of her identity or gender, then that child will need extra help to succeed in education. This is the equity issue: the poorest people may need additional resources to convert educational capabilities (such as the ability to attend school) to educational functionings (such as actually being able to read and reason).

The capabilities approach does not propose a universally agreed-upon set of indicators to gauge basic educational capabilities. However, there are various useful principles for thinking about what constitutes a minimum standard of educational quality. The EdQual Research Program, which focused on improving quality in low-income countries, offered this definition:

> A good quality education is one that enables all learners to realize the capabilities they require to become economically productive, develop sustainable livelihoods, contribute to peaceful and democratic societies and enhance wellbeing. The learning outcomes that are required vary according to the context but at the end of the basic education cycle must include threshold levels of literacy and numeracy and life skills including awareness and prevention of disease.
>
> (Tikly 2010)

Box 9.1 Basic capabilities for education

- **Literacy**: being able to read, write, and use language
- **Numeracy**: being able to count, measure, and solve mathematical questions
- **Sociality and participation**: being able to establish positive relationships with others and participate in social activities without shame
- **Learning dispositions**: being able to concentrate, pursue interests, complete educational tasks
- **Physical activities**: being able to exercise and engage in sports activities
- **Science and technology**: being able to understand natural phenomena and use technological tools
- **Practical reason**: being able to relate means and ends and reflect critically on one's and others' actions

Source: adapted from Terzi (2007)

This definition leaves open the possibility for societies to decide their own outcomes beyond the minimum basic level. But the implication is that an adequate education must ensure that people have certain skills. These skills must include 'functional life skills' such as being able to provide shelter and assure sufficient nutrition for oneself and/or one's family. Every person must have certain minimum cognitive skills, too, which are not just literacy and numeracy but also the ability to access new information (Young 2009). Many of these skills – including social skills to live in harmony with one's community – are subsumed into Lorella Terzi's (2007) proposed list of specific 'basic capabilities for educational functionings.' (See Box 9.1) This list is certainly open to debate as to what it includes and how it could be measured and operationalized. The importance, however, is to consider how programmes to improve education relate to these proposed fundamental entitlements.

What works to improve education?

While there are a number of specific programmes that have demonstrated successes in improving education and reducing poverty, there is no 'one size fits all' policy. Some programmes do a better job of increasing access to schooling, helping to meet the goal of universal primary enrolment. Other programmes are more relevant to improving learning outcomes, so that the quality of the education children receive is adequate. Many times, these goals do not overlap, so that improvements in access do not necessarily translate to improvements in quality. Therefore, programmes must be selected for their fit to an individual society's conditions – blanket recommendations are of little utility. Moreover, many scholars who have studied the challenges of education in developing countries affirm that simply putting more financial resources into existing systems will not produce markedly better outcomes. For instance, increasing teachers' salaries or the availability of computers does not automatically translate to more student learning. To achieve real improvement, educational systems must often be reformed, including incentive structures for teachers, how schools are managed and held accountable, and how data on student progress are gathered. Because there is no magic bullet to ensure optimal poverty reduction through education, we will focus on just a few promising strategies, programmes whose positive outcomes have been most convincingly demonstrated.

The past several decades' impressive gains in primary enrolment have come thanks to a variety of initiatives to expand access to children whose backgrounds might previously have hindered them from attending school. Building schools has been a logical first step in expanding access, and while rural and marginalized areas may sometimes still lack adequate school facilities, international development policy now increasingly focuses on other means of ensuring that children attend school and stay in school. Reducing the costs of attendance is a consistent objective that can be met by providing uniforms and textbooks (so families do not have to pay for them), or eliminating school fees. After school fees were eliminated, primary enrolment jumped by 307.4 per cent in Ethiopia, 95.5 per cent in Tanzania, 68 per cent in Uganda and 49 per cent in Malawi (see Bentaouet-Kattan 2006, Morgan *et al.* 2014). One of the most effective models worldwide for reducing costs and incentivizing school attendance are conditional cash transfers (CCTs). These programmes give low-income families money conditioned upon the family meeting certain goals, such as ensuring that daughters regularly attend school. The amount of money families receive is usually fairly small, around ten per cent of the household's consumption level. CCTs have been implemented in some 28 countries, including nearly all countries in Latin America, plus a handful in Africa, Asia and the Middle East.

The most famous CCT programme is Mexico's Prospera, formerly known by several other names. It works by specifically targeting poor families (at first in rural areas, now in urban areas too), and mothers and daughters: the subsidies families receive for keeping their children in school are higher for girls. The payments typically start in the third grade, and their amount varies – including, for example, a grant to buy food – but the total can sometimes equal what one of the parents earns in a month from work. The money is given directly to the families rather than channelling it through a local intermediary, which reduces the potential for corruption. Besides regular school attendance, the conditions also include routine visits to a health clinic, where the children are vaccinated, weighed, and given vitamins. Mothers have to attend basic health classes covering issues such as nutrition and sanitation. Studies have repeatedly documented this programme's positive effects. It increased school enrolment on average by 3.5 per cent, with larger effects in increasing enrolment in grade six, which improved by 11.1 per cent (Schultz 2004). Boys who participated in Prospera starting at age nine completed a year more of schooling than boys not in the programme. Girls who began participating at early ages received 0.7 more years of schooling. Child labour for boys decreased, though not for girls (Behrman *et al.* 2011).

Studies of CCTs in other countries have found even larger effects. In Nicaragua, time in school increased 18 per cent for children aged 7–13. In Bangladesh, time in school increased by 27 per cent for girls aged 11–18, and in Pakistan the increase was 38 per cent for primary school girls (Orazem 2012). The CCT in Ecuador decreased child labour by 17 per cent in addition to increasing school enrolments by 10 per cent (Schady 2006). In Malawi, a CCT helped girls add the equivalent to one-sixth of a year of schooling and increase their test scores; daily attendance also rose by eight percentage points (Baird *et al.* 2011). A scholarship programme for girls in Cambodia worked similarly to a CCT, giving awards equivalent to 45 USD each to families whose daughters had good attendance and good grades in school. This programme led to significant increases in enrolment for girls from the poorest households, whose enrolment actually surpassed girls from the richest households (Filmer and Schady 2006, 2014). Other indicators of child and family welfare also improved, such as increased health-care visits, better nutrition, and vaccinations.

While CCTs have achieved some excellent results in getting children in school and encouraging them to stay there, such programmes do have limitations. They have been shown mostly to improve access, but not consistently to improve learning outcomes. So though they help get kids in school, CCTs do not necessarily ensure quality learning. CCTs are also relatively expensive, since in large countries such as Mexico they can involve monetary transfers to millions of families. CCTs also require a reasonably effective government administrative system to manage them. For these reasons, they have been more commonly implemented in middle-income countries that have greater financial resources and greater governmental capacity. Though CCTs are often beneficial, there are other programmes to improve access that may be more cost effective for low-income countries.

One widely useful, often highly cost-effective policy that can improve access and outcomes in school actually begins before formal schooling. Early childhood development (ECD) programmes can bring very positive benefits for children such as boosting cognitive skills, nutrition and health status, and levels of school attainment. This is particularly important because deficiencies in these areas contribute to early grade repetition, dropping out, and delayed intellectual development. Strong ECD has also been associated with gains in lifetime earnings (see i.a. Barnett 1995, Anderson *et al.* 2003, Heckman 2006). A programme in the Philippines aimed specifically at disadvantaged families serves as an example of what ECD can accomplish. Day-care centres were set up to serve as pre-schools and provide health services including micronutrient supplements. Participants in the programme were visited in their homes by health workers who provided immunizations among other services. Parents were educated about best practices in raising their children. Schools were also involved through workshops for teachers and administrators to train them in better skills relevant to ECD. An analysis of the programme's results showed that over six years, children displayed satisfactory physical and cognitive development, and as students their test scores improved by 12–15 points (Armecin *et al.* 2006, Yamauchi and Liu 2012). This Philippine ECD programme thus successfully managed to improve children's access to school via improved health and nutrition, as well as their learning outcomes.

Whether separately or as part of such ECD programmes, health interventions in general can be an inexpensive way of addressing both access and learning problems. Deworming and nutrition supplements combat a very common reason for why school-age children do not attend school, namely poor health. Moreover, when children are better nourished and enjoy better overall health, they are likely to have better learning outcomes as well, at least theoretically. When children are deficient in certain nutrients such as iodine or zinc, their cognitive development can be diminished. And when you do not feel well for whatever reason, it is very difficult to concentrate in school and do good work. According to estimates, health interventions such as deworming can cost as little as 50 cents per child per year, and school nutrition programmes also have modest costs, estimated at USD 23.25 per year per child (Orazem 2012). More evidence needs to be gathered on the outcomes of specific interventions, however. Deworming's results have been questioned, for example, and school feeding programmes have a mixed record. Providing free meals at school increased attendance and enrolment in a number of countries. But there have not been consistent improvements in learning outcomes or other measures of cognitive development (Jomaa *et al.* 2011). Because good health is essential for children to attend school and learn, such programmes may be promising particularly for the poorest populations in a given country, though as yet there is no consensus on the best way to improve health to promote educational achievement.

Obviously, even if children manage to attend school, they will not learn very much unless a teacher is also present. Indeed, studies in countries such as the United States and China have pointed to teacher quality as the single most important in-school factor for explaining students' achievement (see i.a. Rockoff 2004, Hanushek and Rivkin 2006, Akiba *et al.* 2007). Given the problems in the developing world with teachers' absenteeism and inadequate professional preparation, how can policies incentivize teachers to do their job better and hold them more accountable for student learning outcomes? Merely raising teachers' salaries may help improve morale and attract more able people to the profession, but is not always effective.

As an example, Kenya instituted a bonus pay scheme so that teachers would be rewarded as their students' test scores improved, but an analysis found that teachers focused on preparing their students mostly to do better on the test, at the expense of other lessons. In contrast, a pay-for-performance programme in India did see increases in teachers' classroom time and student achievement, but at present a workable model to incentivize better teaching through pay increases has not been conclusively established (Kremer and Holla 2008, Muralidharan 2012). To combat the persistent problem of teachers not showing up for work, a surprisingly simple programme was introduced in India: students were given a camera so they could take a picture that was stamped with the date and time to verify that their teacher was present on that day. Teachers' salaries were then made conditional upon adequate attendance based on these data. The study by Duflo et al. (2012) found that teacher absences declined from 44 per cent to 21 per cent once this programme was put in place. Student achievement on tests also improved. Such forms of monitoring teachers' performance will be vital to attain the improvements in learning that have eluded too many students in the developing world even with their increased access to schools.

One reason that teachers in many developing countries have been able to get away with deficient job performance is that they have strong teacher unions able to exert political pressure on local and national governments; the same dynamic can occur in high-income countries as well (Glewwe and Kremer 2005). Several countries have tried a policy to shake up that political structure, namely hiring teachers on a year-long contract basis. If these contract teachers' absences and other job performance were unsatisfactory, then they would not be rehired. This is another way of strengthening both monitoring and accountability of teachers. In most cases, contract teachers had much better attendance rates than did the civil service teachers (who were long-term hires). Though these contract teachers typically lacked the professional training of their civil service counterparts, nonetheless student test performance also improved under the contract teachers (Muralidharan and Sundararaman 2013, Duflo et al. 2015). Such programmes have also been found to be cost effective, producing large savings in governments' education budgets since the contract teachers are paid less. Some commentators have questioned whether a system of contract teachers would be feasible or fair as a policy over many years, since a cadre of temporary teachers would likely militate for higher pay and many of the same job security and other benefits that regular civil service teachers enjoy. However, with certain other changes such as local hiring of teachers, or hiring teachers on a temporary contract basis with the possibility of eventual long-term contracts, such a programme might work (Pritchett 2012).

There are a number of further policies related to teacher performance that could be adopted to improve learning outcomes. Remedial tutoring, and classes outside the formal schooling system, can be a vital supplement to children's learning. The classes provided by the Indian NGO Pratham are often held up as a model (Banerjee et al. 2007, and see Box 9.2). Likewise, interactive radio instruction (IRI) has proven valuable in a number of countries in Latin America and sub-Saharan Africa. In these programmes, lessons in various subjects such as maths and language are given over the radio. They are 'interactive' because listeners have specific assignments that they complete and then check as the lesson is broadcast. Such programmes have been shown to improve both access to basic education (especially for children in remote areas) and learning achievement (Bosch 1997, Ho and Thukral 2009).

Improving teacher performance is not just about better monitoring and pay, of course. A small but growing evidence base also points to other effective forms of professional and pedagogical support (Reid and Kleinhenz 2015). A programme in Chile trained teachers in practices for early language instruction and classroom behaviour management. As a result, teachers who participated in the programme displayed better

Box 9.2 Pratham

I followed a narrow lane hemmed in by closely-crowded little buildings made of concrete, bricks, cinder blocks, and often whatever other materials were at hand. These sometimes slapdash structures rose two or three stories above the lane, pressed so tightly together that I could glimpse only fragments of the hazy sky above. Also overhead, electricity and other cables skeined from house to house, their thick, coiled masses jerry-rigged and a little threatening. The footpath itself was made of broken bits of stone or concrete, the heavy rains leaving frequent puddles of dirty standing water – or sometimes the puddles may have been undrained sewage, judging from their foul smell. My guide was leading me into one of Mumbai's poorest slums, where she acted as a local coordinator for Pratham's activities. Inside the densely-packed houses, in tiny, often dark rooms, people ran businesses, cooked meals, sold necessities, tended to children, listened to the radio, lived their lives. Somewhere in that labyrinth of lanes, we headed to a modest room that Pratham rented to provide educational services to the residents of the neighbourhood. Since most of the residents were Muslim, the class I observed was conducted in the Urdu language: several children around 8 or 9 years of age sat on the floor and listened to their teacher explain concepts of basic maths. The children were attentive and appreciative as they performed exercises with rulers and other tools to learn their measurements. A bright, smiling woman probably in her middle twenties taught them. Though her training as a teacher mostly came from the short preparation courses of a few weeks' duration that Pratham offered, I could see that she was a natural, and my guide told me that this teacher was reputed to be one of Pratham's best in Mumbai. The class she was teaching that morning was non-formal and supplemental for the children, since they would attend regular government schools in the afternoon.

Pratham is the largest non-governmental organization in India, and one of the most respected education-focused NGOs in the world. Its programmes are wide-ranging, including vocational skills training for young adults, English instruction for both children and adults, urban learning centres such as I visited, and other initiatives such as household surveys throughout many communities in India. I also visited two of Pratham's early childhood education centres elsewhere in Mumbai. Since most Indian children, especially from poor backgrounds, do not have access to pre-school, Pratham's programmes are important for boosting children's school readiness. I observed as one of Pratham's teachers led very young children in recitations in English of things like the numbers and months. In another centre, as the youngest children were taught in one part of the room, several girls who were a little older sat quietly in a corner and read from books. After a while, a teacher would come over to discuss what they had read. The energetic coordinator of this centre told me that Pratham's programmes helped not only the children who studied in them, but also the local women who taught there. These women were usually volunteers, sometimes receiving a modest salary, but they reportedly enjoyed the work because it employed people from the community and helped to ensure that girls got an education. These hard-working teachers had clearly decided that the diverse educational opportunities Pratham provided could help them better their lives and the lives of others.

classroom productivity, feedback quality and sensitivity to students' needs; however, there were no evident improvements in student achievement (Yoshikawa *et al.* 2015). Low-skilled teachers especially need more support to learn best pedagogical practices. Teachers in a Liberian programme received clear guidelines to improve the quality of reading instruction in primary schools, and their students showed strong gains in a number of literacy outcomes (Piper and Korda 2011). Other initiatives that have proven beneficial include more practice teaching incorporated into teacher education programmes; ongoing professional development trainings to make curriculum more appropriate for multilingual learners and inclusive for students from disadvantaged backgrounds; and courses for headteachers to help them improve pedagogy in their schools (Barrett *et al.* 2007, Tikly and Barrett 2011, UNESCO 2014a).

Conclusion

Significant progress has been made in improving education as a poverty reduction strategy, though of course much remains to be done. This progress has come in part from the push for universal primary education per Millennium Development Goal 2, which did much to provide school facilities and basic learning opportunities to children around the world. As we have seen, conditional cash transfers are one generally successful means of encouraging enrolment and school completion. Going forward, international policymakers must devote even more attention to the health and other interventions that can keep children in school and help them learn. Health interventions such as micronutrients and various forms of early childhood development programmes are vital to give children the physical wellbeing necessary for adequate intellectual development. Instituting more effective programmes to ensure that teachers are appropriately prepared, properly monitored, and sufficiently incentivized to perform well must also receive greater attention. Accountability mechanisms such as time-and-date photos, hiring short-term contract teachers and expanding remedial programmes have all managed to improve education quality so that children learn as well as they can from the schooling they do get.

From the accepted goal of universal, quality primary education, the international policy community's focus must also now move to expanding access and learning at the secondary and tertiary levels. Primary education has been the agreed-upon minimum floor, but it cannot become a ceiling; as more people in the developing world attain that minimum requirement, they must then be assured a quality secondary education as well. Secondary education is the minimum threshold in high-income countries, and that guarantee should not be denied to people from poorer countries. This next frontier of expanding educational access and outcomes poses a major challenge, since resources for poverty reduction are finite. Therefore, priorities have to be designed to decide which development initiatives to promote at the regional, country and the global levels. A compelling case can be made that education should be a consistent top priority. Education *is* development. It builds human capabilities along multiple dimensions. It contributes to wage increases, productivity growth, health improvements and cognitive gains, which are all essential to escaping poverty and helping people live lives that they value. Though certainly other strategies are useful in targeting particular facets of poverty, education's importance lies in its very broad effects.

Admittedly, achieving large-scale educational improvements in the developing world is a difficult task. One frustration is that few countries have a truly feasible plan for

Box 9.3 Case study: Indonesia

Indonesia (Figure 9.1) is a lower middle-income country that has seen significant advancements in economic and human development since the 1970s. One reason for its progress has been investments in education; Indonesia's record here is illustrative of both the promises and pitfalls of policies to improve educational access and outcomes. Between 1973 and 1978 the Indonesian government constructed more than 61,000 primary schools, and primary enrolment rates for children aged seven to 12 increased from 60 per cent in the early 1970s to 94 per cent by 1984. Universal primary enrolment has nearly been achieved, and roughly 86 per cent of children go on to complete primary education. This major commitment to increasing school access contributed not only to increased years of schooling for the average child, but also to increases in wages. On the whole, poverty defined as low incomes and educational and health deficits declined significantly into the first decade of the twenty-first century. For example, the number of people living below the USD 1.25 poverty line fell by half between 1990 to 2010, from 54 per cent of the population to 20 per cent. Women's literacy grew from 47 per cent in 1970 to 93 per cent by the early 1990s. The increased education of women also lowered Indonesia's fertility rates, as more women entered the labour force and were empowered to exercise greater control over their reproductive lives.

Despite this positive picture, Indonesia faces ongoing challenges in both educational access and outcomes. With universal primary enrolment achieved, the access goal shifted in the 1990s to a minimum standard of 9 years basic education for everyone. This standard has not yet been met, however, because of impediments such as school fees, the costs of uniforms, and significant numbers of students dropping out. According to analyses from the World Bank and others, 46 per cent of Indonesian students who completed primary school were still functionally illiterate, and nearly half could not correctly answer basic maths questions. Similarly, Indonesia tends to score near the bottom of reading, maths and science results on the Program on International Student Assessment (PISA) test. Educational disparities also remain a problem: outside urban areas, and especially outside the higher-income cities on the main Indonesian island of Java, access to schooling beyond primary is often deficient, and quality low. For example, only 55 per cent of children from rural areas continued on to junior secondary school (compared to 80 per cent of children from urban areas), and access to early childhood development services is often very limited outside major cities. Quality of teaching has also often lagged, with inadequate teacher preparation and excessive emphasis on rote learning.

Given that education has already played such an important role in reducing poverty in Indonesia, it is encouraging that policy makers there continue to devote attention to improving the weak spots in access and quality. A number of non-formal educational delivery programmes seek to reach rural areas or adults who may never have received adequate schooling. Programmes to eradicate illiteracy have been broadcast over the radio and television, for instance, or classes have been created to help people with literacy and job-related skill-building. An ambitious law was passed in 2005 to reform teaching, including provisions to improve teacher preparation and accountability. Most ambitiously of all, the Indonesian government committed to devote 20 per cent of the entire national budget to education. Critics question how realistic or efficient that particular goal may be. But it is nonetheless a clear signal of education's acknowledged contribution both to easily-measured improvements in economic development, as well as to less easily-measured but equally valuable improvements in human development.

Sources: Duflo (2001), Oswald Christano and Cummings (2007), Maralani (2008), Chang *et al.* (2012)

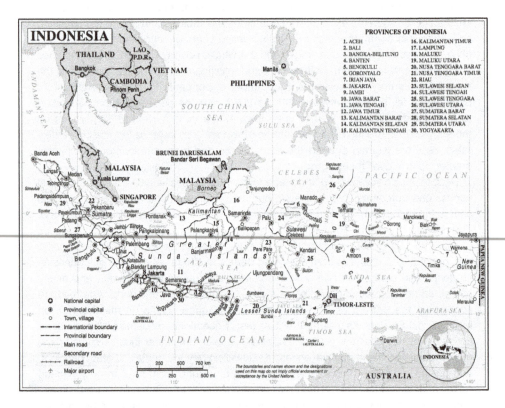

Figure 9.1 Map of Indonesia
Source: Map No. 4110 Rev. 4 UNITED NATIONS January 2004

achieving improvements in learning outcomes. As of yet, most approaches are piecemeal and highly context dependent, as different regions or localities experiment. Reliable data on progress in student learning outcomes are often lacking for many developing countries. Consequently, specific targets for learning improvement, as well as the means for meeting them, are too often vague or ill-conceived. Another frustration is that any progress is likely to be slow. The increases in enrolment that have brought some developing countries near to universal primary enrolment have often taken 30 years to accomplish. Improving learning outcomes may take even longer. According to one analysis, though it may take a few developing countries around 25 years to approach the averages on international tests attained by students in OECD countries, the prognosis for many other countries is much worse. At realistic rates of progress, it could take countries in southern and eastern Africa around 150 years to equal current test score averages in OECD countries (Beatty and Pritchett 2012). Finally, the parts of the world where people are most educationally deprived tend to be the weak and fragile states. Such states are typically too dysfunctional and/or corrupt to expect effective transformation of governmental education provision. Tragically, people caught in conflict and state failure are also prone to see education as not worth the investment, since those societies are so troubled that skills gained through education are often not economically rewarded except via emigration.

None of these problems negates the value of education as a poverty reduction strategy. One thing that policymakers as well as students of development must not forget is that the persistent inadequacies of education in poorer countries are an obvious affront to justice. There is no reason that the world should accept the unfortunate fact that a year of schooling in Togo is so blatantly unequal in its human and economic development effects to a year of schooling in Finland. We have an ethical imperative to ameliorate these egregious disparities in educational outcomes between high- and low-income countries. Perhaps the difficulties of education as a development strategy only reaffirm the necessity to focus improvements on the people who need them the most, namely the poorest. Those most deprived of an adequate education have historically been girls and members of various marginalized groups. Reducing the poverty disproportionately experienced by these excluded people should be a priority for educational policies. Scholarships for girls and people from traditionally underserved groups can encourage enrolment. Recruiting more teachers who are women or from minority groups could further boost enrolment and possibly lead to better learning outcomes. Tutoring, remedial programmes, and other non-formal options for schooling can also open up learning opportunities for those who have otherwise been deprived. Once again, the potential means of combating poverty through education are numerous. The ongoing challenge is to identify what works best, and then to implement expanded, well-designed programmes so that no person in the world should be denied full development of his or her human capabilities because of educational failure.

Discussion questions

1   What does being illiterate or innumerate have to do with being poor? How can getting an education help a person to escape poverty?
2   If, as some scholars have claimed, education's economic benefits to a society are negligible, is it a worthwhile development strategy?
3   Explore the World Inequality Database on Education (www.education-inequalities.org/) to research educational deprivations. Pick a country and examine along which educational indicators it has the severest disparities. Pick an indicator and examine which countries experience the severest disparities in that area.
4   Explore the UNESCO eAtlas of Out-of-School Children (http://tellmaps.com/uis/oosc/) for information on worldwide trends of educational deficiencies. Where are the most children denied their right to education? Where are the most severe gender disparities? Choose a country and read its profile to see how it rates in international comparison.
5   In accordance with the capabilities approach, what do you think should be the minimum threshold of educational attainment to which every human is entitled? How do you

measure that threshold? How does your answer relate to the potential problem of 'adaptive preference', whereby a group of poor, rural children might say that their highest educational aspiration is primary school because that is all that seems realistic to them?

6   How do the specific programmes mentioned in this chapter relate to the ideas of basic capabilities for education?

7   Consider the problems of improving education in fragile or failing states. What are those problems? Do you agree that these problems undermine the potential for improving educational outcomes in fragile or failing states? What are some counter-arguments to the idea that educational investments in such states are unlikely to bring major benefits?

8   Examine the post-2015 development objectives for education. What strengths and weaknesses do you see in those goals?

Further reading

Kremer, Michael, Conner Brannen and Rachel Glennerster. 'The challenge of education and learning in the developing world.' *Science* 340.6130 (2013): 297–300.

Sperling, Gene B., and Rebecca Winthrop. 2015. *What Works in Girls' Education: Evidence for the world's best investment*. Washington, DC: Brookings Institution Press.

Tikly, Leon, and Angeline M. Barrett, eds. 2013. *Education Quality and Social Justice in the Global South: Challenges for policy, practice and research*. London: Routledge.

UNESCO. 2015. *Education for All 2000–2015: Achievements and Challenges*. Education for All Global Monitoring Report 2015.

Unterhalter, Elaine, Rosie Vaughan and Melanie Walker. 'The capability approach and education.' *Prospero* 13.3 (2007). Available at www.nottingham.ac.uk/educationresearchprojects/documents/developmentdiscourses/rpg2008walkermclean9.pdf, accessed May 2016.

Works cited

Akiba, Motoko, Gerald K. LeTendre and Jay P. Scribner. 'Teacher quality, opportunity gap, and national achievement in 46 countries.' *Educational Researcher*, 36.7 (2007): 369–387.

Anderson, Laurie M., *et al.* 'The effectiveness of early childhood development programs: a systematic review.' *American Journal of Preventive Medicine*, 24.3 (2003): 32–46.

Armecin, Graeme, Jere R. Behrman, Paulita Duazo, Sharon Ghuman, Socorro Gultiano, Elizabeth M. King and Nanette Lee. 'Early Childhood Development through an Integrated Program: Evidence from the Philippines.' World Bank Policy Research Working Paper 3922, May 2006.

Baird, Sarah, Craig McIntosh and Berk Ozler. 'Cash or condition? Evidence from a cash transfer experiment.' *Quarterly Journal of Economics*, 26.4 (2011): 1709–1753.

Banerjee, Abhijit, Shawn Cole, Esther Duflo and Leigh Linden. 'Remedying education: evidence from two randomized experiments in India.' *Quarterly Journal of Economics*, 122.3 (2007): 1235–1264.

Barnett, W. Steven. 'Long-term effects of early childhood programs on cognitive and school outcomes.' *The Future of Children*, 5.3 (1995): 25–50.

Barrett, Angeline, Sajid Ali, John Clegg, J. Enrique Hinostroza, John Lowe, Jutta Nikel, Mario Novelli, George Oduro, Mario Pillay, Leon Tikly and Guoxing Yu. 2007. *Initiatives to improve the quality of teaching and learning: A review of recent literature*. Background paper for the Global Monitoring Report 2008, EdQual working paper no. 11.

Beatty, Amanda, and Lant Pritchett. 'From Schooling Goals to Learning Goals: How Fast Can Student Learning Improve?' Center for Global Development Policy Paper 012, September 2012.

Behrman, Jere R., Susan W. Parker and Petra E. Todd. 'Do conditional cash transfers for schooling generate lasting benefits? A five-year followup of PROGRESA/Oportunidades.' *Journal of Human Resources*, 46.1 (2011): 93–122.

Bentaouet-Kattan, R. 2006. *Implementation of Free Basic Education Policy*. Washington, DC: World Bank.

Biggeri, Mario, and Santosh Mehrotra. 'Child Poverty as Capability Deprivation: How to Choose Domains of Child Well-being and Poverty', in Mario Biggeri, Jérôme Ballet and Flavio Comim, eds. *Children and the Capability Approach*. 2011. Basingstoke, UK: Palgrave Macmillan.

Bosch, Andrea. 1997. *Interactive Radio Instruction: Twenty-three years of improving education quality*. Washington, DC: World Bank Group.

Cameron, John. 'Capabilities and the global challenges of girls' school enrolment and women's literacy.' *Cambridge Journal of Education*, 42.3 (2012): 297–306.

Chang, Mae Chu, Sheldon Shaeffer, Andy Ragatz, Joppe de Ree, Ritchie Stevenson, Susiana Iskandar and Samer Al-Samarai. 'Teacher Reform in Indonesia: The Role of Politics and Evidence-Based Policymaking: A Preview', World Bank Report No. 73624-ID, November 2012.

Chaudhury, Nazmul, Jeffrey Hammer, Michael Kremer, Karthik Muralidharan and F. Halsey Rogers. 'Missing in action: teacher and health worker absence in developing countries.' *Journal of Economic Perspectives*, 20.1 (2006): 91–116.

Chiappero-Martinetti, Enrica, and Anna Sabadash. 'Integrating Human Capital and Human Capabilities in Understanding the Value of Education', in Solava Ibrahim and Meera Tiwari, eds. 2014. *The Capability Approach: From theory to practice*. Houndmills, Basingstoke, UK: Palgrave Macmillan.

Comim, Flavio, Jérôme Ballet, Mario Biggeri and Vittorio Iervese. 'Introduction', in Mario Biggeri, Jérôme Ballet and Flavio Comim, eds. *Children and the Capability Approach: From theory to practice*. 2011. Houndmills, Basingstoke, UK: Palgrave Macmillan.

Duflo, Esther. 'Schooling and labor market consequences of school construction in Indonesia: evidence from an unusual policy experiment.' *The American Economic Review*, 91.4 (2001): 795–813.

Duflo, Esther, Pascaline Dupas and Michael Kremer. 'School governance, teacher incentives, and pupil-teacher ratios: experimental evidence from Kenyan primary schools.' *Journal of Public Economics*, 123 (March 2015): 92–110.

Duflo, Esther, Rema Hanna and Stephen P. Ryan. 'Incentives work: getting teachers to come to school.' *American Economic Review*, 102.4 (2012): 1241–1278.

Durston, Susan, and Nice Nashire. 'Rethinking poverty and education: an attempt by an education programme in Malawi to have an impact on poverty.' *Compare*, 31.1 (2001): 75–91.

Filmer, Deon, and Norbert Schady. 'The medium-term effects of scholarships in a low-income country.' *Journal of Human Resources*, 49.3 (2014): 663–694.

Filmer, Deon, and Norbert Schady. 'Getting Girls into School: Evidence from a Scholarship Program in Cambodia.' World Bank Policy Research Working Paper 3910, May 2006.

Glaeser, Edward, Giacomo Ponzetto and Andrei Shleifer. 'Why does democracy need education?' *Journal of Economic Growth*, 12.2 (2007): 77–99.

Glewwe, Paul, and Michael Kremer. 'Schools, Teachers, and Educational Outcomes in Developing Countries', in *Handbook on the Economics of Education*. 2005. Amsterdam: Elsevier.

Glewwe, Paul, Nauman Ilias and Michael Kremer. *Teacher Incentives*. National Bureau of Economic Research, Working Paper No. 9671, 2003.

Hanushek, Eric A., and Steven G. Rivkin. 'Teacher quality.' *Handbook of the Economics of Education*, 2 (2006): 1051–1078.

Hanushek, Eric A., and Ludger Wößmann. 'The Role of Education Quality in Economic Growth', World Bank Policy Research Working Paper 4122, February 2007.

Hart, Caroline Sarojini. 'The Capability Approach and Educational Research', in Caroline Sarojini Hart, Mario Biggeri and Bernhard Babic, eds. 2014. *Agency and Participation in Childhood and Youth: International applications of the capability approach in schools and beyond*. London: Bloomsbury.

Heckman, James J. 'Skill formation and the economics of investing in disadvantaged children.' *Science* 312.5782 (2006): 1900–1902.

Ho, Jennifer, and Hetal Thukral. 'Tuned in to student success: assessing the impact of interactive radio instruction for the hardest-to-reach.' *Journal of Education in International Development*, 4 (2009): 34–51.

Jomaa, Lamis H., Elaine McDonnell and Claudia Probart. 'School feeding programs in developing countries: impacts on children's health and educational outcomes.' *Nutrition reviews*, 69.2 (2011): 83–98.

Kenny, Charles. 'Learning about Schools in Development', Center for Global Development Working Paper 236, December 2010.

Kremer, Michael, and Alaka Holla. 'Improving Education in the Developing World: What Have We Learned From Randomized Evaluations?' mimeo, November 2008.

Levine, Ruth, and Nancy Birdsall. 'On the Road to Universal Primary Education', Center for Global Development CGD Brief, February 2005.

Lewis, Maureen A., and Marlaine E. Lockheed. 'Inexcusable Absence: Why 60 Million Girls Still Aren't in School and What To Do About It.' Washington, DC: Center for Global Development, 2006.

Maralani, Vida. 'The changing relationship between family size and educational attainment over the course of socioeconomic development: evidence from Indonesia', *Demography*, 45.3 (2008): 693–717.

Morgan, Claire, Anthony Petrosino and Trevor Fronius. 'Eliminating school fees in low-income countries: a systematic review.' *Journal of MultiDisciplinary Evaluation*, 10.23 (2014): 26–43.

Muralidharan, Karthik. 2012. 'Long-Term Effects of Teacher Performance Pay: Experimental Evidence from India.' J-PAL Working Paper.

Muralidharan, Karthik, and Venkatesh Sundararaman. 'Contract Teachers: Experimental Evidence from India.' National Bureau of Economic Research, Working Paper No. 19440, 2013.

Nussbaum, Martha. 2011. *Creating Capabilities: The human development approach*. Boston, MA: Harvard University Press.

Oswald Christano, Rita, and William K. Cummings. 'Schooling in Indonesia', in Gerard A. Postiglione and Jason Tan, eds. 2007. *Going to School in East Asia*. Westport, CT: Greenwood Press.

Orazem, Peter F. 'The Case for Improving School Quality and Student Health as a Development Strategy.' Copenhagen Consensus Paper, April 2012.

Piper, Benjamin, and Medina Korda. *EGRA Plus: Liberia. Program Evaluation Report*. RTI International, 2011.

Pritchett, Lant. 'Learning Quality as the Primary Objective.' Copenhagen Consensus Education Perspective Paper, April 2012.

Reid, Kate, and Elizabeth Kleinhenz. 2015. *Supporting Teacher Development: Literature review*. Canberra: Department of Foreign Affairs and Trade, Australia.

Robeyns, Ingrid. 'Three models of education Rights, capabilities and human capital.' *Theory and Research in Education*, 4.1 (2006): 69–84.

Rockoff, Jonah E. 'The impact of individual teachers on student achievement: evidence from panel data.' *American Economic Review*, 94.2 (2004): 247–252.

Saito, Madoka. 'Amartya Sen's capability approach to education: a critical exploration.' *Journal of Philosophy of Education*, 37.1 (2003): 17–33.

Schady, Norbert, and María Caridad Araujo. 'Cash Transfers, Conditions, School Enrollment, and Child Work: Evidence from a Randomized Experiment in Ecuador.' World Bank Policy Research Working Paper 3930, June 2006.

Schultz, T. Paul. 'School subsidies for the poor: evaluating the Mexican Progresa poverty program.' *Journal of Development Economics*, 74.1 (2004): 199–250.

Sen, Amartya. 1999. *Development as Freedom*. New York, NY: Knopf.

Terzi, Lorella. 'The Capability to Be Educated', in Melanie Walker and Elaine Unterhalter, eds. 2007. *Amartya Sen's Capability Approach and Social Justice in Education*. New York, NY: Palgrave Macmillan.

Tikly, Leon. 'Towards a Framework for Understanding the Quality of Education.' EdQual Working Paper No. 27. November 2010. EdQual Research Programme on Implementing Education Quality in Low Income Countries.

Tikly, Leon, and Angeline M. Barrett. 'Social justice, capabilities and the quality of education in low income countries.' *International Journal of Educational Development*, 31.1 (2011): 3–14.

UNESCO Institute of Statistics. www.uis.unesco.org/EDUCATION/Pages/default.aspx, accessed January 2015.

UNESCO. 2014a. 'Teaching and Learning: Achieving Quality for All.' Education for All Global Monitoring Report 2013/4.

UNESCO. 2014b. 'Sustainable Development Begins with Education: How education can contribute to the proposed post-2015 goals.' Paris: UNESCO.

UNICEF Data on Primary Education. http://data.unicef.org/education/primary, accessed January 2015.

UNICEF. 2004. 'Childhood under Threat: The State of the World's Children 2005.' New York, NY: UNICEF.

Unterhalter, Elaine. 'Inequality, capabilities and poverty in four African countries: girls' voice, schooling, and strategies for institutional change.' *Cambridge Journal of Education*, 42.3 (2012): 307–325.

Unterhalter, Elaine. 'Education', in Séverine Deneulin and Lila Shahani, eds. 2009. *An Introduction to the Human Development and Capability Approach*. London: Earthscan.

Vaughan, Rosie. 'Measuring Capabilities: An Example from Girls' Schooling' in Melanie Walker and Elaine Unterhalter, eds. 2007. *Amartya Sen's Capability Approach and Social Justice in Education*. New York, NY: Palgrave Macmillan.

World Bank Group Education Strategy 2020. 'Learning for All: Investing in People's Knowledge and Skills to Promote Development.' Washington, DC: World Bank, 2011.

Yoshikawa, Hirokazu, *et al.* 'Experimental impacts of a teacher professional development program in Chile on preschool classroom quality and child outcomes.' *Developmental Psychology*, 51.3 (2015): 309–322.

Young, Marion. 'Basic capabilities, basic learning outcomes and thresholds of learning.' *Journal of Human Development and Capabilities*, 10.2 (2009): 259–277.

10 The environment and poverty reduction

Benjamin Curtis

Key questions

- How does environmental degradation contribute to poverty?
- What are environmental assets and ecosystem services?
- How do environmental conditions relate to capabilities?
- How can development be sustainable for poor communities and the environment?

Vignette 10.1

We first met Chita and Rosa at a small roadside shack in northern Costa Rica (Figure 10.1). Sitting in a simple structure with a thatched roof and no walls, they were selling artisan products such as elaborately painted, hard-carved wooden masks, gourds carved with intricate designs, and colourful weavings. This was some of the traditional art of their culture: Chita and Rosa both belong to the Maleku indigenous group, a people numbering less than 700 who live in a lush but isolated area of Costa Rica. 'I grew up here in the community so poor that I had to tie my hair up with blades of grass before going to school', Chita said. She is a mother of four who sells her art to make a living. Describing the poverty that older generations of Maleku people faced, she told us, 'My grandmother died giving birth to my mother, so she was raised by another relative and didn't get the opportunities she might have had her mother survived. We were so poor that I only made it through third grade.' Because of Chita's childhood poverty, when she was a teenager she left the community with the first non-indigenous man she met who promised her a better life.

'We grew up poor too', agreed Rosa, 'but in my case, we had an extended family network and everyone pulled together to survive. I grew up proud of being Maleku because my grandmother spent the evenings telling us stories about Maleku myths and customs. We didn't even miss the fact that we didn't have electricity in the house because she told stories every night about our community and its history.' Rosa and Chita both sit on the local school board, and one day they and other community leaders described for us the unique situation of the three Maleku palenques (villages) outside the town of San Rafael Guatuso. Some of the men remembered how when they grew up, poverty was intense: their families didn't have potable water, a decent road to the community, access to credit, or even shoes. Teachers came from outside the community and didn't respect Maleku ways. The Maleku school leaders we interviewed agreed that their community faces different challenges today than did their parents and grandparents. Though

they have made great strides teaching the younger generation about important values of the community – love of nature, respect for elders and the importance of preserving the stories that have been handed down – today young people find themselves chafing for more opportunities than the area can offer. Farming, ecotourism and teaching are the few options available for motivated youth, so many of them leave.

The difficulty of making a living on the lands the Maleku call home points to the complex interrelationships between poverty, capabilities and the natural environment for this community. Farming often generates only a meagre income for Maleku people – and roughly a quarter of all Maleku do not own any land, which means that they cannot grow their own food, and have to find other sources of income. The Maleku have actually been deprived of their land: though they live on a reservation where their land rights are supposed to be legally protected, there are many non-indigenous property owners living on the reserve, such that the Maleku own only 20 per cent of their own reservation. The Maleku teachers we spoke with explained that many of the better-off homes we observed in the area belonged to non-Malekus who moved into the villages over the generations; some of those newcomers even self-identify as Maleku to obtain access to opportunities reserved for indigenous people. The Maleku have also been denied hunting and fishing rights in nearby areas that their people had used for centuries. Beyond

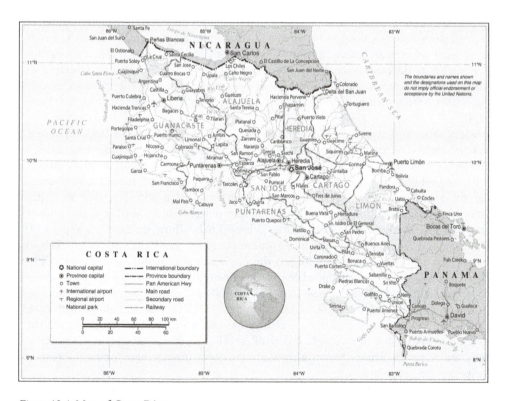

Figure 10.1 Map of Costa Rica
Source: Map No. 4430 UNITED NATIONS December 2010

land deprivation and scarce economic opportunities, environmental degradation has made it harder to maintain some of the Malekus' cultural traditions. For example, certain plants that were traditionally used in spiritual ceremonies, and wood for the traditional palenque structures, are now very difficult to obtain.

The Malekus' story is not unusual. Indigenous peoples throughout the world often face major difficulties in protecting traditional relationships with their natural ecosystem. As colonial powers infringed on indigenous lands, and incipient states expanded their control after independence, indigenous groups in Latin America like the Maleku found their livelihoods, traditions and values in danger of extinction. The Maleku were able to gain title to a small portion of the land they had inhabited prior to the arrival of the Spanish, but poverty in the early twentieth century forced many of them to sell their property to speculators and wealthier, non-indigenous neighbours. Thus land which the Maleku had typically used for communal farming and other household needs was divvied up to private owners. The size of many indigenous groups has been greatly reduced since the colonial epoch, yet their continued presence raises complex questions about environmental justice: how should people be guaranteed access to land and other environmental assets that are essential to their quality of life?

Introduction

We begin this chapter with the example of the Maleku of Costa Rica because discussions about the environment and the capabilities approach involve acknowledging the range of capabilities that are affected by environmental changes, particularly for indigenous people and other marginalized groups, including the poor. Many indigenous groups around the world experience deprivation and unfreedom when they are not able to gather natural resources for traditional medicines or to continue using natural elements found in ecosystems for traditional cultural and spiritual practices (Duraiappah 2002 and 2004).

It may seem surprising that the Maleku have such challenges in Costa Rica, a country known worldwide for its efforts to protect the environment and promote sustainable development. It is particularly famous for its reforestation and conservation efforts, protecting roughly 30 per cent of its territory. Costa Rica is a high human development country according to the HDI, with a score of .766 that is above average for Latin America. It has also done very well on multiple different indicators: it is the highest ranking Latin American country on the Where-To-Be-Born Index (30th out of 80 countries, and ranking above several European countries), and until 2014 it ranked in the top ten of all countries according to the Environmental Performance Index (EPI). Three times Costa Rica has topped the Happy Planet Index, a composite of indicators for ecological footprint, life expectancy and people's self-reported sense of wellbeing. However, most recently Costa Rica has fallen in the EPI because of failures in treating wastewater and responding to climate change. As the example of Chita, Rosa and the Maleku suggests, even in relatively successful developing countries such as Costa Rica, there are many challenges to ensuring that ecosystem management promotes human wellbeing and capabilities.

Environmental conditions and resources are crucial to every person's life, but poor people and indigenous groups depend even more on the natural environment than do the non-poor. This chapter investigates the links between environmental conditions and poverty, and how policies can reduce poverty by targeting those conditions. Costa Rica is our empirical focus: it is a useful model for how countries can address the ecosystemic factors that contribute to poverty. Thus despite the challenges the Maleku are facing, there is hope. At the end of the chapter we will return to the Maleku to show how the people of Costa Rica have worked to mitigate some of the environmental factors that can cause poverty. First, however, the chapter will provide a global overview of how environmental conditions impact poverty. Then it will consider the relationship between the environment, poverty and capabilities. Finally, three case studies will explore how environmentally sustainable projects have promoted human and economic development in Costa Rica.

Understanding key concepts

It is important at the outset to provide definitional clarity for several key concepts. The 'environment' means the living (biodiversity) and non-living (soil, rocks, atmosphere, etc.) components of the natural world, whose interactions are essential for life on earth. The environment provides natural resources and various ecosystem services that in turn provide food, energy, medicine and incomes (DFID *et al.* 2002). 'Ecosystem services' is a specialized term; 'ecosystems' include forests, grasslands, rivers, lakes, the ocean, coral reefs, etc., as well as the biological organisms (such as plants and animals) that live in them. According to the influential analysis of the Millennium Ecosystem Assessment, ecosystems provide four categories of 'services': provisioning, regulating, cultural and supporting (Millennium Ecosystem Assessment 2005). Provisioning services include food, fresh water, wood and fibre, and fuel. Regulating services include how ecosystems purify air and water, mitigate floods and droughts, stabilize the climate and reduce disease. Cultural services encompass recreation and ecotourism, but also spiritual and scientific/educational uses. Underlying the previous three categories are 'supporting services', which refer to environmental factors with an indirect impact on humans such as systems of soil formation, nutrient and water cycling, and oxygen production (see Alcamo and Bennett 2003, esp. chapter 2).

These services that ecosystems provide are critical to all people but particularly to the poor. Though all life depends on ecosystem services, poor people often depend upon them more because of their vulnerability and marginalization. Such services thus constitute key 'environmental assets' for poor people. Environmental assets can include a coral reef, a river, soil, wildlife, a watershed, air, a coal deposit, a forest and many other things. These assets contribute a very wide range of services to the poor, such as food, water, fuel, shelter, health and livelihoods. Poor people often need these inputs as a basic support to life: a lake to fish in, a field to farm, a hillside on which to graze animals, a forest to harvest for fuelwood or building materials. Poor people in rural areas need environmental resources such as fertile land, water, crop diversity, forest products (for fuel, food, medicines, etc.), and protein sources such as fish and wild meat. Poor people in urban areas depend on environmental resources of water (for drinking and washing), energy, sanitation and drainage (DFID *et al.* 2002). Nonetheless, many of the environmental assets the poor depend on they do not privately own – they may be owned collectively (such as national forests) or really by no one (the ozone layer). This means that poor people's access to such resources can easily be threatened by depletion, degradation or deprivation, and it is harder for poor people to assert their rights of access. A particular characteristic of environmental assets relevant to the poor is that those assets are often difficult to substitute. For example, if a forest is cut down or a lake polluted, then the poor may have few or no alternatives for their wood or water (Pearce 2005).

The ultimate goal in protecting ecosystem services and environmental assets for the purposes of poverty reduction is to promote *sustainable development*. Much ink has been spilled debating what this term means; see the further reading at the end of the chapter to pursue those debates. For the purposes of this chapter, though, sustainable development means expanding the substantive freedoms (capabilities) of people today while making reasonable efforts to avoid seriously compromising those of future generations (UNDP 2011: 2; see also Sen 2013). In other words, sustainable development is meeting the needs of today while guaranteeing our grandchildren will have their needs met. Intergenerational justice is a critical aspect of sustainability. What this means is that future generations should not have less freedom than people today – indeed, if the present generation despoils the environment, its impact on people in the future is arguably little different than depriving people of their rights now (UNDP 2011, Ballet 2013). The non-negotiable minimum for justice and sustainability is capabilities: every generation must have the right to develop the same basic capabilities. We will return to the relationships between capabilities, the environment and poverty below, but for now, consider this provocative claim: it may not be necessary that future generations attain the same level of resource use or quality of life as long as the minimal requirements for a good life – as defined by the basic capabilities – are fulfilled (Burger and Christen 2011).

Poverty–Environment relationships

Deficiencies in ecosystem services and environmental assets are widespread, contributing to poverty around the world. Poor people tend to live on 'marginal lands'. Around 1.3 billion people live in areas that are relatively unproductive or ecologically highly vulnerable because of low soil fertility, air pollution and limited access to clean water (World Bank 2002). Almost half of this number are the rural poor (Barbier 2013). This adds up to a lot of people and a lot of land: some 40 per cent of land on the planet has been degraded by soil erosion or overgrazing (UNDP 2011). Deforestation is a major global problem that impacts how poor people live. A billion people on the planet depend on forests for subsistence or income. However, 30 per cent of global forest cover has already been lost, and between 2000 and 2010 an area the size of England was cleared every year (World Resource Institute 2014).

Desertification is another global problem that can make land 'fragile'. It is estimated that the livelihoods of one billion people around the world are threatened by desertification. Already, about 25 per cent of the Earth's territory is desertified, and every year roughly 12 million hectares of land are lost to further degradation (IFAD 2010). Moreover, approximately 1.8 billion people will likely suffer from water scarcity by 2025 (UNDP 2011). Women and girls can be more starkly affected than men, since in rural areas of developing countries, it is often women's job to collect water. As water sources become degraded or depleted, however, women have to walk farther and farther to get the water, sometimes eating up a significant portion of time they could devote to other activities such as education, generating income or working in the home. Problems such as deforestation, desertification and water scarcity will likely increase food prices by 30 to 50 per cent, which will affect everyone on the planet, but hurt the poor the most by making food increasingly unaffordable (UNDP 2011).

Environmental conditions also have a huge impact on health. 'Environmental health' is a term denoting 'aspects of human health, including quality of life, that are determined by chemical, physical, biological, social and psychosocial factors in the environment' (PEP 2008: 10). As one example of the environment's impact on health, every year diseases related to environmental conditions such as respiratory infections and diarrhoea kill at least three million children under the age of five. Some of these conditions, such as unsafe water or lack of sanitation, count among the top 10 leading causes of disease worldwide (UNDP 2011). Overall, it has been estimated that 24 per cent of the global disease burden and 23 per cent of all deaths are associated with environmental conditions (Prüss-Üstün and Corvalán 2006). Many of these problems may be worsened by climate change. For instance, increasing temperatures increase the risks from vector-borne diseases such as malaria and dengue fever. Diarrhoeal diseases are also projected to increase, especially in poorer areas.

There are other impacts of climate change beyond health. Forty per cent of economically active people in the world work in agriculture, fishing, forestry, or hunting and gathering – and most of these people are in poorer countries (UNDP 2011). Because they depend on environmental resources, they are more likely to be negatively impacted by climate change and its effects on those resources. Those effects include reductions in freshwater availability and crop productivity, and increasing sea levels and extreme weather events. Rising sea levels could render islands and low-lying terrain (including much of Bangladesh) uninhabitable, displacing millions of people. Extreme weather events such as droughts, floods and storms can deprive people of their livelihoods, displace them or kill them. In many cases, hotter areas of the world will get hotter and dryer, leading to increased problems with agriculture and food security (Livelihoods and Climate Change 2003). According to some projections, loss of fertile topsoil could reduce agricultural productivity by 50 per cent in some areas (UNDP 2011). Hence climate change may produce yet more malnutrition.

Environmental conditions not surprisingly have a relationship with politics. Competition over land, water and other ecosystem resources can spark conflict, as happened in Rwanda in 1994, Kenya in 2008 or repeatedly in Sudan and the Democratic Republic of the Congo. Furthermore, environmental change – such as temperature rises and increasing water scarcity – have been associated with the likelihood of civil wars (UNEP 2009). As discussed in Chapter 8 on conflict and poverty, conflict is a poverty trap; its particular environmental dimension is a Catch-22 in which 'environmental degradation fuels conflict, and conflict degrades the environment' (UNDP 2011: 58). Evidence also suggests that more democratic political systems (as measured by literacy, political rights and civil liberties) have superior environmental quality such as clean water and sanitation (Gallagher and Thacker 2008). Where inequality of political power is greater, environmental degradation such as pollution is also greater, and services such as access to clean water less (Torras 2006). For poor people, a significant part of the problem is institutions that do not respect their interests with regard to environmental resources. Where people are powerless to stop it, industries or other powerful actors can degrade environmental resources with relative impunity. Poor communities often lack the capacity or institutions to deal with the risks of depletion, degradation and deprivation.

High vulnerability to depletion, degradation or deprivation of the environmental resources on which they depend is one of the factors that make people poor. Such resources can be depleted by unsustainable use; however, because poor people are often vulnerable and have so few assets from which to live, there can be a vicious cycle by

---

Box 10.1 Environmental degradation, health and poverty

- **Indoor air pollution:** Half of the earth's population still uses biomass fuels (such as wood or dung) for heating and cooking. These fuels typically produce smoke that can cause respiratory infections, lung cancer, cardiovascular disease, low birth weight and carbon monoxide poisoning. Indoor smoke contributes to nearly four million deaths a year, especially in poorer countries, most affecting women and children.
- **Outdoor air pollution:** Caused by sources such as industry, transportation, fires or dust storms, outdoor air pollution has many of the same health effects as above. Again, it is the poorest communities that are disproportionately exposed to outdoor air pollution and most susceptible to its ill effects.
- **Water and sanitation:** Dirty water and inadequate sanitation are an enormous problem, contributing to ill health, disability and early death. They lead to malnutrition, parasites, hepatitis, typhoid, malaria and polio, among many other maladies. In countries with low human development, 65 per cent of people do not have adequate sanitation, and 38 per cent lack clean water.
- **Waste:** Whether from industrial, municipal or household sources, inadequate waste disposal has a variety of negative effects on environmental health. Waste can be a breeding ground for vermin and insects. It can contaminate surface water, groundwater and soil. Toxic waste in landfills can lead to cancer, anaemia, mental retardation and various birth defects. Poor people are much more likely to be exposed to these effects because they often live in marginal, disadvantaged areas.

Sources: Pearce 2005, Prüss-Üstün and Corvalán 2006, PEP 2008, UNDP 2011.

---

which their dependence on environmental resources actually depletes those resources. A good example would be with forests. A family needs fuel for cooking, yet if they are poor, they may have no choice but to chop down trees for fuel. However, unless managed in a sustainable way, felling trees can deplete the very resource on which the farmer and his family depend. It is important to note that in terms of depletion, it is rich people who are most responsible for unsustainable exploitation of environmental resources on a global scale. The poor family may be responsible for local depletion of their immediate environmental resources, but the most serious overconsumption of such resources, which affects the entire planet, happens in high-income countries.

Overconsumption of resources on a global or local scale leads to degradation of the natural environment. Degradation means that the quality of the environmental assets on which poor people depend is reduced. Air pollution is an example of how contaminants can degrade an environmental resource – air – which humans and so many other living things need to survive. Pollution of course can also affect water and land, both of which can cause people to become sick. Poor people are again most vulnerable here, since they often will not have the resources to, say, buy bottled drinking water if their stream or well becomes polluted. Nor, if the land on which they live is degraded, can they necessarily just move; they may not have the money or the opportunity to find shelter somewhere else. Deprivation comes about when poor people cannot use environmental assets on which they depend. They are most commonly denied use of those assets by people who are more powerful because of wealth or politics. Poor people often lack legal title to their land, which makes it too easy for them to be forced off it.

The 2011 United Nations Human Development Report used the Multidimensional Poverty Index to examine three areas of environmental assets whose deprivation not only undermined basic capabilities but also constituted 'major violations of human rights' (UNDP 2011: 5). Access to modern cooking fuel, clean water and basic sanitation are conceived as absolute and fundamental entitlements, and therefore as essential to human development. Unfortunately, deprivation in these three areas is very common: 60 per cent of people in developing countries have at least one of these environmental deprivations, and 40 per cent are deprived in two or more. This means that deprivations overlap, intensifying poverty. According to the UNDP's analysis, 29 per cent of people in 109 developing countries are deprived in *all three* of these areas. The people who are most intensely poor along multiple dimensions are found in rural areas. 97 per cent of the rural poor are deprived in at least one environmental area, compared to 75 per cent of poor people in urban areas. Globally, too, multiple environmental deprivations vary, with sub-Saharan Africa the worst affected: 60 per cent of poor people there are deprived across all three dimensions, compared to 18 per cent of poor people in South Asia. In both these regions, the most consistent deprivation is modern cooking fuel, followed by improved sanitation. Overall, environmental deprivations are one of the most powerful reasons why people are poor according to the MPI.

Capabilities and environmental conditions

From the capabilities perspective, environmental conditions are important because they directly impact the opportunities available to people (See i.a. Lehtonen 2004, Sen 2009, Polishchuk and Rauschmayer 2012, Voget-Kleschin 2013). In fact, because environmental conditions help make a range of basic capabilities possible, they are a 'meta-capability' according to Holland (2008). For example, human life (the first basic capability on Nussbaum's list) depends fundamentally on the natural environment for food, water, air and energy. The natural environment is thus crucial to the meta-capability of 'sustainable ecological capacity' that supports most of the other basic capabilities – but which recognizes that the current generation's utilization of environmental services must not unduly disadvantage future generations. Because of the way they underlie and support so many basic capabilities, we should conceive of 'certain environmental entitlements as a matter of basic justice' (Holland 2008: 320).

What then are the minimum environmental entitlements that constitute basic justice, and whose absence can define poverty? Duraiappah (2002, 2004) has specified ten key relationships between ecosystems and wellbeing. These are the capabilities that ecosystems support; if people fall below minimum thresholds in these ten areas, they are in poverty, failing to benefit from the ecosystem(s) as they are entitled. Note that there are many interrelationships between the ten areas listed below. The distinct ecosystem services are often interdependent, and combine to support wellbeing.

1   'Being able to be adequately nourished.' Certain ecosystems provide food, whether through agriculture or hunting and gathering. The rural poor especially depend on

ecosystem services for nourishment, so droughts, pests, other ecological disasters, or being forced off their land can fatally compromise their capability to feed themselves.

2 'Being able to be free from avoidable disease.' As we have seen, environmental conditions have a very large impact on health. No one should have to live in conditions that promote heightened morbidity. When such conditions threaten basic entitlements to health, then people are deprived of basic ecosystem services.

3 'Being able to live in an environmentally clean and safe shelter.' Certain conditions in the ecosystem will also jeopardize this entitlement: pollution, high susceptibility to disease, poor drainage, insecure or marginal terrain, even unacceptable levels of noise. Depletion, degradation and deprivation can all mean that people do not have adequate shelter.

4 'Being able to have adequate and clean drinking water.' Clean water is obviously essential to basic health, which in turn is essential to an enormous range of other capabilities and functionings.

5 'Being able to have clean air.' Likewise, clean air is essential to adequate health and capabilities. Poor people, however, are often deprived of this entitlement. The environmental conditions in which they live – with indoor pollution because they lack access to cleaner cooking fuels, or outdoor pollution because they live in degraded, marginal areas – mean that too often poor people's access to ecosystem services is compromised.

6 'Being able to have energy to keep warm and to cook.' Energy is essential to several other basic capabilities, such as adequate shelter (that provides warmth in cold environments) and nourishment (for preparing food). When an ecosystem does not provide resources to meet this basic entitlement, and people cannot meet it any other way, then they are fundamentally deprived and poor.

7 'Being able to use traditional medicine.' Many poor people depend on traditional medicine since they often lack access to modern, Western health care for cost and other reasons. Many traditional remedies used by indigenous groups come from ecosystem sources, so when those are compromised, so too are poor people's traditional health care and health status.

8 'Being able to continue using natural elements found in ecosystems for traditional cultural and spiritual practices.' This relates to several basic capabilities from Nussbaum's list, such as senses, imagination, thought and emotion. For many people around the world, ecosystems are essential for cultural enjoyment and inspiration, as well as for spiritual practice. When ecosystems are degraded, people's entitlements in this area can be infringed, especially if their cultures are informed by a close relationship with nature.

9 'Being able to cope with extreme natural events including floods, tropical storms and landslides.' Poor people are typically the most vulnerable to such extreme events, and the least able to cope with them. Ecosystem degradation can make such events more likely, thereby disproportionately harming the poor. Healthy ecosystems are essential for adaptation and resilience to extreme events.

10 'Being able to make sustainable management decisions that respect natural resources and enable the achievement of a sustainable livelihood.' People have a fundamental right to participate in management of ecosystem resources that will affect them. If they are deprived of that right, then they are poor. And unfortunately, too often poor people have been denied participation in that management, and been forced into unsustainable resource use that contributes to depletion and degradation.

One of the ways that all of the relationships above affect poor people is that the poor often have few choices. If they are denied the ecosystem service of clean water, for example, they will often lack the money to purchase purified water. Thus they are forced to drink dirty water. Hence from the capabilities perspective, a key aspect in the poverty–environment relationship is unfreedom in terms of what environmental assets you depend on, and how you depend on them (Ballet 2013). If your land becomes degraded, you can't just necessarily go find another field to farm, or move to a new house that isn't sitting on land polluted by toxic waste. This is vulnerability because of a lack of opportunity – in other words, the inability to choose something different beyond the (possibly compromised) environmental resources on which your life depends.

Case studies

The three case studies that follow provide examples of how communities in Costa Rica have worked to promote sustainable development and poverty reduction by managing their environmental assets. The projects each community has undertaken have sought to secure some of the ten freedoms outlined above. The first case study centres on democratic management of a particular ecosystem service, namely water. The second is about how a community with severe environmental disadvantages can ameliorate some of them to reduce poverty. The third discusses how conservation of ecosystem resources can promote sustainable livelihoods.

Case study 10.1 The community water systems of Costa Rica

'The best inheritance I can leave future generations is water', explained Guillermo, the elderly man whose job it is to make sure that the potable water stays crystal clear day after day for his semi-rural community. As he said this, we were high up on the Poás Volcano above his little town of San Roque, visiting the multiple springs that produce the water for his town. Surrounded by dancing blue Morpho butterflies in the dense rain forest that surrounds his water source, he told us that potable water for his great-great grandchildren depends on protecting the springs and watershed. That in turn requires involving the whole community in water management and environmental conservation. Ninety-five per cent of the citizens of Costa Rica enjoy clean water in their homes, more than most other countries in Central and South America. You can just turn on the tap and drink the water (something people take for granted in high-income countries), but which is a basic environmental entitlement that many people throughout the world do not enjoy. Because it is very difficult to have adequate health without access to clean water, Costa Rica has recognized the importance of this entitlement and set up a structure to manage the environmental resources that assure water for today *and* tomorrow.

A state-run company, Aqueducts and Sewage Systems (known as AyA, its Spanish acronym), installs community water systems across the country, but the communities themselves actually run these systems by forming cooperatives. These cooperatives band together the citizens from the local area who want water from the community system; they pay for their water usage but also collectively govern the cooperative that oversees the whole system. Across Costa Rica, there are 80,000 community-managed water systems that provide 20 to 40 per cent of the rural and semi-rural population with water; the denser urban areas are provided water by local municipalities. The distinctive state-civil society partnership between AyA and the community water organizations has not only ensured the basic environmental capability of access to clean water. It has also promoted sustainable management decisions via citizen participation, which in turn strengthens democracy. We had the opportunity to visit three communities at different altitudes up the Poás Volcano of central Costa Rica: Barrio Latino, San Miguel and San Roque. Each community and its water system employees emphasized the importance of local buy-in for protecting water and watersheds for sustainable local water consumption.

Barrio Latino is an urban community in the small city of Grecia, just up from the Pan-American Highway that connects Costa Rica to its northern neighbour Nicaragua and southern neighbour Panama. Many years ago the community's water only arrived in a slow trickle from 11pm to 3am due to a municipal water system that privileged more centralized neighbourhoods over Barrio Latino. Carol Muñoz, the treasurer for the water system, told the story of how Don Freddy Chacón, a community elder, convened the community, proposing that they find their own water source and get the support of AyA to help them build the infrastructure so that they would have water around the clock. Carol recalled,

'Don Freddy remembered that the town used to get its water from a nearby wooded valley, and he started digging in this abandoned valley. He dug and dug and didn't find anything, and then he lay down his shovel and asked God to show him water. Suddenly the water broke through. We have enough water to serve today's 730 families for the next 20 years, including population growth. People identify with the community water system because it's *their* water. So they call when they see there's a leak or if they taste too much chlorine. Furthermore, we're working to educate people about taking care of the water, not just the spring but waste water too. We're encouraging people to recycle cooking oil and not pour it down the drain. We recycle it into bio-diesel. People can drop off their used oil at our office. But there are dangers to our spring: above us on the volcano there are sugar cane farmers who use a lot of fertilizers which can get into the water table. The older farmers – like Don Freddy – have environmental awareness, but sometimes their children have gone to school in the cities and just want to make money from the land. They just see the money. Agriculture in harmony with the environment like their parents did it isn't profitable, and so the younger generation chooses to plant crops that require fertilizers or too much water. This is why it is so important to educate the entire surrounding area about protecting watersheds and buying land around our springs.'

Eager to learn more about how neighbouring communities had worked together to assure their right to water, we headed up the volcano to the springs that supply water to San Miguel, a semi-rural community above Grecia. There, leaders have worked closely with a local landowner whose holdings include the springs that provide water for the community. The community water system has educated the landowner about the importance of keeping cattle away from the springs and farming sustainably so that the springs remain uncontaminated. It is particularly important that animals don't contaminate springs, but it is also vital that ground water run-off not contain harmful pesticides which can poison the natural springs that communities rely on for potable water. The community organization that runs the water system for San Miguel has also worked closely with the local schools to educate young people about the importance of protecting water. Evidence for the effort to involve the younger generation in taking care of the watershed are the signs – around the springs and throughout the community – that encourage disposing of garbage properly and not contaminating water sources. The community itself has participated in community work days to help protect the springs and guarantee that at the point of capture the water is potable and safe.

Even higher up on the Poás Volcano where the community of San Roque draws its water, we visited a dense tropical rainforest where the community has been purchasing and reforesting ever-widening swaths of land around their springs. With only two water system employees, the community has worked hard to reforest these properties with native plants, efforts that are also very important for the preservation efforts of the nearby national park. Community awareness, commitment and resources are essential for the continuity of potable water resources. The community water system is run by its members who elect delegates to provide oversight and hire employees. In the case of San Roque, the community raised thousands of dollars to buy the land adjoining their springs, and followed up by donating thousands of volunteer hours to reforest and preserve the property. It is true that not every community's cooperative has that kind of money, or is as efficient as the ones we visited. Nonetheless, this model of state-civil society partnership through cooperatives has worked throughout Costa Rica – in communities rich, poor, and in between – to support human wellbeing by providing access to crucial environmental resources.

Case study 10.2 The urban settlement of La Carpio

In the 1990s, thousands of Nicaraguans came to Costa Rica, fleeing violence, poverty and political unrest in their home country. Many of these refugees settled in San José, the capital city, occupying a piece of land that was owned by the Carpio family. This land was marginal, with many environmental disadvantages: the area is sandwiched between two deep river canyons and an airport. It is an area prone to landslides and flooding. Open sewage from a nearby neighbourhood runs directly into the river canyons, and flows right by the houses that Nicaraguan emigrants constructed. The poorest people could build only the most insecure structures: dirt floors, recycled tin roofs, walls made of scavenged cardboard and other materials. In the early years, residents of the area told us, the roads of their neighbourhood were muddy and filthy, strewn with trash and sometimes dead dogs. This neighbourhood is called La Carpio. Its population is around 35,000, and it is perhaps the best-known marginalized neighbourhood in the largest city in Costa Rica.

In 2002, the Costa Rican government decided to construct a garbage dump right next to the neighbourhood. Naturally the people living there protested: no one wants to live next to a landfill. However, the government insisted, threatening the people of La Carpio that they could be deported (since most were undocumented Nicaraguans), but also offering them a deal of improved public services if they would drop their opposition to the dump. In the end, the dump was constructed, and now some 200 garbage trucks pass through the neighbourhood daily, carrying hundreds of tons of trash each day. Worse, an enormous pile of garbage rises just on the edge of where people live. The dump has already surpassed its mandated lifespan as well as regulations about how high the pile can rise, yet the rules were rewritten so that the garbage trucks can keep coming. On some days, when the wind blows a certain way, the smell is unbearable. Without proper treatment, the dump can be a breeding ground for rats, insects and other pests. It can also lead to contamination of the water people drink. To cap off the neighbourhood's environmental disadvantages, a sewage treatment plant was also subsequently built next door.

In a way, none of this is surprising. As so often throughout the world, poor people have no choice but to live on the worst land, and their own vulnerability can increase the likelihood that the land will be degraded further. In La Carpio, poverty across a variety of dimensions is very common. More than half the population lives below the national income poverty line. Few people have legal title to their land, which means that some of their most important physical assets such as their house are insecure. Moreover, many of the lots on which people have constructed their houses are actually smaller than the minimum required by law. A fair portion of those houses have been constructed in places where they can be swept away by floods. In general, Nicaraguans in Costa Rica experience higher rates of poverty than do native-born Costa Ricans. They tend to have less educational attainment, higher unemployment, higher fertility rates and worse health outcomes including low birth weight, more malnutrition and inadequate immunizations (see Funkhouser *et al.* 2002, Marquette 2006). Nicaraguans, too, are often subject to discrimination by native-born Costa Ricans. All of these conditions apply in La Carpio. It is a stigmatized area, both by negative popular stereotypes against Nicaraguans and by public policy that has disproportionately concentrated undesirable facilities in the neighbourhood such as the dump or high-voltage electrical cables that pass very close to houses.

The geographical, social and political circumstances of La Carpio combine to threaten many of the fundamental environmental entitlements. In particular, the open sewage and omnipresence of garbage can make it harder to be free from avoidable disease. Pollution, the marginal terrain and even the noise from the nearby airport can compromise being able to live in a clean and safe shelter. Being able to have clean air is obviously threatened by the dump. And because the population of La Carpio is heavily Nicaraguan, hence sometimes undocumented and more vulnerable, it is also more likely to be disempowered, unable to exercise effective management of ecosystem resources. The good news is that in the last 15 years, government, the private sector and civil society have undertaken a variety of steps that have reduced poverty in the neighbourhood and made the environmental entitlements more secure.

These initiatives correspond to several best-practice measures for environmental contributors to poverty in urban areas throughout the developing world (Satterthwaite 2003). For instance, municipal services now provide the infrastructure for sanitation and clean water. The housing stock has also been improved for most people. Most dwellings are now made of brick or concrete, a major upgrade from the days of living in unsafe constructions of cardboard and tin. Now that there is electricity in La Carpio, residents do not have to rely on unclean household fuels for cooking and light. Transport options are also much improved: nearly all roads are paved, and the neighbourhood is connected to the rest of the city by frequent public buses. Paved roads also help with storm and surface water drainage, a step up from the muddy roads of the past, which were more likely to spread waste and excrement.

Community management of its own affairs is also much stronger. The neighbourhood has a number of civil society organizations such as churches and a few NGOs. These organizations contribute significantly to social cohesion, providing specific programmes such as sex education for young people and inclusion for older people. Self-government is also more robust in the form of several neighbourhood councils. Finally, there is a health clinic in the neighbourhood now, funded by the government, which has helped reduce though not eliminate problems of malnutrition and maternal health. The garbage dump, though still an assault on the eyes and the nose, is reasonably well run: the garbage pile is usually covered up, there is pest control and treatment to prevent leakage into water supplies. The company that runs the dump even makes some gestures at corporate social responsibility by providing funds to community organizations within La Carpio.

Not all of La Carpio's problems have been resolved, of course. Though there is a primary school in the neighbourhood, to attend high school young people must take a bus elsewhere, which they cannot always afford. Employment opportunities are lacking, average incomes are generally low, and crime rates are higher than in other parts of San José. Located in such an unfavourable location, this is still marginalized land, and many residents still lack legal title to their property. Pockets of deeper deprivation also persist, particularly for the people who live in the most insecure dwellings down by the river, where female-headed households, larger families with more children, malnutrition and lower incomes are more common. Nonetheless, La Carpio is an example of how community organizations, public services such as water, health and electricity, and some accountability from government and the private sector can mitigate environmental disadvantages. Indeed, because the people of La Carpio have been at least somewhat empowered to demand transparent and responsive government, they have been able to adapt to those disadvantages and make some progress on securing their basic capabilities.

Case study 10.3 Sustainable development in Monteverde

In Costa Rica, the strong laws protecting national parks – which overall are beneficial – nonetheless sometimes have the unintended consequences of alienating local communities who are denied possibilities for sustainably using the forests and other environmental assets. It can be difficult for rural communities near national parks and conservation areas to preserve ecosystems while also developing sustainable livelihoods that generate enough income to meet their basic needs. (See Adams *et al.* 2004 for a summary of the academic research on the challenges of conservation and poverty eradication.) One notable exception is the community of Monteverde. In the midst of Costa Rica's central mountains at almost 5000 feet above sea level and set within a cloud forest, Monteverde is one of Costa Rica's prime tourist destinations. Today Monteverde is a lesson in sustainable development for Costa Rica and beyond. The community has transitioned from agriculture to ecotourism, and while there are substantial environmental challenges in both of those economic and social models, on the whole the people of Monteverde have done an admirable job of trying to protect their ecosystem while also furthering development (see i.a. Baez *et al.* 1996, Farrell and Marion 2001, Davis 2007, Koens *et al.* 2009).

For decades, the relationship of humans to the ecosystem in Monteverde was based in agriculture. Though people had been farming in the area for years, a major change came in 1951, when 12 Quaker families from the United States bought 3,800 acres of mountainous terrain from a Costa Rican mining company. Fleeing the military draft in the United States because of their pacifist beliefs, this group of Quakers chose Costa Rica because it had dissolved its army in the 1940s and promised respite from warmongering and Cold War politics prevalent in the global north at the time. The Quaker community negotiated with the few local farming families and bought many of them out as well. Given the favourable conditions in the area for raising milk cows, the community founded the Monteverde dairy factory (*Productores Monteverde* in Spanish) in 1954, which purchased local milk production and created a wide selection of cheeses. At its height, the company was a major economic engine, employing 200 local people and buying milk from 500 members. Many of the landowners preserved the cloud forest rather than cutting it down, knowing that it was necessary to protect watersheds. Thus back to the 1950s there was a general attempt to manage ecosystem resources sustainably and grow the dairy business with a commitment to a triple bottom line: environment, community and profits.

However, the community also learned that it had to adapt in order to have truly sustainable livelihoods. For example, over time, milk and milk products from bigger companies began to flood the market. According to Sarah Stuckey, a former board member of the company, it was harder for the Monteverde dairy to remain competitive unless it became very big and more industrialized, or became very small and artisanal. In the end, the community decided to sell the dairy, and now it employs about 50 people. Yet, interestingly enough, this was not an economic disaster. The Quaker families from the United States had not remained isolated in their mountain hamlet. They welcomed Costa Rican farming families into the community when land came up for sale, and they continued to educate residents about the importance of conservation efforts and sustainable development, making sure that these messages were prominent in the school and community efforts. They inculcated their values of sustainability and social justice in the community, even founding a local bilingual school whose pedagogy was informed by the importance of environmental stewardship. Though the dairy factory was sold, the community had grown and diversified. Young people from nearby and newcomers drawn by the area's beauty, connection to the environment, and pacifist values wanted more income-generating activities than farming and cattle. Those same values drew many other people to visit Monteverde, and the area grew into an ecotourism hub.

Ecotourism has been defined as 'responsible travel to natural areas that conserves the environment, sustains the wellbeing of the local people, and involves interpretation and education' (TIES 2015). Monteverde mostly succeeds in these three areas. Tourism has given the area's distinctive ecosystem a significant economic value, which incentivizes the preservation of that ecosystem. As the tourist business has grown, it has also provided many people with an income; some 90 per cent of the population now depends on tourism for a living. A few people do still raise cattle and produce milk for local and national consumption, but now there is a new generation of green entrepreneurs who run hotels, restaurants, shops, adventure sports and other attractions. These businesses generate income, create employment opportunities, increase environmental awareness in the tourists who come to visit, and continue the tradition of protecting the cloud forests. Education has long been a priority for Monteverde. Besides the bilingual school the Quakers built, there is also a state secondary school that offers vocational training in tourism, and the Monteverde Institute, which offers a variety of programmes for research, place-based education, and community engagement.

Though most locals think that on balance the tourism boom has been positive, the area's popularity has had some problematic environmental impacts. The building of hotels, shopping areas and other facilities has disturbed wildlife and done some damage to vegetation. The influx of new people coming to live and work in the area has weakened some aspects of the traditional culture as well as the traditions of self-governance. And with all the new people, there is more vehicle traffic, more garbage, and more sewage, which Monteverde's infrastructure is not always equipped to handle. But as Monteverde's residents have learned, being sustainable means learning how to adapt, so the community is working to mitigate the negative environmental impacts. Local councils strive to make better plans for growth, for example. It is a major benefit that much of the money spent by visitors actually stays in the area, rather than benefiting international chains or absentee owners. Similarly, many of the local taxes gathered stay local, which helps fund social services such as a health clinic.

In sum, Monteverde provides many lessons on how the range of ecosystem services can support human wellbeing. The forests help provide water, the fields provide grazing land for cows that provide food, and the biodiversity provides cultural opportunities for tourism that in turn supports livelihoods. Indeed, Monteverde in many ways embodies the 'green trademark' that Costa Rica has claimed for itself. The community's survival – economically, socially, biologically and otherwise – depends on the wealth of its environmental assets. Shrouded in mists much of the year, isolated up in the mountains, with still today very rough roads connecting it to the outside world, Monteverde could be little more than a remote village trying to escape poverty. But its residents have recognized that their environmental assets are what bring prosperity, and therefore that they have to manage those assets in the most perspicacious and sustainable way possible. That management is not always easy or successful, yet without the participation of the people who most depend on the ecosystem's services, it is unlikely the management would ever support their fundamental environmental entitlements.

Conclusion

As these case studies suggest, development can lead to environmental degradation and/or address the environmental conditions that contribute to poverty. In the best cases, development will reduce poverty and support environmental entitlements so that people can live a life that they value. But development often does bring new challenges for managing environmental assets. For instance, Costa Rica's Maleku people have seen a number of their environmental entitlements threatened over the years, including being adequately nourished, having clean water, participating in the management of their own environmental assets, and using traditional medicine and other natural elements for cultural and spiritual practices. In Costa Rica and elsewhere, many indigenous people continue to live on the margins of their societies, suffering as their ecosystems are degraded. However, in many ways the Maleku are actually a success story.

This is not to diminish the deprivations the Maleku have suffered and the difficulties they continue to face in keeping their lands, preserving their culture and providing adequate economic opportunities. But the Maleku leaders we talked to affirmed that their communities are healthier now than they were in previous generations. The Maleku people were in danger of dying out completely in the early twentieth century, but since then their numbers have grown significantly. They now have some powers of self-government and management of their ecosystem resources. For example, the local school board to which Chita and Rosa belong helps ensure that Maleku culture and language are passed on through education. There is a local cooperative to promote economic development, a few NGOs working on land rights and conservation, and the Maleku sit on the national-level organization that protects indigenous interests. Public services have also demonstrably helped reduce poverty in the area. Health centres provide a range of medical care, including programmes combating malnutrition. The community has generally secure access to clean water and reliable electricity. The teachers specifically mentioned that the Maleku do not suffer from information poverty, since they had ample access to cell phones and the internet. The Maleku teachers we talked to affirmed, 'We are not poor.'

Elders do still worry about how many young people leave the community, and how to maintain the culture if the young are not interested. Young people are often more attracted to global youth culture and learning English than Maleku. When they migrate to the cities in search of work, it's difficult to keep their Maleku identity alive.

Nonetheless, sometimes those who leave do return: Chita came back to her village, brought her children, and now works to strengthen the community. 'My mother was indigenous, and we grew up around here. For the past 15 years, I've been back here in the community with my new common-law husband', she said proudly. Rosa's family, too, actively promotes Maleku rights and culture. Her brother, sisters, mother and father, and grandkids all live together in separate houses on the ancestral property. Though her mother doesn't have strong Maleku ancestry and her father is only half Maleku, both grew up following the traditional customs and speaking the language. 'My grandmother had a particular bond with my brother, and she planted a lot of her wisdom in him. Today he is an advocate for our culture and travels widely sharing the stories and customs of our people. But all of my sisters have remained here in the community, and this is where we are raising our children to be good Malekus.'

One of the greatest ongoing challenges for counteracting the relationships between the environment and poverty will be empowering vulnerable people, much as these Maleku leaders have been empowered. Polluting a river or chopping down a forest is more likely to harm the people for whom it is more difficult to adapt (because they have few choices but to live on degraded land), and the very fact that people are deprived of rights to contest pollution or deforestation also makes them poor. Do not forget that this dynamic operates also on a global level: what power do poor people in the poorest countries have to stop environmental degradation caused by rich people in the richest countries? Little to none. One could point to many different statistics to demonstrate how consumption of resources is not only vastly higher in rich countries, but inequitable and unsustainable. For example, countries with high scores on the HDI have a per capita water consumption of 425 litres per day, compared to 67 litres per day in countries with low HDI scores (UNDP 2011). People in the richest countries like the United States and Canada are responsible for 30 times the carbon dioxide emissions of people in countries with low human development. In fact, as the UNDP notes, 'The average UK citizen accounts for as much greenhouse gas emissions in two months as a person in a low HDI country generates in a year' (UNDP 2011: 2).

These facts pose two unavoidable challenges for everyone reading this book. First, what are we doing to assure that consumption levels in poor countries are minimally adequate to assure basic quality of life and equality of opportunities with people in rich countries? Second, are consumption levels in rich countries so high that they are unjust from the perspective of causing negative environmental impacts that harm the quality of life and opportunities of future generations? That environmental conditions at the regional and global levels are often worsening (in part due to climate change) poses a fundamental problem of justice because people in low-income countries have usually done the least to contribute to the worsening conditions, yet they will suffer the most from those changes. It is poor people around the world who will be hurt most by air pollution, disease spread, or the loss of rainfall associated with climate change. They are most likely to be exposed to such problems, and because of their vulnerability, the least able to adapt. And even within poor populations, the negative effects are unequal. The most vulnerable people suffer most. Children, women and the elderly have a higher risk of injury and death from natural disasters. This means that all of us who wish to be ethical global citizens – both in the developing world and in the rich world – must deeply consider the choices we make, the environmental conse-quences of those choices, and those consequences' impacts on the poor and vulnerable everywhere.

Discussion questions

1 Using the above three case studies and the Maleku vignette, describe the opportunities and challenges of the sustainable management of ecosystem services.
2 Which environmental impacts on poverty would you judge to be the most important, and why?
3 Examine the Environmental Performance Index (http://epi.yale.edu/). What exactly does it purport to measure? How do different countries rank? What connections do you see with poverty?
4 What is your reaction to the claims of intergenerational justice with environmental sustainability, such as that overconsumption today equates to oppression of people in the future, or that what matters for people in the future is not equality of resources but equality of basic capabilities?
5 Imagine a scenario where the world has depleted petroleum resources and now only uses what today are called alternative energy sources such as solar energy, wind power and hydro power. In this future world, your grandchildren will likely have less mobility than you do. Will their capabilities be less, more, or equal to yours? What are the justice considerations in this scenario?

Further reading

Biggeri, Mario, and Andrea Ferrannini. 2014. *Sustainable Human Development: A new territorial and people-centred perspective.* New York, NY: Palgrave Macmillan.

Brainerd, Lael, Abigail Jones and Nigel Purvis, eds. 2009. *Climate Change and Global Poverty.* Washington, DC: Brookings Institution Press.

Corvalán, Carlos, Simon Hales and Michael J. McMichael. 2005. 'Ecosystems and human well-being: health synthesis.' World Health Organization.

Hopwood, Bill, Mary Mellor and Geoff O'Brien. 'Sustainable development: mapping different approaches.' *Sustainable Development,* 13.1 (2005): 38–52.

Lessmann, Ortrud, and Felix Rauschmeyer, eds. 2014. *The Capability Approach and Sustainability.* London: Routledge.

Pearce, David, Edward Barbier and Anil Markandya. 2013. *Sustainable Development: Economics and environment in the Third World.* London: Routledge.

Poverty-Environment Knowledge Hub: www.povertyenvironment.net/

Works cited

Adams, William, Ros Aveling, Dan Brockington, Barney Dickson, Jo Elliott, Jon Hutton, Dilys Roe, Bhaskar Vira and William Wolmer. 'Biodiversity conservation and the eradication of poverty.' *Science,* 306 (2004). 1146–1149.

Alcamo, Joseph, and Elena M. Bennett, eds. 2003. *Ecosystems and Human Well-Being: A framework for assessment.* Washington, DC: Island Press.

Baez, Ana L., M. F. Price and V. L. Smith. 'Learning from experience in the Monteverde Cloud forest, Costa Rica.' *People and Tourism in Fragile Environment.* (1996): 109–122.

Ballet, Jérôme, Jean-Marcel Koffi and Jérôme Pelenc. 'Environment, justice and the capability approach.' *Ecological Economics,* 85 (2013): 28–34.

Barbier, Edward. 'Environmental Sustainability and Poverty Eradication in Developing Countries.' In Eva Paus, ed. 2013. *Getting Development Right: Structural transformation, inclusion, and sustainability in the post-crisis era.* New York, NY: Palgrave Macmillan: 173–194.

Burger, Paul, and Marius Christen. 'Towards a capability approach of sustainability.' *Journal of Cleaner Production,* 19.8 (2011): 787–795.

Davis, Jason. *Evolution of Protected Area Conservation in Monteverde, Costa Rica.* Diss. University of Florida, 2007.

Department for International Development, European Commission Directorate General for Development, United Nations Development Programme and The World Bank. 'Linking Poverty Reduction and Environmental Management.' July 2002.

Duraiappah, Anantha Kumar. 'Exploring the Links: the United Nations Environment Programme 2004: Human Well-being, Poverty & Ecosystem Services.' Nairobi, Kenya: United Nations Environment Programme; Winnipeg: International Institute for Sustainable Development, 2004.

Duraiappah, Anantha Kumar. 'Poverty and ecosystems: a conceptual framework.' UNEP Division of Policy and Law Paper. UNEP Nairobi. 2002.

Farrell, Tracy A., and Jeffrey L. Marion. 'Identifying and assessing ecotourism visitor impacts at eight protected areas in Costa Rica and Belize.' *Environmental Conservation*, 28.03 (2001): 215–225.

Funkhouser, Edward, Juan Pablo Pérez Sáinz and Carlos Sojo. 'Social Exclusion of Nicaraguans in the Urban Metropolitan Area of San José, Costa Rica.' Inter-American Development Bank Research Network Working paper #R-437 (April 2002).

Gallagher, Kevin P., and Strom Thacker. 2008. 'Democracy, Income, and Environmental Quality.' Working Paper 164. University of Massachusetts, Amherst, Political Economy Research Institute, Amherst, MA.

Holland, Breena. 'Justice and the environment in Nussbaum's capabilities approach: why sustainable ecological capacity is a meta-capability.' *Political Research Quarterly*, 61.2 (2008): 319–332.

The International Ecotourism Society (TIES). www.ecotourism.org/, accessed April 2015.

International Fund for Agricultural Development. 'Desertification' fact sheet. August 2010.

Koens, Jacobus Franciscus, Carel Dieperink and Miriam Miranda. 'Ecotourism as a development strategy: experiences from Costa Rica.' *Environment, Development and Sustainability*, 11.6 (2009): 1225–1237.

Lehtonen, Markku. 'The environmental–social interface of sustainable development: capabilities, social capital, institutions.' *Ecological Economics*, 49.2 (2004): 199–214.

Livelihoods and Climate Change. 'Conceptual framework paper prepared by the Task Force on Climate Change, Vulnerable Communities, and Adaptation.' The International Institute for Sustainable Development: 2003.

Marquette, Catherine M. 'Nicaraguan migrants in Costa Rica.' *Población y Salud en Mesoamérica*, 4.1 (2006).

Millennium Ecosystem Assessment. 2005. *Ecosystems and Human Wellbeing*. Washington, DC: Island Press.

Pearce, David W. 'Investing in Environmental Wealth for Poverty Reduction.' Poverty-Environment Partnership. September 2005.

Polishchuk, Yuliana, and Felix Rauschmayer. 'Beyond 'benefits'? Looking at ecosystem services through the capability approach.' *Ecological Economics*, 81 (2012): 103–111.

Poverty-Environment Partnership (PEP). 'Poverty, Health and Environment: Placing Environmental Health on Countries' Development Agendas.' Joint Agency Paper, June 2008.

Prüss-Üstün, Annette, and Carlos Corvalán. Preventing Disease Through Healthy Environments. Geneva: World Health Organization, 2006.

Satterthwaite, David. 'The links between poverty and the environment in urban areas of Africa, Asia, and Latin America.' *The Annals of the American Academy of Political and Social Science*, 590.1 (2003): 73–92.

Sen, Amartya. 'The ends and means of sustainability.' *Journal of Human Development and Capabilities: A Multi-Disciplinary Journal for People-Centered Development*, 14.1 (2013): 6–20.

Sen, Amartya. 2009. *The Idea of Justice*. Cambridge, MA: Belknap Press.

Torras, Mariano. 'The impact of power equality, income, and the environment on human health: some inter-country comparisons.' *International Review of Applied Economics*, 20.1 (2006): 1–20.

UNDP. 2011. *Human Development Report 2011. Sustainability and Equity: A better future for all.* New York, NY: United Nations Development Programme.

UNEP. 2009. *From Conflict to Peacebuilding: The role of natural resources and the environment.* Nairobi: United Nations Environment Programme.

Voget-Kleschin, Lieske. 'Using the capability approach to conceptualize sustainable development.' *Greifswald Environmental Ethics Papers*, no. 4, February 2013.

World Bank. 2002. *World Development Report 2003. Sustainable Development in a Dynamic Economy.* Washington, DC: World Bank.

World Resource Institute. www.wri.org/our-work/topics/forests, accessed 24 December 2014.

11 Financial services for the poor

Serena Cosgrove

Key questions

- Why have microfinance programmes become so popular with development agencies?
- Why are financial services – such as credit, savings and insurance – important for microentrepreneurs, marketers and others who earn their income outside of the formal economy?
- What are the major debates about microfinance?
- Why are most clients of these financial services women?
- What is the evidence about microfinance's effectiveness as a poverty reduction strategy?

Introduction

'I've been able to increase my sales and diversify what I sell thanks to the small loan and training I got from Lumana here in our town', said Mary, a Ghanaian micro-entrepreneur who sells salted fish and now dry goods from her home in Anloga, a small town near the ocean. 'And even though I don't know how to read or write, we received business training that taught us how to figure out whether we're making a profit or not, by using small stones to count with', she said proudly. The fact that a low-income, rural woman considers herself better off thanks to the microfinance institution that provided her with business training and a small loan speaks to the possibilities inherent in a range of financial and non-financial services often referred to as microfinance. In developing countries around the world, many poor women like Mary have received small loans, to expand their businesses and build relationships with other microentrepreneurs.

In the mid-1990s, the success of Muhammad Yunus' Grameen Bank in Bangladesh began attracting a great deal of attention: impoverished women in Bangladesh were emerging from poverty and gender oppression through access to small loans and obligatory savings programmes, *and* they were repaying their loans at the rate of 97 per cent, a higher rate than rich men on Wall Street. Referred to as microfinance or microcredit, such programmes provide low-income microentrepreneurs with small loans, savings and other services from rotating credit funds. These funds can be used for microenterprise development, acquisition of technologies and other assets, land purchase, farming and housing construction and improvement. In the years since Yunus won the 2006 Nobel Peace Prize, however, microfinance has also attracted less favourable attention. Critics have claimed that such programmes take advantage of poor people, do little to help them escape poverty, and siphon off development funds from more effective uses. There was even a rash of suicides by people in India who became heavily indebted through microfinance.

Given such controversies, what is the real utility of programmes that promise financial services for poor people? There are certainly good reasons to believe that microfinance *could be* a valuable poverty reduction strategy. In many developing countries a large proportion of the economically active population works in the informal sector, which means that their income-generating activities tend to happen outside of state control, i.e. their businesses do not operate according to regulations on taxation or labour. Many of these income-generating activities are run by women, their average income is low, and their businesses are oriented towards survival, not savings or business growth (Le and Raven 2015). These microentrepreneurs, marketers and craftspeople have little to no recourse to legal protections, labour laws, and security from illegal behaviour such as gang-related activities and drugs and arms trafficking. Historically they have also rarely had access to the services of the formal banking system (loans, savings, retirement accounts) and other financial services (insurance, pension plans), let alone access to formal education, vocational training, and specifically business training opportunities.

The theory behind microfinance is that with access to financial services, poor people may be able to develop income-earning businesses that will lift them and their families out of poverty. For its proponents, part of the appeal of microfinance is often as a 'bottom-up' solution to development, that it can empower people, who are excluded from access to formal financial services, to help themselves. Due to the preponderance of women marketers and microentrepreneurs in the informal sector throughout the developing world, microfinance has predominantly targeted women. Microfinance institutions typically see women as good credit risks because they are regarded as more likely to repay loans due to cultural traits such as obedience and selflessness, often associated with women's caretaking roles. In turn, because of their roles in the family and their communities as mothers and caretakers, increased income for women can translate into improved economic conditions and wellbeing for them as well as their children and communities. Thus another rationale for microfinance is that it has the potential to contribute to human and economic development by empowering women especially.

This chapter examines the theory and rationale for microfinance, comparing them to the evidence for this strategy's impacts on poor people. It centres on the debates that have arisen around microfinance's implementation, impact, and empowerment potential. The chapter first describes the practicalities of receiving services through a microfinance programme, explaining the methodologies, concepts and values behind this type of programming. It then considers the poverty reduction potential of micro-finance through the lens of the capabilities approach. In the final section, the chapter investigates a number of the debates in this area, including the different modes of microfinance (credit-only versus credit-plus), who implements microfinance program-ming, and the goals and ideological assumptions of such programmes. Most importantly, the chapter surveys the evidence on microfinance's effectiveness as a poverty reduction strategy, including whether it does consistently empower women. The chapter's conclusions are based on field research in El Salvador in the 1990s, Zambia in 2011 and Ghana in 2012, as well as a review of recent academic work in many further countries. Ultimately, though such research does sometimes show increased incomes and other positive effects for microfinance clients, additional programming and structural change are often necessary to catalyse longer-term processes of empowerment and development.

Microfinance: examples and definitions

Microfinance typically targets microenterprises, which are characterized by little to no capital invested in the businesses, and a maximum of two to three employees. Francisca's cheese stall, or Mari, José and Rosa Elba's vegetable stalls in El Salvador (described below in Box 11.1) are all examples of microenterprises. Microenterprises cover a wide spectrum of income-generating activities in urban and rural areas: in El Salvador, for example, these businesses included making tortillas; working leather for belts, purses and satchels; selling fruit juices, cheese, milk, soft drinks, fruits and vegetables, shoes, underwear and cosmetics; preparing and selling food; or raising animals for slaughter or resale. Sometimes these businesses were small stores or *tiendas* run from the microentrepreneurs' homes, serving the needs of their immediate neighbours. The small loans that microfinance institutions (MFIs) provide are often intended for use for investment in the microentrepreneurs' businesses: for repairs, expansion, diversification, inventory acquisition, or to acquire such assets as corn mills, a computer or even access to water or electricity for a business run from the home. These loans can also translate into housing improvements when the business or part of it is located in the borrower's place of residence. Some loan programmes don't require that microentrepreneurs invest directly in their businesses because they understand that what might be most useful to the client is paying for her children's schooling or other costs. In addition to loans, sometimes clients choose to work with MFIs because they have savings programmes for personal or business investment goals as well as because of insurance programmes which help clients access health insurance or insurance against crop failures.

Throughout this chapter, and the development literature in general, the terms microfinance, microcredit and microenterprise lending are often used interchangeably, but in strict rigor, the umbrella term is microfinance. Microfinance encompasses a range of financial and non-financial services including microcredit or small loans, savings, insurance, money transfers, other business opportunities such as access to technologies, and sometimes training and accompaniment. Whereas microfinance refers to numerous financial services for clients, microcredit and microenterprise lending are the terms used to refer specifically to the loans (or credit) which clients will pay back with interest to the MFI. Frequently managed by local MFIs (often NGOs), microfinance institutions use a rotating credit fund from which they distribute small loans (typically USD 100–500), collect savings from clients/entrepreneurs, recover the loans with interest, and then expand the number of clients served as the credit fund grows. MFIs often target a particular city or neighbourhood, letting community leaders know about their services. With input and recommendations from local leaders, microfinance promoters from the MFI will begin to build networks of contacts in the community. After an orientation and site visit from the promoter, borrowers are encouraged to form groups with people they know and vouch for, and soon they can access their loans.

In order to minimize administrative costs and increase the commitment of clients to the process, MFIs often use a group method for distributing and recovering the loans. There are two different models that MFIs around the world use to provide credit: the communal bank and the solidarity group. The communal bank, as we will see in Francisca's case, is a small group of borrowers – from 5 to 20 depending on the programme – who apply together for loans, receive training or orientation together, and then commit to the same repayment schedule. In the case of the communal bank model, individuals each put up some form of collateral, be it a television, a refrigerator,

Box 11.1 Becoming a microfinance client in El Salvador

Fifty-four-year-old Francisca is a cheese seller in the marketplace of Apopa, El Salvador, a small city on the outskirts of the Salvadoran capital, San Salvador. Francisca is also a natural leader, a hard worker and a creative microentrepreneur. Though illiterate, she supports her family by selling cheese at an open-air stall near the Apopa municipal market. I met her for the first time when she brought three other marketers – Mari and José, a married couple, and their sister, Rosa Elba – who sell fruits and vegetables near her to attend an orientation meeting at the Apopa office of the NGO FUSAI (Fundación Salvadoreña de Apoyo Integral – Salvadoran Foundation for Integral Support). My initial impression of Francisca was her determination. She did not hesitate to ask Roberto, the FUSAI promoter, questions about FUSAI's microfinance programme when something was not clear; often women do not ask clarifying questions of men, especially educated men seen as belonging to a higher status group, such as professionals.

Francisca had been financing her microenterprise with high-interest loans from one of the many moneylenders working in the Apopa market. Paying an exorbitant interest rate of 10 per cent per day (compared to 3 per cent per month with FUSAI), low-income market vendors end up *dándole de comer al gordo* ('feeding the fat man') instead of feeding their own kids, as Francisca explained. Francisca accurately conveyed the consensus of the group: 'We want a break. We want out from under the loan shark.' So Francisca and the three others applied to become a communal bank and receive loans from FUSAI.

My next meeting with Francisca was accompanying Roberto, the FUSAI promoter, as he checked out the businesses of the potential communal bank members and helped them fill out the application forms. Outside of an already bustling market building, sellers set up boxes and baskets occupying the streets in their allotted areas under black pieces of plastic that had been strung up to protect vendors and shoppers from both sun and rain. It is like entering a different world: a thriving centre of commerce under black plastic. First I walked past Elba and her vegetable stand, then past Mari and José with their vegetables before I saw Francisca, waving a fly swatter over a metal box filled with *cuajada* (farmers' cheese) and little plastic bags of *crema* (sour cream).

Little over a week later, the loans were ready for disbursement. Gathered at the FUSAI office in Apopa, José, Mari, Elba and Francisca prepared to sign the contracts and take their checks for USD 100–150 to the local bank around the corner to be cashed. Francisca turned to me and told me she was getting a headache. Francisca cannot read or write; she has received no formal education. She can just barely write her initials, but that does not qualify as a signature in El Salvador. In Salvadoran banks, a check is not valid to be cashed unless it has been signed. Francisca had to ask one of the other members of her communal bank to accompany her to sign the check for her. Holding her head in her hands, she said to me, 'This is my father's fault. He used to say that it made no sense to send a girl to school just so she could learn to write letters to a boyfriend.' She went on, 'It just hurts my head to know that I cannot sign my own name.' Francisca got Mari to help her sign the cheque, and thus she received her first loan from a microfinance institution.

Francisca gets up at 5am and catches a bus to the outlying municipality of Aguilares where she walks out into the countryside to buy the cheese. By 9am, she is back at the Apopa market selling cheese; she stays at the market until she's sold everything she has, returning home in the mid-afternoon. Slowly, as we got to know each other under the black plastic, Francisca let me take responsibility for the fly swatter, waving it over the cheese, and as the weeks went by, I joined her in singing out the many qualities of the cheese for sale that day. By the end of my fieldwork stint, Francisca began to talk about the problematic relationship with her common-law husband. She no longer sleeps with him. He doesn't contribute financially to the household anymore. She would just put his things out in the street, but his name is on the title to the house. Recently, he got angry at her and slammed her hand in the door, injuring her fingers. 'What can I do to leave him?' she asked me. Francisca is also concerned about her three teenage sons. Trying to keep them occupied after school so they don't get into trouble, she has apprenticed them to a baker. They earn some money, get job experience and keep their distance from the gangs.

As the primary income-earner for her family, Francisca struggles to make ends meet and provide a home for her sons. Though beset by a number of problems – from the abusive husband to gang activity in her community – not only did her income increase during her loan period, but she was able to increase her inventory by 15 per cent. As I followed her progress after the loan disbursement, she told me that sales were up, she had increased inventory, and felt she had increased the amount of money she took home at the end of the day. 'I feel rested working with FUSAI', she said explaining how she felt less economic stress now that she was not depending on the loan shark. 'I was drowning working with the loan shark.'

(Adapted from Cosgrove 1999a and 1999b)

or simply the income-generating potential of their microenterprise. The solidarity group – or the peer lending group as it is also called – is used for borrowers who have no assets to put up for collateral. In this case, a group of clients (the group size can vary) commits to covering each other should one of them not be able to make a repayment. Group pressure, and the social bonds that connect the borrowers, keep members repaying their loans on time. The solidarity group model often includes an obligatory savings programme which can be used to repay delinquent accounts. In cases where borrowers may not have immediate access to funds, they often take extraordinary measures to find the payment to avoid the shame of defaulting, even for one payment. Since women predominate in the informal sector, most microfinance clients are women. And because of culturally-coded messages about the caretaking and maternal responsibilities of being a woman as well as the class-coded messages about respect for authority, women tend to be very responsible loan clients. In fact, they repay their loans better than men and usually invest more of their profits in the health and welfare of their families.

Many microfinance programmes focus solely on providing credit, and they are referred to as credit-only programmes. Some programmes include obligatory savings programmes of five to ten per cent on the amount loaned. However, given the need of clients for basic financial services, MFIs have begun to offer additional financial services such as different savings programmes, health insurance, and insurance in case of personal,

Table 11.1 Types of microfinance and associated services

Microfinance and associated services			
Financial services		Related services, also referred to as credit-plus	
Financial services	Importance for entrepreneurs served	Additional services	Importance for entrepreneurs served
Credit-only: microcredit or small loans	Clients, like Francisca mentioned above, who just want loans	Business skills and strategies training	Provides clients with knowledge for managing their businesses better
Savings programmes	Many programmes include savings programmes for clients so they can begin to build their own capital for their businesses or other personal and family-related needs	Entrepreneurship and community engagement training	Training for how clients' businesses can expand or diversify and contribute to development in their communities
Insurance (health, life, disaster) and pensions	Because so many clients are not employed in formal sector jobs with benefits and often do not meet prerequisites to be served by the formal banking sector, they find these services useful for unexpected illnesses in the family, weather shocks that affect crops, and long-term planning	Training and programming related to clients' other capabilities such as women's empowerment and rights, health and hygiene, citizen participation and advocacy, and green technology	Serves to connect clients' individual businesses to address bigger challenges that limit their capabilities and contribute to poverty

familial emergencies or crop failures (Zeller and Sharma 2000). There are a number of programmes providing additional services other than financial ones especially when targeting low-income women; these programmes are often referred to as credit-plus and can include health-related trainings or medicine, vocational training, business skills enhancement (business basics, marketing or entrepreneurship, for example), gender awareness workshops, or specific workshops on best practices for particular kinds of microenterprises (Table 11.1).

Microfinance programmes exist around the globe, and not surprisingly, there can be a lot of variation in how the programmes work. The most well-known microfinance model is the Grameen Bank in Bangladesh, whose solidarity group programmes have loaned more than USD 17 billion for self-employment purposes, with repayment rates approaching 100 per cent (Grameen Bank 2015).

Bangladesh is also the home of two other important microfinance institutions called Building Resources Across Communities (BRAC) and Proshika Human Development Centre. According to Lamia Karim's research, there are over 21 million women in a country of 140 million being served by MFIs in Bangladesh (2011). The work of ACCION International in the Americas includes the ACCION NGO-credit network and the commercially successful, credit-only institution BancoSol. Also active in Latin

Box 11.2 The importance of an array of financial services, by Julian Fellerman

The expansion of financial services beyond microcredit has been a major focus for the microfinance sector in recent years. Savings and insurance products tailored to the needs of the world's unbanked have been at the forefront of this expansion.

Emblematic of this larger trend is MiCredito, a Nicaraguan MFI which has developed an array of savings and insurance products into its core microcredit offerings. When a new client takes out a microloan with MiCredito, they automatically enrol in a life-insurance plan funded by a small percentage of their loan repayments to the MFI. MiCredito has also partnered with Banco de America Central (BAC), a larger regional bank, to begin offering new and existing clients a syndicated debit card option. These saving and insurance products serve a dual purpose: in the case of insurance, the product serves to create a stronger 'future-orientation' among clients wherein long-term financial planning is literally built in to the loan repayment plan. The debit card is one of the most fundamental tools in the financial inclusion arsenal; specifically, access to a savings account with no required minimum balance improves MiCredito's clients' ability to manage repayments by reducing transaction costs associated with storing and moving money. Most importantly, though, is the role of the MFI savings account as a pre-requisite step in the client's journey towards banking with a formal financial sector institution.

I had the opportunity to witness the transformative power of savings in action during a field visit to Maribel, one of MiCredito's clients in Rivas, Nicaragua, located about 20 miles north of the Costa Rican border. Maribel relocated to Rivas after spending most of her life living on the outskirts of the colonial city of Leon. After much of her family fell victim to the Counter-Revolutionary forces during the Nicaraguan civil war of the 1980s, she was forced to relocate to this economic hub in southern Nicaragua. 'I escaped from there with nothing in terms of money. We had a few family friends down here (in Rivas) where we stayed for a few years trying to rebuild', she comments. Maribel began to realize her homemade tortillas were gaining popularity in her new community. This led her to start an artisanal tortilla enterprise she now operates out of her home. She's taken out multiple microloans from MiCredito to fund the expansion of her increasingly popular business, with a small percentage of each loan repayment depositing into her savings account. When I asked her about her experience as a MiCredito client, she expressed particular gratitude for the savings account option: 'This has really changed things for me. As small business owners, we want a safe place to store our money – however, because many of our businesses are so small, our options for a formal savings account are often limited.'

According to Maribel, this savings cushion has also come in handy as a means of smoothing out her personal consumption during lulls in the business. She says she has greater peace of mind because of the increased preparedness she feels in the event of a financial emergency. This peace of mind from something so seemingly basic as a savings account has fundamentally changed the outlook of this budding entrepreneur.

Box 11.3 The Grameen Bank

As of 2013, the Grameen Bank in Bangladesh had almost 129 million USD in capital, 22,000 employees, 8.5 million borrowers and 2500 branches. The Grameen Foundation has its headquarters in Washington DC, and it works to replicate the Grameen model around the world. (Data taken from the Grameen Bank and Foundation websites.)

America, with many national affiliates, is FINCA International. In Central America, governmental offices, non-governmental organizations and private sector credit associations provide credit throughout the region from rotating credit funds that are managed by the communities themselves, NGOs or governmental institutions. In Indonesia, the country-wide programme Bankya Rakyat's Unit Desa System has been successfully implemented by the government (Boomgard and Angell 1994). Interestingly, Bankya Rakyat Indonesia requires that clients buy life insurance so that their loans can be repaid in the case of illness or death (Zeller and Sharma 2000).

Many of the bigger microfinance institutions – such as Grameen and BRAC – focus on small loans and if they have a savings programme, it is an obligatory one, serving more as 'a down- payment on a loan and a screening device' (ibid: 159) than as a flexible savings account tailored to the borrower's accumulation needs. Catholic Relief Services and other international non-governmental agencies, such as CARE and Caritas, have promoted models of lending and saving in the developing world that are built with capital from a group of women themselves: women organize as a group and pool their own savings and then loan it out to group members. This way they do not have to rely on an outside source for their capital. These models are called SILCS (savings and internal lending communities) and ROSCAS (rotating credit and savings associations). Microfinance efforts can also be found in the developed world: there are successful MFIs in the United States, such as the Working Capital model in Boston and Ventures in Seattle, a non-profit that provides microloans at graduated levels and individual development accounts, matching client savings 2:1.

Box 11.4 Microfinance and business training in Ghana

Lumana is an MFI in Ghana (Fgure 11.1) that operates on a credit-plus model with small communal bank groups. Once they are approved for a loan, but before they receive any money, these groups attend a three-day business training in the local language. This training includes basic accounting appropriate even for illiterate clients, as well as instruction in personal savings. Obligatory micro-savings are built into Lumana's model to help clients with goal setting, such as saving for children's education or home construction. Once they have completed the training, Lumana sets up a bank account for each group, and each member gets the equivalent of about USD 60 for their first loan. Lumana charges an interest rate of 24 per cent, compared to 30 to 90 per cent that other banks or MFIs offer. If clients successfully repay in 6 months (with a 2 month grace period), they become eligible for larger loan amounts. At the time of research, Lumana's repayment rate was 94 per cent.

To assess impacts, Lumana administers a 'Progress Out of Poverty' survey every year to each client, which is based on a Grameen Foundation instrument adapted for Ghana. It asks questions about the total family size, the highest grade level completed by the female head of the household, the construction material of the roof, the main source of drinking water for the household, and whether the household owns a working stove, radio or a few other household goods. Besides gathering some additional items of financial data, Lumana also employs people from the local community to act as case managers. These managers are mostly recent university graduates whose local contacts and knowledge of the language are essential for understanding clients' lives and maintaining good community relationships.

In the little seaside village of Dzita we met one of Lumana's clients, Alice, a very sharp, friendly woman who has a number of income-generating activities. Alice buys fresh fish, smokes it, then sells it. She also has a store, sells corn and regularly travels to the nearby country of Benin to buy small crabs that she can resell in Ghana's capital of Accra. The day we met her, Alice was sitting alongside her mother smoking shrimp on a big pan over a fire. She said that she learned you have to have multiple business strategies to survive, since if sales aren't good in one area, you can compensate with another. Women who had taken loans just for their shrimp business have had trouble repaying, she noticed.

Alice is in a lending group with four other women, and she has taken out four loans from Lumana. She had very positive things to say about her experience with microfinance: 'you can take in a big amount and pay back small.' She found Lumana's business training useful because 'it tells you what to do with your money', and 'how to attract customers and market yourself'. If she hadn't had that training, Alice said, she wouldn't know how to spend better and save. She noticed how some women spent their loans on personal or family needs and had trouble repaying, but she was determined to use her loans to invest so she could bring in more income. She wants to use her next loan to increase her family's farming productivity so they can have more beans, corn and groundnuts to sell especially in the off-season when they fetch a higher price. With her savings, Alice has already bought a refrigerator for the house, and her next goals include saving for her kids' university education and to buy land for a guest house to rent out.

On a market day, Alice wakes up as early as 3am to smoke fish so that she's done by 7am. She also has to get her store ready and her kids off to school by the time she leaves for the market, usually before 8am. She spends the entire day selling, while her mother minds the store and takes care of the younger kids. Alice usually gets home after 7pm, when she cleans up, spends a little time with her children, then goes to sleep so she can get up early and start again the next day. Her family lives in her husband's house, but he works at a hospital in Accra, a few hours away. Alice's husband comes home only a few times per month, and she says she doesn't really miss him, though she does like it when he's home. They make their decisions on finances and family matters together. Alice is obviously a hard worker: she developed her businesses while she was raising three small children. Though her life is by no means easy, it is more secure and comfortable in part, she thinks, because of microfinance.

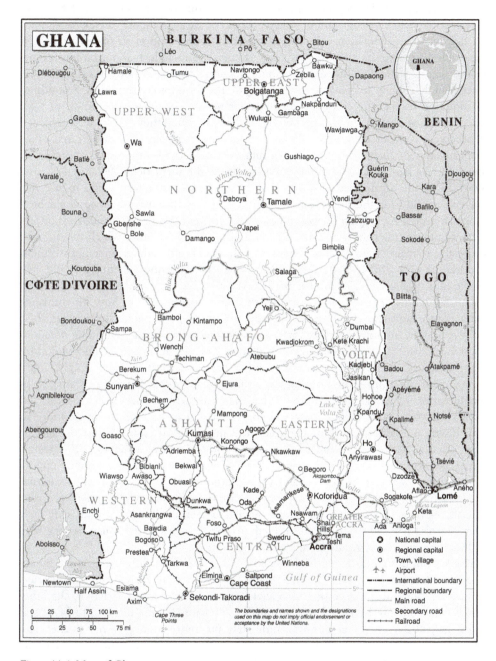

Figure 11.1 Map of Ghana

Source: Map No. 4186 Rev. 3 UNITED NATIONS February 2005

Microfinance and capabilities

From an economic development perspective, how microcredit and related financial services could help lift people out of poverty should be clear. In theory, these programmes can help people generate income, but also smooth consumption so that they are less vulnerable to economic shocks. Economic shocks can include major spending events such as illness, weddings, funerals or natural disasters (drought, floods, hurricanes) that affect a family's ability to generate income or produce food for consumption. Smoothing consumption means, for example, helping poor people get the same amount of food every month, so that they don't go hungry in a month when they've had an emergency or otherwise run out of money. Though small loans can help, it is more often other financial services such as savings and insurance that provide important resources so clients survive hard times which plague vulnerable and poor people (Zeller and Sharma 2000). From the capabilities perspective, all of these potential effects could reduce risk and vulnerability for the poor. This is why Tseng says that microfinance could be a 'shock absorber': by helping people to cope with emergencies or other sudden shortfalls in consumption, microfinance can bring financial stability, without which people may not be able to realize their goals or valued capabilities in health, education, empowerment or other life plans (2011: 244). Therefore, microfinance's economic effects should give people more agency to live the life they choose.

The capabilities approach adds a further theoretical perspective to how microfinance could reduce poverty. By strengthening the ability of poor people to manage their money, and by raising their incomes, microfinance can actually promote freedom (Roodman 2012). It can do so in several different ways. First, higher incomes and more secure finances can expand a variety of other life opportunities. Very simply, more money often opens up more possibilities. As mentioned above, financial security helps people withstand shocks that can limit what they can do with their lives. Second, and more concretely, with higher incomes, poor people may be able to invest more in their health and education. This is money as a means to an end: not just the end of more physical assets or growing one's business, but the end of achieving more robust human development (Zeller and Sharma 2000). Third, by expanding economic opportunities, microfinance may also expand various other social and political opportunities. The reason here is that with more secure finances, the poor may be less prey to corrupt officials, or they may be able to escape restrictive social/cultural situations that limit their choices. This latter idea relates directly to the fourth way that microfinance may promote freedom, specifically by empowering women.

Think again of Francisca: her loan helped her actualize the capability to earn a living. The microfinance institution FUSAI helps people such as Francisca break barriers preventing them from accessing financial services because of restrictive eligibility requirements like not being able to sign one's own name. Giving the loan to Francisca, which helped her grow her business, ultimately put more money in her pocket, and gave her the power to make her own financial decisions. In the big picture, Gilardone *et al.* argue, microfinance can 'increase women's incomes and facilitate their financial independence, stabilize their entrepreneurship activity notably by training, but also, and maybe especially, improve their status within the family and strengthen the respect of themselves, and finally, favour their capacities of auto-organization and thus, their capacities of expression and claiming' (2014: 245). This is the theory of how microfinance can enhance capabilities, and it does have some empirical support, as we will see below.

However, even in Francisca's case, there are a number of reasons for caution. Yes, she's doing better with her business thanks to the loan and mutual support from her communal bank, but does she have more freedom and options to choose the life she wants, given that she faces gendered and institutional limitations imposed by poverty, including oppressive gender roles, a lack of education, and high levels of insecurity due to gang violence? Moreover, how much has microfinance helped with other contributors to Francisca's poverty, such as personal safety? In fact, there are some ways that a small loan may *reduce* clients' freedoms. For example, it does undeniably lock people into sometimes severe contracts and potentially lead them into debt spirals. It is also possible that solidarity groups can actually be coercive, disempowering at least as much as they empower. For example, if you are a member of a solidarity group and you cannot repay your loan, the group may seize your belongings, leaving you worse off than before you joined. This potentially disempowering aspect of microfinance suggests that the feel-good stories one often encounters on promotional web sites can have a dark side – and it points the way to the many debates about this poverty reduction strategy.

Microfinance debates

There is no denying microfinance's powerful, intuitive appeal: reduce the limitations around credit, savings and insurance for poor people, and they will be able to build or expand businesses, increase their incomes and escape cycles of indebtedness from high-interest loans. It may even be an impressive vehicle for women's empowerment. Furthermore, because of the mounting criticism of bilateral aid (large aid flows from one government to another), microfinance is often seen as a decentralized, bottom-up strategy that does not rely on big aid commitments making it to the local level: once an MFI has established a rotating credit fund either through donations, an investment, or a loan itself, it can grow to serve more borrowers if it is managed efficiently. There is no shortage of cases such as Mary's, Francisca's or Alice's where a microfinance client is able to make her business more lucrative and attain greater control over her life in the process.

Nonetheless, there are also many analysts who disagree with microfinance proponents' claims for its effectiveness. In fact, there are a number of contentious debates that swirl around the utility of microfinance as a poverty reduction strategy. I will examine four specific areas of debate: (1) the arguments about the most effective models for providing microfinance to clients; (2) the critiques that arise from examining the world views or underlying ideologies of microfinance programmes; (3) the discussions about whether or not microfinance empowers its clients, especially impoverished women, or places them under more pressure as they have to repay the loans or risk being shamed in their communities; and (4) the long-term effectiveness and impact assessment of microfinance programmes on loan clients, their communities, and developing world economies in general. Through studying these debates, we will examine the best research on the outcomes of microfinance to understand the pros and cons of this strategy. Given that there is no 'magic bullet' to reduce global poverty, the essential question is this: under what conditions can microfinance most benefit its clients and contribute to the expansion of their capabilities?

Credit-only or credit-plus?

A familiar debate in the sector has been whether financially sustainable credit-only programmes are preferable to a broader array of services including savings and insurance or more expensive credit-plus programming in which borrowers access financial services and educational opportunities. Some MFIs have promoted a credit-only model in part because it may be easier for financial institutions to manage since it does not include the range of training, solidarity and other development inputs with which they may not have experience. This minimalist model of the credit-only approach emphasizes the financial sustainability of the programme's loan portfolio via the expansion of borrowers served. The focus is simply on providing credit to a population that needs it. As Muhammad Yunus himself said, 'The fact that the poor are alive is clear proof of their ability . . . So rather than wasting our time teaching them new skills, we try to make maximum use of their existing skills' (1999: 135). Credit-only is attractive to certain donors because of the focus on loan portfolios' financial sustainability, and the ability to serve larger numbers of borrowers resulting from the relatively limited services provided.

However, critics allege that other sustainability concerns, such as the long-term sustainability of borrowers' businesses and communities, are more likely to be neglected by the credit-only approach. Zeller and Sharma (2000) argue that the poor and near poor need savings and insurance more than they need credit. Advocates of credit-plus approaches insist that when little attention is given to the cultural, economic, institutional and political factors that contribute to poverty and a lack of social protections for clients, their families and communities, individual borrowers may see an increase in consumption, but other contributors to poverty will persist. Models using the credit-plus approach, while more costly, aim at promoting human development for greater economic and non-economic sustainability in the long-term. There is evidence from around the world about the impact of additional financial services and training programmes in conjunction with business training. In Peru, women borrowers increased their business knowledge and demonstrated likelihood to stay with the MFI offering the training compared to a control group without training who demonstrated lower levels of retention (Karlan and Valdivia 2011). In Vietnam, business training did increase business performance overall, and the heterogeneity of women microentrepreneurs explains why some – such as isolated rural entrepreneurs – showed more satisfaction with the training than those in the lowlands (Le and Raven 2015).

Though it generated much discussion in the 1990s and 2000s, the ongoing relevance of the credit-only versus credit-plus debate is as a reminder that programming must respond to the needs of the clients, their cultural context and the scope of the programme. One of the risks with a one-size-fits-all model is that it does not have the flexibility to respond to clients' needs. If cultural practices and gender hierarchies mean that women are not supposed to touch money, then programming will have to focus on cultural change and consciousness raising among women *and* men. If the community faces significant violence – such as gang violence and/or gender-based violence – it would be important to have an alternative to saving money at home and possibly gender sensitivity training for clients, their spouses and family members before simply giving women money. However, if the clients have years of experience selling in markets and other places, but credit constraints prevent them from growing their businesses, then a programme restricted to small loans with low interest might be appropriate.

The issue of credit-only versus credit-plus is also related to the question of which organizations should implement microfinance programming. Presently, there is a range of different institutions running such programmes. Initially, non-governmental organizations and mission-driven, for-profit institutions like the Grameen Bank which only serve impoverished borrowers were the primary providers of microfinance. But as time went by and governmental agencies and the formal banking sector saw that microfinance was profitable and addressed an important need in their communities, new actors joined the ranks. The pros and cons are multiple. When government agencies run microlending programmes, they can assure that programming fits into local, regional and national development plans, and coordinate ways to leverage the resources of all government agencies working in those communities. However, governments should not use microfinance projects as an excuse to decrease programming that provides citizens with basic social protections. Other MFIs also need to make sure that their efforts fit into broader development goals when instituting a microlending programme. For instance, in the Salvadoran town of Nejapa, local NGOs and the municipal government worked together efficiently towards common goals. As NGOs provided microentrepreneurs with loans and business skills and knowledge, the mayor raised money to rebuild the municipal market building. By the time the building was finished, many marketers had expanded their businesses, happy to relocate to the new building (Cosgrove 2002 and 1999a).

When established financial institutions develop programming for low-income clients, they are meeting a need in the community by expanding services they already provide. Banks do not have to go through an intensive learning curve about the financial management of a loan fund, though they do have to develop client-sensitive materials and services. Because some microentrepreneurs do not read or write, banks need to understand that they cannot require microentrepreneurs to sign or fill out extensive forms; they need to streamline requirements. When an NGO, on the other hand, decides to include microlending as part of their programming, they often have to train staff and establish the necessary systems to manage the fund efficiently. But the NGO is probably better suited to administering additional services clients may need such as education, vocational training, health workshops and consciousness-raising groups. And finally, NGOs play an important role in the strengthening of civil society and its ability to monitor government fulfilment of rights and obligations. If an NGO manages a microfinance programme well, it can generate additional resources for other kinds of programming, thus serving clients and the community better.

Ideological disputes around microfinance

The credit-only versus credit-plus debate, along with the issue of which organizations should operate which kinds of microfinance programmes, are mostly practical in nature. Another contentious area with microfinance as a poverty reduction strategy deals more with ideology and competing worldviews. No matter the strategy, it is always important to assess the worldview of its proponents. A particular worldview does not necessarily render a poverty reduction strategy ineffective; rather, the imperative is to understand the motivations behind actions as well as the long-term vision for the future. Microfinance, like virtually any other strategy, is not free of politics. The politics come in choosing this approach over other interventions; in promoting individual businesses over collective enterprises; in starting small and scaling up programmes and client numbers. We should not simplistically presume that increasing the assets and income of poor microentrepreneurs is good for communities, and that incorporating this sector of society into the broader economy can thereby promote development. The reason is that microfinance may not only be about getting microentrepreneurs capital to build their businesses at fair interest rates.

To the contrary, critics raise concerns about how ideological assumptions and political views of neo-liberal development inform much of the popularity of microfinance. For example, Isserles (2003) contends that microfinance facilitates devolving state responsibilities of welfare and development to MFIs, thereby putting poor communities' social protections at risk. The potential problem with doing so is that it avoids the structural problems confronting a country by enforcing a bootstrap ideology in which poor people must generate their own opportunities and their governments are let off the hook for fulfilling their social contract. The microcredit revolution hit the front pages of newspapers as bilateral aid agencies were requiring that the governments of developing countries implement structural adjustment programmes to qualify for additional grants and loans. In order to make governments more streamlined and foster increased economic competition, structural adjustment policies compelled governments to privatize state businesses, cut spending, layoff state employees, eliminate subsidies for basic food items and decrease social protections and welfare programmes. Expecting state employees who have been laid off to start microenterprises to make ends meet is deeply problematic. How realistic is it to assume that almost anyone can earn a living by running their own business? Moreover, for those already stuck in poverty, the price increase of basic food goods sometimes associated with structural adjustment strained any possibility they had of moving out of poverty. How much help can a small loan provide in these circumstances?

Also, because women – often the most subordinated members of societies – make up the majority of microlending borrowers, it is important to consider how they might be affected differently than male borrowers. For instance, in her feminist critique of microfinance, Isserles suggests that targeting women because they repay loans and invest more in families is actually idealizing women and lowering expectations of men: 'This instrumental approach to women as conduits for credit . . . plays on, and reinforces, traditional cultural notions of womanhood, with women seen as moral guardians of the household and policers of recalcitrant men' (2003: 48). Thus while focusing on women for microfinance programmes has the potential of empowering them, it also has the potential of saddling them with new debt, new responsibilities and new problems as they challenge traditional norms around women handling money.

Many critics of microfinance also criticize how the managers of the credit funds charge interest to borrowers. They ask how it can be considered 'development' to charge poor people for services. For instance, Karim's research (2011) in Bangladesh has raised concerns that the contradictory impulses of making profit get entangled with helping the poor. Furthermore, microfinance periodically attracts controversy over usurious interest rates that new players – particularly the formal banking system – are charging clients (MacFarquhar 2010). For many in the sector, especially the mission-driven NGOs, interest rates hover at roughly 1–3 per cent per month (12 to 36 per cent per year), but the new players from the banking system and for-profit companies are charging interest sometimes above 75 per cent annual average rate. However, these rates are still less than what moneylenders charge, which stands at 120 per cent annual average in Bangladesh, for example (Karim 2011).

This debate over interest rates is not new. Many microfinance proponents – including Muhammad Yunus – as well as critics of microfinance chastise banks and companies that charge excessively high interest rates. This argument applies to both the formal banking system and MFIs. For the formal banking system and for-profit businesses investing in microfinance, critics again ask if something that enriches investors and stockholders should be considered 'development' for poor people. For the NGOs and municipal programmes that charge the more moderate 12 to 36 per cent annual interest rates, on the other hand, interest provides them with an important income stream for improving and expanding programming, especially for their clients. First, these rates are not exorbitant compared to what other moneylenders charge. Second, microloans can generate higher costs for lending organizations than bigger loans do for banks. It seems fair that microcredit organizations be able to cover their costs with the interest generated. The issue is complicated because when microcredit organizations make a profit, they may put it to the service of their mission. As in the case of FUSAI (the Salvadoran Foundation for Integral Support), the organization that gave Francisca a loan, the organization was able to support difficult-to-fund development programming from the profits of the microcredit fund. Is this usurious?

Debates about empowerment

The claim that microfinance empowers women is contentious in part because of differing definitions of 'empowerment'. There can be an economic dimension to empowerment when women have more money to spend and more power within the household to influence decisions over how to spend that money. However, even if they are earning a higher income, women may not have control over their income if they live in a patriarchal culture where financial decisions are made by fathers, husbands or sons. Empowerment can also be social, such as through strengthening a woman's social capital, normative influence and social cooperation (Sanyal 2009). Social capital refers to kinship and other social networks, connections that can help people in all kinds of ways. Normative influence refers to the ability to influence not just financial but other decisions, practices and values. Social cooperation is related to the idea of solidarity, helping women help other women. Moser (1993) offers a useful, summative definition of empowerment as women increasing their capacity for self-reliance, their right to determine choices and their ability to influence the direction of change by gaining control over material and nonmaterial resources. In theory, microfinance can empower women by giving them control over income, strengthening their community relationships and influence, and breaking down restrictive cultural norms about gender roles. What, however, does the evidence show – does microfinance truly and consistently empower women?

There is a wide range of qualitative studies and stories that affirm microfinance's empowering effects (see Sanyal 2009, Duvendack *et al.* 2011 for a review). These studies typically find, for instance, that the perception of women within their communities does change because of their participation in microfinance. Women have reported improved feelings of self-worth and a sense of increased agency. They have secured ownership over household assets and acquired financial management skills. There is also evidence that participation in microfinance increases mobility, trust, social capital and women's ability to organize for positive community change. As an example, in Sanyal's research, groups of women that had come together via microfinance began intervening to stop domestic violence and underage marriages. Increased social capital for women can thus lead to positive outcomes for the whole community, in addition to the benefits of generosity, a safety net and mutual support for the women microfinance clients themselves. A big caveat is necessary for all these findings, however: most of these qualitative studies focus on individual programmes in particular places, and have been criticized for their generalizability to other programmes in other places. This means that conclusions about empowering effects for microfinance may be too highly contextualized, or insufficiently rigorous, to enable us to say broadly and definitively that microfinance does empower.

In fact, according to quantitative and more generalizable evidence, microfinance does not consistently empower women. One reason is that though a woman may be the microfinance client, she may not actually end up controlling the money she receives (whether as a loan or as income from her enterprise). In various studies, women attained only limited control over household finances. Women in Bangladesh, for instance, often gave their loans to their male relatives, assuming the debt but not the ability to decide how the money gets spent (Karim 2011; see also Goetz and Sen Gupta 1996, Banerjee *et al*. 2013). According to some researchers, women can even be disempowered by microfinance. Karim (2011) argues that credit makes women more dependent on men, exposes them to shaming and dishonour if they don't repay, and puts them into debt. Evidence from one study even found that women microfinance clients suffered increased violence from the men in their lives (Schuler, Hashemi and Badal 1998). The solidarity group lending model can also potentially have negative effects. Such groups can exclude new entrants, stifle innovation ('this is how we have always done it'), and exclude women along ethnic, political, religious and other types of difference (Mayoux 2001).

As with the qualitative research mentioned above, here too a caveat is necessary. In large-n, quantitative studies, a likely reason that empowering effects of microfinance have not consistently appeared is because of the research design. Few studies have been able to isolate when empowerment effects are due to the microfinance programme itself, or due to other aspects of the programme (such as education for literacy, numeracy, or about gender norms). Even when women do attain increased spending capacity, that does not necessarily mean increased ability to chart the future, to participate in decisions that affect their bodies and lives, and to work at the community or collective level towards mutual goals.

What then to conclude from this debate? Think of microfinance's empowerment potential in terms of capabilities. It is certainly conceivable that microfinance could enhance a woman's capabilities, for instance by increasing her income, raising her social status or strengthening her decision-making power. All three of these areas could support a woman's capability to live a life that she values. Microfinance programmes have the potential to contribute to valuable freedoms, to empower women to have greater agency. However, there is no really rigorous, generalizable evidence that microfinance programmes consistently do so. (Tseng 2011; see also Lewis 2004, Selinger 2009) They may do so in some cases, but even then it is not clear that the empowering effects come from the actual financial services of the programme (the loan, micro-savings and/or insurance) or the non-financial services such as training or programming related to other community needs such as health or women's rights. In reality, the empowerment effects most probably come from the non-financial aspects, such as increased access to training, attention to gender issues, health and hygiene, all of which are more likely to help women address the challenges they and their communities face.

Earlier in this chapter we read about Francisca and her market stall in El Salvador. For her, there was no business training, technical assistance or attention to social issues affecting the loan clients. Low-interest loans can help some clients increase income simply by cutting the amount they pay for loans from moneylenders, but Francisca had difficulties at home in terms of an abusive partner and a community plagued by gang violence. The loan helped Francisca get out of the vicious cycle of the moneylenders, but she still cannot read or write, nor was she empowered to address the domestic or community challenges. For reasons such as these, microfinance programmes ought to emphasize the 'credit-plus' model, with specific gender-focused programmes to promote human development. Many players in the microfinance sector have recognized this concern. As one example, Global Partnerships, a Seattle-based NGO, raises money for investment in credit-plus MFIs in Latin America, to offer both training and credit to support long-term empowerment and sustainable development in the region.

A last facet of the empowerment issue is that borrowers may very well not escape from the moneylenders or the indebtedness trap because they have the opportunity to take out multiple loans from different MFIs to pay off pending loans. Until the rise of microenterprise lending in the early 1990s, Salvadoran marketers, for example, could only turn to local moneylenders for their credit needs, but now they have many MFIs competing to give them loans. Yet, there are valid concerns that women have traded the trap of the moneylenders for the trap of microfinance, borrowing loans to repay loans. This is why other impact assessment questions are so important: are borrowers actually increasing profits and assets? Are they investing profits in their families or using loans to pay for shocks and then having to take out loans to repay the initial loan? Though these questions, too, are debated, a close look at the evidence will provide the most reliable answers.

Microfinance's impacts at the micro and macro levels

Research about the impacts of microfinance programmes has evolved significantly over the last three decades. It has moved from analysing the financial performance of MFIs and sharing anecdotes of clients' success stories to more systematic quantitative and qualitative research strategies which attempt to measure whether microfinance efforts increased the incomes and capabilities of participants. Contradictory conclusions about the impact of programmes often stem from different research methodologies as well as different time, geographic and cultural settings where studies have been carried out. There is a growing application, though, of large-n quantitative methods using randomized controlled trials. These studies measure whether clients have increased their income, business and assets by comparing their progress to a control group of similar standing who did not receive loans. The Poverty Action Lab at the Massachusetts Institute of Technology was one of the first to carry out this kind of research for microfinance. In 2005, researchers began a baseline study in 104 marginalized neighbourhoods in Hyderabad, India and then the Indian MFI, Spandana, formed lending groups and dispersed loans to eligible women in 52 of the 104 neighbourhoods (Banerjee *et al.* 2013). After 12 to 18 months, researchers resurveyed households across the 104 neighbourhoods to see if there were differences between the credit-receiving neighbourhoods and the control neighbourhoods.

What did they find? According to this influential study, the positive effects of microfinance are modest at best. There was no rise in overall average monthly expenditures for the microcredit neighbourhoods, but there was an increase in expenditures on durable goods – assets such as refrigerators, televisions, carts, sewing machines etc. – and new businesses increased by one-third. Such findings contrast with the many inspiring stories one hears from more anecdotal, qualitative studies. Ultimately, the different methods, and the sometimes contradictory findings, mean we must become educated interpreters of data. What is being compared? What indicators are used to make comparisons? What are the cultural mores that could influence how borrowers use their loans? How honestly will the borrower participate in a survey or a conversation when interviewed by a local researcher or foreigner? Keeping these questions in mind, we will carefully survey the research on micro- and macro-level impacts, with a focus on capabilities. Micro-level impacts refer to the effects on individuals and families. This is where, according to the theory behind microfinance, we would expect to see the strongest effects in poverty reduction and enhancement of capabilities.

In reality, microfinance's theoretical positive effects are only sporadically confirmed: impacts tend to be mixed. Sometimes microfinance does lead to business creation or growth, but it does not consistently lead to increased or 'smoother' consumption (see i.a. Dichter 2006, Chowdhury 2009, Bateman 2011, Milana and Ashta 2012, Banerjee 2013). A few of the studies that Van Rooyen et al. (2012) deem most rigorous do find that microfinance increased incomes, but many of the studies they examine reject that finding, and one even found that microfinance decreased incomes in some cases. On the other hand, micro-savings do sometimes have positive economic effects by helping poor people increase their assets (Barnes et al. 2001a, Adjei et al. 2009). This evidence is promising because micro-savings does not come with the freedom-reducing potential downside of debt and the harsh consequences of default. Micro-savings may not boost people's incomes or consumption in the short term in the way a microloan can, but there is evidence that micro-savings may actually contribute more to developing microenterprises than microloans do (Dupas and Robinson 2009). Microfinance has also in a number of cases helped families to have more secure housing. People became more likely to own their home, to make improvements to it, and even to acquire rental units for additional income (Barnes et al. 2001a, Lacalle Calderón et al. 2008, Brannen 2010). This means that microfinance has supported the capability to have secure shelter.

Another area of generally positive impact is health, where several reliable studies have found that microfinance strengthens capabilities. When coupled with education and training on health practices, microfinance programmes reduced the incidence of diarrhoea and encouraged the use of mosquito nets and contraception. People in these programmes also saw reductions in the amount of days they were unable to work due to sickness, and the total number of episodes of sickness (Van Rooyen 2012). Similarly, there is evidence that microfinance programmes can support improved food quality and nutrition, though the research consensus is not strong here. For example, in Tanzania and Rwanda, microfinance clients saw increases in meal quality, and in Zimbabwe the poorest clients began consuming more nutritious food (Barnes et al. 2001b, Lacalle Calderón et al. 2008, Brannen 2010). A key reason for improvements in health and nutrition is that microfinance can (though it does not always) lead to increased control for women over household expenditures (Duflo 2003).

In contrast, microfinance programmes do not appear consistently to promote human development in the area of education. The research actually shows contradictory impacts. Sometimes microfinance is associated with higher household expenditure on education and increased school enrolment for children. In other cases or countries, however, those positive effects are absent. Sometimes, in fact, microfinance has negative impacts on education. In both Malawi and Uganda, for example, children's school attendance declined: boys had to repeat primary grades, fewer girls entered school, and families were unable to pay their school fees (Barnes *et al.* 2001a, Shimamura and Lastarria-Cornhiel 2010). There are even some suggestions that microfinance contributed to a higher incidence of child labour as families put their children to work in the family business (Tseng 2011).

Turning to the macro level, most of the research cited above focuses solely on the impact of the loans on individual clients; relatively fewer studies examine the macroeconomic impact of the programmes. At first, this could be explained by the fact that many microfinance efforts were restricted to target areas of individual non-governmental organizations. However, sometimes participative development plans in which loan clients, MFIs and municipal councils work together to increase local economic activity can lead to economic growth for the municipality (Cosgrove 2002). As an illustration, for the municipality of Nejapa (a 30 minute trip from the capital of San Salvador), microfinance tied to infrastructure development was a successful strategy for catalysing the local economy. Wary of the motives of the Salvadoran private sector and international companies, the mayor of Nejapa concentrated economic development planning on local production – agriculture, animal husbandry, petty commodity production and the buying and selling of products by local people. As marketers strengthened their businesses with microcredit and technical assistance, the municipal government designed and built a new market building for them. Now, Nejapa is a destination for those seeking *pupusas* and other traditional dishes at lunch time and on national holidays.

This research points to the potential for municipal-level impacts of successful microfinance models, though its small scale limits its generalizability. Other researchers have examined impacts at the regional level since many formal banks and other commercial lenders have joined NGOs in the field of microfinance. This is what Nargiza Maksudova (2010) calls integration with national financial systems. Because the microfinance industry is no longer a marginal actor, can it act as a 'locomotive for economic growth'? (ibid: 5). In a number of countries, Maksudova saw a positive relationship between microfinance and economic growth, but this trend decreases when there is credit saturation, i.e. competition between MFIs for clients.

Maksudova's research raises another important macro question, namely who is actually benefiting from microfinance. Globally, MFIs show an increase in loan amounts but not new clients. This means that instead of reaching out to the traditionally 'unbankable', efforts are focused on growing businesses that are already doing well. If this is the case, then how many people have been lifted out of poverty? Is microfinance really responding to the voices, concerns and hopes of the poor? In a study about the impact of microfinance in Bolivia, Mosley (2001) argues that yes, income increased for clients, and in fact, between 10 and 20 per cent of clients surveyed passed over the poverty line. Nonetheless, he acknowledges that those in extreme poverty, especially the rural poor, did not have access to credit. This claim – that the poorest of the poor are getting left out of the potential benefits of microfinance – has been corroborated by Karim (2011), who notes that in Bangladesh MFIs are increasingly targeting middle-class borrowers with a better chance of repayment than women in extreme poverty.

Looking over all of this evidence, what are the key takeaways? Microfinance *can* have positive effects in boosting incomes, supporting entrepreneurship, acquiring durable goods, smoothing consumption, improving health and helping people have more sustainable livelihoods (Terberger 2013). All of these things can help expand people's freedoms, contributing to economic and human development at the national and household levels, and supporting capabilities at the individual level. However, relatively few of the microfinance programmes analysed around the world reliably do have these effects. Microfinance does not typically help the poorest of the poor. Nor is micro-savings in itself a sufficient strategy to reduce poverty: how could poor people save if their incomes don't adequately cover consumption to begin with? And microfinance does sometimes have negative impacts, whether through encouraging deeper debts or reduced expenditures on education (Barnes *et al.* 2001a; Waelde 2011).

As one further element in this mixed bag, remember that microfinance does appear to have respectable macro effects, contributing to a society's financial system in a variety of ways that go beyond poverty reduction. MFIs can help small and medium-sized enterprises that previously had limited access to banking services, and the mushroom-like growth of MFIs worldwide has provided jobs and professional financial training for many employees. Should then microfinance be pursued as a poverty reduction strategy? The answer is yes, but programmes must be carefully adapted to their societal context and have realistic expectations. They should also be transparent, flexible and rigorously evaluated, and they must be designed to minimize harm. These recommendations obviously apply to any poverty reduction programme. Additional financial services and credit-plus programmes do have the most potential to enhance people's capabilities through trainings, health interventions and a conscious focus on multiple aspects of empowerment for women. Ultimately, what may help the poor more than loans is cash grants or conditional cash transfers. (See Fiszbein *et al.* 2009 and the discussion of CCTs in this book's Chapter 9 on education.)

Conclusion

Microfinance's potential is more limited than its most ardent admirers would like to believe. It is certainly not ineffective, but its objectives must be realistic: if development efforts seek to promote increased capabilities and functionings for all, microfinance can play a role, but those efforts must address the structural roots of poverty and lack of social protections for the most vulnerable in society. This requires integrated, participative community development as well as community, municipal and state funding. It requires participative development planning with a gender perspective and awareness about how other forms of social difference exclude people. Poor people in developing countries, especially women and those marginalized by ethnicity, religion, geographic location and class, face a rough road to reach empowerment. Income generation can be a piece of that project, but so is eradicating discriminatory practices and endemic structures that keep people and their communities in poverty. Microfinance can help women and their families increase income, savings and assets, but unless they have control over how their increased income gets spent, and their empowerment is part of an integrated plan of human development, these achievements will only help them get by, surviving from one day to the next. Increased survival chances are a good thing, but empowerment means being able to make choices over one's life and contributions to one's community.

Even if microfinance does not always live up to its inspiring reputation as a means of poverty reduction, it does have a lot to teach us about the development sector more broadly. It shows how ideologies play into poverty reduction strategies. Microfinance has a particular appeal to those who believe in the bootstrap ideology of giving individuals the economic tools to lift themselves out of poverty. Microfinance also shows how rigorous evaluation methods have been introduced through research using randomized controlled trials and produced more conclusive evidence for impacts. In this sense it is a test case for the push towards more intensive assessment of development programme outcomes. However, microfinance also shows how conflicts over evaluation methodology can play out, namely through disputes over the relative limitations and strengths of qualitative and quantitative evidence that pit individual empowerment stories on the one hand against large-n, quantitative studies on the other.

The debates around microfinance also point to larger conflicts over what really matters in poverty reduction: is it increasing incomes, empowerment however defined, improving health or education, or securing basic capabilities? These goals are not mutually exclusive, but which to emphasize does involve hard choices. Making those hard choices requires a systematic, careful study of what clients or participants want, what works, as well as transparency in methodology, epistemology and ideology. The sometimes inconclusive results of such research illustrate the need for caution even with the question of 'what works to reduce poverty'. What works in some cases may not work in others. Similarly, programmes may work according to some definitions of success but not others – and those definitions can again depend on the goals and the stakeholders. There is no one-size-fits-all poverty reduction strategy, as we emphasize throughout this book.

Microfinance and its associated debates remind us that poverty reduction is hard, contentious, riven by competing interests and rarely clear-cut. In the end, a fundamental question to ask is whom anti-poverty programmes such as microfinance actually help. It can happen – and has sometimes happened, in the case of microfinance – that big players have become involved, and their interests have eclipsed the interests and priorities of poor people. Nonetheless, the lives of poor people must always remain in the foreground, and poverty reduction should focus on helping the poor to have a life that they value. Francisca in El Salvador, and Mary and Alice in Ghana, all see some value in microfinance. But each of them would also say that microloans and other financial services are only one small part of ending poverty in their communities.

Discussion questions

1   In what areas (income, consumption, education, health, etc.) does microfinance have the most consistently positive effects? In what areas does it have few consistently positive effects, or actually cause harm?

2   What might be the circumstances when a microfinance programme would not be appropriate for a given situation or group of people?

3   How would you define 'empowerment' for a marketwoman or microentrepreneur in the developing world? For a small business owner in a high-income country? For yourself? How do capabilities considerations play into your definitions?

4   What do you see as the pros and cons of having local, non-governmental organizations manage microfinance programmes versus government agencies or for-profit companies?

5   If you were to carry out a research project to measure the impact of a microfinance programme, what indicators would you choose to measure, what kinds of research methods would you use, and why?

6   Microfinance activity: depending on the size of the group, divide into three sub-groups (a credit committee, a communal bank group comprised of individual microentrepreneurs seeking loans, and an outside assessment team). Let the entire group know the total amount available for loans and the maximum amount for an individual loan. Then, give each sub-group 15 minutes to prepare. The credit committee will need to agree on what criteria are necessary to make a loan. The members of the communal bank group will select their individual business ideas and ideal loan amounts based on their real experiences and skills. The outside assessment team will consider what indicators would need to be assessed to measure the effectiveness of increasing income for college students. For the next 15 minutes, the different potential members of the communal bank will present on their proposed business ideas and credit needs. Then the credit committee will interview the potential communal bank members: weeding out risky investments and announcing loans. The members of the assessment group will comment on the challenges of assessing the impact of the loans.

Further reading

Banerjee, Abhijit, and Esther Duflo. 2012. *Poor Economics: A radical rethinking of the way to fight global poverty*. Philadelphia, PA: Public Affairs.

Bornstein, David. 1996. *The Price of a Dream: The story of the Grameen Bank and the idea that is helping the poor to change their lives*. New York, NY: Simon & Schuster.

Collins, Daryl, Jonathan Morduch, Stuart Rutherford and Orlanda Ruthven. 2009. *Portfolios of the Poor: How the world's poor live on $2 a day*. Princeton, NJ: Princeton University Press.

Robinson, Marguerite. 2001. *The Microfinance Revolution: Sustainable finance for the poor*. Washington DC: World Bank.

Yunus, Muhammad. 1999. *Banker to the Poor*. New York, NY: Public Affairs.

Works cited

Adjei, Joseph Kimos, Thankom Arun and Farhad Hossain. 'The Role of Microfinance in Asset-Building and Poverty Reduction: The Case of Sinapi Aba Trust of Ghana.' University of Manchester. (2009).

Banerjee, Abhijit Vinayak. 'Microcredit under the microscope: what have we learned in the past two decades, and what do we need to know?' *Annual Review of Economics*, 5.1 (2013): 487–519.

Banerjee, Abhijit, Esther Duflo, Rachel Glennester and Cynthia Kinnan. 'The miracle of microfinance? Evidence from a randomized evaluation.' National Bureau of Economic Research Working Paper 13–09, April 2013.

Barnes, Carolyn, Gary Gaile and Richard Kibombo. 'The impact of three microfinance programs in Uganda.' Development Experience Clearinghouse, USAID, Washington, DC (2001a).

Barnes, Carolyn, Erica Keogh and Nontokozo Nemarundwe. 'Microfinance program clients and impact: An assessment of Zambuko Trust, Zimbabwe.' Washington, DC: Management Systems International (2001b).

Bateman, Milford. 'Microfinance as a development and poverty reduction policy: is it everything it's cracked up to be?' Overseas Development Institute Background Note, March 2011.

Boomgard, James J., and Kenneth J. Angell. 1994. 'Bank Rakyat Indonesia's Unit Desa System: Achievements and Replicability', in María Otero and Elisabeth Rhyne, eds., *The New World of Micro-Enterprise Finance: Building healthy financial institutions for the poor*. West Hartford, CT: Kumarian Press. 206–228.

Brannen, Conner. 2010. *An impact study of the Village Savings and Loan Association (VSLA) program in Zanzibar, Tanzania*. Diss. Wesleyan University.

Chowdhury, Anis. 'Microfinance as a poverty reduction tool-a critical assessment.' United Nations, Department of Economic and Social Affairs (DESA) working paper 89 (2009).

Cosgrove, Serena. 'Levels of empowerment: marketers and microenterprise-lending NGOs in Apopa and Nejapa, El Salvador.' *Latin American Perspectives*, 29.5 (2002): 48–65.

Cosgrove, Serena. 1999a. *Give them the credit they deserve: Marketwomen and the impact of microenterprise lending in the municipalities of Apopa and Nejapa, El Salvador*. PhD Dissertation, Northeastern University.

Cosgrove, Serena. 1999b. 'Engendering Finance: A Comparison of Two Micro-Finance Models in El Salvador', in Kavita Datta and Gareth Jones, eds., *Housing, Finance, and Gender in Developing Countries*. London: Routledge.

Dichter, Thomas. 'Hype and hope: the worrisome state of the microcredit movement.' *The Microfinance Gateway* (2006). Prepared by the QED Group, LLC, and International Resources Group for review by the United States Agency for International Development.

Duflo, Esther. 'Grandmothers and granddaughters: old-age pensions and intrahousehold allocation in South Africa.' *The World Bank Economic Review*, 17.1 (2003): 1–25.

Dupas, Pascaline, and Jonathan Robinson. 'Savings constraints and microenterprise development: evidence from a field experiment in Kenya.' No. w14693. National Bureau of Economic Research, 2009.

Duvendack, Maren, Richard Palmer-Jones, James G. Copestake, Lee Hooper, Yoon Loke and Nitya Rao. 'What is the evidence of the impact of microfinance on the well-being of poor people?' London: EPPI-Centre, Social Science Research Unit, Institute of Education, University of London, 2011.

Fiszbein, Ariel, Norbert Rüdiger Schady and Francisco H. G. Ferreira. 2009. *Conditional Cash Transfers: Reducing present and future poverty*. Washington, DC: World Bank.

Gilardone, Muriel, Isabelle Guérin and Jane Palier. 'The weight of institutions on women's capabilities: how far can microfinance help?', in Flavio Comim and Martha C. Nussbaum, eds. 2014. *Capabilities, Gender, Equality: Towards fundamental entitlements*. Cambridge: Cambridge University Press.

Goetz, Anne Marie, and Rina Sen Gupta. 'Who takes the credit? Gender, power, and control over loan use in rural credit programs in Bangladesh.' *World Development*, 24.1 (1996): 45–63.

Grameen Bank, Historical Data from June 2015, www.grameen-info.org/monthly-reports-06–2015/, accessed June 2015.

Isserles, Robin. 'Microcredit: the rhetoric of empowerment, the reality of "development as usual".' *Women's Studies Quarterly*, 31.3/4 (2003): 38–57.

Karlan, Dean, and Martin Valdivia. 'Teaching entrepreneurship: impact of business training on microfinance clients and institutions'. *The Review of Economics and Statistics* 93.2 (2011): 510–527.

Karim, Lamia. 2011. *Microfinance and its Discontents: Women in debt in Bangladesh*. Minneapolis, MN: University of Minnesota Press.

Lacalle Calderón, Maricruz, Silvia Rico Garrido and Jaime Durán Navarro. 'Estudio piloto de evaluación de impacto del programa de microcréditos de Cruz Roja Española en Ruanda.' *Revista de Economía Mundial*, 19 (2008): 83–104.

Le, Quan, and Peter Raven. 'Teaching business skills to women: impact of business training on women's microenterprise owners in Vietnam.' *International Journal of Entrepreneurial Behavior and Research*, 21.4 (2015).

Lewis, Cindy. 'Microfinance from the point of view of women with disabilities: lessons from Zambia and Zimbabwe.' *Gender and Development*, 12.1 (2004): 28–39.

MacFarquhar, Neil. 2010. 'Banks Making Big Profits from Tiny Loans.' *The New York Times*, 3 April 2010.

Maksudova, Nargiza. 2010. 'Macroeconomics of Microfinance: How Do the Channels Work?' (October 1, 2010). CERGE-EI Working Paper Series No. 423. Available at SSRN: http://ssrn.com/abstract= 1699982, accessed 28 November 2010.

Mayoux, Linda. 'Tackling the down side: social capital, women's empowerment and micro-finance in Cameroon.' *Development and Change*, 32.3 (2001): 435–464.

Milana, Carlo, and Arvind Ashta. 'Developing microfinance: a survey of the literature.' *Strategic Change*, 21.7–8 (2012): 299–330.

Moser, Caroline. 1993. *Gender Planning and Development*. London: Routledge.

Mosley, Paul. 'Microfinance and poverty in Bolivia.' *The Journal of Development Studies*, 37.4 (2001): 101–132.

Roodman, David. 2012. *Due Diligence: An impertinent inquiry into microfinance*. Washington, DC: Center for Global Development.

Sanyal, Paromita. 'From credit to collective action: the role of microfinance in promoting women's social capital and normative influence.' *American Sociological Review*, 74.4 (2009): 529–550.

Schuler, Sidney Ruth, Syed M. Hashemi and Shamsul Huda Badal. 'Men's violence against women in rural Bangladesh: undermined or exacerbated by microcredit programmes?' *Development in Practice*, 8.2 (1998): 148–157.

Selinger, Evan. 'Does Microcredit 'Empower'? Reflections on the Grameen Bank Debate.' *Human Studies*, 31.1 (2009): 27–41.

Shimamura, Yasuharu, and Susana Lastarria-Cornhiel. 'Credit program participation and child schooling in rural Malawi.' *World Development*, 38.4 (2010): 567–580.

Terberger, Eva. 'The Microfinance Approach: Does It Deliver on Its Promise?', in Doris Köhn, ed. 2013. *Microfinance 3.0. Reconciling Sustainability with Social Outreach and Responsible Delivery*. Heidelberg: Springer.

Tseng, Chuan Chia. 2011. *Microfinance and Amartya Sen's capability approach*. Diss. University of Birmingham.

Van Rooyen, Carina, Ruth Stewart and Thea de Wet. 'The impact of microfinance in sub-Saharan Africa: a systematic review of the evidence.' *World Development*, 40.11 (2012): 2249–2262.

Waelde, Helke. 'Demasking the impact of microfinance', Gutenberg School of Management and Economics, University of Mainz, Germany: manuscript available at www.macro.economics.uni-mainz.de/RePEc/pdf/Discussion_Paper_1115.pdf, accessed 3 October 2016.

Yunus, Muhammad. 1999. *Banker to the Poor*. New York, NY: Public Affairs.

Zeller, Manfred, and Manohar Sharma. 'Many borrow, more save, and all insure: implications for food and micro-finance policy.' *Food Policy*, 25.2 (2000): 143–167.

12 Conclusion

Ethics and action – what should you do about global poverty?

Benjamin Curtis and Serena Cosgrove

Key questions

- What are some important ethical principles in relation to reducing poverty?
- What are some prominent arguments for why we should or should not work to reduce poverty?
- What are some concrete actions you can take to fight poverty at home and abroad?

Introduction

If you are reading this book, you are most likely privileged and probably live in a high-income country. You hopefully have never experienced the deprivations of basic capabilities that constitute absolute poverty. But what kind of world would you want to live in if you *didn't* have a comfortable life? What would you think the world's moral obligations towards those living in poverty should be if you yourself were poor? The philosopher John Rawls (1999) famously proposed that we should evaluate standards of justice from the perspective of a 'veil of ignorance'. This perspective asks us to consider what kind of society we would want to be born into if we didn't know what kinds of advantages we would have. If you didn't know what your class, race, gender, sexual orientation, disability status and income were going to be, then what societal arrangements would you insist on? How would you want rights and resources to be distributed?

Though the veil of ignorance test is typically applied to think about what justice might look like in a particular society, it can also fruitfully be applied on a worldwide level to consider standards of global justice. It can be too easy for people living in rich countries to disregard the ethical implications of poverty. If I have enough to eat, decent health, a middle-class income and secure civil rights, how likely am I genuinely to sympathize with the plight of people who don't have those things? Because if we live comfortably we may be ignorant or dismissive of the needs of the poor, we need to think very carefully about our ethical duties in this world with widespread poverty and massive inequities. This topic has for decades provoked debates among philosophers, politicians and development professionals. The debates, however, are not purely theoretical. They have a direct relevance to all sorts of poverty reduction policies, whether to alleviate a famine, to end a genocide, to intervene in a war or to pursue projects that may alter a way of life.

It is essential to think through issues such as the veil of ignorance: considering how to reduce poverty also requires considering ethics. This book is in fact founded upon a sometimes implicit, sometimes explicit ethics. Though we of course think that it is imperative that everyone who reads this book – and everyone around the world – should work to reduce poverty, that basic position is actually rather simplistic. There are so many questions underlying that position, questions such as: What do we owe people at a minimum? What do we owe people *beyond* the minimum? Who is the 'we' that owes? When do we stop owing – is it when people have attained sufficiency or equality, and if so, of what? Of outcomes or opportunities? Such questions are considered in depth by development ethics, a subfield of development studies. Here we will examine only a few provocative issues and thinkers in this subfield, and provide few definitive answers, so further investigation is certainly warranted (see i.a. Gasper 2004, Crocker 2008, Gasper and St. Clair 2010). The chapter begins with an analysis of a number of ethical principles relevant to poverty reduction, then examines several debates about what individual and global ethical obligations should be. Finally, the chapter translates principles into action, suggesting what you personally can do to help reduce poverty.

Ethical principles

Though development ethics is vital for helping to think through why and how we should work to reduce poverty, it does not always provide easy answers. Some of the answers, including a few we consider in this section, are challenging. But that is to be expected when the questions are themselves very difficult. One text on development ethics actually defines the field in terms of the questions it asks: development ethics 'seeks to engage in debates around basic ethical questions: what are the costs of change and who bears them? How can we decide when costs are outweighed by gains? Who has the right to intervene, by what procedures, and to promote what ends? What is social improvement? What fundamental changes are desirable or undesirable?' (Penz, Drydyk and Bose 2011: 36). Do not expect that any one of those questions will have a single right answer – what is 'right' in any given situation may sometimes depend on the situation. However, some general principles should guide thinking on those questions. According to Penz *et al.*, 'ethically responsible development' depends on seven essential values: human wellbeing and human security, equitable development, empowerment, cultural freedom (such as with the rights of indigenous peoples), environmental sustainability, human rights and anti-corruption practices. These values have guided many of the topics and much of the discussion in this book, and we have explored their application to most of the poverty reduction programmes we have highlighted.

However, these values are admittedly broad, and by no means exhaustive. An ethical consideration of the rationale for reducing poverty must plumb deeper to some basic principles of ethical action. We must ask, why do most people in high-income countries not care very much about the wellbeing of children in low-income countries? Even more starkly, why do most people in high-income countries put less value on the lives of children in low-income countries? It is difficult to deny that this is the normal state of affairs. According to UNICEF statistics, some 19,000 children die every day from causes related to poverty, which translates to 13 children every minute. Why are more people not outraged by that fact? Were you aware of that number before you read this book? If you weren't, then why not? If you read that statistic now and don't resolve to do something about it, why not? One simple answer to these questions is that it's often hard to care about people you don't know. We tend to feel few or no obligations to faceless people. This is a deeply rooted psychological reason for why more people are not outraged by the statistics on child mortality.

There is a more powerful reason, however, which relates to ethics: most people don't regard human lives as equal. Most people will regard the lives of children in their immediate community as more worth saving than the life of a child in some far-off, poverty-stricken country, with all the stereotypes that image provokes. Therefore, a bedrock ethical principle in relation to poverty is that all people truly are equal, that their lives have equal value; call this 'humanist egalitarianism' (Gilabert 2012: 9). An ethical global citizen recognizes the humanity of all people around the world, and acknowledges the implications of equally valuing all humans' lives. One of those implications is that principles of global justice extend across humanity and bind all people to certain responsibilities (Nagel 2005). Where there is injustice, where there are people whose lives are being threatened by extreme poverty, then those who can help must help. This global, moral responsibility to help people who are suffering can be motivated by two further principles: assistance and restitution. The assistance principle insists that because wealthier people around the world have the means, and poor people around the world have the need, the wealthy have a duty to help the poor (see Chatterjee 2004, Barry and Øverland 2009). The restitution principle asserts that wealthier people are actually doing things that harm poor people and exacerbate poverty, and therefore they have a duty to help those in need. The rationale and application of both these principles will be explored in greater detail below.

Global justice, whether impelled by the assistance or restitution principles, demands an effort to reduce poverty. In order for that effort to be ethical, in turn, it must involve three more principles: solidarity, non-elite participation, and decent sufficiency for all. These three principles were espoused by Dennis Goulet (2006), one of the founders of development ethics; they have also threaded throughout this entire book, and continue to play out in the discussion which follows. Solidarity begins by recognizing the equal value of all human lives, proceeding from there to acknowledge the obligation, per the assistance principle, that those who are better off must help those who are worse off. Practicing true solidarity, however, entails a genuine and possibly difficult commitment on the part of those who are well off. It means 'institutionalizing the principle that the world's wealth belongs to all its inhabitants, on the basis of priority needs, not on geographical accident or on different technological abilities to extract or exploit resources that some groups enjoy over others' (Goulet 2006: 166–167). This amounts to a redistribution of global resources, such that those in rich countries may have to give up some of their luxuries to ensure that the poor have equitable access to food, education, health care and other basic entitlements. The implication of this principle is that rich countries, and the people in those countries, may have to go on an austerity diet: we may have to accept reductions in our standard of living in order to raise the standard for the poor.

The next of Goulet's principles, 'non-elite participation', means that reducing poverty involves empowering poor people. Poor people must be empowered not just to help guide development projects. They must be empowered to make decisions for their own societies, families and bodies; they must be fully empowered so that they can choose a life that they have reason to value. Recall that one of the definitions of poverty is lacking that power in certain key areas. It follows, then, that a fundamental ethical principle is that poor people participate in efforts to address their own poverty. The poor must never be mere objects of poverty reduction policies: they must be *subjects* in those policies, with their own agency and voice included. Finally, 'decent sufficiency' entails that everyone will have equitable access to the resources that can ensure human wellbeing such as food, shelter, medicine, etc. This principle entails not just a minimum threshold of resources so that no one is poor – it also entails a minimum threshold of rights and/or capabilities. A world where everyone has enough of the resources essential for a dignified human life is a world where no one is denied basic capabilities to live the life they choose. It is also a world, in Goulet's framing, that will live more sustainably, so that resources and opportunities will be adequately guaranteed not just for this generation but for future ones as well.

These principles ground the fundamental claim that people in poverty must be assisted, that injustice must be righted. How, though, should justice and injustice be defined? One powerful way is via human rights. International humanitarian law and the Universal Declaration of Human Rights lay out the different civil, political, social, cultural and economic rights to which all people are entitled. These include familiar civil and political rights such as the freedoms of speech and assembly, prohibitions against torture, and the right to vote. As we mentioned in Chapter 1 and have suggested throughout this book, there are other guarantees besides, including rights to education, shelter, health care and access to employment. When countries sign the international treaties framing human rights and join the United Nations (which has certain human rights guarantees as part of its charter), they are obligated to respect and protect those rights within their own boundaries. Human rights thus involve a substantial body of agreed-upon norms as well as various international institutions to promote those rights (Nickel 2007). Ensuring that everyone enjoys the 'decent sufficiency' of basic human rights is a vital way of defining global justice.

Human rights are not merely legal provisions, however, nor do the relevant obligations fall solely on countries. Human rights have a moral force beyond any formal legal commitments. This goes back to the idea of the fundamental equality of all human beings. Basic morality insists that we not torture, that we not let people starve, that we not deprive them of political agency, dignity or the possibilities of earning a livelihood. Because of this inherent moral force of human rights, individuals have a duty to respect and protect them. Thus a just society, and a just person, works to uphold human rights – and injustice means violating those rights. In many ways, as this book has argued, poverty violates basic human rights. Therefore, we *all* have a duty to fight poverty.

Debates about ethical obligations

It might seem easy to acknowledge that duty in an abstract, non-committal way: sure, extreme poverty and gross inequality are deplorable, and we should do something about them. But the admonishment to 'do something' is far too vague. We need to move beyond lazy slogans. Anyone reading this book should aspire to think more deeply about both their obligations to reduce poverty and the actions they can take to that end. Thinking more deeply requires considering arguments and counter-arguments about those obligations. This section surveys several relevant debates without, however, offering final adjudications on which perspectives are 'right'. Though some arguments here are stronger than others, readers should think through their own evaluation of the contending perspectives.

To begin with, Peter Singer (2009) has posed a famous thought problem about a drowning toddler which forces us to interrogate our commitment to the ethic of assistance. This is the scenario: you have just bought a pair of very expensive, very nice shoes, and you are out for a walk in the park. You come across a toddler drowning in a pond, and you are the only person around who can save the child. Getting to him in time means you run into the water and ruin your new shoes. Probably everyone will say yes, they would save the toddler rather than their new shoes. That in fact is the morally justifiable answer. However, Singer claims that almost everyone in the rich world every day chooses to save their shoes. His point is that for the amount of money we spend on a luxury item such as shoes, or a nice restaurant, or an expensive vacation, we could easily save a poor child's life. And yet very few of us will give up that vacation or new pair of shoes or fancy phone.

The fact that so many people in high-income countries shirk the ethic of assistance has led Singer to propose what he calls a Reasonable Standard of Giving (RSG). This standard calculates how much money you should give to reduce poverty, based on your total annual income. While most people in the rich world can afford to give something, Singer insists that the richest people need to give the most – and if they did, they could easily provide enough money to end extreme poverty around the world. For example, according to Singer's calculations, if the top 10 per cent of income earners in the United States gave away between a third to a tenth of their incomes (which would still leave most of them with a very comfortable standard of living), they could raise USD 404 billion. While it is easy for those who are not rich to claim that wealthy individuals need to pitch in more than they do, even those of moderate incomes are not off the hook. If we could skimp on some of the luxuries we enjoy in order to help the poor but we choose not to, then 'we are doing something wrong', Singer says (2009: 19). Singer's basic principle is that we have a duty to reduce suffering when we can do so at a minimal cost to ourselves.

If Singer's ideas compel us to consider more deeply our obligations to assist those in poverty, Thomas Pogge (2008) pushes even further with an argument relying on the restitution principle, which holds that we have a duty to reduce poverty because we are responsible for creating it. Pogge sees poverty as a human rights violation in which nearly everyone living in the rich world is complicit. As Pogge explains, 'we are *harming* the poor if and insofar as we collaborate in imposing an *unjust* global institutional order upon them. And this institutional order is definitely unjust if and insofar as it foreseeably perpetuates large-scale human rights deficits that would be reasonably avoidable through feasible institutional modifications' (Pogge 2005a: 5). Pogge's argument takes many of the basic statistics of poverty – which we have referred to throughout this book, and which include the estimate that 18 million people die a year because of poverty-related causes – as evidence of massive human rights violations. He claims that there are hundreds of millions of people who are being denied basic rights, living in conditions below what a fair, proportional distribution of resources among the world's population should be. Why do some have so much and others have so little? Pogge argues that a major reason is that global institutions have been designed to benefit the rich (which includes all of us who live in high-income countries) and disadvantage the poor.

Pogge bases his argument that the rich world has systematically impoverished the global south on several points. First, rich countries are rich in part because of massive historical injustices such as colonialism which demonstrably made many exploited parts of the world poorer, such as sub-Saharan Africa. Second, history aside, rich countries are harming poor people right now. They do so through the institutional economic order that reproduces the 'radical inequality' in the global distribution of resources (Pogge 2005a: 4). The rich countries largely control the World Trade Organization (WTO), which enforces protectionist trade barriers including tariffs, quotas, anti-dumping mandates, and subsidies to domestic producers that favour rich countries. WTO rules also limit poorer countries' access to drugs, software, seeds and biological technologies that could reduce poverty. Global institutions create trade relations disadvantageous to poor countries by compelling them to open up their markets to rich countries' exports, while doing much less to open rich countries' markets to poorer countries' exports.

In Pogge's view, the global economic order is structured through international negotiations 'in which our governments enjoy a crushing advantage in bargaining power and expertise' over poorer countries (Pogge 2007: 27). According to McNeill and St. Clair (2009), organizations such as the WTO and the World Bank actively resist arrangements more favourable to poorer countries because the powerful northern elite that controls those organizations wants to protect its own interests. Finally, Pogge alleges that the anti-democratic and corrupting effects of the resource curse are in large part the fault of rich countries. The economies of rich countries consume resources from poor countries, but payments for those resources rarely benefit the poorest people in low-income countries. Instead, payments typically just benefit the elite, and rich countries care very little whether rulers in those countries are democratic. Rulers in countries whose economies are highly dependent on natural resources often oppress their people, which in turn creates situations where the people have to resist with force, leading to armed conflict that exacerbates poverty.

We should not assume that only distant international institutions are guilty: the guilt also falls on us because we in the rich world are partly responsible for the policies that our national governments take. Pogge explains that 'the fact that we choose to remain ignorant, choose to allow important structural features of the world economy to be shaped by unknown bureaucrats in secret negotiations cannot negate our responsibility for the harms that our governments inflict upon the innocent' (Pogge 2005b: 79). Therefore, we have a duty to influence our national governments and to lobby international organizations to create a global institutional order that is more just for the poor. While we should work for institutions that do not violate human rights, we must also provide financial compensation for the harm we have caused. This means that governments in the global north should provide restitution to countries in the global south. Individuals, too, have a duty here. Pogge does not go as far as Singer in specifying the amounts that people must contribute, but he claims that it should be easy to raise the roughly USD 300 billion it would take to eradicate extreme poverty.

Pogge's perspective is certainly provocative, and not surprisingly it has attracted a fair amount of criticism (Vizard 2006, Schweickart 2008, Jaggar 2010). For example, critics retort that Pogge does not make a meaningful distinction between when global institutions actively harm the poor, or when they simply fail to reduce poverty adequately. The idea is that a failure to reduce poverty is not morally equivalent to actively causing poverty. Another criticism holds that Pogge puts too much blame on countries in the global north, failing to hold countries in the global south accountable for good governance. Pogge, though, explains that problem through the metaphor of a 'strong headwind' in which 'national policies and institutions are indeed often quite bad; but the fact that they are can be traced to global policies and institutions' (Pogge 2008:

149). As a last means of questioning this perspective, remember the debate on foreign aid in Chapter 2 on development and its debates. It is possible that the idea to raise USD 300 billion for poverty eradication is unrealistic because aid money may be spent inefficiently.

Some thinkers would counter Pogge by rejecting both the ethics of assistance and restitution. Among the most famous cases in development ethics is the debate Garrett Hardin waged in the 1970s with Peter Singer (among others) over 'lifeboat ethics'. Hardin (1974) insisted that we have a duty *not* to help the poor because doing so will only increase suffering. Hardin constructed a metaphor in which rich countries are like lifeboats, and swimming in the sea around the lifeboats, trying to get in, are the poor people of the world. What should the lifeboat passengers do in this situation? The way Hardin sets up the problem is to stipulate that the lifeboat can only carry 60 people, and it already has 50 people inside. There are a hundred people swimming in the sea. If you could only save ten of them, how would you choose which people to save? In Hardin's view, any choice you make will be problematic for all kinds of reasons. If you try to let too many people crowd onto your lifeboat, they will overwhelm the carrying capacity, and you will all drown. According to Hardin, the most defensible choice is to keep only the 50 people in the boat and let no more in, since that will give the best possibility for survival for those already in the boats. If you feel guilty about not helping those poor people swimming in the sea, then Hardin says you need to get out of the lifeboat: give up your place to one of the swimmers, and go swim yourself.

Hardin referred specifically to food aid, though his argument is relevant to poverty reduction efforts more generally. In his view, countries such as Bangladesh were overpopulated, and they needed to bring their populations down. Every new mouth to feed in countries with weak economies and high rates of population growth means that there are fewer resources for the people already alive. This assumes that available resources are not expanding quickly enough to meet the needs of the growing population. The growing population makes everyone's life worse, and therefore the population needs to stop growing. The famine that Bangladesh experienced in the 1970s would halt that growth, resulting in a population size the country could sustain. Aid would only worsen the situation by keeping people alive who would be dependent on handouts, which moreover could encourage poor people to continue having children, resulting in yet more mouths that they could not adequately feed. His conclusion was that rich countries should not undertake aid projects that only put further pressure on limited resources, thereby threatening to sink the existing lifeboats.

Hardin also denies the ethic of restitution by claiming that we don't have inter-generational obligations for past injustices. Even if our ancestors may have perpetrated colonialism, that does not mean that people today owe restitution. 'We are all the descendants of thieves', Hardin claims, and 'we cannot remake the past'. Given those facts, and that the world's resources have been fundamentally inequitably distributed, 'we must begin the journey to tomorrow from the point where we are today. [. . .] We cannot safely divide the wealth equitably among all peoples so long as people reproduce at different rates. To do so would guarantee that our grandchildren and everyone else's grandchildren would have only a ruined world to inhabit' (1974). Thus Hardin makes a surprising argument relating to sustainability: the wellbeing of future generations depends upon *not* helping the poor today. Since he wrote his essay on lifeboat ethics, some of Hardin's assumptions have been proven wrong. For instance,

Bangladesh's population is actually larger now than it was in the 1970s, yet it is not experiencing a famine.[1] Nonetheless, there are certainly still people, such as acolytes of the philosopher Ayn Rand, who insist that helping the poor simply makes them dependent, thereby perpetuating poverty. In this view, because charitable assistance can bring more harm than good, it is not a moral duty.

A final argument for action on global poverty has less to do with ethics than with self-interest. Paul Collier, for one, has argued that the wellbeing of people in rich countries is threatened by a situation in which nearly a billion people worldwide live in extreme poverty. The rich world is threatened by fragile states that can harbour terrorists, such as in Afghanistan; threatened by armed conflict that spills over borders, breeding destruction, political and economic instability; threatened by outbreaks of disease in countries lacking the resources to deal with them, such as Ebola in Sierra Leone; and threatened by massive population movements spurred by climate shocks, war or economic migration. The problem of global poverty matters, Collier writes, 'and not just to the billion people who are living and dying in fourteenth-century conditions. It matters to us. The twenty-first century world of material comfort, global travel, and economic interdependence will become increasingly vulnerable to these large islands of chaos' (Collier 2007: 4–5). According to this perspective, poverty, its discontents, and the bad institutions associated with it will increasingly put at risk even those of us living complacently in the rich world. Therefore, to help ourselves, we must help those in poverty.

What should you do?

Whether you find most compelling the arguments about the ethics of assistance or restitution, or the self-interest motivation, they all urge us to take action to reduce poverty. Indeed, libertarian or social Darwinist perspectives of Hardin's ilk notwithstanding, it is very difficult to deny the moral imperative to help people who are in extreme poverty. Is it not a basic humanitarian duty to aid those who are desperate? If you accept that we all have moral obligations here, then how can you do your part to reduce global poverty? There are actually many different things you can do, and some of them are easy enough that it is hard to justify doing nothing. Our list proceeds on a scale from a relatively simple engagement to actions that demand a deeper, ongoing commitment to promoting global justice. You should determine what you will do based on your own resources, values, aspirations and conscience.

Give money

This is the easiest, most common recommendation for helping to reduce poverty, and it is a reasonable place to start. Giving money to an organization working either in your home country or abroad is something that almost everyone can afford to do. For example, if a few times a week you go to Starbucks or eat out for lunch, consider skipping one of those times and putting the money aside to donate. Over a month, giving up one coffee a week will add up, and over a year, it could add up to a respectable donation. Peter Singer urges everyone to give *at least* 1 per cent of their annual net income to charities, though those with higher incomes should give more. The website www.thelifeyoucansave.org has a calculator for how much you should give to charity based on your income. Besides your individual giving, you can also form a

Box 12.1 Poverty and basic humanity

In Chapter 1, we promised to return to two fundamental questions in the Conclusion. The first was the question of what counts as the basic minimum capabilities necessary for an adequate human life. The second was the question of what it means to be a human living in poverty. Most of the chapters have considered these questions in one way or another, and though we would not pretend to arrive at conclusive answers to such big and fundamental issues, we can offer a few final thoughts.

If you have read all the preceding chapters, does it seem like there are, could be, or should be basic capabilities with minimum universal standards? Would it be possible for the world to agree upon such standards? It's possible that the answer is 'no', that ideas of an adequate human life simply differ too much from culture to culture, society to society, ever to allow for universal definitions. Note, however, that some universal standards *have* been adopted. Take the Universal Declaration on Human Rights, for instance: dozens of countries around the world have ratified the core provisions of this declaration, though there are indeed countries that have abstained or agreed to only some of the rights in the list. Nonetheless, the valorized body of international human rights law suggests substantial agreement on basic entitlements that no human being should be deprived of.

If human rights seem too abstract to serve as measures for poverty reduction, then consider the Millennium Development Goals and their successors, the Sustainable Development Goals. These detailed lists of very specific indicators have also been agreed upon by nearly all of the world's countries. This means, for example, that there is an effectively universal belief at the global level that everyone should attain a minimum of food consumption, that everyone should complete primary school, that all children should be able to be immunized against measles, that everyone who has HIV/AIDS should have access to treatment, and that everyone should have access to safe drinking water. The Multidimensional Poverty Index is another widely respected measurement tool based upon minimum thresholds, and it was directly inspired by ideas of fundamental entitlements that can support basic capabilities.

Inevitably there will be disputes about which capabilities are 'basic'. In many countries around the world, including the United States, there is disagreement about whether women should have reproductive rights including access to birth control and abortion. Certainly in practice many societies do not guarantee freedoms of speech, association or religion. And within reason, minimum standards can be societally specific. However, in our view, there are incontrovertibly some capabilities that every human being must be guaranteed, so that no one falls below minimum thresholds in key areas such as health, education and political rights. The world has already agreed on many of these areas and many of the indicators. Although there is still room for debate on some details, societally specific variation should not be an excuse to resist minimum guarantees for all human beings.

The reason is that despite whatever cultural differences, there is also broad agreement on what constitutes basic humanity. Qizilbash emphasizes that 'there is some notion of a distinctly *human* life, which crosses culture and time, and this must guide us in formulating the precise standards for what is basic to any human flourishing' (1998: 12). Philosophers have of course argued for millennia over what defines a human life. But one powerful idea is that humanity depends in part on dignity. Dignity is something inherent to all human beings, something we all want for ourselves, something that makes our life precious (Bernardini 2010). It is a worth we all have simply by virtue of being human. For Nussbaum, dignity means 'being endowed with capacities for activity and striving' (2008). It means being able to enjoy certain fundamental freedoms of action, key opportunities to shape one's own life.

To be a human living in poverty, then, means that you are denied basic capabilities to which every human being is entitled. Living in poverty often means a denial of your dignity, since dignity is predicated on having agency and freedom. And when your dignity is denied, so too is your humanity, since being human means having dignity. In this way, poverty is an affront to the very definition of being human. This is not to imply that people in poverty are in any way 'less human'. Quite the contrary: the poor are human beings just like the rest of us, they are our brothers and sisters, but they are deprived of the opportunities to realize a fully flourishing human life that everyone should enjoy. Every human's life is equal, it is predicated on a fundamental dignity, which means having the basic capabilities to live a valued life. Poverty deprives us of those capabilities, of that dignity, and therefore robs us of an important aspect of our humanity.

giving circle and/or motivate other people in your network to give. A giving circle is typically a group of people who agree to donate to a common cause. Giving circles help to raise larger donations for an organization, and they also can strengthen the donors' commitment both to the cause and to making regular donations. You can also encourage other people to give just by talking about the organizations you believe in and why you think it's important to donate. You don't have to be aggressive: people are often swayed by example, so if you donate regularly and generously and are open about it, you can influence other people to be more generous as well.

How can you find a good organization to give to? We recommend that you first identify an issue that you really care about. Perhaps from reading this book you have latched on to the issue of global health, or women's rights, or education. Whatever the issue might be, think about what you are most committed to, and then identify the organizations that work on that issue. We have mentioned many commendable organizations in this book, from Pratham to Catholic Relief Services to PATH. You should research any organization you're interested in to find out more about its activities. That research can be as in-depth as you want it to be, such as exploring the details of the organization's website including its annual reports, or it can be relatively easy. A simple way of evaluating an organization is to check out its listing at sites such as www.charitynavigator.org, www.givewell.org, or www.guidestar.org. These sites offer ratings systems that are partly inspired by the trend of 'effective altruism', which seeks to create evidence-based strategies to evaluate the most impactful ways of improving the world (Singer 2015). You should be aware of critics' claims that such ratings systems overemphasize how much organizations spend for programmes versus administrative or fundraising costs. Nonetheless, the three sites listed above are all reputable and useful. Finally, if you have no strong preference as to an issue or organization, then consult the list of recommended organizations at www.thelifeyoucansave.org and www.givewell.org.

Volunteer

While giving money is something nearly everyone can do, giving time involves a deeper commitment. Active work to reduce poverty and promote social justice has the power to make more visible change – not just for the poor, but for you too. Volunteering for an organization can help it reach its goals of improving people's lives. Volunteering can also give you skills, and the transformative experience of working for the benefit of others. For this reason, we believe that if you possibly can, you should *always* volunteer. As with many of our recommendations, you can strive to make this a lifelong habit. The admonition to 'think globally, act locally' fits in here. You might not be able to work to reduce poverty in some far-off country on a regular basis. However, you can routinely give your time and energy to an organization with projects abroad. Or you can give your time and energy to an organization that works to fight poverty in your own community.

Volunteering can be relatively uncomplicated, such as working an hour or two a week at a local soup kitchen, or tutoring kids at a high-needs school a few times a month. Your commitment can go much deeper, too, such as by helping an organization with whatever basic, unglamorous tasks it consistently needs like cleaning or maintenance; by contributing specialized skills you might have, such as accounting, marketing or social media; or by contributing expertise (and usually fundraising assistance) through serving on an organization's advisory board. How do you find worthy volunteer opportunities? Often a university will have a community service office to partner with organizations that need volunteers. Alternatively, United Way is a community network operating throughout North America; consult your local branch's website for its list of local organizations with volunteer opportunities. Idealist.org is another site with many searchable, localized volunteer opportunities. Or if you're interested in volunteering abroad, www.volunteerinternational.org is a good place to start.

Make different choices

You can also help fight poverty by making different choices in your daily life about how you consume. Remember that people in the rich world consume planetary resources at a drastically more intensive rate than do people in lower-income countries. We thereby contribute to the radical inequities in the distribution of those resources. Thus we need to change how we consume. To begin with, pollution from humans' carbon consumption is partially responsible for climate change; therefore, drive less, if possible. Take public transportation more. Also, make sure that you recycle and re-use. Many communities now have respectable recycling programmes. Encourage your friends, family, school and/or workplace to participate in those programmes. Better yet, work to expand those programmes. Does your community separate yard waste and food scraps from other trash for use as compost? Doing so is another way of reducing the amount of garbage that goes to landfills, and hopefully consuming more sustainably. Consuming more sustainably also means making other choices, such as eating less meat. The huge industrial cattle, pig and chicken farms in North America are often responsible for heavy water use and pollution, not to mention cruel conditions for the animals. If everyone in the world ate as much beef as North Americans do, the strain on the planet's resources would be unsupportable. You can consider working in other ways, too, for a more just and sustainable food system. Get involved with a community garden, for instance, to help support more local agriculture and food sources.

When you shop, seek out fair trade products. Fair trade is a standard promoting greater equity in international trade by improving conditions for marginalized producers and workers in the global south particularly. Look for products that are labelled fair trade, whether coffee, bananas, chocolate, flowers, or many others. Ten Thousand Villages is a fair trade retailer with shops throughout North America, as well as an online portal where you can buy many different fair trade-certified items such as jewellery, clothes and furniture. You may also consider buying from companies that operate on a 'buy one, give one' business model. The idea behind this model – whose most famous exponents include Toms Shoes and Warby Parker eyewear – is that for every purchase you make, the company donates a product to a needy person or community. While this strategy can be beneficial, it has also drawn much criticism, so you should research the particular company you're buying from and its donation practices. Finally, consider consuming less by doing a 'buy nothing' day (or week), once a year or even more often. Encourage other people in your social network to consume less. It is true that your consumption choices may not immediately better the lives of poor people. However, the point is to adopt practices that make you a more considerate global citizen, aware of and committed to acting in the interests of the poor at home and around the world. Working for a more just society really can start with something as simple as eating less meat.

Study programmes

If you are reading this book, you may already be embarked upon a study programme connected to poverty or international development. Regardless, we hope that this book is only a beginning for your engagement with these issues. Keep learning about poverty, what causes it and how to reduce it. Consider pursuing a major relevant to international development, or social work or sociology for poverty domestically. Besides a formal course of study, keep learning by reading the best newspapers such as the *New York Times* or the *Guardian* – follow the news outside of your home country, pay attention to events in the global south, read articles that deal with poverty and injustice. Follow a good blog or Twitter feed of organizations such as CARE, Oxfam or the Center for Global Development. Look at the 'Further reading' suggestions in the chapters throughout this book and continue to explore the topics that most interest you. Go to lectures at your local university or sponsored by other organizations in your community. Many cities in the United States have a World Affairs Council, for instance, which routinely bring interesting speakers knowledgeable about global development topics.

It is also extremely important to study global poverty by spending time in a developing country, if you can. There is no substitute for talking with poor people, and learning first-hand about their lives, troubles, successes and aspirations. Particularly if you want to pursue a career in international development, you must gain international experience. You should study abroad, whether in formal university courses or by doing an international internship. Generally speaking, the more time you spend abroad, the more you'll learn. However, there are also shorter-term opportunities. Global Brigades is the largest student-led sustainable development organization in the United States, offering a number of valuable study and service-learning programmes doing international development work. Global Visionaries is an organization with programmes in Central America for high-school and gap-year students, and there are many similar outfits. You could also consider the 'reality tours' offered by Global Exchanges, which are open to a wide age range and focus on specific issues such as human rights in the countries visited.

Educate

If you have devoted real energy to learning about global poverty – by reading this book, by taking various classes, by doing development work abroad or by whatever other means – then another way you can work to combat poverty is by educating others. Talk to your family, your friends, your co-workers, any community groups you belong to. What do you tell them? Explain to them that poverty is best conceived as the deprivation of fundamental freedoms, the denial of basic capabilities to which we are all entitled. Explain how poverty is multidimensional and needs to be measured not just by income but by a range of other indicators in health, education and civil rights. Talk about what good development looks like, and examples of effective poverty reduction programmes. Mention why empowering women and girls is so important for reducing poverty, and how that can be accomplished. Give the rationales from this chapter for why we all have a responsibility to reduce poverty – encourage people in your social networks to think about their own ethical obligations in relation to suffering and injustice around the globe. Combat the common misunderstandings that one hears so often when uninformed people talk about poverty. People aren't poor just because they're lazy, assistance doesn't merely make them dependent, poverty isn't mainly a result of cultural pathologies, foreign aid doesn't always go down a rat hole, people can't just lift themselves up by their own bootstraps to get out of poverty and so on. Remind people that there are universal human rights and basic capabilities that are violated not only abroad but at home, too.

Educating others about poverty doesn't mean that you have to become a professional teacher, though that would certainly be an admirable career ambition. Nor does it mean that you have to be a hectoring nuisance who annoys everyone by bringing up poverty in every conversation. Be informed, judicious and strategic. If in conversation friends or family are expressing ignorant things about poverty, gently correct them with examples from this book or your own reading and experience. Be prepared to provide a compelling argument and evidence for your more informed perspective. Suggest an article or book that people might read – or share an article when you come across a good one. Every so often, instead of watching an entertaining but shallow popcorn movie with a group, watch something that actually deals with issues related to global poverty, whether it's a documentary or fiction, and then spark a discussion about those issues. Demonstrate leadership and organize a movie or speaker event at your school, workplace or community group. The objective is to give other people the chance to learn some of the same things that you have learned about global poverty, and there are many ways to accomplish that goal.

Advocate

If you are ready to push your engagement with poverty issues to a still deeper level, then you need to start talking to people in power. Educate public officials about poverty and what you think should be done about it. For all the outsize role that rich donors play particularly in American politics, many politicians will actually still listen to you even if you're not rich, especially if you're a voter in their district. Do a search to determine which politicians represent your local area. You can focus on the municipal level, the state/provincial/regional level and/or the national level. Call or visit your politicians' offices, send them an email or a letter. Sending a personal email or letter (i.e. not a form letter) is most likely to get attention. Go to city hall meetings or other public forums where policy that can impact poverty is being discussed. Then speak up! It is not hard to make your voice heard, and you truly can make an impact even as one individual.

What should you tell your politicians? At the most general level, you could urge them to increase funding to support anti-poverty programmes worldwide. The United States in particular is a laggard when it comes to foreign aid. Polls show that Americans think that 28 per cent of the federal budget goes to foreign aid. That belief is utterly deluded; a more accurate number is that the United States spends only 0.19 per cent of its GNI on development assistance. The internationally valorized target is 0.7 per cent. The United States is shamefully below that figure, and far outdistanced by leaders such as Norway and Sweden, which give over 0.9 per cent of their GNI. Beyond increasing funding, you can get more specific with your advocacy. Tell politicians to decrease subsidies for agribusiness, which are often grossly unfair to farmers in the global south. As one famous example, it has been estimated that thanks to subsidies the average cow in the European Union earns around USD 2.60 a day, which means that European cows earn more money than the approximately two billion human beings who live on less than two dollars a day. Similarly outrageous stories could be told about agricultural policies throughout most high-income countries. Advocate not just for more funding for health and education programmes abroad, but remember the needs of people in your own country. Push for equitable education funding for children in disadvantaged areas, mental health programmes and shelters for the homeless, vocational training to help those who are unemployed. Oxfam is an organization that often does excellent advocacy work – pay attention to its campaigns and get involved when you can.

Agitate

If you are willing to educate and advocate for global justice, then you may be willing to agitate for it as well. Agitating means not just learning, not just caring, not just speaking up. It means working actively to make a positive change. It means taking some risks, challenging entrenched and complacent power structures. It means making a deeper, lasting commitment to change. It means taking on leadership roles and building coalitions to make a collective impact. Agitating means fighting against forms of injustice whether in your own backyard or far away. You might participate in a march for human rights, or stage a rally against unethical corporations. You might launch a campaign to encourage your university to divest from fossil fuel industries. You might lead protests against income inequality or for immigration reform. You might join an existing organization such as Oxfam, RESULTS, One.org or InterAction and work in their campaigns. You might create a new group that focuses on a specific poverty issue that you care deeply about. You might start a social enterprise that can respond to a carefully determined community need. You might spend a period of time living in solidarity with people marginalized by poverty or discrimination. Doing this kind of work to promote justice means that you must think deeply about what really matters to you, and what kind of life you want to live. There are many different ways you can be a 'changemaker', and though none of them may be easy, probably nothing else in life is more rewarding than when you give yourself and your energies to help other people.

What do you agitate for? Besides whatever specific issue(s) to which you might dedicate your activism, we urge you to remember that reducing poverty ultimately depends on securing people their freedoms. These are the fundamental freedoms of the basic capabilities, all of which support the most important freedom, which is the freedom to live a life that one has reason to value. Because we are human beings, we are all entitled to basic rights such as minimum standards of housing, health, education, control over our own bodies, and political agency. These capabilities are basic because they make all sorts of other valuable choices possible. Take just one example: girls' education. Education, remember, promotes better health outcomes. It helps people have more secure economic livelihoods. It leads to greater support for democracy and tolerance for diversity. Education combats ignorance, which is a form of poverty. Education empowers – it helps support a girl's freedom to choose a life for herself.

Conceiving of anti-poverty work in this way requires changes in both the discourse about poverty and in practical policy approaches. These changes are happening in some places. For example, about half of the countries in the world have a right to health care in their constitutions. Some, such as South Africa, even have constitutional rights regarding basic shelter. The United States Constitution recognizes neither of these rights. Among many politicians as well as the general public, this change in discourse and policy practice has yet to occur. It would be a worthy effort not just to think about how American society might be different if citizens had a basic right to housing – but also to work towards that right. Again, an adequate standard of global justice insists that whatever basic rights we want for ourselves we must guarantee to everyone around the world, and vice versa. The objective must be that no one anywhere lives in the absolute poverty defined by the deprivation of those basic rights and capabilities.

Conclusion

Studying global poverty, it is possibly unavoidable and probably essential to consider global justice. Any sincere effort to think about how to reduce poverty requires an ethical framework. That ethical framework can provide the fundamental motivation for poverty reduction, even if there are different and not always congruent ethical perspectives on this issue. As we have seen, some writers argue from the assistance ethic: in effect, people around the world who are suffering from poverty are part of our human family and as such, we should do for them what we would do for a family member who is suffering. Other writers emphasize the restitution ethic. The former colonial powers and the leading countries of the global north have benefited so much from the global south – through cheap primary commodities, cheap labour and cheap products – that they have structured the international system to preserve their own advantages, which actually creates poverty. There is also the legal and moral framework of human rights treaties which commit our governments (and urge us as individuals) to prevent violations to those rights posed by poverty and suffering. Finally, the self-interest argument holds that if you live comfortably in a high-income country, and you want to continue to enjoy that life, then you must work to reduce global poverty. Otherwise, conflict, terrorism, disease outbreaks, and mass migrations from poorer countries will put your lifestyle at risk.

These are all big, broad arguments for why we should work to reduce poverty, but they actually give us relatively little ethical guidance for *how* to reduce it. For that guidance, we must rely on the principles of solidarity, non-elite participation and decent sufficiency for all. These principles underlie ethically responsible development, which in turn must be based on standards of equity, empowerment, cultural freedom, environmental sustainability and human wellbeing. Even with all these ideas in mind, we should always remember that doing poverty reduction and development work is hard. This is one reason why some writers insist that intervention will only prolong suffering, especially because northern countries so often get it wrong. It is important to acknowledge this perspective too. Well-intentioned but naïve meddling in people's lives, helping people to eat for one day while failing to address long-term structural causes of poverty, really can do more harm than good. Nonetheless, we prefer to err on the side of action rather than inaction. All human lives are equal, and the ethos of humanist egalitarianism demands that we try to prevent avoidable suffering. Where human rights are being violated, where people are being denied basic capabilities to lead lives that they value, then we have a responsibility to act.

You of course must make your own choices, even if it is to do nothing, to remain complacent. What you should not do is *not* decide. You should ask yourself: what am I going to do? Given the massive injustices in the world, at home and abroad, what are you going to do about them? Whatever you decide, you should make a commitment. Write down what you're going to do. Don't be vague – be specific as to exactly what you will do. Plan for how you will accomplish whatever you've written down. If you write it down, you are more likely to commit, and more likely to follow through. After you've written it down, then tell someone else about your commitment. Make your commitment public. Decide to take action, and then take it. Fanciful as it may seem, it is true that one person can make a difference. You don't have to change the world; perhaps all you have to do is change yourself. Ultimately, we can all be part of a solution to global poverty, and if we are good global citizens, we all have an obligation to do so.

Discussion questions

1   What are some ethical, moral and political reasons for fighting poverty? What arguments would you use to persuade someone about the importance of this goal?

2   What are some different potential meanings of 'global justice' that you take from this chapter?

3   What would you do in Hardin's lifeboat scenario? What is your reaction to this line of argument?

4   What is your evaluation of Pogge's perspective? Would you agree with his critics that a failure to reduce poverty is not morally equivalent to actively causing poverty, and therefore entails different obligations?

5   If you were given a billion dollars to end global poverty, what specifically would you do and why? Would your answer change if you only had a thousand dollars to spend? If so, what does that difference tell you about strategies for poverty reduction?

6   Go to this site: www.globalrichlist.com/. Enter your or your parents' annual income. What are the results? What else can you learn from the facts on this page, and how do they impact your understanding of yourself and your obligations in relation to global poverty?

7   Go to this site: www.givingwhatwecan.org/. How are charities evaluated, what recommendations are there for donors, and what do you think about the suggestions for getting involved?

Note

1   Famines rarely happen because of a lack of food, and more typically because of a lack of democratic political structures (Sen 1981).

Further reading

Daley-Harris, Shannon, Jeffrey Keenan and Karen Speerstra. 2007. *Our Day to End Poverty: 24 ways you can make a difference*. San Francisco, CA: Berrett-Koehler.

Deneulin, Séverine. 2014. *Wellbeing, Justice and Development Ethics*. New York, NY: Routledge.

Illich, Ivan. 'To hell with good intentions.' An Address to the Conference on InterAmerican Student Projects (CIASP) in Cuernavaca, Mexico, on 20 April 1968.

Pogge, Thomas. 'World poverty and human rights.' *Ethics & International Affairs* 19.1 (2005): 1–7.

Satz, Debra. 'What do we owe the global poor?' *Ethics & International Affairs* vol. 19.1 (2005): 47–54.

Unger, Peter K. 1996. *Living High and Letting Die: Our illusion of innocence*. New York. NY: Oxford University Press.

Works cited

Barry, Christian, and Gerhard Øverland. 'Responding to global poverty: review essay of Peter Singer, The Life you can Save.' *Journal of Bioethical Inquiry*, 6.2 (2009): 239–247.

Bernardini, Paola. 'Human dignity and human capabilities in Martha C. Nussbaum.' *Iustum Aequum Salutare*, 6 (2010): 45–51.

Chatterjee, Deen K., ed. 2004. *The Ethics of Assistance: Morality and the distant needy*. Cambridge: Cambridge University Press.

Collier, Paul. 2007. *The Bottom Billion: Why the poorest countries are failing and what can be done about it*. Oxford: Oxford University Press.

Crocker, David A. 2008. *Ethics of Global Development: Agency, capability, and deliberative democracy*. Cambridge: Cambridge University Press.

Gasper, Des. 2004. *The Ethics of Development: From economism to human development*. Edinburgh, UK: Edinburgh University Press.

Gasper, Des, and Asuncion St. Clair, eds. 2010. *Development Ethics*. Farnham, UK: Ashgate.

Gilabert, Pablo. 2012. *From Global Poverty to Global Equality: A philosophical exploration*. Oxford: Oxford University Press.

Goulet, Denis. 2006. *Development Ethics at Work: Explorations 1960–2002*. London: Routledge.

Hardin, Garrett. 'Lifeboat ethics: the case against helping the poor.' *Psychology Today*, September 1974. Available at: www.garretthardinsociety.org/articles/art_lifeboat_ethics_case_against_helping_poor. html, accessed May 2015.

Jaggar, Alison, ed. 2010. *Thomas Pogge and His Critics*. Cambridge, UK: Polity Press.

McNeill, Desmond, and Asunción Lera St. Clair. 2009. *Global Poverty, Ethics and Human Rights: The role of multilateral organisations*. London: Routledge.

Nagel, Thomas. 'The problem of global justice.' *Philosophy & Public Affairs*, 33.2 (2005): 113–147.

Nickel, James W. 2007. *Making Sense of Human Rights*, 2nd edn. Malden, MA: Blackwell.

Nussbaum, Martha. 2008. 'Human Dignity and Political Entitlements.' Chapter 14 in *Human Dignity and Bioethics: Essays commissioned by the President's Council on Bioethics*. Washington, DC. Available at: https://bioethicsarchive.georgetown.edu/pcbe/reports/human_dignity/chapter14.html, accessed August 2015.

Penz, Peter, Jay Drydyk and Pablo S. Bose. 2011. *Displacement by Development: Ethics, rights and responsibilities*. Cambridge, UK: Cambridge University Press.

Pogge, Thomas. 2008. *World Poverty and Human Rights: Cosmopolitan responsibilities and reforms*, 2nd edn. Cambridge: Polity Press.

Pogge, Thomas. 2007. 'Severe poverty as a human rights violation.' In Thomas Pogge, ed. *Freedom from Poverty as a Human Right: Who owes what to the very poor*. Paris: UNESCO. 11–53.

Pogge, Thomas. 'World poverty and human rights.' *Ethics & International Affairs*, 19.1 (2005a): 1–7.

Pogge, Thomas. 'Severe poverty as a violation of negative duties.' *Ethics & International Affairs*, 19.1 (2005b): 55–83.

Qizilbash, Mozaffar. 1998. 'Poverty: Concept and Measurement.' Research Report Series #12. Sustainable Development Policy Institute.

Rawls, John. 1999. *A Theory of Justice*. Cambridge, MA: Harvard University Press.

Schweickart, David. 'Global poverty: alternative perspectives on what we should do – and why.' *Journal of Social Philosophy*, 39.4 (2008): 471–491.

Sen, Amartya. 1981. *Poverty and Famines: An essay on entitlement and deprivation*. Oxford: Oxford University Press.

Singer, Peter. 2015. *The Most Good You Can Do: How effective altruism is changing ideas about living ethically*. New Haven, CT: Yale University Press.

Singer, Peter. 2009. *The Life You Can Save: How to do your part to end world poverty*. New York, NY: Random House.

Vizard, Polly. 'Pogge vs. Sen on global poverty and human rights.' *Éthique et économique/Ethics and Economics*, 3.2 (2006): 1–22.

Index

Locators in italics refer to figures and those in **bold** to tables.